REFRAMING LATIN AMER

REFRAMING LATIN AMERICA

*A Cultural Theory Reading of the
Nineteenth and Twentieth Centuries*

ERIK CHING
CHRISTINA BUCKLEY
AND ANGÉLICA LOZANO-ALONSO

UNIVERSITY OF TEXAS PRESS, AUSTIN

LIBRARY OF CONGRESS CATALOGING-IN-PUBLICATION DATA

Ching, Erik Kristofer.
    Reframing Latin America : a cultural theory reading of the nineteenth and
twentieth centuries / Erik Ching, Christina Buckley, and Angélica Lozano-
Alonso. — 1st ed.
        p.   cm.
    Includes index.
    ISBN 978-0-292-70933-1 (cloth : alk. paper)
    ISBN 978-0-292-71750-3 (pbk. : alk. paper)
    1. Latin America—Civilization.   2. Spanish American literature—
History and criticism.   3. Postmodernism.   4. Culture.   I. Buckley,
Christina, 1969–   .   II. Lozano-Alonso, Angélica, 1973–   .   III. Title.
F1408.3.C44   2007
980—dc22

                                                              2006038417

To all our students in Interdisciplinary Studies 75:
Issues in Latin America

CONTENTS

What Are We Doing and Why
Are We Doing It? A Preface

Modernism, postmodernism, discourse, deconstruction, hegemony, hybridity, hermeneutics, semiotics, episteme. Even for someone trained in cultural theory these terms can be daunting. For the novice, they can be downright alienating. This book has two goals: to define and explain the basics of cultural theory, or postmodernism, and to demonstrate its usefulness in interpreting nineteenth- and twentieth-century Latin America.

This book grows out of an undergraduate seminar we teach at Furman University, a liberal arts school in South Carolina. We find that most of our students entering the seminar have heard of postmodernism and cultural theory but lack a working knowledge of them. We are happy to report that none of them has left ignorant, although, admittedly, not all of them have agreed with us as to cultural theory's explanatory merits. In fact, some have left firmly opposed to it, choosing to retreat to the safety of modernity; others have left unsure, waiting for more information to declare a verdict. Still others have strongly accepted its claims and now see themselves and their world in a new way. It is not of great concern to us whether our students agree with us by the end of the course. We simply want to make cultural theory and postmodernism accessible to them so they can decide for themselves. The same objective drives this book.

Its structure follows closely that of our seminar, which we designed to ease the encounter with cultural theory and postmodernism. A main introductory section lays out some central issues. The remainder is divided into two parts. The first is dedicated to theory and consists of brief excerpts from key works in cultural theory. Some of these address specifically Latin America; others are more general. The second part consists of excerpts from some of Latin America's principal writers in the nineteenth and twentieth centuries, including Domingo Sarmiento, José Martí, Rómulo Gallegos, Elena Garro, and Che Guevara. Anyone familiar with Latin America will recognize these authors as key figures in Latin American history and/or literature. Indeed, their writings commonly appear in anthologies. So what makes our approach different? Why have we included the same authors that anthologists have selected repeatedly? We will show that what matters is not *what* is read, but *how* it is read. Using our section on theory as a guide, we will demonstrate how to read these works from a cultural theory perspective. We will then show how this approach results in new interpretations of modern Latin American history and culture.

The introductory sections of the book prepare the reader to interpret its deliberate mixture of primary and secondary sources that cuts across the traditional theory/text hierarchy. We should point out here that it is not our goal to offer a comprehensive survey of particular time periods, authors, or literary styles. We leave those goals to anthologies and historical surveys. To that end, we have divided our coverage into only five areas:

1. Liberalism (mid-to-late nineteenth century)
2. Nationalism (late nineteenth through mid-twentieth century)
3. Socialism (1959–1989)
4. Magical realism (1960s and 1970s)
5. Testimonials (1970s–1990s)

These areas are ordered chronologically and cover most of Latin America's modern era, which dates back to independence from Spain in the early nineteenth century (with a few exceptions, like Brazil and Cuba). They obviously are not comprehensive, and they represent an admixture of historical eras and literary styles. We have made these choices because they allow us to explain cultural studies and then apply its theories to a series of readings in the confines of a short book.

Our selections have another objective, which is to show the prevailing trend in Latin American intellectual and political circles over the past two centuries to incorporate a broader swath of the population into the center of power. Authors in the mid-nineteenth century were typically privileged white, propertied males, but by the end of the twentieth century, the definitive protagonist had become dark-skinned, poor, and female. But our cultural studies reading of this progression will illustrate how ideologies and power structures can betray authorial intentions. Sometimes, attempts at liberation contain elements of exclusion and hierarchy.

The excerpted writings are drawn from a variety of genres, including but not limited to essays, novels, short stories, and personal testimonies. We have also included film analyses and other secondary critical essays on primary texts. Each of these is preceded by a brief, or not so brief, introduction written by us to provide some guidance for our readers. At the end of the book, we offer a few concluding thoughts inspired by questions typically asked by our students as we approach the end of our term together.

We assume that readers of this book already understand the basic contours of Latin American history, but such knowledge is not essential. For those who do not know Latin America or who are interested in a refresher, we recommend reading a historical overview alongside this book, such as John Charles Chasteen's *Born in Blood and Fire* (New York: Norton, 2006) or Will Fowler's *Latin America 1800–2000* (New York: Oxford UP, 2002).

The seminar experience has been a constant source of intellectual growth and pleasant interaction. We and the students who assisted in writing this book have enjoyed the challenge of trying to recreate the seminar here. We hope the following pages demonstrate and perpetuate the sentiment that went into it.

Acknowledgments

This book has been a group effort. It grew out of Interdisciplinary Studies 75: Issues in Latin America, the capstone seminar in Latin American Studies at Furman University. The course is taught every spring and offered mostly to graduating seniors as the final project in their Latin American Studies concentration—Furman's version of a minor. The book before you is a variation of the reader we have used in the seminar over the past five years, beginning in spring 2001 when Erik Ching, one of the coauthors, became chair of Latin American Studies, which carries with it the responsibility of teaching IDS75.

The seminar, as well as the Latin American Studies concentration, had been in existence since the late 1990s because of the efforts of a variety of visionary faculty who wanted to broaden the curriculum. Our initial acknowledgment, therefore, is extended to Bill Teska, formerly of Furman's Biology Department, David Bost of Modern Languages and Literatures, Cleve Fraser of Political Science, and the many other faculty who have been involved in building and maintaining the Latin American Studies concentration over the years.

Thanks to a grant that Furman University received from the National Endowment for the Humanities to promote interdisciplinary teaching and curricular development in the humanities, Ching was able to apply for and receive the necessary additional funding to invite a colleague from the Modern Languages and Literatures Department to co-teach the course and promote its interdisciplinary character. The colleague was Charles Boyer, whose expertise lay in twentieth-century Mexican narrative. Charles has since left Furman University to fulfill his teaching mission in greener pastures, but we express our heartfelt thanks to him for the efforts he put into designing the first version of the course reader that eventually morphed into this book. A significant portion of the present manuscript bears his imprint.

After Charles left, Ching received a second year of funding from NEH and invited two other colleagues from the Modern Languages and Literatures Department to continue the co-taught, interdisciplinary nature of the seminar. They are the coauthors of this book, Christina Buckley and Angélica Lozano-Alonso. Following Ching's departure as chair of Latin American Studies in 2003, Lozano-Alonso assumed the mantle and has carried on valiantly. When NEH funding ran out, it was only because of the generous support of the dean's office that we were able to maintain the presence of multiple faculty members in the seminar, and so we would like to extend our appreciation to former Dean A. V. Huff and current Dean Tom Kazee for recognizing the worth of the seminar and supporting it with the necessary resources. Had it not been for that support, we would not have been able to continue with the classroom efforts that ultimately led to this book. Additionally, the departments of History and Modern Languages and Literatures at Furman supported the project, financially and otherwise, being especially understanding of the extra-departmental demands that Latin American Studies placed on our time. So, to the successive chairs in History, David Spear and Marian Strobel, and to David Bost, the chair of Modern Languages and Literatures, we express our thanks. In particular, we are indebted to David Bost for taking the time to examine the reader and for believing in its broader value. He insisted that we develop it into a manuscript; had it not been for his supportive prodding, we might not have pressed forward. Additional financial support for copyright permission costs was provided by Furman University's Research and Professional Growth Committee, as well as by Furman's Department of Modern Languages and Literatures.

Various colleagues near and far have given us invaluable insight and advice. Richard Letteri of Furman's Communications Studies Department has been not only a long-standing friend but also a constant source of intellectual engagement. He read and provided extensive comments on various portions of the book. Other friends and colleagues at Furman provided advice as well, and for their suggestions, especially in the realm of theory, we thank Nick Radel and Vincent Haussman of Furman's English Department. We are also grateful to Marvin D'Lugo, Professor of Spanish and Screen Studies at Clark University, for lending us his advice in the initial stages of narrowing down theoretical texts to consult for reference and for inclusion in excerpted form in the book. We would like to thank the editorial staff at the University of Texas Press, especially Theresa May, Allison Faust, Mary LaMotte, and Tom Lacey, an excellent copy editor, for their constant support. The two outside readers for the University of Texas Press provided valuable insights. One of them was anonymous, and thus we can only direct a thank-you here for the thorough and informed comments s/he provided. The second reader identified himself, so we thank Arturo Aldama of the Ethnic Studies Department at the University of Colorado, Boulder, for his suggestions.

Individually, Ching would like to acknowledge the benefit of a week spent at the University of North Carolina, Chapel Hill, in the College Teacher Workshop program sponsored by the Duke/UNC Consortium of Latin American Studies. Various faculty at Duke and UNC, including John Charles Chasteen, offered advice. The efforts spent during that week devising a sample syllabus for a course dealing with cultural studies in Latin America contributed to the development of the IDS75 seminar.

In large part, our own professors and mentors have inspired us in our teaching of the seminar and our writing of this book. Ching would like to thank his two main advisors in Latin American history, David Rock at the University of California, Santa Barbara, and Héctor Lindo-Fuentes at Fordham University. Buckley would like to take this opportunity to thank her former professors from Tulane University and the College of William and Mary for being role models as educators and scholars. She is especially grateful for the mentorship of Susan Martin-Márquez and Ana López, without whom cinema may have remained two-dimensional. The generosity and humanity with which they shared their expertise made it a privilege to study with them and continue to make it a privilege to count them as friends. She is also indebted to her parents, John and Kathleen, educators as well, for paving the way for a life of fulfillment through learning, and to her tíos, Stephen Strobach and Natividad Reyes, for teaching her the indispensability of social justice through their everyday practice of its principles.

Lozano-Alonso would like to thank her former professors from the University of Colorado and Cornell University. In particular, she would like to thank her graduate school professors who first introduced her to these theoretical approaches and taught her by example about the importance of connecting pedagogy with research: Debra A. Castillo, John Kronik, and Edmundo Paz-Soldán. She is indebted to her parents, Anthony G. Lozano and Leticia Alonso de Lozano, for her love of teaching and learning. A special thanks to Anthony G. Lozano for his help with editing the final manuscript.

Ultimately, of course, it is to our students in IDS75 to whom we owe the greatest thanks. Needless to say, this project would have been impossible without them. Their reactions to and experience with the various manifestations of the text and our accompanying pedagogy provided the primary impetus behind our revisions. Students have been directly involved in various phases of the project, including contributing essays that improved some of the final introductions. We would like to single out Andrew Barron for his writing and researching efforts in the spring of 2003. Additionally, we would like to thank Donté Stewart for his help and enthusiasm with scanning and editing our primary sources in the summer of 2003 and for being a wonderful teaching assistant in spring 2005. Morgen Young helped to improve the quality of some of the images. We would like to recognize the class of spring 2004 in particular for helping us with the introductions, especially Mike Overby, Emily Dean, Kelsey Worrel, Donté Stewart, and Janie Parnell.

We extend our appreciation to the various presses who granted us permission to reprint texts or images. Although a cost was commonly associated with most of the permissions, some, such as the Center for Latin American Studies at Arizona State University, graciously recognized the educational mission of this project and reduced their normal prices. We would like to thank Stuart Hall for granting us permission to use his work and Jim Heimann for his assistance with one of the images from Mexico.

Finally, we would to like to thank our respective partners—Cathy Stevens, Peter Nieuwenhuizen, and Anthony Tiberia—for their patience, encouragement, ever-present support, and frequent insight into the contents of this project.

With regard to all those who have helped bring this book to fruition, any oversights are solely our responsibility.

PART I

Introduction(s)

Post What?! (Not) An Abbreviated Introduction

The image of an attractive young woman (Fig. 1.1) appears on the cover of a recently published book about El Salvador. The book provides a nonfictional survey of the people, culture, and history of El Salvador for English-speaking readers. Its intended readership is university students or the general public looking for an overview. We think the book is quite good. The author expresses strong regard for the people of El Salvador, and the content of the book demonstrates his extensive knowledge of the country and its customs. We can only assume that the image chosen for the cover is meant to express the author's intention of providing a factual and sympathetic overview. But to what extent does this photograph accomplish its task? Does it present a vision of Salvadoran reality?

On the one hand, these questions are easy to answer. The image is a photograph of a real Salvadoran woman and real flowers. Indeed, this scene is ubiquitous in El Salvador. The country's tropical climate allows flowers to grow easily, and many young women can be found carrying bunches of them, often because they sell them in public markets. In this sense, the photograph does offer us a slice of El Salvadoran reality.

But the image contains multiple meanings, which the author and publisher may or may not have been aware of when they chose it. This visual representation of El Salvador is part of a long and complicated history in which the lands and peoples of Latin America have been depicted as female, especially in images intended for North American and European audiences. Such images depict Latin America and relations between it and North America/Europe through a historic lens of gendered power relations.

FIGURE I.I   *From the cover of* Culture and Customs of El Salvador. *New York: Greenwood, 2001*

A classic example of depicting Latin America as female is a drawing (Fig. 1.2) from the late 1570s by the Flemish Renaissance painter Jan van der Straet of Vespucci's discovery of America. Titled *America,* the drawing depicts Latin America as a prone female nude, over whom stands a European explorer who is armored and fully clothed. He carries the instruments that enabled him to discover America—a sword, a cross, and an astrolabe—that are symbols of Europe's belief in its superiority over the world in military, religious, and scientific terms. The caption for the drawing, "Americus rediscovers America; he called her once and thenceforth she was always awake," clearly makes the explorer the active agent in the scene, whereas female America is a passive recipient awaiting Europe's orders. Just above America's raised arm is another scene that further establishes the power relations in the drawing. This depiction of cannibalism supposedly being practiced by other Americans is evidence that, in the eyes of the artist, America is a barbarian in desperate need of Europe's civilizing and commanding presence.[1]

Latin America is also depicted as female in an editorial cartoon (Fig. 1.3) that appeared in *Puck* magazine in 1896 on the eve of the war between the United States and Spain. The illustration is meant to be at once serious and funny. It portrays Spain, the United States, and Cuba, then a Spanish colony, as actors in a melodrama. Cuba is a young, attractive damsel in distress, fearing a darkly dressed Spanish villain. A virile Uncle Sam represents the United States, which is stepping in to save her from a miserable fate. Obviously, the author of this editorial cartoon is telling his readers that Cuba should be freed from Spanish domination and that the United States is the nation to do the job. But in the cartoon, as in countless others throughout the years, a Latin American nation is illustrated as a young defenseless female and the United States as a strong male hero.[2] At the heart of this image resides a gendered hierarchy in which a woman is depicted as weak and needing male protection. Such a depiction parallels the image the United States has of itself as a world power and its tendency

FIGURE I.2   America *(ca. 1580). An engraving by Theodor Galle following an original drawing by Jan van der Straet (ca. 1575). Plate courtesy of Burndy Library, Norwalk, CT*

FIGURE 1.3 *Editorial drawing by C. Jay Taylor in* Puck *magazine, June 3, 1896. The caption reads, "Stand back, there, gol darn ye!—If you force this thing to a fifth act, remember that's where I git in my work!"*

to think of Latin America as a place to be controlled and dominated. Not so coincidentally, European colonial powers employed a similar gendered imagery to portray lands in Africa and Asia around the turn of the century.

Another issue that arises from the image in the El Salvador book is that the young woman is holding a bundle of red roses, another very complicated image with a long history. Red roses are a widely recognized symbol of passion. When a young woman holds them in her arms, especially near her chest and stomach, they take on meanings of fertility and sexual invitation. Because the young woman stares directly at the camera and the background is washed out so as to draw the viewer's eyes directly to hers, this sexualized effect is enhanced. Such depictions of Latin America were common in advertisements, among other things, intended to sell products to North Americans or to draw them as vacationers to Latin America. This imagery made Latin America out to be an inviting and bountiful playground full of mysterious but safe sensuality. A recent book, *Mexicana: Vintage Mexican Graphics*, presents a compilation of these types of images from Mexico, and even calls them "iconic" due to the frequency and timeless consistency with which they appeared.[3] The book shows that through the years Mexico was displayed repeatedly in advertisements for goods and tourism as a light-skinned, often scantily clad, sensuous-looking female. One of the images advertised a spa (Fig. 1.4). According to Jim Heimann, author of *Mexicana*, that image dates from the late 1940s or early 1950s and is similar to others appearing in thousands of other brochures and advertisements produced at the time that targeted U.S. tourists who were just beginning to have the time, money, and means to travel to Mexico in greater numbers.[4] Once again, Latin America is feminized, and a woman appears as an exterior representation of a general principle, rather than as a fully developed, autonomous person.

So, to what extent does the photograph of the young Salvadoran woman capture something real about El Salvador? Our argument in this book is that the possibility that the photograph could capture reality is moot. We are not concerned with whether such an image is accurate or inaccurate, or whether it depicts a real, surreal, or even false El Salvador. Instead, we are interested in the way its representation contains multiple meanings, many of them unintended. We do not believe that the intention of an author (or in this case, the photographer and cover designer) or an audience must be conscious for meaning to exist and be transmitted. For example, we assume that neither the person who took the picture, the publishers who decided to use it on the cover, nor the intended readership necessarily possessed conscious knowledge of the long and complex history of young, attractive Latin American women being presented to North American audiences. Nevertheless, the image is inevitably charged with multiple and complex meanings. We contend that representations like this photograph construct places like El Salvador, rather than reveal their objective or true nature. Our goal in this book is to study the process through which these constructions come to be.

Daniel Mato, an Argentine-born theorist now working in Venezuela, once said, "Latin America doesn't exist."[5] By this provocative statement Mato meant that Latin America is an identity and that, like all identities, its meaning is constructed by the people who try to define it. Mato decided to dedicate his career to exploring the process by which meanings come

FIGURE 1.4 *An advertisement for Ixtapan Spa, Mexico (ca. late 1940s or early 1950s). Scan provided by TASCHEN America*

into existence, rather than trying to determine the true, singular meaning of Latin America and then to convince people of the accuracy of his discovery. The same motive inspires this book.

Postmodernists or cultural theorists (we will distinguish between them in a moment) view the world differently than do modernists, or theorists operating in the modernist tradition. Modernists take as their fundamental premise the idea that truth exists independent of human interpretation. Gravity, for example, exists whether or not people are aware of it and despite how they interpret it. It is a truth; the question is whether human beings will be able to figure it out. Modernists accept as their main objective the discovery of truth, typically through the scientific method. They also believe that any right-minded person would want to adjust society's norms according to those truths; thus, even for modernists who consider themselves unconcerned with politics, their studies have deep political implications. For example, they believe that if we know that gravity exists, we should order our society according to that truth and reject all other nonsensical explanations for why apples fall from trees. Modernist scholars in the humanities and social sciences approach the social and literary world in the same way that scientists view the natural world. They believe it to contain truths that can be discovered and then used to orient society for the better.

In contrast to modernists, cultural theorists contend that lived reality is a social construct in which meaning does not exist as objective truth but resides in our individual and collective interpretations. Cultural theorists seek to understand how presumed truths and long-held assumptions come into existence and how they operate within ever-changing social values and norms. In a manner of speaking, they contend that the truth of everything is relative to the interpretive lens used to view it. They do not deny that apples fall from trees or that gravity exists, but they examine the pathway by which we arrive at those unassailable truths and wonder whether it is lined with social construction. Cultural theorists are accused by their modernist adversaries of refusing to stand for anything, of wallowing in a sea of relativism and do-nothingism. On the contrary, however, cultural theorists do take strong stands, but they insist that we recognize the ever-tenuous nature of any truth claim.

LANGUAGE SHOCK

If this seems confusing, don't worry. Our goal by the end of this book, if not by the end of this introduction, is clarity. One of the first challenges in trying to understand cultural theory is to move beyond language shock. Cultural theorists appear to communicate in a private language composed of many familiar words but indecipherable to the untrained ear. Not only do laypeople and students complain about their apparent incomprehensibility, academicians at the highest level have accused cultural theorists of saying nothing to one another in a self-referential language that no one understands, not even the theorists themselves. In the words of one critic, "Much deconstructive criticism [a major facet of cultural theory] . . . now seems to be self-indulgent and self-absorbed, and ultimately uncommitted to anything that matters."[6]

Discourse provides a clear example of this linguistic challenge. Before cultural theory, discourse was an innocent, somewhat formal word meaning a speech, serious conversation, or the interconnected language of a particular field, such as scientific discourse or medical discourse. Today, it refers to a system of rules governing the constitution of knowledge and the way in which people give meaning to their surroundings. Whereas use of the word previously assumed simply a full command of the English language, today it indicates a cultural theory perspective, and the mere utterance of the word can polarize an audience.

A defining moment in this language clash between modernists and postmodernists occurred when Alan Sokal, a physicist at New York University, pulled a hoax on the journal *Social Text,* one of the premier journals in cultural studies and literary theory in the early 1990s. Sokal submitted an article entitled "Transgressing the Boundaries: Toward a Transformative Hermeneutics of Quantum Gravity."[7] It ostensibly argued, among other things, that gravity was a social construct and did not exist as the natural law we have assumed it to be. Shortly after *Social Text* published the article, Sokal declared it a hoax. He confessed he had no understanding of what he wrote but had cobbled together a variety of words and catchphrases commonly used by literary critics and postmodern theorists. Sokal's actions set off a firestorm of debate and turned him into a cause célèbre for cultural theory's critics. As one of them put it, his hoax was "the greatest exposé of postmodern asininity."[8]

Critics are not alone in recognizing the linguistic challenges of cultural theory. A microindustry has emerged for the publication of encyclopedia-length books that define key concepts in the field. The existence of these texts shows that cultural theorists themselves acknowledge the need to decipher their own language and homogenize the often disparate meanings of commonly used terms.[9]

So if the language of postmodernism/cultural theory is so confusing, why do its adherents bother using it? Perhaps the simplest answer is that old meanings cannot explain new concepts. For example, how could someone in the medieval era, steeped in the language of God's will, a cosmology like the Great Chain of Being, and monarchism understand a modern political theorist's views of democracy, individual liberty, and equal rights before a natural law? Similarly, how could a postmodern theorist explain the social construction of reality and the deconstructed individual with modernist concepts of objective truth and individuality? Oftentimes, only a different vocabulary can explain something new.

THINKING BIG: POSTMODERNISM VERSUS CULTURAL STUDIES

Cultural theory, cultural studies, and *postmodernism*—they are not quite synonymous, even though they are often used interchangeably, as we have done to this point. It is difficult to confine *postmodern* to a single definition, but for the sake of argument we are going to begin by associating it with a historical era, roughly the mid-1960s to the present. The beginning of postmodernity is often traced to the 1940s, or even to the turn of the twentieth century. In any event, the postmodern era represents a deep and fundamental change in human existence.

When Western civilization entered the modern era, roughly in the late fifteenth and early sixteenth centuries, human existence changed simultaneously in almost every arena: economics, politics, society, art, philosophy, and more. People in Western society began to see themselves and the world around them in quite different ways than did their premodern ancestors of the Middle Ages. Postmodernists contend that this same degree of change was taking place in the late twentieth and now in the early twenty-first century. They do not consider themselves proselytizers of a new idea or some New Age religion. Instead, they contend that postmodernity is upon us whether we like it or not, just as modernity confronted its premodern predecessors five hundred years ago whether they liked it or not. One of the debates among postmodernists is whether this transition is a global phenomenon or something peculiar to Western civilization. Some Latin American scholars are suspicious of postmodernism as yet another form of intellectual imperialism by Europe and North America. Indeed, this is an issue we will address in greater depth.

Modernists, or those people who think the modern era is still alive and well, naturally reject the postmodernist claim as a silly but threatening idea that has the potential to erode the core values of civilization, Western or otherwise. In turn, postmodernists see their modernist opponents as holdouts, unwilling or unable to see the changes taking place all around them. Although it has not always been articulated in as many words, this disagreement between modernists and postmodernists has been at the center of the so-called culture wars of the past two decades. The battles in this war will not let up anytime soon, so to learn about postmodernism and cultural theory is to enter into this contested terrain about deeply fundamental issues. As just one example, as we write these words, our local newspaper has printed an editorial by a syndicated columnist decrying the threat represented by postmodernists. The editorialist claims that our nation's most prestigious liberal arts universities are failing to teach "the literary canon" and "the fundamental events in Western civilization," and instead are offering a "free fall of reinterpretation . . . cheap politics . . . [and] political correctness."[10]

Cultural studies is usually associated with the Centre for Contemporary Cultural Studies (CCCS) at the University of Birmingham in England between 1963 and 2002. During its heyday in the 1970s, the center, which is often referred to simply as the Birmingham school, played a major role in developing and disseminating frameworks for interpreting texts and cultural practices within the English-speaking world and beyond. Many scholars at the CCCS who studied contemporary affairs accepted that the contemporary era was witnessing a fundamental shift in human existence; they were called postmodernists. But cultural studies is not synonymous with postmodernism. Instead, cultural studies signifies a loose set of methodologies from which the critic can choose, such as feminism, poststructuralism, ethnography, postcolonialism, Marxism, semiotics, and many others, including postmodernism. This strategy proved highly effective and prolific, and many scholars from the CCCS developed their own theories, concepts, and methods, such as Stuart Hall in his seminal work, *Encoding/Decoding.*[11]

Generally, scholars operating in the cultural studies tradition are identified as cultural theorists, and they concern themselves with issues of identity construction and textual production. Cultural theorists do not necessarily hold that the contemporary world is transitioning out of modernity, as postmodernists do. But they interpret texts from an interdisciplinary or nondisciplinary perspective that usually challenges modernist notions of identity, textual truth, and knowledge. Since that is our goal in the present book, and since we are now at the point where we can distinguish between the terms, we will avoid *postmodern* and use the more appropriate *cultural theory* to define our interpretive approach.

Students who approach cultural theory from a non-Western perspective will recognize a tendency to frame much of the discussion within a European or U.S. framework. Indeed, you will note that many of our examples are drawn from academic debates or from popular American culture. One reason for this is that most of our readers live in the United States; thus, we find it easier to introduce alien concepts with familiar references. But another reason is that understanding postmodernity requires a solid understanding of modernity, which is closely tied to European and U.S. history, for better or worse. With these issues in mind, and as a nod to the notorious rejection by cultural studies and the Birmingham school of the difference between high art and popular culture (which we will explain later), let's open up the discussion by considering a recent Hollywood blockbuster.

THE MATRIX: BLACK LEATHER, COOL ACTION, AND MAYBE EVEN SOME CULTURAL THEORY

Few films in the recent past have generated more scholarly as well as general interest among moviegoers than *The Matrix.* It is quickly becoming the *Star Wars* of the early twenty-first century, a widely viewed film that defines a pop culture generation. *The Matrix* is a science fiction drama combining stylized violence and hip fashion with some probing questions about the state of lived existence. It asks whether the world we know and assume to exist (Earth in the late twentieth and early twenty-first centuries) really does exist.

The film revolves around the main character, Neo, played by Keanu Reeves. He is a nondescript computer programmer for Metacortex, a massive software firm in Manhattan. On the side he is a computer hacker who makes extra money selling illegal programs. Shortly after the film begins, Morpheus, played by Laurence Fishburne, contacts Neo through his computer. Neo has heard of Morpheus and believes him to be a legendary computer hacker, but as we are about to learn, Morpheus is much more than that. When Morpheus informs Neo that "the Matrix has you," Neo responds, logically, by asking, "What is the Matrix?" When he accepts an invitation from Morpheus to learn the answer, his and our (the audience's) wild ride to a new understanding of the world begins.

Morpheus tells Neo that nothing he has experienced in his life has been real. All the sights, sounds, smells, emotions, and memories that he associates with lived reality have been constructions. Morpheus says that the natural laws Neo assumes have governed his daily life do not, in fact, exist. He demonstrates this by instantly changing their surroundings. At one moment they are sitting in a room in New York City talking and the next they are standing on a rock ledge on the side of a cliff. When Neo asks, "This isn't real?" Morpheus responds, "What is real? How do you define real?" He continues, "If you are talking about what you can feel, what you can smell, what you can taste and see, then real is simply electoral signals interpreted by your brain."

Up to this point in the film, roughly thirty minutes after it begins, *The Matrix* has offered a cultural theory perspective. A central premise of cultural theory is the deconstruction of presumed reality. It contends that the reality we know does not exist and that the forces we assume to determine our existence—individual will and natural law—are social constructions rather than objective truths. Instead, cultural theorists argue that our lived experience is defined by discourses, a term we have mentioned and will define further. A widely read primer on postmodernism by Walter Truett Anderson is entitled *Reality Isn't What It Used to Be*.[12] Neo must have been thinking as much, as the world he knew was coming unraveled at the hands of Morpheus.

It is quite evident that the makers of *The Matrix* are aware of their dabbling in cultural theory. At one point early in the film, the camera zooms in on a book called *Simulacra and Simulation* by Jean Baudrillard, which Neo uses to stash his earnings from computer hacking.[13] This book has made an important contribution to cultural theory. In it, Baudrillard argues that nothing is original, that everything is a copy of everything else. This idea strikes at the heart of modernity, which searches for origin and celebrates the originality produced by individual creative genius. The filmmakers also make a deft reference to television, which cultural theorists consider symbolic of the postmodern era. Morpheus uses a TV to explain the Matrix to Neo, showing that reality can be changed as quickly as a television channel.

Despite its enticing potential in the first thirty minutes, *The Matrix* abandons its cultural theory pretenses and becomes a typical man-against-machine, sci-fi, modernist epic. Morpheus tells Neo that the world is controlled by a computer system endowed two centuries ago with artificial intelligence. This computer learned how to convert human beings into a usable power source, but because it needed to keep them docile it fills their minds with an artificial reality created by a computer program called the Matrix. Morpheus is a rebel commander trying to free humans from their captivity. Because he knows the Matrix to be a fabrication, he is able to tap into Neo's consciousness and show him the truth. This is a very modernist conceptualization. The world that Neo thinks to be real may not be, but behind the facade is a very real world of computer control and human-on-machine warfare. Furthermore, there is somebody or, in this case, some-*thing* responsible for the fabrication. Cultural theorists contend that no individual or group controls the construct, that behind it there is no reality, only more constructs.

If we ignore the modernist premise of the film *The Matrix* for a moment, we can read Neo's exposure to the Matrix itself as analogous to a modernist's initial exposure to cultural theory. The Matrix can be seen as modernity and Neo's grueling and painful journey of being unplugged from it as representative of the disequilibrium accompanying first-timers' exposure to cultural theory. They learn that the solid ground of modernity upon which they had placed so much confidence is failing them. Even worse, there is nothing to replace it. At least Neo has a real world of computers and warfare to fall back upon. A modernist learning about postmodernism is afforded no such consolation. Marshall Brennan, author of another introductory study of postmodernism, seemed to predict this sensation when he titled his overview of cultural theory *All That Is Solid Melts into Air.*[14]

The Matrix also offers a character who is symbolic of people who reject cultural theory and remain in the comfortable surroundings of modernity. This is Cypher, another human that Morpheus liberated. But Cypher finds life as a rebel—miserable living conditions and a constant threat of discovery and subsequent death—far from desirable, so he decides to betray his fellow rebels in exchange for being returned to the artificial pleasures of the Matrix. The only difference between Cypher and someone who rejects cultural theory is that Cypher knows the Matrix to be a construct. People who reject cultural theory tend to do so because they believe modernity's claims about a true and objective world.

A FEW TERMS

Before we go any further in defining cultural theory's deconstruction of reality, we should take a moment to agree on the meaning of the terms moder*nity* and modern*ism*. Modernity refers to the state of affairs (the economy, society, politics, etc.) associated with the modern era, roughly 1500 to the late twentieth century. Modernism refers to the cultural expression of that state of affairs, such as rococo, romanticism, and surrealism. To use an analogy, capitalism and science are to modernity as Michelangelo's *David* is to modernism. This same formula applies to the terms postmodern*ity* and postmodern*ism*. The former is the state of economic, political, and social affairs that has been steadily emerging since the 1960s, whereas the latter refers to the cultural expression of that condition. To rephrase the analogy, discourse and globalism are to postmodernity as the photography of Cindy Sherman and the prints of Andy Warhol are to postmodernism. As a quick side note, we need to be careful with the terms *modernism* or its Latin American variant *modernismo,* which refer to a specific period of cultural and artistic production in the late nineteenth and early twentieth centuries. Examples of this artistically prolific era include the poetry of Ruben Darío and Ezra Pound, the paintings of Piet Mondrian, the architecture of Ludwig Mies van der Rohe and Le Corbusier, the novels of James Joyce and Virginia Woolf, and the music of Arnold Schoenberg. It is unfortunately confusing that this single era would bear the same name as the broader five-hundred year epoch, but many scholars consider it appropriate because they see modernism and *modernismo* as having produced some of the most representative examples of modernist cultural expression.

DEFINING *MODERNITY,* OR 500 YEARS OF HISTORY IN A FEW PARAGRAPHS

Trying to define *modernity* in a few brief paragraphs is like trying to tell the history of a nation in an hour, but it is possible to simplify this process by focusing on two of modernity's most central concerns: the individual and natural law. Arguably, few words uttered in the history of modernity have been more definitive than those of René Descartes (1596–1650): "I think, therefore I am." With these words, Descartes gave rise to the notion of the rational subject, the modern individual, which became the basis for the entire modernist project. Descartes cannot be credited single-handedly with discovering the modern individual. For centuries, Western scholars and theologians, Saint Thomas Aquinas (1225–1274) not least among them, struggled to reconcile Christian faith with classical notions of reason. But it is not without good cause that the modern individual is sometimes called the Cartesian subject after Descartes, for he more than anyone else gave it specific and clarified meaning.

The beauty of his idea lay in its simplicity. Confronted with conflicting interpretations of the world and human nature, Descartes proposed that we had to abandon all that we knew and start over with only that which we could know for sure. In what would become a perfectly modernist exercise, Descartes sought out a foundational point of origin that would then serve as the starting point for all subsequent inquiry. He concluded that the one thing he knew for sure was his own consciousness, his own existence and capacity to reason. Therein was born the modern, rational subject. It is important to understand that Descartes did not believe he was inventing an idea. If the subject were merely an idea, it would be malleable and transitory. Rather, Descartes believed the subject was an indisputable fact, a truth that existed prior to his discovery. Although he did not articulate it in so many words, Descartes believed the discovery of the modern subject was akin to the discovery of a natural law, like gravity. Thus, he was not unlike a modern scientist, discovering fundamental truths about the world. It is for this reason that he is credited, along with Francis Bacon (1561–1626) and others, of giving birth to the modern scientific method.

Obviously, the modern subject is closely related to natural law, the second foundation of modernity. Few readers will find any reason to dispute the claim that the world is composed of natural laws that exist objectively, or prior to human interpretation. Gravity, to use our prior example, has been around forever, but it is only in the relatively recent past that human beings (such as Isaac Newton) gained knowledge of its existence in the form of a mathematical equation. We can attribute this modern concept of an objective, truthful world existing a priori, or prior to, human interpretation to the scientific revolution (roughly 1550–1650). The early scientists believed they discovered a world functioning like a machine, according to natural laws that awaited unveiling through the scientific method. Suddenly, the world was no longer a great mystery to be understood solely through moments of religious revelation. Early scientists, and indeed their recent counterparts, marveled at the harmony of nature. They believed the material world, as an expression of this harmony, provided them with the raw material to conduct experiments and thereby expose the truths about natural law.

The idea that the world is composed of objective truths that exist prior to human interpretation is known as an essentialism, which derives from a belief in ontologies, that things have predetermined properties or truths that are available to be discovered. In the words of Diana Fuss, an English professor and theorist, "Essentialism [is] a belief in the real, true essence of things, the invariable and fixed properties which define the 'whatness' of a given entity."[15] The exercise of discovering ontological and essentialist truths is known as *hermeneutics,* or "the science of interpretation."[16] The term is often closely associated with theological studies because biblical scholars used its principles to seek out the oldest religious texts under the premise that these original texts were the closest they could get to God's true meaning, to religious truth. They rejected secondary copies and translations in favor of going straight to the primary sources in their original language. Therefore, biblical hermeneutics is a sort of Cartesian approach to reading scripture; it assumes ontological truth and seeks out a foundational moment to discern it.[17]

Throughout this text, *hermeneutic, essence,* and *essentialism* will appear frequently because we use them to indicate a modernist approach. Hermeneutics is embedded in an unqualified acceptance of ontological principles, and modernity is nothing if not a hermeneutic exercise in search of essence. Modern science offers the most explicit example. In believing that natural laws exist whether or not human beings have managed to decipher them, scientists perceive empirical research as an objective means to crack nature's code. Modernists in the humanities and social sciences take a hermeneutic approach to their study of society and literature.

Despite this apparent dichotomy between modernist and postmodernist approaches to truth and knowledge, we should point out that a school of thought resides within cultural theory that contests the clean break with modernity. Associated with Jean François Lyotard and other scholars, this perspective claims that postmodernism and cultural theory grow out of intellectual traditions within modernity in which truth, self, and identity were already being "decentered."[18] For instance, Karl Marx, arguably one of the most modernist thinkers of all time, observed in an often-cited quote that "men make their history, but they do not make it just as they please; they do not make it under circumstances chosen by themselves, but under circumstances directly encountered, given and transmitted from the past."[19] According to this school, postmodernism, for all its claims to destabilizing truth claims, ends up sounding a lot like modernity in telling us that discourses exist and shape our lives. In other words, postmodernism is seen not as *anti*modernism or as nihilistic, but as bearing a strong intellectual inheritance from modernity. As some of our students have observed, the truth claim of postmodernity is that there is no truth. In this regard, postmodernity is in many ways another discourse. We will address these variances in the rest of this introduction, but we prefer to emphasize here, for the sake of clarity, the modernist/postmodernist dichotomy. At the core of modernity are the individual rational subject and natural law. Modernists believe that the basic purpose of life is to exercise our capacity for reason, which allows us to know more about natural law and the individual and to change the world for the betterment of all. As straightforward and beneficial as this modernist framework might sound, it is precisely the assumed truths of modernity that cultural theorists challenge as being loaded with complexity and alternative meanings.

ONE CHALLENGE TO MODERNITY: EDWARD SAID'S ORIENTALISM

We have found the book *Orientalism* by Edward Said (1935–2003), a former professor of literature at Columbia University, to provide an effective introduction to cultural theory.[20] *Orientalism* has become one of the most widely read and central works in the field. It was not published until 1978, by which time many of the key figures in cultural studies and postmodern thought—Michel Foucault, Jacques Derrida, Jacques Lacan, and Roland Barthes—had completed their career-defining works. But among *Orientalism*'s assets are its accessibility and wide-ranging implications.

Said was a scholar of nineteenth-century British literature, which is highly canonical. Most people who enter the field, including Said, consider it to be an essential subject for the English-speaking world and for humanity as a whole. Said was born in Palestine, but trained for his PhD at Harvard University, where he wrote his doctoral dissertation on Joseph Conrad, author of *The Heart of Darkness* (1902), a book that many scholars place squarely in the English canon. As Said progressed through his research, he found himself questioning celebratory assumptions and formulating the theory that led to *Orientalism*.

In the process of reading one text after another, Said noticed a curiously consistent reference to the Orient, and especially today's Middle East, throughout nineteenth-century British literature. Not surprisingly, given Britain's status as a colonizing empire, most of these references were negative; the Orient was described as strange, dark, oversexed, tradition-bound, and ultimately inexplicable. But more important than the positive or negative nature of these images was the simple discovery of the Orient's constant reappearance in nineteenth-century literary texts.

The more Said read, the more obvious the references became. He noted many consistent qualities of this image, including its immutability over time and its appearance in every literary genre, including novels, poems, and essays, among others. As might be expected, this image appears in virtually every work purposefully relating to the Orient. But what fascinated Said most was the Orient's appearance in works that had no ostensible relationship to that part of the world. The authors of these works employed references to the Orient in various ways but often as a literary device, such as a metaphor or an analogy. From Said's perspective, books that seemed to be about one subject suddenly took on meaning in another realm altogether. Their central theme became secondary to what lay between the lines, in the margins, or behind the scenes. Said, like other postmodernist literary critics, used the words as tools to expose what lay behind them.

Said's work shows that the qualities associated with the Orient needed no explanation; they were universally understood and accepted. Nineteenth-century Britons believed these qualities to be factual and existing prior to their encounter with them. In other words, they considered them to be ontological truths. An example is a line in *Don Juan*, a poem written in 1819 by Lord Byron: "The darkness of her Oriental eye,/Accorded with her

Moorish origin." Lord Byron endows his character with a complete set of essentialized characteristics, however stock they might have been, by simply giving her an "Oriental" eye. In nineteenth-century Britain, his readers believed the Oriental to be a universal and real type of human character. They accepted his reference without question and understood it without explanation. An example of Orientalism from a Latin American writer can be seen in the 1913 poem "Nipona" by the Chilean poet Vicente Huidobro. It celebrates the inherently exotic nature of a young Japanese woman.

While it is one thing to discover the Orient reappearing as an image in literature, it is quite another to explain why it does. When Said eventually did put words to the phenomenon, cultural studies had a powerful argument in its corner. Said drew upon studies in cultural theory to identify the Orient's consistent presence as a discourse, and he named that discourse *Orientalism*. Said was referring to a system of rules that determined how nineteenth-century Britons understood and defined the Orient. Orientalism represented British society's ongoing "conversation" about the Orient and the ensuing impression that was taken to heart collectively by the people of that time and place. It was not conspiratorially created by a group of people with an ax to grind against the Orient, sitting in a dark room smoking cigars. Rather, it was an image created unconsciously in the collective social mind through repeated encounters with a wide range of sources. Much as we turn to television or the Internet today, nineteenth-century Britons read literature to gain an understanding of their world. Orientalism was merely an idea born from the collective contributions of everyone who had anything to do with literary production—authors, readers, publishers, critics, politicians, diplomats, Middle Eastern scholars, people who had extensive firsthand knowledge of the Orient—by those who had never set foot there and by the public at large, including those who had never read a word in their lives. Said's arguments about Orientalism showed how the idea of discourse brought to life the adage "Everything is connected to everything else."

Said showed that ideas about the Orient were ideas only; furthermore, these ideas literally created what were assumed to be a priori truths. In other words, Said found that the British were constructing the Orient while believing they were describing it objectively. Orientalism provides a concrete example of the difference between modernist hermeneutics and the cultural theory alternative (which we will soon call *semiotics*). Modernists, or hermeneuticians, as they can be called, argued that there was an objective truth about the Orient well before Britons bothered with it. Whether any modernist authors had discovered that truth was open to debate, they believed it was out there to be found. Thus, a constant feature of life during the Modern era was a debate among the various interpreters of any given idea as to whose version was superior, according to its accordance with truth.

Cultural theorists reject this modernist exercise. They argue that there is no true Orient, only the collective renderings of its interpreters. Because everything had to pass through the lens of interpretation, all the British had were their interpretations; there was no Orient a priori. Instead of quarreling about whose version is more correct, cultural theorists ask how particular versions come to be.

ANOTHER CHALLENGE TO MODERNITY: ROLAND BARTHES AND DEAD AUTHORS

By arguing that discourses governed the perceptions of nineteenth-century British authors, *Orientalism* draws upon a foundational argument in cultural theory, the notion of the "death of the author," which was first published in an essay in 1968 by Roland Barthes (1915–1980).[21] Barthes asked a simple question: What happens to authors if discourses govern how they view the world? Who actually writes when an author puts pen to paper? Is it the author or the discourse? Barthes said it was discourse. In his world, the author, metaphorically, had died. Born in her or his stead was the reader— all of us who, by virtue of our participation in the collective exercise of discursive construction, are involved in the authorial process, no matter how tangential to it our role might be.

Barthes' ideas clash directly with modernity's notion of authorship. According to modernists, a text reflects the intentions of its author. Literary critics were like detectives, scholarly versions of Sherlock Holmes, who used their rational skills to seek out the truth in the form of the author's intentions, thereby gaining insight into the process of creative genius. Who, a modernist might ask, selects the words and writes them down? Who constructs the sentences, thinks of the overall story, and pulls together random ideas to create a coherent narrative? It could be no one else but the author, of course.

Cultural theorists reject this notion by asking what directs an author to make her or his selections. Can authors be omniscient, knowing every connotation, every possible motivation behind and implication of their selected thoughts, words, and ideas? To a cultural theorist such complete awareness is impossible, and they see the modernist notion of authorship, and the entire body of modernist literary interpretation, as resting precisely upon this fanciful idea. When reading, modernist literary critics commonly ask, What is the true meaning of this text? What was the author trying to say? In response, a cultural theorist might ask, What does it say about the interpreter that her or his interpretation depends upon authorial intention? Cultural theorists want to know which discourses were operating at the time and place the author wrote and what these discourses reveal to us through the words on the page. Even thoughts that seem completely original come from some place and this place is in some way familiar, however unconscious that familiarity might be. To the question of what leads authors to make their selections, cultural theorists respond by citing convention or discourse.

Cultural theorists often investigate authorial intention. But they interrogate that intention by seeking out the broader historical and discursive context in which it operates. Conventions and discourses come from some place: they have a history, and cultural theorists are in search of it. By this logic, cultural theorists should welcome a similar interrogation when it is directed at them by other scholars. After all, they, as authors, cannot possibly be aware of every discourse that informs their selective process. One example of that is the microfield that has emerged around Orientalism, including analyses of Said and his original work, and analyses of the analyses.

Consider the words before you. How could the three of us writing these words have been aware of what governs our selections? Why, for example, did we choose *The Matrix* to introduce our concepts of modernity and cultural theory? To modernists, asking such questions is tangential, even irrelevant. It strikes them as a downward spiral of endless interrogation that never provides answers—a sort of secular literary hell. As one critic put it, "[Postmodernists] tangle themselves up in a perpetual regression of qualification." [22] But to cultural theorists, such ongoing interrogation is the purpose of intellectual inquiry. They want to constantly draw out connections and question truth claims, exposing them as temporal and transitory. The moment we stop doing so, they argue, we begin falling back into modernist traps. In the words of Edward Said, "I take criticism so seriously as to believe that, even in the midst of a battle in which one is unmistakably on one side against another, there should be criticism, because there must be critical consciousness if there are to be issues, problems, values, even lives to be fought for. . . . Criticism must think of itself as life-enhancing and constitutively opposed to every form of tyranny, domination, and abuse; its social goals are noncoercive knowledge produced in the interests of human freedom." [23]

DISCOURSING ABOUT DISCOURSE:
THE FOUNDATION OF CULTURAL THEORY

Discourse is a difficult concept, but it is critical to understanding cultural theory. In brief, a discourse is a set of rules or organizing principles we use to structure meaning and determine value. It is our interpretive framework, the lens through which we view everything in the world. Cultural theorists contend that discourses come from all of us and that they constitute us; yet, none of us necessarily controls them, nor for that matter are we even aware of them. If we can set aside the modernist pretenses in *The Matrix* for a moment, the description by Morpheus of the computer program at the center of the film sounds a lot like discourse: "The Matrix is everywhere. It is all around us. Even now in this very room. You can see it when you look out your window or when you turn on your television. You can feel it when you go to work, when you go to church, when you pay your taxes." Said's Orientalism is a classic example of a discourse. It was the interpretive framework that nineteenth-century Britons used to view the Orient, and especially the region we now call the Middle East. Nobody in nineteenth-century Britain, however, was necessarily aware of its existence; they did not talk about an Orientalist perspective. But as Said has since shown us, that perspective did nevertheless exist and shaped the way successive generations of Britons defined the Orient.[24]

Some people more than others have the capacity to influence discourse. For example, one sentence uttered by the president of the United States on national television probably influences discourse more than all the words in this book. But this doesn't mean the president controls discourse any more than we do, or that he is any more aware of it than we are. The same principle applies to people in history. They, too, were governed by discourses, although they had no idea of their existence. The only advantage we have today, thanks to the studies of people like Barthes and Said, is our knowledge that discourses exist. We are like Neo awakening from our captivity in the modernist Matrix. We cannot know all the discourses affecting us at any given moment; nor, for that matter, can we gain control over the ones we do recognize. But at least we can see them for the constructs they are, and this gives us a chance to be more involved in their transmission and transformation.

Discourses exist as a result of social interaction. They originate in our efforts to make sense of the world and communicate our ideas. Discourses are constructed during any conceivable form of human communication— in writing, speech, gesture (such as body language), image (such as photography, film, and painting), and so forth. We belong simultaneously to countless discursive communities, called "societies of discourse" by Foucault, that share some form of communicative interaction.[25] Our largest conceivable discursive community is the human race, but the communities that affect us more directly are smaller—nations, regions, cities, families, ethnic or cultural groups, audiences of a particular art form, etc. Said's nineteenth-century Britons are a good example of a discursive community.

If all this discussion about discourse were just about literature, it might not warrant a strong objection. But, unfortunately for modernists, the implications of these ideas strike at one of the cores of modernity, the Cartesian subject. A question logically emerges from Said's and Barthes' ideas on the death of the author: What is the difference between an author of words and an author of actions? Cultural theorists respond that there is no difference. If an author bases creative decisions on interpretive frameworks derived from discourse, then isn't an actor (that is, simply somebody living in the world), basing her or his behavioral decisions on an interpretation of the world also derived from discourse? If so, then a "dead" author is synonymous with a "dead" actor, or a "dead" Cartesian subject.

This linkage of authors and subjects takes on special salience in Latin America, where so many political leaders began their careers as authors and intellectuals. Do they suddenly escape discourse and become omniscient subjects when they leave their writing studios and enter the presidential office? Of course not. As presidents, they base decisions on a discursively framed interpretation of the world, just as they did their creative decisions in their former lives as authors. This logic holds true for all of us. We base our decisions on our interpretations of the world and our sense of self, both of which originate in discourse. Discourse writes through the author, and it acts through the actor.

Think of this issue on a very personal level. Think of all the decisions you make in your life: who you date or marry, what you do for a living, what clothes you wear, how you decorate your room, what you eat, what books you read or which TV programs you watch, and so on. Cultural theorists contend that we make these decisions based on convention, learned behavior, and socially defined rules and norms, even if the society defining those rules is very small, such as a group of friends or a family. According to cultural theory, we are no different than authors who make decisions about putting certain words on a page; we are discursively constituted authors of our actions.

WHERE IS THE REAL ME?! IDENTITY

We are now ready to move on to the issue of identity, and more specifically, to identity categories, which will assume center stage for the remainder of this book. With these few introductory pages behind us, we can now be more specific about the goals of this book. In short, it is about how authors over the past two centuries have constructed Latin American identity. These writers, all of them major literary and political figures, described Latin America, or portions of it, in the belief that they were availing their readers of truths. In disseminating their discoveries, these authors were driven by a deep civic responsibility. They wanted to share their ideas with their fellow citizens in hopes of building support for public policies that would accord with these truths and thereby improve society for everyone. In other words, they were modernists. In this book we will show how these authors operated within discursive fields and constructed identities, rather than discovering them.

We have said that René Descartes was foundational in the "discovery" of the individual, in the modernist conception of that word. Thereafter, thinkers in the seventeenth and eighteenth centuries like John Locke and Jean-Jacques Rousseau, among others, theorized social and political systems in accordance with this newly discovered individual. But it was the Romantics, in the first half of the nineteenth century, who pushed the notion of the individual to unprecedented heights. They said that each individual was a distinct being, possessing an essence or core that was uniquely theirs. The Romantics certainly credited their early modern forerunners for discovering individuality and for releasing it from the confines of premodernity. But they believed early modernists had limited humanity's potential with an overly mechanistic approach to life, a legacy of the scientific revolution. This stifled true individual expression, according to the Romantics. They advocated releasing the individual from the bounds of early modern convention, calling for the exploration of humanity's more complex, emotional side. Borrowing from Descartes, the Romantics insisted that each of us feels distinctly and, therefore, that each of us exists uniquely.

We can see the presence of this Romantic individual even now, in the early twenty-first century. Take, for instance, the following example from Joseph Bailey, author of numerous books about relationships and personal health:

> Most of us go through life gaining only glimpses of our true or natural self. . . . Our true self is the essence of who we are, unencumbered by history or culture or learned ideas of who we think we are. That true

self is without limitations. It can never be damaged or tarnished—but it can be out of our awareness. When we are conscious, even partly so, of our true self, we're connected to a deeper intelligence that is often called wisdom, instinct or intuition.[26]

More influences than simply Romantic ideas of the individual went into Bailey's thinking here. There are hints of meditative Eastern religions, but if we set those aside for the moment and read the words in isolation, we can hardly find a more explicit expression of the idea of the modern individual. These words express the belief that each person has some true, unique self, which she or he calls an essence. This essence is revealed when people are stripped down to their very core. It is immutable, beyond the influence of culture and society. In the self-help tone of the article, the author is advocating slowing down and listening to this essence as an important life skill.

Romantics would have found nothing to dispute in Bailey's description. They and their successors in the late nineteenth and twentieth centuries did not believe individual essence to be an idea or a fabrication. Rather, like Descartes before them, they believed that human uniqueness was ontological truth; their description of it provided a deeper and more accurate understanding of humanity. They believed, as modernists do, that this essence could be discovered and described, and they set out to do that as both artists and scientists.

We can see a continuation of this belief in the work of Sigmund Freud, the founder of modern psychoanalysis. In the early twentieth century, Freud argued that he discovered human beings to be partly, if not largely driven by their unconscious, which he called the id. Freud's pronouncement of this discovery came as a shock to many modern individuals, who believed their identity and decision making were consciously determined. Instead, Freud insisted that inside each of us is an entity that we know nothing about and that, without proper management, will influence what we do and who we are more than our conscious self. But, luckily for modernity, Freud had a reassuring answer. He said that with proper technique, namely scientifically based psychoanalysis, we can decipher our respective ids and be in a position to control them. So instead of throwing the modern self to the dogs of unconscious drives, Freud empowered modern individuals to gain even more control over their identity. It is for this reason that Freud is considered by many, including himself, to be one of the two or three most important architects of modern identity.

We have seen, then, how modernity has given rise to the notion of individual identity and to the idea that there is at the core of every person a fundamentally unique individual. But—and this is important—a tremendous paradox exists at the core of these modernist notions of identity, and it is on this paradox that most of this book will be centered. While modernity claims to have discovered and released the Cartesian individual, it has simultaneously cemented individuals into rigid and unyielding categories of group identity. Cultural theorists use the term *essence* to refer to these categories, and they accuse modernists of engaging in acts of essentialism or essentialization.

WHERE IS THE REAL US?! GROUP ESSENCES

For modernists, individuals possess not only a unique core or essence, but certain groups of people can be defined by traits shared by their individual members. As these traits are intrinsic, they are immutable and ontological; in other words, they exist prior to our perception of them. Like natural law, they simply exist. Therefore, according to modernists, essences can be identified and described by modern techniques; namely, the scientific method. While the number of these essential categories is vast, cultural theorists have so far tended to focus on only a few, and of those we have selected four for this book: race, class, gender, and nation.

We might think of modernists conceptualizing essentialized identities as dog breeders talking about different types of dogs. They consider each breed to have a distinct set of characteristics that is intrinsic, immutable, or essential. One breed is high-energy, another is relaxed; one is highly intelligent, another is unresponsive, and so forth. After the discovery of genetics in the mid-twentieth century, these traits were referred to as genetic in origin, whereas previously it was thought that they were simply passed along "in the blood," as was often said. What distinguishes each breed, even before its inherent traits are manifested in behavior, is physical appearance. When we see a dog that looks like a Jack Russell terrier, we expect it to behave according to its inherent Jack Russell essence.

Modernists' conceptualizations of race, class, gender, and nation have functioned very similarly to breeders' classifications of dogs. Modernists believed that each of the varying subgroups of these four categories were distinguishable as physical types and that these corresponded to immutable essences. They set races apart by skin color, hair texture, and various other physical features; genders by sex organs and body parts; classes by bloodline or possession of property; and nationalities, which can be a bit more abstract, by the physical manifestations of a national people. Modernists argued that there existed, for instance, a white race and a black race, a male

FIGURES 1.5 AND 1.6   *An ethnically diverse group of Cuban people come together in Céspedes Park, Santiago de Cuba, 1991. Photographs by Erik Ching*

gender and a female gender, a class of owners and a class of workers, and varying nationalities—French, German, American, and so forth—and that each of these physical groupings corresponded to inherent characteristics. There was something essentially black about people with the physical manifestations of darker skin and kinkier hair. Not surprisingly, throughout most of modern Western history, the dominant paradigm portrayed black essence negatively; admittedly, however, there have also been positive contrasts that were no less essentialistic.

The other categories of gender, class, and nation were similarly dichotomized and essentialized. The basic rule was that when a person observed the physical markers of a particular group, she or he could safely assume that beneath that manifestation was an essentialized foundation. Or when the physical marker was not evident or was covered up, the essence still applied. So even if a black person could have been "whitened," the essential quality of blackness was still determinant. Or if a proletarian was dressed up in a rich person's clothes, the essential proletarian traits remained intact.

Essences, according to the logic of scientific modernism, were not ideas or inventions of the mind, but naturally occurring qualities that could be defined and classified just like any other naturally occurring ontology. So when modernists set out to map the physical world, they also defined and classified these varying human types. One of the enduring features of modernity has been a constant debate over the true meaning of these respective categories. Questioning their existence, however, was not part of the equation; at least not until late, late modernity in the latter half of the twentieth century.

Two recent novels provide easily accessible examples of racial essentialism. The first is *The Shot*, published in 1999 by Philip Kerr, a highly successful thriller writer whose four prior novels have all been put into development for film. Mary, one of Kerr's characters in *The Shot*, is from Jamaica and is of Chinese and African ancestry. Kerr identifies her as "a Chigro—half Chinese, half Negro—born in Kingston, Jamaica. In her it was a spectacularly successful combination for she was as beautiful and athletic as she was intelligent and industrious." [27] Setting aside the reference to beauty for the moment, it is evident that Kerr believes he is communicating in a universally truthful language of race, that people of Chinese and African ancestry have immutable traits. In the case of black people, the norm is athleticism; and in the case of Chinese or Asian people, it is intelligence and industriousness.

The second example is Laura Esquivel's 1989 novel *Como agua para chocolate* (*Like Water for Chocolate*). The story, set in early twentieth-century

Mexico, revolves around the lives of three sisters, one of whom, Gertrudis, possesses a sense of rhythm quite distinct from the rest of her family. This always perplexed the family and the rest of the community, for how could three girls with the same parentage and social upbringing possess such different capacities for dance? The novel reveals that Gertrudis was conceived when her mother had an affair with a man who "had Negro blood in his veins."[28] But, as chance would have it, her physical appearance did not reveal her mixed racial heritage, and almost no one, not even Gertrudis, knew how different her ancestry was; hence the confusion. The idea being put forth by the narrator is that her black essence could not be hidden, and it expressed itself in the form of "rhythm and other qualities."[29] Whether Esquivel believes in this racial essentialism herself, or whether she simply endowed her narrator with a belief in it, is another matter, but various analyses of her book have taken her to task for this uncritical use of race to define the character of Gertrudis.

Another example of racial essentialism was provided in 2006 by Arnold Schwarzenegger, the governor of California. A closed-door meeting with members of his staff was recorded and a copy of the tape was secretly released to the Los Angeles Times. On the tape of the meeting, Schwarzenegger is heard speculating with Susan Kennedy, his chief of staff, about the nationality of state Assemblywoman Bonnie Garcia. He called Garcia naturally feisty because of her race. "I mean Cuban, Puerto Rican, they are all very hot," Schwarzenegger was quoted as saying in the Los Angeles Times. "They have the, you know, part of the black blood in them and part of the Latino blood in them that together makes it."

One of the principal objectives of cultural theorists is to expose essentialisms as constructs rather than truths. Regarding race (we set aside gender, class, and nation for a moment), cultural theorists contend that it is nothing more than an idea, a discourse. They demonstrate this through what they call deconstruction, or decentering. They "interrogate" racialized terms and the premises upon which they are based. In short, they take them apart. A cultural theorist might first take a historical approach to the idea of race, illustrating when, where, and why its modernist conceptualizations came into existence. Race is proved to be a historically contingent idea, a concept dependent upon peculiar social, political, economic, and cultural contexts in a particular place and time. They might show how the idea of race entered into society's collective consciousness and then later, when it became a discourse, how it shaped subsequent "discoveries." One of the things cultural theorists have shown us is how discourse, or portions of a discourse, can be resilient. The belief in white supremacy provides one good example.

But as discourses are ultimately nothing more than ideas or mental constructs, they can also change according to the shifting needs of the discursive communities that use them. Cultural theorists seek out these changes as further proof of the existence of discourse. They point, for example, to the variations in meaning of the term *black* in different national or regional contexts. They show that it means one thing in the United States and another in Brazil; that it meant one thing in Brazil in the 1960s, and another since 2000; or that it meant one thing in southern Brazil since 2000 and another in northern Brazil. How, cultural theorists ask, can there be a true and objective quality to race if a uniformly held meaning of it, beyond the unfortunate consistency of white supremacy, has never existed?

Modernists respond to this type of criticism with an appeal to the scientific method, saying that the quest for truth is often long and arduous. They believe that we can expect only that, at any given moment, multiple interpretations of racial essence will exist simultaneously. The challenge, a modernist would insist, is to determine which one is correct and then use it to eradicate the others. Cultural theorists reject the idea that any one of these constructs is any more accurate than the other. Instead, they insist that each is nothing more than a variation on a common discursive theme, the variations of which reflect the needs of distinct discursive communities and eras.

Cultural theorists also expose essentialism as discursively constituted by revealing the tendency of essentialists to "collapse" categories. A text, for example, might superficially discuss race but at the same time comment on nation, class, or gender. A writer from a nineteenth-century Latin American country might discuss indigenous peoples, describing their traits, the qualities that make them indigenous, and so forth. This writer might mention that the majority of indigenous people in his country are lower class and that they constitute an important proportion of the nation's population. Suddenly, by association and without ever having explicitly set out to do so, the writer has made a major declaration about his nation's identity, linking it to essential qualities of class and race. And by commenting on his own nation, the author might also be making a broader commentary about Latin America and/or the United States and Europe, as it is not uncommon to use such broad comparisons. We can assume, of course, that authors sometimes make these associations purposefully, but the theory of the death of the author invalidates the attempt to identify intent in writing. So cultural theorists are interested in exposing these associations as revelations into the inner workings of discourse.

WHERE IS THE REAL LATIN AMERICA?!

The focal point of this book is Latin American identity in the nineteenth and twentieth centuries. So in addition to race, class, gender, and nation, we are adding Latin America to our list of modernist identity categories. We might define this as a multinational identity, referring to the group of nations and peoples in the Western Hemisphere that are south of the United States. For the past two hundred years, Latin America, like most of the rest of the world during that time, has been dominated by modernist conceptualizations of identity and modernist attempts to discern ontological truths. Whether or not they set out with the purposeful and conscious intent to do so, virtually every author during the modernist era participated in a broad project of seeking out the truth about Latin America.

As modernists, these various interpreters debated among themselves as to who possessed the most accurate version of Latin America. Sometimes this debate was overt and purposeful, as in the case of the renowned treatise on Mexican identity by Octavio Paz in *The Labyrinth of Solitude*.[30] Other times, the debate has been less direct, even accidental, as authors simply set out to write a story or comment on their lives, families, towns, or regions, but then found that their commentaries, as texts, operated in a broader whole of interpretation.

In this book, we provide selections from roughly a dozen examples spanning the past two centuries and fit each text into its respective historical era and/or literary movement. Some of these eras and movements will likely be new to someone unfamiliar with Latin American history, but some might be quite recognizable. For instance, we find that even people who possess limited knowledge of Latin America have heard of magical realism, a literary movement dating back to the 1960s and 1970s, or at least of one of its main contributors, Colombian author Gabriel García Márquez. He was one of a number of magical realist authors to win a Nobel Prize during this so-called boom in Latin American literary production. We will demonstrate how magical realist authors were part of a massive, collective, albeit uncoordinated attempt to reveal the true Latin America. Our goal is to illustrate these modernist foundations and show their ideological and discursive makeup.

Hopefully, it is evident by now that we do not distinguish between fiction and nonfiction in our interpretation of texts. Regardless of the intellectual tradition from which it originates, whether it be fiction, drama, poetry, history, sociology, politics, or some other genre, almost every text produced in the nineteenth and twentieth centuries participates in the modernist

exercise of trying to discover the true Latin America. A text's genre or intellectual tradition might be worth noting in that it can shed insight on the
distinct discursive communities to which its authors belong, or to whom
it is directed. But to argue, as modernists are wont to do, that one field of
production, such as literature or history, is better equipped to reveal truth,
is an untenable proposition. Likewise, to argue that certain forms of so-
called high culture (like poetry) possess greater capacity to reveal the truth
than "low" culture (like pop fiction or film) also lacks credibility. Drawing
on Barthes' theory of the death of the author, every writer is subject to discourse and every text is part of a collective expression of discursive production. We are in pursuit of those discourses.

ANOTHER FORM OF IMPERIALISM? LATIN AMERICA AND CULTURAL STUDIES

The exercise of interpreting modern Latin America from a cultural theory
perspective does not lend itself to scholarly consensus. Modernists reject
it out of hand, and even cultural theorists disagree as to how it should be
conducted. For instance, within the broad community of Latin American
scholars, a sort of division exists as to which theoretical traditions are best
suited to interpreting Latin American identity. A group of these scholars,
many of whom are either from Latin America or work there, suggests that
the contributions to cultural studies from U.S. and European academic institutions might have limited applicability for Latin America.

The scholars in this group are far from homogeneous in their approaches,
and they are not necessarily organized. Their work has been published
throughout Latin America, and little of it has been translated into English,
so it remains relatively unknown to U.S. and European scholars—although
anthologies published in 2001 and 2004 promise to give it wider exposure.[31]
What unites these scholars is a shared belief in the existence of a distinct
Anglo/North American variant of cultural studies, often referred to simply
as U.S. cultural studies, and in the idea that this so-called school has failed
to incorporate intellectual traditions from Latin America.

This claim might seem surprising, given that an important impetus behind the development of cultural studies in U.S. and European intellectual
circles was the insistence that modernist scholarship was too limited in
focus and needed to include more and differing perspectives. Nevertheless,
Neil Larsen, one of these scholars, puts the issue in the form of a question:
"Do the various critical theories often termed 'postmodern' enable us to
make better sense of contemporary Latin American reality, or do they merely

continue a covertly imperializing practice of assimilating Latin American or postcolonial culture itself to critical canons that the latter have had no hand in establishing?"[32]

The wording of this question raises a number of issues at the core of the debate. One of them concerns the historically unequal relationship between Latin America, the United States, and Europe. Scholars like Larsen wonder to what extent academic communities in the United States and Europe are able to escape this broader imperial ethos, however critical of it they might be. For instance, Larsen identifies cultural studies in the United States and Europe as a "critical canon." His doing so is, of course, ironic because cultural theory supposedly rejects canons as modernist hierarchies. But Larsen is trying to draw attention to the fact that, from the perspective of Latin American scholars, the academic system in the United States and Europe can seem quite imperial and exclusive. Scholars in the United States and Europe, compared with their Latin American colleagues, have disproportionate access to the financial resources necessary for research and publication. Thus, much of the academic dialogue about cultural studies and Latin American studies occurs in the United States and Europe and excludes Latin American scholars and their ideas. Furthermore, as cultural studies has moved more into the academic mainstream in the United States, allowing it to function "canonically," Larsen's question suggests that its adherents are wrapped up in broader institutionalized issues within the academy in which preserving intellectual authority assumes priority.

Larsen is something of an opponent of cultural theory, and his observations about U.S. cultural studies fit into his broader belief that modernist frameworks retain some liberating qualities for Latin America. But a large contingent of those scholars who share Larsen's critique of U.S. cultural studies do not share his faith in modernism and believe that cultural theory offers valuable insights on Latin American identity. They do, however, point out an additional problem for U.S. cultural studies: It ignores a long and well-developed tradition of cultural studies in Latin America.

Daniel Mato is one of these scholars. Argentine by birth but now working as an academic in Venezuela, Mato says he first came to the United States in 1991 on a faculty exchange program and was surprised to discover that his North American colleagues defined him as a cultural studies scholar: "The research I [had] been recently doing received here a name that was new to me, 'Cultural Studies.' Surprisingly for me, I began being introduced as a 'Cultural Studies scholar.'" Mato was disturbed by this experience. He believed that his intellectual training in Latin America was organic, but in

the United States it was "consumed," labeled, and fit into a foreign intellectual tradition. "How might it have happened," he asked, "that all that
we thought we had invented or consciously adapted . . . had, in fact, been
invented in one place, Birmingham (UK), and then re-engineered in the U.S.
and exported to the rest of the world?"[33] Other contemporary scholars, like
the Colombian Jesús Martín Barbero, the Argentine Beatriz Sarlo, and the
Argentine/Mexican Néstor García Canclini have reiterated Mato's sentiments, insisting that they were doing cultural studies before they knew the
label existed.[34]

   Mato's concern is that U.S. cultural studies is being imposed on Latin
American scholars rather than being created by them or in consultation
with them. This, he argues, recreates the classic imperial act of fetishiz-
ing Latin America, of seeing it as an exotic object to be observed, not as a
subject of its own making. As Mato put it, "If what our English-speaking
colleagues are seeking in Latin America are their peers, not their followers,
then the focus has to be made on a diversity of intellectual practices that
are not necessarily related to the English-speaking tradition of Cultural
Studies."[35] Mato wonders if U.S.-based scholars of Latin America, whether
or not they are of Anglo or Latino descent, might be "Orientalizing" Latin
America.

   Scholars like Mato, Martín Barbero, Sarlo, and Canclini contend that the
roots of their so-called cultural studies frameworks are indigenous to Latin
America, dating back at least to the early twentieth century, when politically engaged intellectuals like José Martí in Cuba or José Martiátegui in
Peru devised broadly inclusive philosophical traditions to challenge social
and political hierarchy. Their contributions, while still very modernist, laid
the foundation for later scholar-activists like Paulo Freire in Brazil, Roberto
Fernández Retamar in Cuba, and Angel Rama in Uruguay, who devised intellectual traditions that matured alongside the schools of cultural studies
in the United States and Europe. Furthermore, critics of the so-called U.S.
school of Latin American cultural studies point out that the characteristics
typical of postmodernist literature in the United States and Europe ("decentering the subject, dissolving borders among literary genres, reader's participation, among others") were being practiced by Latin Americans already as
part of their modernist literary movement.[36]

   Reaction from the so-called U.S. school of Latin American cultural studies has varied. Some worry that the Latin American critics are falling into
old traps of essentializing Latin American identity and the scholars suited
to study it. Others insist that Latin Americans have long been contributing
to U.S. and European cultural studies traditions. Marc Zimmerman, a Latin

Americanist at the University of Houston, has promoted this argument, contending that "European theory has brought key perspectives to a table Latin Americans helped build." Zimmerman uses the example of Stuart Hall, long-time director of the Birmingham school, as an example. Hall, who is Jamaican-born, drew upon the work of Ernesto Laclau, an Argentine, to revise the renowned theoretical premises of Antonio Gramsci, a Sardinian/ Italian. Zimmerman questions how this could be defined as an Anglo or U.S. intellectual tradition.[37] Zimmerman's critics would argue that Hall is an exception to the norm.

In addition to issues of academic tradition and institutionalized power relationships, there is also a serious intellectual aspect to the debate. The Latin American school accuses its U.S. counterparts of subscribing to a more extremist version of cultural theory, in which most everything is decentered and seen as discursively constituted, whereas Latin Americans advocate for retaining more empirical standards and centered identities.

A comparison to feminist criticism in the United States and Europe might help clarify the nature of the debate. On the one hand, feminist critics played a key role in the development of cultural studies and postmodern theory in the 1960s and 1970s. Perhaps not surprisingly, this coincided with the civil rights movement and expanding opportunities for women and minorities. Women were participating in the making of history to an unprecedented degree, thereby moving them from the periphery to the center. In theoretical terms, they were becoming "centered" or were able for the first time to claim identity as Cartesian subjects. But some feminist theorists noted the distressing coincidence that just as women were making these momentous gains, cultural theory came along and decentered the self and turned the subject into a discourse. The goals that women's rights activists had struggled to achieve for so long seemed to be vanishing into the thin air of discourse. Feminist criticism has remained a central part of cultural studies, but this issue provided an opportunity for cultural theorists to act on their own words and recognize that every new position, no matter how progressive it might seem, has the potential to mask hierarchical power relations, regardless of the conscious intent of its authors.

Latin American critics of U.S. cultural studies have confronted a similar problem. Their homelands are still struggling to achieve developmental parity with the United States and Europe. They ask to what extent it is possible to be postmodern and to decenter all the old modernist identities without having had the chance to be fully modern. Just as feminists were concerned about the decentered self, some Latin American scholars are concerned that a rampant embrace of cultural theory would erode the few empirical defenses they have, such as nation or class, against the raw economic and military power of the developed world.

This debate has pushed them to propose a sort of third way that avoids unbridled decentering but remains attentive to the problems of essentialism. This theoretical position has revolved around terms like *hybridity* and *locality*, or local knowledge, and is commonly associated with García Canclini and the Argentine Walter Mignolo, among others.[38] Its basic premise is that intellectual traditions have to allow room for local conditions, or concrete local interests, to make an impact; people on the margins or the periphery have to be able to talk back to the metropolis and its globally oriented propositions. Ideally, a sort of constant dialogue would occur between local and global in which, at the very least, Latin American theorists could explain why certain aspects of U.S. cultural studies strike them as unproductive, if not threatening, and more a defense of U.S. and European power than a constant state of criticism.

The Latin American scholars advocating this third way find common cause with a sector inside the European and U.S. cultural studies tradition. One scholar to whom they often refer is Stuart Hall. In particular, they identify with Hall's arguments about establishing a place from which to begin any discussion and analysis. Hall contends that people, be they as individuals or in groups, have to acknowledge that they come from some place, even an intellectual tradition or cultural background, which makes them who they are. As long as they do not essentialize it, Hall argues that they need to use that place as their entry into the sea of discourse and shifting identities. Once they have this point of departure, they are ready to move onto the next temporary place. Without some place, Hall argues, people will be talking from nowhere. More recently, the Ghanaian-born philosopher K. A. Appiah has been advocating an approach to identity similar to Stuart Hall's.[39]

A similar idea is also found in the excerpt in Chapter 7 from David Parker, who examines the issue of class. In describing class identity as a social construct, Parker approaches language from the perspective of Mikhail Bakhtin (1895–1975), the Russian theorist who argued that language is neither an entirely closed system that controls its human interlocutors nor an entirely open one that is subject to human whim. In other words, every aspect of language arrives with a history, or comes from some place that limits human ability to dictate its meaning at will. But human beings are not simply at the mercy of language and convention; they are capable of affecting and influencing them both. Thus, according to Bakhtin, language is a two-way street between its own history and the desires of its contemporary interlocutors. In adopting this approach, Parker stakes out a middle position between the fully-in-control rational subject and the fully discoursed, de-centered self.

Hall's and Parker's arguments are very similar to the theories of hybrid-ity and local knowledge being advanced by Latin American theorists. Those arguments validate the specificities of local issues, while remaining atten-tive to generalizing global trends.

NOTES

1. For a good analysis of this image, see Louis Montrose, "The Work of Gender in the Discourse of Discovery," *Representations* 33 (Winter, 1991): 1–41; reprinted in Stephen Greenblat, *New World Encounters* (Berkeley: U of California P, 1993) 177–217.

2. For more images, including this one from *Puck*, see John J. Johnson, *Latin America in Caricature* (Austin: U of Texas P, 1980), chap. 3.

3. Jim Heimann, *Mexicana: Vintage Mexican Graphics* (New York: Taschen, 2002).

4. Jim Heimann, e-mail with the authors, 1 Nov. 2005. The authors would like to thank Mr. Heimann for assistance.

5. Daniel Mato, "Latin American Intellectual Practices in Culture and Power," lecture delivered at the King Juan Carlos I of Spain Center, New York University, 1 Oct. 2000 <http://www.nyu.edu/gsas/dept/latin/Mato_program.pdf>.

6. Christopher Butler, *Postmodernism: A Very Short Introduction* (New York: Oxford UP, 2002) 28.

7. Alan Sokal, "Transgressing the Boundaries: Toward a Transformative Hermeneutics of Quantum Gravity," *Social Text* 46/47 (Spring/Summer 1996): 217–252.

8. Jonah Goldberg, "Facts and Firemen: An Accidental Phrase Leaps Glo-riously from Controversy," *National Review Online*, 18 Jan. 2002 <http://www.nationalreview.com/goldberg/goldbergprint011802.html>.

9. See Tony Bennett, Lawrence Grossberg, and Meaghan Morris, *New Keywords: A Revised Vocabulary of Culture and Society* (Oxford: Black-well, 2005); Peter Sedgewick and Andrew Edgar, eds., *Cultural Theory: The Key Concepts*, 2nd ed. (New York: Routledge, 2005); and Julian Wolfrey, *Critical Keywords in Literary and Cultural Theory* (Chicago: Taylor & Francis, 2002).

10. Suzanne Fields, "Political Correctness Is Suffocating True Liberal Edu-cation," *The Greenville News*, 4 Nov. 2003: 7A.

11. For a good introduction to the history of the CCCS and its main meth-odologies, see Patrick Branlinger, *Crusoe's Footprints: Cultural Studies in Britain and America* (New York: Routledge, 1990). Some of the seminal es-says related to the theories, methods, and critiques of cultural texts related to cultural studies, including Stuart Hall's work "Encoding/Decoding" can be found in Lawrence Grossberg, Cary Nelson, and Paula Treichler, eds., *Cultural Studies* (New York: Routledge, 1992); Simon During, ed., *The Cul-*

tural Studies Reader (New York: Routledge, 1993); Meenkshi Durham and Douglas Kellner, eds., *Media and Cultural Studies: Keywords* (Malden, MA: Blackwell, 2001). For those interested in learning more about the main theorists and debates concerning the relationship between postmodernism and poststructuralism, see Christopher Norris, *Deconstruction and the "Unfinished Project of Modernity"* (London: Athlone, 2000); Steven Best and Douglas Kellner, *Postmodern Theory: Critical Investigations* (New York: Guilford, 1991).

12. Walter Truett Anderson, *Reality Isn't What It Used to Be* (San Francisco: Harper, 1990).

13. Jean Baudrillard, *Simulacra and Simulation* (Ann Arbor: U of Michigan P, 1994).

14. Marshall Berman, *All that Is Solid Melts into Air* (New York: Simon, 1982).

15. Diana Fuss, *Essentially Speaking: Feminism, Nature and Difference* (London: Routledge, 1989) xi–xii. For a quick definition of essentialism, see Brian Cliff's description on the Emory University's English Department Web site from spring 1996 <http://www.english.emory.edu/Bahri/Essentialism.html>.

16. David Guralink, ed., *Webster's New World Dictionary* (New York: Simon & Schuster, 1980) 656.

17. We should also point out that the term *hermeneutic* has had different meanings in various intellectual traditions. In twentieth-century continental philosophy, it has had semiotic overtones in what has come to be identified as *phenomenology*. According to this school of thought, a "hermeneut," the reader or interpreter of a text, is always recognized as being historically situated; thus, "no matter how 'close' she claims to be to identifying the conditions of its [the text's] production, [she] will always be mediated by [. . .] historically constructed assumptions and expectations." Clive Cazeaux, ed., *The Continental Aesthetics Reader* (New York: Routledge, 2000) 65. Throughout this text, the version of hermeneutics that we employ emerged from literature classrooms, where it meant the search for the author's original intentions as the litmus test for authentic, original, accurate, and, above all, good literary analysis. It is for this reason that we will use the terms *hermeneutic* and *modern* more or less interchangeably.

18. Jean François Lyotard, *The Postmodern Condition: A Report on Knowledge* (Minneapolis: U of Minnesota P, 1984).

19. Karl Marx, *The 18th Brumaire of Louis Bonaparte* (Moscow: Progress, 1972) 120.

20. Edward Said, *Orientalism* (New York: Pantheon, 1978).

21. "Death of the Author" was originally published in 1968 but appeared in translation in English for the first time in Roland Barthes, *Image-Music-Text* (New York: Hill & Wang, 1977).

22. Butler, *Postmodernism* 28.

23. Edward Said, *The World, the Text and the Critic* (Cambridge: Harvard UP, 1983) 34.

24. For a brief and convenient definition of discourse, see Paul A. Bové, "Discourse," in Frank Lentricchia and Thomas McLaughin, eds., *Critical Terms for Literary Study* (Chicago: U of Chicago P, 1995).

25. Michel Foucault, "The Order of Discourse," ed. M. Shapiro, *Language and Politics* (New York: NYUP, 1984) 108–138.

26. Joseph Bailey, "Deep Listening," *Natural Health* (Nov/Dec 2003): 105, which is adapted from his book, *Slowing Down to the Speed of Love* (New York: McGraw-Hill, 2003).

27. Philip Kerr, *The Shot: A Thriller* (New York: Atria, 2000) 34.

28. Laura Esquivel, *Like Water for Chocolate: A Novel in Monthly Install-ments, With Recipes, Romances, and Home Remedies* (New York: Double-day, 1992) 137. Originally published in Spanish in 1989.

29. Esquivel 180.

30. Octavio Paz, *The Labyrinth of Solitude: Life and Thought in Mexico*, trans. Lysander Kemp (New York: Grove, 1961); first published in Spanish as *El laberinto de la soledad* (1950).

31. Ana Del Sarto, Alicia Ríos, and Abril Trigo, eds., *The Latin American Cultural Studies Reader* (Durham: Duke UP, 2004); Pedro Lange-Churión and Eduardo Mendieta, eds., *Latin American and Postmodernity: A Con-temporary Reader* (Amherst, NY: Humanity, 2001).

32. Neil Larsen, *Reading North by South* (Minneapolis: U of Minnesota P, 1995) 189; see also, Del Sarto 729.

33. Mato 7–8.

34. Mato 11, 49.

35. Mato 49.

36. Lange-Churión and Mendieta, *Latin American and Postmodernity*, 33.

37. Marc Zimmerman, "Transnational Crossings and the Development of Latin American Cultural Studies," Latin American Cultural Activities and Studies Arena Web site, University of Houston, 25 July 2005 <http://www.hfac.uh.edu/mcl/faculty/zimmerman/lacasa/Estudios%20Culturales%20Articles/Marc%20Zimmerman.pdf>. See also Zimmerman's "Cultural Studies and Transnational Process: The French Connection," coord. Cata-lina Castellón and Cristián Santibáñez y MZ, *Estudios culturales y cues-tiones de globalización*, LACASA 2004, 15 Sept. 2005 <http://www.class.uh.edu/mcl/>.

38. Néstor García Canclini, *Hybrid Cultures: Strategies for Entering and Leaving Modernity* (Minneapolis: U of Minnesota P, 1989); Walter Mignolo, *Local Histories/Global Design: Coloniality, Subaltern Knowledges and Border Thinking* (Princeton: Princeton UP, 2000). See also Mignolo's most recent exploration of Latin American identity, *The Idea of Latin America* (Oxford: Blackwell, 2005).

39. K. A. Appiah, *The Ethics of Identity* (Princeton: Princeton UP, 2004).

CHAPTER 2

Saussure, Signs, and Semiotics, or Lots of Words That Begin with S

With that broad description of cultural theory behind us, we will now turn to a more detailed and diagrammatic comparison of essentialism and semiotics. We take as our starting point the turn of the twentieth century, when empiricism achieved its greatest influence on the humanities. This is the era when architecture and art took an industrial turn, as seen in French art nouveau and art deco; when ethnographic studies merged science with humanistic anthropology; and, perhaps most notably, when the naturalistic movement in literature asserted that novels are akin to laboratories in which authors, like scientists, conduct experiments on their subjects (characters and plot) to discover new laws of existence (denouements).

Linguistics also witnessed a scientific turn in the early twentieth century. At the center of this movement was Ferdinand de Saussure (1857–1913), a Swiss linguist whose approach came to be known as semiotics, or the language of signs.[1] Before Saussure, linguistics tended to be an exercise in etymology. Scholars believed the meaning of a language could be discovered by seeking out the historical origins or genealogy of words. The modernist foundations of etymology should be quite clear. Believing that languages had ontological meaning that could be scientifically discovered, etymologists were prototypical hermeneuticians, or essentialists. Saussure ruptured this approach by defining words as belonging to a system of what he called signs. He insisted that everything in the world, every sound, image, gesture, thing, etc., is a sign. In short, Saussure argued that the entire material world and every attempt by human beings to communicate with one another about it consist of signs. This might sound like the ranting of a harmless academic, and Saussure's ideas did indeed remain relatively unknown and obscure for many years after his death in 1913. But his theories experienced a renaissance in the 1950s and 1960s when emerging postmodernist scholars saw the revolutionary implications of his work. His theories cracked the modernist system and contributed to the advent of cultural theory and postmodernism.

According to Saussure, a sign consists of two inextricable parts: the *signifier* and the *signified*. The signifier is the vehicle that carries a mental concept, such as a word, a wink, a photograph, an expression, etc. The signified is the abstract idea or the meaning that is attached to the vehicle. For example, the way one crosses one's legs (the signifier) conjures the abstract idea of femininity or masculinity (the signified), and the union of the two (the gesture plus the mental impression associated with it) is known as the sign.

Saussure's primary contribution to cultural theory is his assertion that the relationship between signifier and signified is at once arbitrary and conventional. By this he means that there is no inherent or natural connection between the language we use and the objects or ideas to which words refer (the relationship is arbitrary). Thus, meaning (the signified) is not built into the signifier but emerges from our collective norms and cultural practices (convention). Saussure never used *discourse* to define how that meaning is determined, but hopefully you can see how well his ideas would fit with that term once it became available in the 1960s.

Because the relationship between signifier and signified is culturally determined, we can expect their relationship to vary across time and space. The notion of feminine/masculine (the signified) associated with certain types of leg crossing (the signifier) will differ from place to place and from one time period to another. The manner in which one crosses one's legs will signify differently (will count for different meanings) between, say, rural and urban New York, between the northern and southern United States, between North and South America, between America and Europe, and between the West and Asia (variation across space). Similarly, leg-crossing styles and their respective meanings were different in the United States in the 1950s compared with today (variation across time). Given that the nature of signs is therefore arbitrary, we can expect the relationship between signifier and signified to be in a constant state of flux. Although any given sign might be quite durable, even lasting centuries without much change, others might be much more fleeting. Ultimately, however, all signs can and will vary.

Even though Saussure challenged the etymological approach to language, his sign system possessed some deeply modernist characteristics. He was a structuralist. He believed that linguistic communication exhibited traits, or structures, that were universal to all human beings, regardless of the different cultures or eras in which they lived. As a structuralist, Saussure wanted to discover these universal and underlying principals.

Saussure's structuralism might seem to contradict his insistence on the arbitrary yet conventional nature of sign systems; indeed, this is why his ideas represent an important development in the transition to postmodernism. But he himself was not a postmodernist or cultural theorist. Much like Sigmund Freud, his contemporary, Saussure ruptured some aspects of modernist thinking while reinforcing others. In the 1960s, scholars who used his ideas to develop the first stages of cultural theory rejected his structuralism but retained his ideas about the arbitrary yet conventional nature of creating meaning. For that reason, scholars like Jacques Derrida (1930–2004), who can be described as a poststructuralist linguist, became founding figures in cultural theory.

Using the leg-crossing signifier, we can compare a pre-Saussurian (essentialist or hermeneutic) and post-Saussurian (semiotic) approach to notions of femininity and masculinity. A hermeneutician would argue that ontological male and female essences exist, and the way a person crosses one's legs reflects an innate masculine or feminine state. In contrast, a semiotician would reject the idea of intrinsic traits and contend that the playing out of feminine and masculine roles does not arise from the awakening of women and men to their true essences but is a performance that is both learned from others and then practiced to ensure one's place in the culturally constructed gender structure. Semioticians do not deny the existence of anatomical, hormonal, and physiological distinctions between individuals. They do point out, however, that these distinctions become imbued with relative values given the prevailing gender discourse. In this way, notions regarding what counts as feminine and what counts as masculine create women and men, rather than the other way around. So, if a boy crosses his legs "like a girl," he becomes like a girl, according to convention. We are being a bit facetious in making that claim, of course, but anyone who has been through grade school knows that a boy who exhibits what are thought of as feminine qualities will come under suspicion of lacking innate masculinity. He will be readily derided with insults that pertain to that don't-be-such-a-girl logic.

CULTURAL THEORY IN SEVEN SIMPLE GRAPHS

By depicting this comparison between essentialism/hermeneutics and semiotics as graphs, we can better see how Saussure's ideas revolutionized

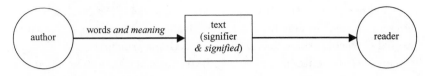

GRAPH 2.1

literary theory. From an essentialist approach, an author is thought to write the words of his or her novel on the page and to imbue specific meaning into them. According to this model, authorial intent exists.

According to the essentialist view, the author writes the text, consciously placing words *and* meaning onto the page, the reader receives these words, and then tries to decipher the author's inhered meaning (see Graph 2.1). It is the job of the reader to get as close to the original intent of the author as possible (like a scholarly Sherlock Holmes, as in our analogy). Whoever accomplishes this task best is recognized as possessing the most accurate interpretation of the work. Likewise, the best authors are regarded as those who have the best or deepest meanings within their texts. They are honored with Nobel Prizes and other literary awards. Naturally, there is intense debate among modernist critics as to which authors are best or which readers possess the most accurate interpretation. Some believe that Argentine author Jorge Luis Borges was the greatest writer who ever lived; others think his work is unnecessarily complex and insular trash. But all such debate is done in the name of discovering ontological truth.

Semiotics contends that meaning is constantly shifting; thus, it is impossible for the author to attach specific signifieds to signifiers. Authors do not fix meaning into the words they write. If they did, the meaning of a text would remain static across distinct eras and cultures. But this is a false assumption because some books are banned in some countries and not in others. Consider the story "Pierre Menard: Author of *The Quixote*" by Borges. The narrator of the story considers Menard's unfinished version of *Don Quixote* (the famous novel written by Cervantes in roughly 1600) to be better than the original, even though Menard's is an exact, line-by-line duplicate of portions of the novel. The narrator's justification for this seemingly ludicrous position is that Menard, a twentieth-century French writer, immersed himself in sixteenth-century Spanish language, politics, and culture in order to write the copy. In other words, he claims that the *Don Quixote* written by Cervantes becomes "infinitely richer" when read through the filter of more than three centuries of intervening history. The story by Borges speaks to the "Death of the Author" essay by Barthes, in

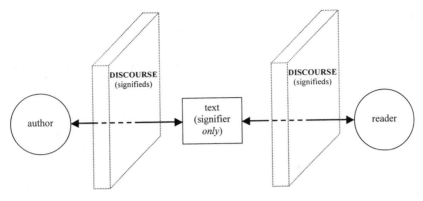

GRAPH 2.2

that two texts with exactly the same words, but written in distinct eras, take on differing meanings. Semiotically speaking, context assigns variable meanings to the same words and renders the author a context/construct within which the reader's act of interpretation occurs.

Semioticians argue that authors simply record the words (signifiers) onto the page, and the meaning of those words (signifieds) gets attached at the moment readers see them. Does this mean that the truth once held by the author now resides with the reader? No, that would be a simple reversal of the essentialist model. Semioticians recognize that the intent of readers (i.e., their interpretive framework) is subject to discourse just as the intent (creative process) of authors is. Everyone is at once author and reader. Cultural theorists do not abandon the fact that authors write with intent. Rather, they invite us to focus on the discursive context that gives rise to intent (see Graph 2.2).

Instead of looking to the intentions of authors to find the meaning of words in a text, semiotic readers look to the discourses that inform the writing, discourses which may or may not overlap with those informing their reading. They still read the text, of course, but they see its meaning residing in discourse rather than authorial purpose. Graph 2.2 represents the way in which multiple discourses act as an obstacle through which words must pass from the author to the text and back again. Discourse develops and changes based on the inputs of authors and readers. It is simultaneously dependent upon us and independent of us. (Remember our brief discussion of David Parker in the introduction and his Bakhtinian approach to language.) In this way, semioticians posit that meaning is contingent rather than stable and that meaning lies outside author, text, and reader. Graph 2.2 also represents Barthes' critique of the modern author. When authors write books and readers read them, consciously or unconsciously, each is creating the text through a discursive filter as well as contributing to changes in discourse.

If authors cannot attach specific meaning to their texts, and readers can do so only for themselves, how do we explain that different readers come up with similar interpretations of the same text? Moreover, what if this interpretation more or less corresponds to the author's description of the text, as discovered, say, in an interview with the author? A semiotician would say, in that case, that authors and readers might belong to similar discursive communities. It is quite conceivable that readers and authors who share cultural contexts will share similar interpretations of texts. In other words, they will be mutually affected by a similar array of discursive constructs. A reader from an alternative discursive community, or one who has been trained in interpreting discourse, might come along and see a radically different meaning in the text.

Part of the fun of cultural studies comes from acknowledging that no one is above discourse. Semiotic readings not only discern discourses out of which a text emerges, they also strive to remain aware of the discourses that drive their own readings. Yet, no matter how much any one of us is aware of the presence of discourse, no one is omniscient or able to be aware of the infinite ways in which our interpretations are discursively constituted. Thus, any reader who analyzes a text and shares that analysis in a public forum (a conversation, a written publication, etc.) exposes himself or herself to the same discursive reading that she or he performed on an original author (see Graph 2.3). Edward Said, for example, and his critique of nineteenth-century English literature had many critics, and those critics had critics.

Said analyzed nineteenth-century British authors and found them to be operating under an Orientalist discourse. His readers came along and found Said himself to have been affected by a whole range of discourses that colored his reading of literature. According to one critique, he failed to take into account British women writers, who seemingly operated under a different sort of Orientalism. Critics of the critics of Said noted that such analyses tended to reinforce the Oriental/Occidental dichotomy rather than challenge it, as was Said's original purpose.[2] So each successive reading reveals another level of discursive construction anonymously influencing any given author or critic, whose inputs in turn contribute to shifts in discourse.

Critical theorists insist that the semiotic model is not limited to literature and politics but applies to everything in the world—material, ideological, and otherwise (see Graph 2.4). But if we depict the hermeneutic model graphically, nature becomes the author, the material world becomes the

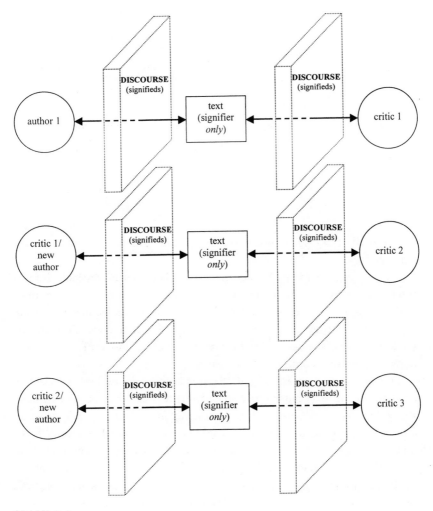

GRAPH 2.3

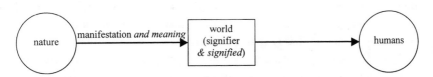

GRAPH 2.4

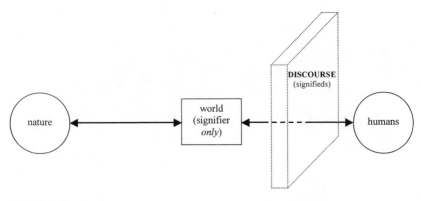

GRAPH 2.5

text, and all of us—scientists, observers, critics, and so forth—become the readers.

The essentialist model insists that truth about nature precedes human interpretation. So any signifier would have the signified (meaning) contained within it. In this model, the task for humanity is to receive nature's meanings through observation, discover nature's original code through the modernist exercise of scientific inquiry, and then, as modernists, structure our social world according to those truths.

In contrast, the semiotic model contends that nature does not contain ontological truths because those so-called truths can only be read through the discursively constituted lens of human interpretation. The physical world is only a signifier and its meaning (signified) is to be found in the realm of discourse (see Graph 2.5). Our exercise as semiotic observers is to study those discourses to better understand how physical manifestations are being interpreted. In Graph 2.5 we have removed the discourse obstacle between nature and the world, unlike Graph 2.3 in which a second box of discourse stands between the author and the text or between the critic and the text. This is because discourse does not "write" the world through nature in the same way that it writes these texts through authors and critics. But discourse does dictate how we as readers interpret nature and the material world, in the same way that it affects how we interpret texts.

This discussion of nature as author can be applied to our current exercise of identity construction, and in particular to the issue of race, or the variations in human physical appearance that we have come to understand as racial traits—hair texture, skin color, and facial features. Our author is once again nature (or, in this case, genetics), and skin color is our physical example (see Graph 2.6).

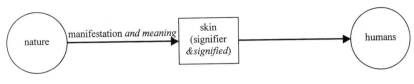

GRAPH 2.6

An essentialist reading insists that nature stamps meaning onto skin color. Darker or lighter skin means something, and it is the job of human observers to discover that objective reality. Once we discover that meaning, we should apply it to our social world. A semiotic approach contends that skin color contains no objective meaning but takes on meaning only within the context of the discursive lens used to view it (see Graph 2.7). We have removed the discourse box between nature and skin in Graph 2.7 for the same reason that we removed it from the interval between nature and the world in Graph 2.5.

In American history, for example, we have seen this lens alter meaning, as darker skin was used to justify enslavement, to prove three-fifths human status, to validate the notion of separate but equal, and in some regions, to prove superiority. Across cultures and time periods, the meaning of darker skin has changed from the scathing to the complimentary, from the inferior, strange, evil, or primitive to the pure, innocent, simple, or noble, and so forth. Essentialists are necessarily disturbed by these seemingly vast discrepancies, but ultimately they see them as evidence of an ongoing process of refinement. They believe that, with the proper scientific tools, the more accurate interpretations (i.e., those that accord more closely with objective truth) will trump inferior interpretations. The challenge for essentialists is to figure out which of these are indeed accurate.

In contrast, semioticians see this variation as evidence of the arbitrary nature of signs. They stress the importance of studying history to witness this process of change so we can understand that discourses come and go and that what remains when they disappear is only the skeleton of construct.

We could insert any identity category into the rectangles labeled skin in Graphs 2.6 and 2.7 to construct models of essentialisms. For instance, does their possession of female sex organs and hormones mean that women are intrinsically more volatile than men? Are poor people naturally lazy? Since the United States is the most powerful nation in the world, might it have superior physical traits compared with people in all the other countries? Semiotics allows us to see that the associations between signifiers and signifieds are discursively, not inherently, determined. When put into practice,

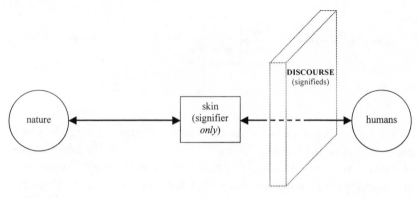

GRAPH 2.7

semiotic inquiry leads us to ask different questions. How and when did female sex organs become associated with volatility? What vested interests are served by asserting that laziness is an intrinsic trait of the poor? Who decides the criteria for most powerful nation? In the case of Latin America, we do not ask whether Latin Americans are truly violent, poor, good dancers, great musicians, exotic, passionate, or closer to nature, but how those labels came to be applied to them.

NOTES

1. Saussure's main work was published posthumously in 1916 as *Course in General Linguistics* (Paris: Payot). It actually consists of a compilation of notes taken by his students of his lectures at the University of Geneva between 1906 and 1911. It was first published in Spanish in 1945 by the Buenos Aires publisher Losada and then in English in 1959 by various publishers such as Oxford's Pergamon Press and New York's McGraw-Hill and has since been translated and reprinted many times.

2. See Alexander Lyon Macfie, *Orientalism: A Reader* (New York: NYUP, 2002).

CHAPTER 3

Narrating about Narrative

We are now ready to close this introductory section with a discussion of *narrative*, a critical aspect of semiotic readings.

A narrative is a story, the sort of tale we tell one another about our world and ourselves. Most narratologists, those who study narrative, would agree with this short and simple definition. That consensus, however, evaporates as soon as the discussion moves to more substantive issues, such as origin, structure, and meaning. Some define narrative strictly as novels, short stories, or other specific literary forms. Others take a broader approach and accept most forms of communication, from the most sophisticated literature to bedtime stories, jokes, and songs, as narrative. Not surprisingly, they often equate it with discourse: being around us all the time and constructing our visions of the world and ourselves in it, yet not necessarily under our control. As you might have guessed, narrative interpretation has become a point of contention in the debates between modernists and cultural theorists.

Modernists tend to view narratives from a scientific perspective, believing them to be composed of fundamental elements, such as plot, setting, character, narrator, and tone, among others. They also tend to insist that narratives follow universal patterns, having a beginning, middle, and end, or an introduction, climax, and resolution. They believe the best way to understand a narrative and to gain access to its inner truths is to break it down into individual pieces, not unlike a biologist taking apart a cell.

Modernist narratologists focus on cause and effect, how a story is told and constructed. If an essentialistic reading of a story could be represented as a formula, it might look something like $a + b = c$, where a and b

represent different elements of the story and c is the end result. For hermeneuticians, deciphering a narrative is like solving a math equation with one clear answer. The answer to the equation is a number, and the solution to a narrative, for them, is its internal truths, those kernels of enlightenment that supposedly reside at the core of every worthwhile piece of literature. According to hermeneutics, the challenge before readers and critics is to decipher the code and discover that deep meaning.

It might seem impossible to describe narrative in terms of objectivity and science because it is, ultimately, an aesthetic form, an artistic expression in which standards of quality would seem to vary according to individual taste. How can there be a standard of measure for narrative?

Establishing this standard is precisely what essentialist literary theorists and critics, many of whom are authors themselves, seek to achieve. As the supposed experts in the field, they are its arbiters of quality, and they strive to agree upon standards that will be used to distinguish good narrative from bad. In expressing their opinions, often in the form of debates among themselves, they are like scientists setting out to prove the validity of their claims. They see themselves weeding out the false ideas and half-truths of bad narrative and inaccurate criticism from the objective truth of good narrative and accurate criticism. Those critics who apply this perspective in education believe that they are training the reading public so it, too, can enjoy access to the inner truths of narrative.[1]

The quintessential expression of this debate over quality occurs in the creation of a literary canon, the body of work that represents the best and most significant forms of narrative. These supposedly set the standards for future work. Creating canonical lists and subsequently debating one another concerning the validity of a list are common exercises among modernist narratologists and critics.

Frank Raymond Leavis (1895–1978) was one of the best-known modernist literary critics. He firmly believed in the existence of a literary hierarchy and in objective standards for quality narrative. He sought out those works that met standards and disregarded the rest as unworthy or as pop culture trash. Leavis embraced the notion of a literary canon, and he believed that critics and narratologists had critical roles to play in preserving canonical standards. He defended his position on this issue strongly because he believed that the finest literature and the best critics had the power to transform the world for the better. In the words of a student of his work:

> Leavis revealed a lifelong aggressive certainty about the high place
> and central importance of literary criticism in solving the crisis of the

twentieth century. Leavis wished to establish a true way, a single comprehensive standard for all English literature, a canon of works which
realized true values, values of life (responsiveness, vigour, subtlety, wit)
that are at the same time literary values.[2]

So specific were the standards of the canon according to Leavis that by
the time he had finished narrowing his list of the best authors only five
remained on it: Jane Austen, George Eliot, Henry James, Joseph Conrad,
and D. H. Lawrence. Leavis is still criticized, even by his admirers, for his
elitism, but he is also recognized as one of the most influential figures in
twentieth-century literary criticism. For modernist critics like him, the ultimate criterion for inclusion in the canon is the extent to which a work of
narrative reveals something about the human condition through its unique
aesthetic form or through its subject matter. Good narrative supposedly reveals something about who we are, where we come from, and where we
are going. In the hermeneutic framework, both author and critic are types
of scientists, finding out truths about the ontological world and revealing
them through narrative and their analyses of it.

To understand how modernists and postmodernists interpret literature
differently, imagine a window. And imagine the builder of the window to be
the author, the glass to be the written word, and the scene outside to be the
human experience represented by the narrative. Just as we can choose between an essentialist and a semiotic reading of narrative, so can we choose
to focus only on the glass itself, or on the glass, the framer, and the scene
outside all together.

In 1925, Spanish philosopher José Ortega y Gasset (1883–1955) published
his influential *The Dehumanization of Art*.[3] As a high modernist, he created
a window metaphor to critique artists who produced realist art as well as
their admirers. Ortega y Gasset was opposed to realism because he believed
it failed to represent the complex nature of humanity and the universe. He
was adhering to the central premise of modern art: by distorting what we
take to be the real appearance of something we get closer to its true reality.
Therefore, he opposed the idea of art as a transparent windowpane and embraced abstraction by authors and narratologists operating in the modernist
tradition, believing that only their highly complicated forms possessed the
appropriate subtlety to gain insight into the true human condition.

Although Ortega y Gasset's window metaphor is a useful way to depict
the relationship between meaning and artistic production, his use of this
metaphor is problematic for cultural theorists because of his highly elitist
view of art. According to him, the uncultured masses of society favored

realist art because they thought they could understand it, but only an elite few could truly appreciate the finer aesthetics of artistic abstraction, as it was expressed in modern art.

Like Ortega y Gasset's desire to find the purest art form, essentialists and hermeneuticians focus on the windowpane in and of itself, valuing most highly the narrative that they believe reveals truths about the human condition. Just as the purity of the glass improves our vision of what we see through it, essentialists believe that the more precise or flawless the author's narrative, the less aware we are of the author and the more we learn about humanity. This does not mean the narrative style has to be simplistic or obvious, as evidenced by Ortega y Gasset's defense of modern art. After all, *Ulysses,* the highly challenging work by James Joyce (1922), regularly appears atop canonical lists of Western narrative.

In *Framing the Sign,* Jonathan Culler offers a cultural theorist's approach to the window metaphor. He compares the context and discourse surrounding each work of art or narrative to the frame of a window. An important distinction between Culler and Ortega y Gasset is that, as a cultural theorist, Culler is not interested in revealing the most pure art form. He is looking to expose the discourses that shape each narrative. Culler wants our understanding of narrative to go beyond mere context, such as the historical events surrounding the creation of a text. Instead, he encourages the reader to consider the work semiotically by examining the role of discourse in it. As he explains:

> The expression *framing the sign* has several advantages over *context:* it reminds us that framing is something we do; it hints of the frame-up ("falsifying evidence beforehand in order to make someone appear guilty"), a major use of context; and it eludes the incipient positivism of "context" by alluding to the semiotic function of framing in art, where the frame is determining, setting off the object or event as art and yet the frame itself may be nothing tangible, pure articulation.[4]

Semioticians like Culler insist that the frame, the articulation, or the discourse always mediates the scene or the narrative. A person who chooses to focus solely on the glass itself, or the scene outside as transparent reality, rather than also examining the elements constructing and refracting the image, misses this crucial point. Whereas Ortega y Gasset and other essentialist modernists believe that there are more or less accurate representations of the human experience, Culler and other cultural theorists do not rank narratives. Instead of assuming the existence of an ontological world and then looking for narratives that reveal it, semiotic narratologists reveal how narratives create meaning. In other words, the scene outside comes into existence only as a result of the creation of the frame and the glass.

Semiotic approaches to narrative reject the typical essentialist emphasis on plot, narrators, and/or tone. They focus on how these elements come together to construct meaning and discourse. If a semiotic reading of narrative were to be plotted as a formula, it would look like $x \rightarrow y$, where x and y represent different elements of a story, and the arrow symbolizes the process by which x becomes y. Unlike in the essentialist equation of $a + b = c$, there is no solution, but rather a constant process of uncovering how meaning comes to be.

Besides rejecting the idea that narratives and their authors can reveal truths about an ontological world, semioticians reject the notion of a literary canon. While they might agree that certain narrative styles, or certain pieces of literature, are exceptional, semioticians view canons as saying much more about the people who assemble them than about the works being included or excluded. They believe that constructing notions of literary standards runs the risk of allowing hegemonic power to exclude dissenting voices, discourses, and aesthetics. Semioticians seek to include more voices and styles, not wanting to silence those with less access to power. The more open we remain to a multiplicity of aesthetic standards, the greater our potential to understand the meaning of reality as a social construct.

On the whole, semioticians ask very different questions about narratives than their essentialist counterparts do. Essentialists look to narratives for authenticity, truth, affirmation of the human experience, and authorial intention. Semioticians want to expose ongoing constructs.

Some of the semioticians' key questions are asked by Jonathan Culler in another work of his called *Literary Theory: A Very Short Introduction*. We cite some of these questions here and embellish them with some of our own. Afterward, we offer further examples of this difference in objectives by applying both essentialist and semiotic readings to the writings of El Inca Garcilaso de la Vega and the literary movement called magical realism.[5]

"Who speaks?" (Culler, 87) Is it a first-person narrator or an observer of the events? A character within the novel or an omniscient narrator? Keep in mind that a text can focus on a particular character and be told by an omniscient narrator.

"Who speaks to whom?" (88) Who is being narrated to? Are readers implied or are they constructed characters within the text? An audience can be implied from the era when the text was published. As we approach texts from

other centuries, we may find that some of the cultural references evident to an author's contemporaries now require explanation.

"Who speaks when?" (88) Does the narration occur at the same time as the events or has there been a lapse? In Bernal Díaz del Castillo's *A History of the Conquest of New Spain,* the author, a retired soldier of the Mexican conquest in the early 1500s, narrated the events years after they occurred but with seemingly perfect recollection. Though Díaz del Castillo remains an invaluable source, readers must question whether a person could remember a series of events with such accuracy decades later.

"Who speaks what language?" (88) This question can be understood in terms of national languages. Though we consider languages to be equal in terms of their ability to communicate information, all are not social equals. A social hierarchy of languages closely parallels the power of those who speak them. For instance, a text written in English will have more possibilities for worldwide distribution. It is not just coincidental that the majority of research on Latin American literature is written in English, as there are more academic presses and readers in the United States than in Latin America. Latin American authors who have gained the most recognition are those who have been translated and published in English. We cannot separate the act of writing from the publication process and its power imbalance with regard to production, marketing, distribution, and reception of a book. In terms of issues like class, social position, dialects, and regionalism, consider a text from Latin America about an indigenous community. The book is written in Spanish, the language of the conquerors. More than likely, the targeted audience will be urban Spanish speakers, not the people depicted in the text. The political implications of this system need to be addressed when seeking the broader position of the narrative.

"Who speaks with what authority?" (89) In general we accept the authority of the author/narrator, unless we are given reason not to believe him or her. Traditionally, people who have composed in writing were "lettered citizens," a term coined by the Uruguayan critic Angel Rama to describe those who have held authority in writing and narrating, i.e., well-educated, middle- to upper-class criollo men. (See Chap. 10 for more on Rama.) Someone who is illiterate or who does intensive manual labor has less leisure time to devote to writing. People who traditionally lacked access to the written word, however, finally began to tell their stories near the end of the twentieth century in what is known as testimonial literature. These

perspectives and narrative styles tend to differ greatly from the styles and contents of works produced by "lettered citizens."

"Who sees?" (89) This question should not be understood as point of view. It refers to whose perspective is presented, or how the narration is focused. We distinguish between point of view and focus because sometimes the narrator can focus the narration on a character other than on him or herself (see *Celsa's World*, excerpted below). Focus is similar in function to the frame of a window. Considering the focus of the novel contributes to our understanding of its discursive construction.

Semiotic narratologists challenge the essentialist assumption that narratives are stable. They look for contradictions within narrative to reveal multiplicity of meaning, for the ways in which a narrative reflects discourses and thus is subject to constant variations in interpretation. Semioticians often read texts against themselves to expose how a narrative constructs identity and meaning through contradiction. A claim by a narrative written in Spanish that it represents Mayan people and their worldview may diverge from what the text actually does.

Another common essentialist practice that semioticians reject is the close biographical study of the author in order to gain access to the truths of a text. The logic behind this practice originates in the essentialist belief that an author's intention instills meaning in a text. Therefore, the truths of a text are to be found in the author's life and thought. Because semioticians embrace the notion of unintended meaning and of the death of the author, they do not privilege biographies. But they nonetheless remain very interested in historical context, both that pertaining to the author and to the period in which a text was produced. Semioticians ask, Where is the author from? What is his or her education? What is his or her economic situation? What is the historical context in which she or he is writing? What are the author's political views? Who makes up the author's audience? What was the author's access to the national discourse? Semioticians do not ask these questions with the goal of unearthing the true intentions of the authors or finding out how the human condition is uniquely captured. Their objective is to reveal the discursive framework within which authors operate. They expose the elements that constitute the windows through which authors see.

Many of the authors included in the chapters that follow, for example, were educated, white or mestizo men who at the time they were writing, or shortly thereafter, became political leaders in their countries. As a result, the influence of their writing on national discourses became much greater. We also include the work of an uneducated indigenous peasant woman who traditionally has been excluded from national discourse.

Consider the historical context and biography of El Inca Garcilaso de la Vega, known as the first successful mestizo writer. He was born in Cuzco, Peru in 1539 to an Incan princess and a Spanish military captain. He spent the first part of his life with his mother's family in Cuzco. As a result, he was bilingual in Spanish and Quechua, an indigenous language spoken in the Andes Mountains. At the age of 22 he moved to Spain and shortly thereafter began to write about indigenous culture, religion, and myths for a Spanish audience. His unique bicultural and intellectual background gave him a different perspective on the Conquest than that of his Spanish contemporaries. He celebrated indigenous culture and endeavored to show that it was not as barbaric as the conquistadors had characterized it. Yet, in his writings he claimed to be in agreement with the principal Spanish chronicles of the Conquest and insisted that his goal was simply to include some additional information. Though he strikes a careful balance between indigenous beliefs and Catholicism, he also describes Catholicism as the only true religion. While El Inca's writings have been subjected to many differing essentialist analyses, modernists generally agree that he presents an authentic version of indigenous culture because of his family background. His nickname, "El Inca," comes from his indigenous heritage.

Semiotic readings of El Inca Garcilaso de la Vega consider other aspects of his work. Instead of seeing El Inca as an authority because of his genetic background or his ability to tap into the true indigenous experience, semioticians consider how he was an outsider in Spanish society and that his writings were an attempt to provide him with legitimacy. They focus on the many contradictions in the text. El Inca claims that his interpretation fundamentally complements the Spanish chronicles, yet the text is also a celebration of indigenous culture. He presents a different version of the Conquest, while claiming that it is not new. He contests the imposition of colonialism on a rich and ancient culture, while denying that he does so. Furthermore, El Inca was writing during the Spanish Inquisition and had to be careful to avoid being accused of heresy, which makes his defense of the Catholic Church ever more complex.

Semiotic analyses also consider El Inca's intended audience. He directed his text to a particular audience; otherwise, he would have had difficulties finding a publisher and a readership. His texts might have been quite different had he been writing for an indigenous rather than a European audience. El Inca's writings can be read as his attempt to situate himself between two cultures without offending the dominant one. Semioticians find interesting his constant attempts to negotiate the differing discourses and argue that his identity, as well as indigenous identity itself, is being constructed through the narrative process. Hermeneutic analyses tend to accept the stability of his identity and thus read him as being either an accurate or inaccurate observer of Peru's ontological reality.

Another way to consider the discursive foundation of narrative is to examine the ideology of an entire literary movement. Consider one of Latin America's most important literary movements, the Boom. In the 1960s and 1970s, Latin American authors gained worldwide recognition for their innovative narrative form, known commonly as magical realism. Promoters claimed that Boom authors had developed an authentic narrative style owing to Latin America's distinct history and mixed cultural identity. Boom texts commonly question linear time, thereby drawing upon indigenous interpretations of time as circular. They also commonly accept magic as part of everyday life. This is often read as drawing upon pre-Hispanic religious beliefs, their mystery and incomprehensibility to Western audiences. Boom authors tend to make protagonists from prostitutes, the poor, or from indigenous people. This multiplicity of voices allows contributions from those traditionally excluded from literary attention. These characters talk in their vernacular, incorporating local expressions and speech patterns. For all these reasons, the texts are regarded as a celebration of the uniqueness of Latin America; at the same time, they are considered technically complex and are defined as high culture.

Essentialist readers tend to focus on the extent to which Boom authors captured Latin America's authentic ontological essence. Given the many Nobel Prizes they won and the extent to which magical realist works have been accepted into the canon, it is evident that most critics believe the Boom to have achieved its goals of authentic expression.

Semioticians do not deny the value of Boom literature, and they acknowledge its achievement in bringing international recognition to Latin American writers. But they question why its distinct narrative form was so widely embraced by international audiences. Some semiotic interpreters have suggested that magical realism reveals more about foreign expectations for Latin America than about Latin America itself. They contend that the Latin America portrayed by Boom literature is an exotic, irrational place where time is circular and magic is a part of daily life, rather than a place of modern reason and science. From a semiotic perspective, essentialist readers in the United States and Europe who embrace the Boom might be doing so because it meets their expectations of Latin Americans as passionate, deviant, magical, mystical, and, most important, different. But Boom literature was consumed avidly by international readers and by Latin Americans, and in great quantities at that. Many Boom authors became national heroes or cultural icons and many complicated and interesting questions were raised as a result. Were Latin American readers defining themselves through the lens of "otherness" that was being nurtured in an international arena of expectation about Latin America?

The Boom is even more problematic when we consider its authors' backgrounds. Almost to the last, they are middle- or upper-class white or mestizo men who have traveled widely. Many of them have lived outside Latin America for many years and many have held high political positions inside their home countries. Though they claim to represent Latin America's heterogeneous condition, they are actually highly homogeneous and represent a distinct minority. Rarely have they been excluded from political, social, or economic power, and rarely have they lived the lives of the characters they create in their writings. This does not mean that a rich, white, urbane male is incapable of writing about a poor, rural, Indian woman. But when virtually all of the Boom authors are rich, white, urbane men, their claims about revealing the authentic Latin America become more problematic.

In short, a semiotic approach examines how narrative constructs cultural meanings and identities. This text will examine readings on the basis of how their narration creates meanings and defines identities, not on authorial intention. As readers, we will be challenged to interpret the text not in terms of what the author claims to believe or to portray, but rather on what these claims reveal about the author's lens. How do narrated ideas become part and parcel of the events portrayed, and how is the meaning of this reality in a state of constant flux? No longer does narrative belong only to the written world. It becomes the stuff of everyday telling, listening, acting, reacting. It is all around us all the time.

NOTES

1. Theorists who argued for the need for aesthetic literary standards are said to belong to the school of New Criticism. Some of these are: Ivor Armstrong Richards, William Epson, F. R. Leavis, Kenneth Burke, John Crowe Ransom, Allen Tate, Yvor Winters, Cleanth Brooks, R. P. Blackmur, William K. Wimsatt, Jr., and René Wellek. It should be noted that Wimsatt and Monroe C. Beardsley wrote a famous article, "Intentional Fallacy," which argues that conflicts over interpretation of a work cannot be resolved by returning to the author's intentions and should focus on the work itself. William K. Wimsatt, Monroe C. Beardsley, "The Intentional Fallacy," *The Verbal Icon* (Lexington: U of Kentucky P, 1954). See <http://www.wordiq .com/definition/New_Critics> for a definition of intentional fallacy.

2. J. Docker, "How I Became a Teenage Leavisite and Lived to Tell the Tale," ed. J. Docker, *In a Critical Condition: Reading Australian Literature* (Ringwood, Austral.: Penguin, 1984) 17.

3. José Ortega y Gasset, *The Dehumanization of Art; and Other Essays on Art, Culture and Literature* (Princeton: Princeton UP, 1948); in Spanish as *La deshumanización del arte. Ideas sobre la novela* (Madrid: Revista de Occidente, 1928).

4. Jonathan Culler, *Framing the Sign: Criticism and Its Institutions,* (Norman: U of Oklahoma P, 1988) xiv.

5. Jonathan Culler, *Literary Theory: A Very Short Introduction* (New York: Oxford UP, 1997).

PART II

Theory

CHAPTER 4

An Opening Jaunt: El Salvador in 1923

To open our theory section, imagine taking a trip to Latin America. Our guide is Harry Foster, a North American, and our destination is El Salvador in the early 1920s. Our guidebook is Foster's *A Gringo in Mañana-land*, a description of his travels that he published in 1924. It may seem strange to begin this theory section with a primary text, but we have chosen to do so for two reasons. First, we aim to encourage readers to recognize all texts as discourses. Second, we seek to provide a case study of identity essentialism that will prepare them for the denser theoretical explanations that follow.

At the time of Foster's travels to Central America in the 1920s, many people in the United States saw Latin America (and especially Central America) as a frontier, just as Britons saw Africa or the Orient in the late 1800s. It was a place full of unknowns and potential discoveries, where anyone with a sense of adventure and determination could supposedly find himself or herself, make a pile of money, or bring back stories worth telling to the curious folks back home. It is probably not a coincidence that shortly after the so-called closing of the Wild West, travelers and businesspeople from the United States began directing their attentions southward to Latin America. Subsequently, travel narratives became a popular form of literary activity and a common way to share information about other parts of the world. Harry Foster was one of those writer-adventurers.

He was born in Brooklyn, New York, on October 31, 1894 and attended Newton Academy and Lafayette College. While in college he joined ROTC and in 1917 he left to fight in World War I. After returning from Europe, he was posted on the U.S.-Mexican border where he finished his military career. In 1919, while still a young man, he traveled throughout Latin America.

This initial travel experience provided the material for his first book, *Adventures of a Tropical Tramp*. He eventually traveled to many places across the globe, including Latin America, the Caribbean, and Southeast Asia, returning to New York only for short periods of time. Before he died at the young age of 36, Foster became a prolific writer, producing seven travel memoirs, a magazine, and a play.[1]

The excerpt that follows is drawn from Foster's brief trip through El Salvador in 1923 as part of a longer trip through Mexico and Central America that led to the writing of his third book, *A Gringo in Mañana-land* (1924).[2] Foster had a great affection for Latin America and its people, which is evident in his writings. He also had a hearty sense of adventure. He enjoyed the process of discovery and relished the opportunity to bring home stories of new things. Foster was an insightful and astute observer, but he viewed Latin America and its people through a particular lens, through a particularly constructed window, to borrow from our previous analogy. It is this lens that we are interested in understanding here, not to agree or disagree with Foster, but to know the filter through which he viewed Latin America.

Notwithstanding the fact that Foster liked Latin America and its people a great deal, he viewed them with cultural biases not uncommon among early twentieth-century North Americans. Much of what he sees inspires in him a sense of superiority and a feeling of relief that he does not have to actually live in the wretched conditions he encounters. Foster relies on a great many generalizations and cultural biases. For example, he points out that the roads are not paved and that the driving is more dangerous. Then he accuses all the drivers of being reckless, a generalization showing cultural bias. To explain why Central America can't develop he describes the "comic opera" of "internal bickerings" among its countries, despite the fact that "the whole five could be lost in Texas."[3] This territorial comparison does not go unnoticed by his implied audience, the U.S. citizen, whom he prompts to compare the "unity" of their vast nation with the inherent division of such "tiny" countries as those in Central America.[4] A caption under a photo of an indigenous women carrying a bucket reads, "In these pleasant tropical countries no peon girl escapes maternity."[5] He refers to the Central American as a walking contradiction who, "like the Mexican, is both an idealist and a materialist [as] [h]e sees no inconsistency in being both devoutly religious and frankly immoral."[6]

From our perspective, much of Foster's comments are uncomfortable to read, but to be fair, we can't expect him to view El Salvador outside the norms of his time. But we are interested in identifying the essentialism in his text, as distinct from generalizations or cultural biases. Foster rests many of his descriptions on an essentialist foundation, revealing the modernist framework at the core of his interpretation. For example, he often implies that the behavior of Central Americans reflects inborn character traits. He categorizes animals and people alike as "half-breed" and uses the term "to mate" to describe the marital practices of "peons." The most revealing of his essentialisms occur when he collapses essentialist identities together and allows them to reinforce one another. When he writes that "the peon *girl* without a partner is the *daughter* of a rather sensuous *race*, and of a *race* that is not inclined to work when an easier living is to be obtained" (our italics), he links class and race such that a poor girl becomes a racial type rather than a member of an economic category.[7]

A semiotic reading pays attention to the moments when Foster's text speaks against itself. For example, he criticizes the people of El Salvador for generalizing about all "gringos," proving that he is aware of the problems of stereotyping. He is not deterred, however, from writing stereotypical descriptions of Salvadorans. If we further examine what he means by "internal bickerings," we can see both the essentialisms and the contradiction in the Foster text, of which he is unaware. While wondering why Central Americans don't escape overpopulation in one nation by "gravitating" over into the next, he concludes that "the people of all these nations are like those of the Balkans in their hatred for one another." He bases this conclusion on a conversation with a Salvadoran he meets on a train who tells him he should never go to Guatemala because the people there are scoundrels. This revelation prompts Foster to recall that Guatemalans he had spoken to previously characterized Salvadorans in a similar manner. In describing the details of this bickering, he points to the absurdity of the essentialisms that Central Americans carry for one another. Yet, he does not reveal the absurdity of essentialisms in general and essentializes the people of Central America even further.

HARRY FOSTER, "A GRINGO IN MAÑANA-LAND"[8]
IV

A few hours of leisurely travel brought me to San Salvador, the capital of El Salvador.

It was a warm, sunny capital, only a trifle over two thousand feet in altitude, extremely low for a Central American city. Its population numbered only some fifty or sixty thousand. Its people, being of *mestizo* composition, did not affect the barbaric raiment of the Guatemalan Indians. The half-breed maidens wrapped themselves in filmy shawls of pink or blue, but after the blazing *serapes* of the previous country these garments seemed colorless. The city itself was somewhat drab. A few of its structures were of the heavy masonry found elsewhere in Central America, and its Governmental Palace was imposing in its wealth of marble columns, yet the city as a whole—being another favorite objective of the local earthquakes—was constructed mainly of wood and corrugated iron, even to the cathedral, which, although painted to suggest stone, was convincing only at a distance.

But it was a decidedly pleasant city, with many parks and tinkling fountains. Pretty *señoritas* were abundant. Priests in black robes—unrestricted by law in this country—were to be seen everywhere. Men walked through the marketplaces ringing dinner bells, and carrying little boxes containing a tiny image of the Virgin, to whom one might bow for a penny. Horse cars rattled through the streets with much crackling of the drivers' whips. There was music each night in the *plaza,* and flirtation beneath the palm trees. The tropic air was balmy and soothing. About the whole city there was an atmosphere of contentment—and a touch of that fictional romance which the traveler craves.

VI

The Central American, like the Mexican, is both an idealist and a materialist. He sees no inconsistency in being both devoutly religious and frankly immoral.

He is quite apt to use the name of his favorite saint as a fitting title for his gin-mill. He employs it as a harmless ejaculation. He may even resort to it for emphasis, as in the case of an advertisement I recall, which endorsed a Charlie Chaplin moving picture with the phrases: "Is it funny? Jesus, Joseph, and Mary!" And, among the lower classes, he is quite apt to regard any religious holiday as a fitting excuse for over-indulgence in liquor.

It is frequently charged throughout these countries that the great waves of illegitimacy follow the principal church processionals, which fact is not a reflection upon the church, but upon the inability of the *peons* to associate the ideas of religion and personal behavior. In fact, the common people see nothing essentially wrong, or even unusual, in illegitimacy itself. In Nicaragua, the newspapers in publishing a list of births, distinguish each new citizen with the candid "legitimo" or "ilegitimo," and the latter outnumber the former by two or three to one, a ratio which holds good for all these countries.

It must not be assumed from these statements, however, that all Central America is a hotbed of immorality. In discussing any moral question, a writer must indicate which social class he has in mind. In any of these countries there is a distinct division between the aristocrat and the *peon.*

In aristocratic circles, a man has every privilege, and a woman none. It is assumed, in Latin fashion, that boys will be boys. Lest girls be girls, their virtue is assured by a close chaperonage. A man of wealth may keep several establishments in town beside his regular home, if bound upon a journey, he may take with him some other lady in order that his wife may be spared the discomforts of travel. The wife remains a model of propriety. Here prevails the double standard.

In *peon* circles, both sexes share something more of equality. They mate usually without the formality of marriage. Should they prefer to change partners from time to time, they do it casually, yet this is the exception rather than the rule. In some cases, a woman objects to any ceremony, preferring to remain free of ties, so that in case her new spouse proves a drunkard or a wife-beater, she can leave him, for there is no divorce in most of these countries. In some cases, they would prefer the marriage ritual, but cannot afford it. And in most cases, although free to change partners, they remain faithful throughout life. Women in this class, so long as they have a consort, are apt to be as loyal as the women of the upper classes. Illegitimate children, consequently, are more a result of these informal unions than of a general promiscuity.

Yet promiscuity is not unknown. The *peon* girl without a partner is the daughter of a rather sensuous race, and of a race that is not inclined to work when an easier living is to be obtained. In this land of tolerance, little stigma attaches itself to her or to her children if she takes up prostitution as a career. In most Latin-American countries, she is restricted to a certain segregated district, but she is recognized by the police as a legal and useful member of the community. The *gente decente,* or decent people, as the aristocrats describe themselves, may not invite her to their homes, but the gentlemen may sometimes call at hers.

If, in San Salvador, she chooses to ply her trade before the presidential palace, what matters it? She does not molest the president. And if she chooses also to join a religious procession, and return immediately to her profession, the Central American sees nothing inconsistent therein. What has religion to do with one's personal affairs? [. . .]

VIII

If these people seldom criticize harshly, however, they are very fond of gossip. The women especially have few interests to discuss, and infinite leisure for the discussion.

There were some fifteen *señoras* and *señoritas* at my hotel in San Salvador, the wives or daughters of guests, all of them built to resist earthquake, who spent the entire day sitting in a chair upon the patio veranda, without amusement or occupation. Anglo-Saxon girls, with nothing to do except to wait for a husband to come home from work, would have gone insane, but these of Salvador were passively content. None of them ever read anything; in fact only a very few people of either sex ever seem to read anything in these countries; few of them ever sewed or knitted; all of them were quite satisfied with their peaceful existence.

During the absence of their husbands, they were extremely circumspect. When spouses were present, they might greet me with a pleasant, "Good morning." When alone, they affected not to see me. Since the Latin-American gentleman, unless patently snubbed, fancies always that a lady must be encouraging amorous advances, they had learned to be extremely cautious.

But they all had a great curiosity about the United States—which newspapers had taught them to regard as a country whose population spent most of its time in a divorce court—and they were eager to ask me questions. Wherefore they would gather in a body, and reassured by the security of numbers, occasionally surround me for purposes of conversation.

Since the feminine mind runs mainly to romance, their questions were rather personal. The women here always wish to know whether the man they meet is married or single, and if single, whether he has a sweetheart. On the theory that the lack of a sweetheart would interest them most, I had always answered questions in the negative, but in San Salvador I discovered that by inventing one I merely interested them the more. The news spread rapidly, and within two minutes every woman in the hotel was present to ask further questions about her.

"Is she beautiful?"

"No, she's about as ugly as they make them."

That provoked much discussion. These strange *gringos* did not care for beauty! Had one not seen many an American bringing with him a wife that no Latin would have wed?

"But what does she look like? Six feet tall! *Dios!* And wears number ten shoes! *Ay, caramba!* Do you really love her?"

Night after night they asked questions about her, until I regretted her invention. If friends or relatives came to see my inquisitors, the entire story had to be repeated again. I finally decided to let her marry another. But this merely invited further inquiries.

"Are you not disconsolate? No! Ay, what unfeeling creatures are the Americans! And she married a man of ninety years for his millions! How commercial the *gringos!*"

Sympathy and comfort were offered in abundance. Each of the ladies seemed to have a friend or relative who was suggested as a substitute. I was forced to decline the suggestions.

"We are merely waiting, my sweetheart and I, until the old millionaire dies. Then we shall inherit his wealth, and live happily ever after."

There was a moment of shocked silence. Some one suggested that I was joking, but was immediately overruled by the others. This, they insisted, was a common practice in the United States. Anything was possible among Americans! And was I not even jealous that I must wait while my beloved lived with another?

"Not at all. I've cabled a second girl, and she'll be my wife until the first one is free. We do that regularly."

My love affairs became the sensation of the community. And the story did not reach the breaking point until the first girl, in the furor of her love for me, announced in an imaginary cable that she had poisoned her husband, and that the millions were ours. Even then, there were several doubtful inquiries as to whether I really meant it. And when I confessed that the whole story was fictitious, they were vastly disappointed. It was all so in keeping with their visions of the United States that they wished to believe it.

IX

In all of these women one observed a strangely child-like quality.

When better conversational subjects were exhausted, several of them requested that I guess their ages. Oddly enough, in this land where frankness is seldom encountered, women make no effort to hide the number of their years. Perhaps it is because their personal vanity, so very manifest in younger girls, practically ceases after marriage has been achieved.

One of them I judged to be fifty. To please her I guessed forty. She proved in reality to be thirty-two. They grow old so quickly here. Yet in their manner they retain toward men that air of a child toward a parent. Should a husband see fit to discuss with them any serious subject, they listen in awed admiration to his opinions, exclaiming occasionally, "I see! Ah, I understand!"

It would probably offend the average Latin American to discover that his spouse knew as much about anything as he did himself. He likes the role of the patient mentor. He prefers that his wife be a gentle pet rather than a comrade. I dined one day with a Salvadorian gentleman and his wife; the lady, who came from one of the leading families, had been educated abroad and had traveled extensively; yet the gentleman, although he conversed quite brilliantly with the men at the table, chattered only playful nonsense to his wife. In consideration of his pride, she artfully concealed the fact that she was his intellectual equal.

Now and then one reads in our newspapers or magazines about the equal suffrage movement in Mexico or the organization of a new women's club in Chile. But such innovations have yet to gain an extensive following. With the same conflict of idealism and materialism that distinguishes Latin-American men, the women may verbally deplore their lack of liberty but are in reality quite satisfied with it. They are of a race which is inclined to follow the easiest course, and the easiest course is to attach themselves to some convenient man and allow him to worry about life's problems. In these pleasant tropical countries no girl of the lower classes escapes maternity; most girls of the middle classes, not being over-critical about whom they marry, can land some one; even in the more particular aristocratic circles the spinster is a rarity. The wife usually has her own way when questions arise about the household or the children. Beyond that she is quite content with complete male dominance. And she is passively happy.

DISCUSSION QUESTIONS

• Consider the influence these discourses have on how the United States thought about and continues to think about Latin America. In what ways is Foster's travelogue representative of past and current Western constructions of Latin America?

• How does Foster react to Latin American essentializations of the United States? Based on his presentation of El Salvador, is this reaction justified?

• What do Foster's observations suggest about the U.S. view toward Latin Americans at this time? In what ways is Foster subject to and participant in the constructive process of discourse?

• Consider Foster not only as an individual writer but also as part of a much larger print culture that wrote about Latin America in a similar way. What effect do these travel narratives have on the audience's perceptions of Latin America? Could these texts eventually shape Latin Americans' ideas about their own identity and who they are as a people?

• On two occasions Foster refers to Latin Americans as a race, although the contexts to which he refers are not rooted in racialized difference. What does this reveal about the essentialistic nature of his interpretive framework?

• What might Edward Said have said about Harry Foster?

NOTES

1. Biographical information on Foster was drawn from the Web site of Dixon-Price, a publishing house, 23 Aug. 2004 <http://www.dixonprice .com/ATTpage.htm>.

2. Harry Foster, *A Gringo in Mañana-land* (New York: Dodd, Mead, 1924).

3. Foster 223.

4. Foster 223.

5. Foster 236.

6. Foster 228.

7. Foster 230.

8. Excerpt is from 224–237.

Be Here (or There) Now

Before launching into our five identity categories of race, class, gender, nation, and Latin America, we shall turn our attention to a brief excerpt from Stuart Hall, one of the worlds' foremost theorists on identity.

Destabilizing identity structures, a primary objective of cultural theory, can be an alienating experience. What once seemed unwavering and true suddenly becomes tenuous and shifting. Hermeneuticians and modernists, who reject postmodernism, are quick to accuse cultural theorists of eradicating identities so much that we are left adrift on a sea of constructs. In short, they accuse postmodernism of being entirely impractical. One of Stuart Hall's main contributions to cultural theory has been to provide a practical way to conceptualize identity from a cultural theory perspective.

Hall's professional career is closely tied to the Centre for Contemporary Cultural Studies (CCCS), the Birmingham school we mentioned in our introduction. He became its director in 1968, and under his tutelage the center emerged as the focal point of the emergent field of cultural studies, a place where theories of postmodernism were applied to the study of contemporary issues. Not surprisingly, the center and its teachings also became a focal point for debate. Defenders of modernist methodologies and teaching styles considered it a haven for fringe scholars trying to pass off intellectual shenanigans as legitimate academic inquiry. If the center's ideological foundation was not enough to inspire detractors, its occasional application of its theoretical approaches to the classroom fanned the flames of opposition. For example, a former student recalls one of the more memorable lectures on queer theory being "given by a well-stacked, tattooed, skinhead Ph.D. student wearing a clear plastic suit."[1] But such legendary stories should not detract from (perhaps they should enhance) the center's reputation among many scholars as a place of serious academic inquiry and as a major contributor to the development of new and influential ideas.

The excerpt that follows is taken from an edited version of a speech Hall delivered at Hampshire College, in Amherst, Massachusetts, in 1989. Hall addresses the issue of identity primarily from the perspective of ethnicity, but with the overarching objective of conceiving of identity in a way that does not fall into the traps of either the old modernist notions of the true self or of the completely discursive deconstruction. Hall, of course, rejects modernist notions of the self, or the rational Cartesian subject, but he also criticizes extreme postmodernist arguments in which "the Self is a kind of *perpetual signifier* ever wandering the earth in search of a *transcendental signified* that it can never find."[2]

Hall's solution to this modernist/postmodernist dichotomy is to acknowledge that all people indeed come from some place: they have a history, culture, or community that has framed their conceptualization of the world. Hall believes these places to be constituted discursively, their meaning always in flux. But these places or locations, however temporary and fleeting they might be, are all that we have at any given moment, and Hall argues that we have to use them as a starting point for any discussion or analysis. Without that place, Hall argues, there would be no position from which to begin, and we would indeed become nothing more than a series of fractured constructs scattered to the winds of discourse.

> There is no way, its seems to me, in which people of the world can act, can speak, can create, can come in from the margins and talk, can begin to reflect on their own experience unless they come from some *place*, they come from some history, they inherit certain cultural traditions. . . . You have to position yourself *somewhere* in order to say anything at all.[3] [Hall's emphasis]

It might seem contradictory that Hall, a cultural theorist, would instruct people to acknowledge their identity and use it as a point of reference. But he does not portray this identity as originating in some indelible true self or remaining the same for perpetuity. Quite the contrary. He insists that we recognize the temporality of who we are at any given moment and that we momentarily embrace it as the only place from which we can come at that instant. Rather than being distressed by this impermanence, the new postmodern self will be comfortable with it, ready to acknowledge the limits of personal identity claims as well as any truth claims.

Hall grounds his theoretical elaborations regarding identity in what he calls the "process of identification." By this he means that identity is a gradual awareness of self as contingent upon cultural, historical, and political contexts. Using specific autobiographical anecdotes, he asserts that knowing oneself is not accomplished through the search for a so-called true inner self, but through an understanding of how we are positioned and how we position ourselves at any given moment by the recognition of others. This positioning is Hall's contingent and temporal place, and he illustrates it by examining his own process of identification.

When he first immigrated to England, Hall identified himself as a respectable, lower-class Jamaican. The first time he returned to Jamaica, his mother urged him not to think of himself as an immigrant back in England. It was the precise moment—and not before—of his mother's suggestion that the English most likely perceive him as an immigrant that it occurs to Hall to identify himself as an immigrant. He became an immigrant at the moment that he saw himself as one and was seen as one.

Hall also considers the process he underwent in understanding the shifting meaning of his skin color. He explains that, until the 1970s, Jamaicans never considered themselves to be black. For a modernist reader, Hall's absence of a black identity prior to the 1970s may be surprising; after all, his skin color did not change. What did change was the value attached to black skin as a signifier. In the 1970s, Hall's skin color took on political meaning; thus, it became a difference that made a difference. Hall in turn attempts to teach his own biracial son to locate himself in an unfixed place from which he can understand the world and recognize who he is in the world at that moment. Hall recounts the moment that he hails his son as Black (with a capital *B* to indicate an idea, not a skin color), and the latter retorts that he is brown (with a lowercased *b* to indicate that he fails to recognize the cultural, historical, and political definition of his temporal place of identity.) In these ways, Hall insists that both his son and his audience recognize and embrace the contingency of identity as the temporary place of self-discovery.

Hall applies his theory to individual identities and to collective ones like race, class, gender, and nation. He demonstrates this with the case of England's national identity under Margaret Thatcher's government. He argues that Thatcherism defined English national identity in an essentialist way as a nationalist response to the growth of immigration. Ironically, it is precisely when England was divested of its colonies in the 1950s that its formerly colonized citizens began to immigrate and function as a constant reminder of the loss of England's glorious past. This immigrant presence, often of nonwhite, racialized groups, in and of itself is a constant challenge to contemporary English identity. On the one hand, the immigrants are a reminder of England's lost colonial glory; on the other hand, they can never return to the colonies they left behind without having been changed by their experience in England. Hall proposes that under Thatcherism there are two different ways of understanding ethnicity. The old ethnicity, the one in power, consists of a modernist notion of fixed identity; the new ethnicity recovers the past only temporarily in seeking out that sense of place. Hall proposes that we reject essentialist understandings of identity and celebrate the new ethnicity that allows subjects to situate themselves discursively.

It is this acknowledgment of a temporary place of origin that makes Hall's argument so important. Indeed, it is one of the most important arguments in this book and a foundation we will return to repeatedly. In Hall's understanding, every subject's identity is discursively situated; like discourse, it will change over time and space. It is this constant process of transformation that Hall celebrates and defines as the postmodern self.

STUART HALL, "ETHNICITY: IDENTITY AND DIFFERENCE"[4]
The Return of Identity [. . .]

Let me start by saying something about what seems to have been the logic of the way in which we have thought and talked about questions of identity until recently. The logic of the discourse of identity assumes a stable subject, i.e., we've assumed that there is something which we can call our identity which, in a rapidly shifting world, has the great advantage of staying still. Identities are a kind of guarantee that the world isn't falling apart quite as rapidly as it sometimes seems to be. It's a kind of fixed point of thought and being, a ground of action, a still point in the turning world. That's the kind of ultimate guarantee that identity seems to provide us with.

The logic of identity is the logic of something like a "true self." And the language of identity has often been related to the search for a kind of authenticity to one's experience, something that tells me where I come from. The logic and language of identity is the logic of depth—in here, deep inside me, is my Self which I can reflect upon. It is an element of continuity. I think most of us do recognize that our identities have changed over time, but we have the hope or nostalgia that they change at the rate of a glacier. So, while we're not the fledglings that we were when we were one year old, we are the same sort of person.

Disruption of Identity

So where does the recent disruption of identity come from? What is displacing this depth—the autonomous origin, point of reference, and guaranteed continuity that has been so long associated with the language of identity? What is it about the turbulence of the world we live in that is increasingly mirrored in the vicissitudes of identity?

While, historically, many things have displaced or decentered the stable sense of identity that I just described, I want to focus on four great decenterings in intellectual life and in Western thought that have helped to destabilize the question of identity. I'll attach particular names to three of them, just for convenience sake. I don't want to say they alone did it, but it is quite useful to summarize by hooking the ideas to a particular name. The fourth cannot be attached to a single name, but is just as important.

Marx begins the de-centering of that stable sense of identity by reminding us that there are always *conditions* to identity which the subject cannot construct. Men and women make history but not under conditions of their own making. They are partly made by the histories that they make. We are always constructed in part by the practices and discourses that make us, such that we cannot find within ourselves as individual selves or subjects or identities the point of origin from which discourse or history or practice originate. History has to be understood as a continuous dialectic or dialogic relationship between that which is already made and that which is making the future. While Marx's argument deconstructed a lot of games, I'm particularly interested in his impact on the identity/language game. Marx interrupted that notion of the sovereign subject who opens his or her mouth and speaks, for the first time, the truth. Marx reminds us that we are always lodged and implicated in the practices and structures of everybody else's life.

Secondly, there is the very profound displacement which begins with Freud's discovery of the unconscious. If Marx displaced us from the past, Freud displaced us from below. Identity is itself grounded on the huge unknowns of our psychic lives, and we are unable, in any simple way, to reach through the barrier of the unconscious into the psychic life. We can't read the psychic *directly* into the social and the cultural. Nevertheless, social, cultural and political life cannot be understood except in relationship to the formations of the unconscious life. This in itself destabilizes the notion of the self, of identity, as a fully self-reflective entity. It is not possible for the self to reflect and know completely its own identity since it is formed not only in the line of the practice of other structures and discourses, but also in a complex relationship with unconscious life.

Thirdly, we must consider Saussure and his model of language and linguistics which has so transformed theoretical work. Saussurian linguistics suggests that speech—discourse, enunciation itself—is always placed within the relationships of language. In order to speak, in order to say anything new, we must first place ourselves within the existing relations of language. There is no utterance so novel and so creative that it does not already bear on it the traces of how that language has been spoken before we opened our mouths. Thus we are always within language. To say something new is first of all to reaffirm the traces of the past that are inscribed in the words we use. In part, to say something new is first of all to displace all the old things that the words mean—to fight an entire system of meanings. For example, think of how profound it has been in our world to say the word "Black" in a new way. In order to say "Black" in a new way, we have to fight off everything else that Black has always meant—all its connotations, all its negative and positive figurations, the entire metaphorical structure of Christian thought, for example. The whole history of Western imperial thought is condensed in the struggle to dislocate what Black used to mean in order to make it mean something new, in order to say "Black is Beautiful." I'm not talking about Saussure's specific theories of language only. I'm talking about what happens to one's conception of identity when one suddenly understands that one is always inside a system of languages that partly speak us, which we are always positioned within and against.

These are the great figures of modernism. We might say that if modernity unleashes the logic of identity I was talking about earlier, modernism is modernity experienced as trouble. In the face of modernity's promise of the great future: "I am, I am Western man, therefore I know everything. Everything begins with me," modernism says, "Hold on. What about the past? What about the languages you speak? What about the unconscious life you don't know about? What about all those other things that are speaking you?"

However, there's a fourth force of destabilization. This could be given a variety of names. If you wanted to stay within the episteme of Western knowledge, you could say Nietzsche. But I want to say something else. I want to talk about the de-centering of identity that arises as a consequence of the end of the notion of truth as having something directly to do with Western discourses of rationality. This is the great de-centering of identity that is a consequence of the relativization of the Western world—of the discovery of other worlds, other peoples, other cultures, and other languages. Western rational thought, despite its imperializing claim to be *the* form of universal knowledge, suddenly appears as just another episteme. To use Foucault's words, just another regime of truth. Or Nietzsche's, not absolute Knowledge, not total Truth, just another *particular* form of knowledge harnessed to particular forms of historical power. The linkage between knowledge and power is what made that regime True, what enabled that regime to claim to speak the truth about identity for everyone else across the globe.

When that installation of Western rationality begins to go and to be seen not as absolute, disinterested, objective, neutral, scientific, non-powerful truth, but dirty truth—truth implicated in the hard game of power—that is the fourth game that destabilizes the old logic of identity.

Post-Identity? Cover Stories

There is some language for the notion of doing without identity all together. That is my somewhat unfavorable reference to the extreme version of post-modernism. The argument is that the Self is simply a kind of *perpetual signifier* ever wandering the earth in search of a *transcendental signified* that it can never find—a sort of endless nomadic existence with utterly atomized individuals wandering in an endlessly pluralistic void. Yet, while there are certain conceptual and theoretical ways in which you can try to do without identity, I'm not yet convinced that you can. I think we have to try to reconceptualize what identities might mean in this more diverse and pluralized situation [. . .].

Identity, far from the simple thing that we think it is (ourselves always in the same place), understood properly is always a structure that is split; it always has ambivalence within it. The story of identity is a cover story. A cover story for making you think you stayed in the same place, though with another bit of your mind you do know that you've moved on. What we've learned about the structure of the way in which we identify suggests that identification is not one thing, one moment. We have now to reconceptualize identity as a *process of identification*, and that is a different matter. It is something that happens over time, that is never absolutely stable, that is subject to the play of history and the play of difference [. . .].

If I think about who I am, I have been—in my own much too long experience—several identities. And most of the identities that I have been I've only known about not because of something deep inside me—the real self—but because of how other people have recognized me.

So, I went to England in the 1950s, before the great wave of migration from the Caribbean and from the Asian subcontinent. I came from a highly respectable, lower-middle-class Jamaican family. When I went back home at the end of the 50s, my mother, who was very classically of that class and culture, said to me, "I hope they don't think you're an immigrant over there!" I had never thought of myself as an immigrant! And now I thought, well actually, I guess that's what I am. I migrated just at that moment. When she hailed me, when she said, "Hello immigrant," she asked me to refuse it and in the moment of refusal—like almost everything my mother ever asked me to do—I said, "That's who I am! I'm an immigrant." And I thought at last, I've come into my *real* self.[5]

And then, at the end of the 60s and the early 70s, somebody said to me "These things are going on in the political world—I suppose you're really Black." Well, I'd never thought of myself as Black, either! And I'll tell you something, nobody in Jamaica ever did. Until the 1970s, that entire population experienced themselves as all sorts of other things, but they never called themselves Black. And in that sense, Black has a history as an identity that is partly *politically* formed. It's not the color of your skin. It's not given in nature.

Another example: at that very moment I said to my son, who is the result of a mixed marriage, "You're Black." "No," he said, "I'm brown." "You don't understand what I'm saying! You're looking to the wrong signifier! I'm not talking about what color you are. People are all sorts of colors. The question is whether you are *culturally, historically, politically* Black. That's who you are."

The Other

So experience belies the notion that identification happens once and for all—life is not like that. It goes on changing and part of what is changing is not the nucleus of the "real you" inside, it is history that's changing. History changes your conception of yourself. Thus, another critical thing about identity is that it is partly the relationship between you and the Other. Only when there is an Other can you know who you are. To discover that fact is to discover and unlock the whole enormous history of nationalism and of racism. Racism is a structure of discourse and representation that tries to expel the Other symbolically—blot it out, put it over there in the Third World, at the margin.

The English are racist not because they hate the Blacks but because they don't know who they are without the Blacks. They have to know who they are not in order to know who they are. And the English language is absolutely replete with things that the English are not. They are not Black, they are not Indian or Asian, but they are not Europeans and they are not Frogs either and on and on. The Other. It is a fantastic moment in Fanon's *Black Skin, White Masks* when he talks of how the gaze of the Other fixes him in an identity. He knows what it is to be Black when the white child pulls the hand of her mother and says "Look momma, a Black man." And he says "I was fixed in that gaze." That is the gaze of Otherness. And there is no identity that is without the dialogic relationship to the Other. The Other is not outside, but also inside the Self, the identity. So identity is a process, identity is split. Identity is not a fixed point but an ambivalent point. Identity is also the relationship of the Other to oneself.

Difference(s) [. . .]

So the notion that identity is outside representation—that there are our selves and then the language in which we describe ourselves—is untenable. Identity is within discourse, within representation. It is constituted in part by representation. Identity is a narrative of the self; it's the story we tell about the self in order to know who we are. We impose a structure on it. The most important effect of this reconceptualization of identity is the surreptitious return of difference. Identity is a game that ought to be played against difference. But now we have to think about identity *in relation to* difference. There are differences between the ways in which genders are socially and psychically constructed. But there is no fixity to those oppositions. It is a relational opposition, it is a relation of difference. So we're then in the difficult conceptual area of trying to think identity *and* difference.

The Thatcher Project

So, how can one think about identity in this new context? [. . .] When I first started to write about Thatcherism in the early 70s, I thought it was largely an economic and political project. It is only more recently that I understood how profoundly it is rooted in a certain exclusive and essentialist conception of Englishness. Thatcherism is *in defense* of a certain definition of Englishness. England didn't go to the Falklands War inadvertently. It went because there was something there about the connection of the great imperial past, of the empire, of the lion whose tail cannot be tweaked, of the little country that stood up to the great dictator. It's a way of mythically living all the great moments of the English past again. Well, it happens that this time it had to be in the South Atlantic, miles away from anything—

in a little corner of the globe that most English people can't identify on the map.

The Return of the Repressed

So it's a very profound part of the Thatcher project to try to restore the identity that in their view *belongs* to Great Britain—Great Britain, Inc., Ltd.—a great firm, Great Britain restored to a world power. But in this very moment of the attempted symbolic restoration of the great English identities that have mastered and dominated the world over three or four centuries, there come home to roost in English society some *other* British folks. They come from Jamaica, Pakistan, Bangladesh, India—all that part of the colonial world that the English, just in the 1950s, decided they could do without. Just in the very moment when they decided they could do without us, we all took the banana boat and came right back home. We turned up saying "You said this was the mother country. Well, I just came home." We now stand as a permanent reminder of that forgotten, suppressed, hidden history. Every time they walk out on the street, some of us—some of the Other—are there. There we are, *inside* the culture, going to their schools, speaking their language, playing their music, walking down their streets, looking like we own a part of the turf, looking like we belong. Some third generation Blacks are starting to say "We are the Black British." After all, who are we? We're not Jamaicans any more. We have a relationship to that past, but we can't be that entirely anymore [. . .].

Ethnicities: Old and New

What does all that I've been saying have to do with ethnicity? I've left the question of ethnicity to the last because ethnicity is the way in which I want to rethink the relationships between identity and difference. I want to argue that ethnicity is what we all require in order to think the relationship between identity and difference. What do I mean by that? There is no way, it seems to me, in which people of the world can act, can speak, can create, can come in from the margins and talk, can begin to reflect on their own experience unless they come from some *place*, they come from some history, they inherit certain cultural traditions. What we've learned about the theory of enunciation is that there's no enunciation without positionality. You have to position yourself *somewhere* in order to say anything at all. Thus, we cannot do without that sense of our own positioning that is connoted by the term ethnicity. And the relation that peoples of the world now have to their own past is, of course, part of the discovery of their own ethnicity. They need to honor the hidden histories from which they come. They need to understand the languages which they've been not taught to speak. They need to understand and revalue the traditions and inheritances of cultural expression and creativity. And in that sense, the past is not only a position from which to speak, but it is also an absolutely necessary resource in what one has to say. There is no way, in my view, in which those elements of ethnicity that depend on understanding the past, understanding one's roots, can be done without.

But, on the other hand, there comes the play of difference. This is the recognition that our relationship to that past is quite a complex one, we can't pluck it up out of where it was and simply restore it to ourselves. If you ask my son, who is seventeen and who was born in London, where he comes from, he cannot tell you he comes from Jamaica. Part of his identity is there, but he has to *discover* that identity. He can't just take it out of a suitcase and plop it on the table and say "That's mine." It's not an essence like that. He has to learn to tell himself the story of his past. He has to interrogate his own history, he has to relearn that part of him that has an investment in that culture. For example, he's learning wood sculpture, and in order to do that he has had to discover the traditions of sculpturing of a society in which he has never lived.

So the relationship of the kind of ethnicity I'm talking about to the past is not a simple, essential one—it is a constructed one. It is constructed in history, it is constructed politically in part. It is part of narrative. We tell ourselves the stories of the parts of our roots in order to come into contact, creatively, with it. So this new kind of ethnicity—the emergent ethnicities—has a relationship to the past, but it is a relationship that is partly through memory, partly through narrative, one that has to be recovered. It is an act of cultural recovery.

Yet it is also an ethnicity that has to recognize its position in relation to the importance of difference. It is an ethnicity that cannot deny the role of difference in discovering itself [. . .].

We need a place to speak from, but we no longer speak about ethnicity in a narrow and essentialist way.

That is the new ethnicity. It is a new conception of our identities because it has not lost hold of the place and the ground from which we can speak, yet it is no longer contained within that place as an essence. It wants to address a much wider variety of experience. It is part of the enormous cultural relativization of the entire globe that is the historical accomplishment— horrendous as it has been in part—of the twentieth century. Those are the new ethnicities, the new voices. They are neither locked into the past nor able to forget the past, neither all the same nor entirely different. Identity *and* difference. It is a new settlement between identity and difference.

Of course, alongside the new ethnicities are the *old* ethnicities and the coupling of the old essentialist identities to power. The old ethnicities still have dominance, they still govern. Indeed, as I tried to suggest when I referred to Thatcherism, as they are relativized their propensity to eat everything else increases. They can only be sure that they really exist at all if they consume everyone else. The notion of an identity that knows where it came from, where home is, but also lives in the symbolic—in the Lacanian sense—knows you can't really go home again.[6] You can't be something else than who you are. You've got to find out who you are in the flux of the past and the present. That new conception of ethnicity is now struggling in different ways across the globe against the present danger and the threat of the dangerous old ethnicity. That's the stake of the game.

DISCUSSION QUESTIONS

• What is the difference between the old and the new ethnicity? Can one be categorized as an essentialist understanding of identity and the other as semiotic?

• Hall writes, "I am, I am Western man, therefore I know everything." In what way is he referencing the modernist notion of the Cartesian rational subject with this quote, and how does he challenge the legitimacy of that notion?

• What does Hall's description of Thatcherism tell us about the role of the nation in shaping the identity of its individuals?

• How does Hall's description of the role of the Other in identity help us rethink race, class, gender, and nation?

• Although Hall does not address the issue of Latin American immigration to the United States, how might it compare with his description of immigration to Great Britain?

• What is this place that Hall says we have to come from, and why is the idea of it so central to his entire argument?

• Hall says that the very postmodern or cultural theory concept of the "de-centering of the self" traces its origins to a modernist intellectual tradition. Think back to our introductory section(s) and consider the significance of this claim for understanding debates between modernists and cultural theorists and for the Latin Americanist challenge to so-called U.S. cultural studies.

NOTES

1. This episode is cited on the Vocabulary of Culture Web site, devoted to CCCS (1963–2002), consulted on 4 March 2005 <http://www.jahsonic .com/CCCS.html>.

2. Stuart Hall, "Ethnicity: Identity and Difference," ed. Geof Eley and R. Suny, *Becoming National: A Reader* (New York: Oxford UP, 1996) 344.

3. Hall 347.

4. Excerpt from Hall 339–341, 344–349.

5. Hall's reference to his mother's "hailing" him draws upon a classic argument put forth by the Algerian/French political philosopher, Louis Althusser (1918–1990), in his essay, "Ideology and Ideological State Apparatuses: Some Notes Toward an Investigation." Althusser drew upon Jacques Lacan's notion of the unconscious and the construction of the self to argue that identity can be constructed by processes of external identification. For instance, when we stop because a police officer hails us, our internal self becomes shaped by external ideologies.

6. Hall is referring to Jacques Lacan (1901–1981), a French psychoanalyst generally associated with approaching psychoanalysis from a cultural theory or poststructuralist perspective. Hall's reference to the Lacanian "symbolic" refers to Lacan's idea that we are born into and raised in social systems (i.e., discursively constituted social norms) that then construct our identities for us.

CHAPTER 6

Identity Construct #1: Race

In the early 1990s, Cornell West, a U.S. academician, wrote *Race Matters*, the title of which is a play on the word *matter* as both noun and verb.[1] West rejects racism and even the existence of race, so to him race does not matter. But he recognizes that ideas about race have affected and continue to affect, if not to dominate, life in the United States, so he believes in the need to study racial matters. He challenges those people who believe the United States has rectified its long history of racial injustice; West informs them that, unfortunately, race does still matter.

The wordplay in the title of his book and the issues he addresses in his work provide good points of entry for our exploration of essentialistic and semiotic interpretations of race in Latin America. Essentialists who believe in race, whom we can call "racialists," believe in racial essences. They hold the view that humans can be divided into distinct groups based on fundamental and immutable traits. These differences can be most easily determined by physical features, such as skin color and hair texture, but even if these physical features are not obvious, racial essence is still present. Racialists believe that racial divisions are objective characteristics of human existence, not mere social conveniences. Thus, for a racial essentialist, having lighter or darker skin reflects a distinguishing essence.

It is worthwhile to differentiate racists from racialists. Racists hold a hermeneutic view on race, but believe one racial group to be superior and tend to advocate discrimination against the supposed inferiors. One obvious example of a racist is a white supremacist. A black supremacist or an Asian supremacist is also technically a racist. But as many scholars of race point out, in a society where access to power is often determined by one's race, minority groups (blacks, Asians, Hispanics, etc.) lack the capacity to actively discriminate against whites. These scholars therefore encourage us in the United States to reserve the term *racist* for people with economic and social power, typically whites, and to identify supremacists of disenfranchised minority groups as xenophobes or bigots, or as just downright ignorant.

A racialist is someone who holds a hermeneutic view on race and believes in racial essences but does not necessarily think these differences should be a basis of discrimination or separation. Racialists believe in race but are not inherently racists. The danger in this view is that a belief in racial essence easily lends itself to discriminatory views, regardless of intent. For this reason, Lawrence Blum, a professor of philosophy at the University of Massachusetts and a scholar of racial issues, titled his recent book *"I'm Not a Racist But . . .": The Moral Quandary of Race.*

In the first of two excerpts from his work in this chapter, Blum lays out a series of beliefs that constitute racial essentialism in the United States in the nineteenth century. What he writes is directly applicable to Latin America. Blum's nine-point typology reflects issues specific to the nineteenth century. His reference to biology would not be part of his list if it were based on ideas from the sixteenth or seventeenth century. But this view from the nineteenth century more or less synthesizes modernity's generalized belief, dating back roughly five hundred years, that racial difference is an essentialism.

Some scholars consider Blum's list inapplicable to Latin America because North American views on race were supposedly developed from a truly deep-seated racism based on notions of essentialism and immutable traits. Racial issues in Latin America purportedly lacked essentialism and were based solely on a cultural recognition of physical difference. This argument has had many advocates and with good reason. Places with distinct histories will produce different views on race. But a counterargument has been steadily growing and arguably is now more accepted. One of its advocates is Peter Wade (also excerpted in this chapter), who argues that regardless of the almost infinite variations on racial views, not only between North America and South America but also within these regions, the commonality of all racialist interpretations is that they rest upon a foundation of essentialism rooted in Western modernity.

Some essentialists reject the idea of race and therefore believe their hermeneutically racialist ancestors had it wrong. Contemporary biologists and geneticists constitute one important part of this group. They argue that there is no connection between the genes that produce the physical traits associated with race and any other aspect of human identity. Therefore, having darker or lighter skin means nothing more than having any other physical feature, such as height, weight, or body shape. Still, the racialist idea continues to hold fast in many minds throughout the world.

Race offers a rare moment when semioticians and hermeneuticians (at least the nonracialist variety) agree on something: race is a social construct and not an objective fact. Semioticians, of course, see this social construction as being rooted in discourse, something no hermeneutician could accept. Regardless, a foundation for agreement is there. The second part of the excerpt from Lawrence Blum outlines the social constructivist interpretation on race. Blum might not be a cultural theorist per se because he does not specifically link ideas about race to discourse, but he nevertheless provides a succinct and clearly worded deconstruction of racial essentialism. When reading that selection, note that Blum compares race to gender and nation, two other identity categories we will explore.

Because social constructionists like Blum define race as nothing more than an idea, they are particularly interested in studying its history. By demonstrating that a particular idea ebbs and flows in accordance with social convention, social constructionists believe they bolster their argument about race as a figment of society's collective imagination. They argue that the variety of views on race reveals more about the peculiarities of time and place than any ontological truths about human nature. Wade and Blum both offer an extended survey of the history of racialist ideas in their studies, although we have decided not to excerpt those sections because we lack the space for them. Their work reveals to us that historical studies on race and the origin of racial ideas are numerous and diverse. For example, one major school of thought links the origin of racism to material issues, mainly the trans-Atlantic slave trade and the economic necessity of cheap labor. Another traces its origins farther back, even to biblical times, and to long-held cultural assumptions in Western societies that associate blackness with evil. Regardless of these variations in interpretation, there is a widespread agreement that Western modernity and its economic, scientific, and imperial mandates bear responsibility for the consolidation and globalization, if not the origin, of racial essentialism.

We will not try to untangle conflicting interpretations about the origin of racial essentialism. We would point out that much of the research on this subject was done before the notion of essentialism, in its cultural theory context, was more widely accepted in the academy. Thus, much of the historical research on race seeks out references to skin color but does not necessarily identify racial essentialism. Recent research, based on a more semiotic approach, advances an argument about the genesis of essentialist thinking and places Latin America at its inception. For that reason, we will outline the basics of that argument.

The study in question is an academic article written by Jorge Cañizares Esguerra, a history professor at the State University of New York, Buffalo.[2] He argues that the origin of racial essentialism can be traced to colonial Mexico and Peru in the 1500s and 1600s. The context for the emergence of essentialist thinking was the consolidation of a distinct demographic population within the maturing colonial society known as criollos, or creoles. These were people of Spanish descent born in the Americas. They considered themselves pureblooded Europeans, meaning that no one in their families had intermixed with Indians, though they had been born and raised in the Americas rather than continental Europe. They were contrasted with the *peninsulares*, Spaniards born and raised in Spain who came to the Americas to administer the colonies but who often did not stay there and returned home to Europe.

This takes on significance in the context of Spain's need to justify its exploitation of Indian populations primarily for labor purposes. At the time of the Spanish Conquest, people defined one another according to how they interpreted the Bible, astrology, and the natural environment. Eventually, these would be replaced by more scientific arguments based in Europe's emergent modernity, but until then they served as the primary tools for defining humanity. The Bible was understood as providing God's word on how people were constituted; thus, on the proper social order as well. In a society heavily reliant on religion, as Europe was in the late 1400s and early 1500s, the Bible was deemed the first and foremost authority on questions pertaining to human identity. But the challenge for Spain's and Portugal's colonization of the Americas was that the Bible did not mention the New World or its inhabitants. Hence, Spanish and Portuguese intellectuals turned to astrological and environmental interpretations. It was believed that people's makeup was determined by the stars under which they were born or the natural environment in which they were raised. Excessive heat or humidity had specific effects on people, as did dryer, colder climates, and certain astrological patterns.

At the outset of Spanish colonization, the peninsular/creole divide did not exist. Basically everyone was a peninsular, and classifying people in the colonial project was not that difficult; there were only Europeans and Indians. Even though the Bible did not mention Indians specifically, the astrological and natural environmental arguments allowed Spaniards to comfortably rest on a distinction between the two. Indians supposedly grew up in an inferior natural environment and under astrological signs that allowed for their exploitation at the hands of the Spaniards. But after two or three generations of Spanish people living and raising families in the Americas, the old classifications no longer sufficed. According to the arguments based on astrology and natural environment, creoles were no different than Indians.

Not surprisingly, peninsulars recognized this issue, and driven by a need to preserve the economic basis of the empire and the exploitation of Indian labor, they began to develop views that discriminated against the creoles. Basically, they defined creoles as lesser forms of humanity for having been born and raised in the Americas, even though they were physically indistinguishable from peninsulars. The creoles did not passively accept these developments. They responded to peninsular discriminations by reversing the astrological and natural environment arguments, and then by inventing the idea of racial essentialism. Eventually, this so-called racial divide contributed to the creole fight for independence. Starting in the mid-to-late 1500s, creole intellectuals argued that America's astrology and nature were superior to Spain's. But this argument did not allow creoles to maintain their supremacy over Indians because in theory Indians now shared the same superior astrological and natural origins. It was in seeking to resolve this issue that creoles moved on to the second, essentializing phase of their response.

Creole intellectuals argued that Indians were somehow fundamentally different from people of European descent. They were not able to define specifically what that difference was, but in so many words it was the internal, bloodline essence of Indians that set them apart. An explanatory analogy that one of these emerging creole racialists used was that fire (from nature and astrology) responds to green wood (Indians) and dry wood (people of Spanish descent) differently. Unable to define specifically the origin and cause of this difference, these creole intellectuals turned to physical differentiation. Suddenly, darker skin, blackish hair, and certain other physical features (like a larger nose) became markers of Indian identity and essential inferiority. The modern notion of race in Latin America was born.

Cañizares Esguerra shows the birth of such a discourse. He does not attempt to explore the possible multitude of discourses that might have contributed to the essentialist thinking of these nascent creole racialists. Neither does he try to argue that they invented racial essentialism for the first time, or that the ideas of these creoles in Peru and Mexico were responsible for the emergence of racial essentialism throughout Western modernity. But Cañizares Esguerra's argument represents a pathbreaking moment in racial studies. Rooted in a more semiotically driven methodology that considers human bodies as signifiers to be assigned signification, and sensitive to the idea of essentialism, Cañizares Esguerra was able to read the writings of these creole intellectuals in a new way. Consequently, he illustrates Latin America's participation in the creation of modern Western racial essentialism.

Social constructionists and semioticians certainly recognize the incredible durability of racialist arguments over the past five hundred years. They take note of how racialist essentialism was globalized along with the spread of Western modernity. But they are also quick to point out that racialist ideas, being social constructions or discourses, are highly flexible and adapt to local and regional needs; thus, they tend to focus much of their research efforts on finding these variations.

Despite the steady onslaught of social constructionist arguments, racialist views have proven highly resilient; indeed, so has racism. But in the latter half of the twentieth century, owing to populist political movements and the realization of the horrors of the Holocaust, the legitimacy of racism, and even of racialism, has been in retreat. But human beings have still needed ways to explain the distinctions that typify the complex fabric of human coexistence. So as references to race have declined, alternative terms have risen instead. Arguably, ethnicity is now the most widely accepted and commonly used among these.

Ethnicity is supposedly a more neutral term that lacks the historic legacy of race and refers to cultural identity or place of origin rather than immutable traits in the blood. Even for those people who have no awareness of the concept of essence, the term seemingly avoids essentializing people and instead defines them with respect to their cultural grouping. Thus, according to this approach, people of African descent in the Americas are no longer defined as being part of the black race but as belonging to cultural groupings, such as of African American, or African Caribbean, or African Brazilian, depending on where they lived and what cultural group nurtured their identity.

Ethnicity is the subject of the excerpt by Peter Wade, a professor of social anthropology at the University of Manchester, who has devoted much of his professional life to the study of race and ethnicity in Latin America. Wade's main argument is that ethnicity suffers from many of the same essentialist foundations as does the term *race*. Wade demonstrates how essentialism, as a sort of foundational modernist discourse, has affected the issue of ethnicity.

Wade's discussion is particularly important in the context of Latin America, especially to the issue of *mestizaje*, which we will define at greater length in our discussion of nation. But briefly, *mestizaje* originally referred to the racial mixing of Indians and Europeans that began with the Spanish (and Portuguese) conquest in the late 1400s and early 1500s and that continues to the present day. Within Latin American history, which has been typified by a strict racial hierarchy, mestizos held a middling position. They were not as high as pure Europeans but neither were they as low as Indians. As we will see, one of the problems with defining society along racial lines was that physical characteristics that supposedly distinguished mestizos from other racial groups (especially Indians) were not always so obvious. Thus, *mestizaje* became as much a cultural identity (an ethnicity of sorts) as a racial identity. Throughout Latin American history, racial essentialism and cultural identity have constantly intermingled and mutually reinforced one another. This has held deep implications during the era of populist nationalism in the early twentieth century. The nationalist populist movements celebrated *mestizaje* and the idea of a mixed or heterogeneous society over the racially hierarchical societies of the past. But their intentions for inclusiveness and social leveling often became confused with underlying racial essentialism. The discourse of race and essentialism profoundly influenced the interpretations of society in these movements, contrary to their designers' apparent plans.

LAWRENCE BLUM, *I'M NOT A RACIST BUT . . .*[3]
[Part One]

THE ELEMENTS OF CLASSIC RACIAL IDEOLOGY   Here, then, are the elements of the "classic," nineteenth-century conception of race in the United States:

1. Human beings fall into a small number of ancestral groupings called "races," linked historically to certain geographical regions of the globe. These are natural, discrete, fixed subdivisions of humanity. These races are radically distinct in character from one another. Every human being is a member of one and only one race.
2. Races differ from one another in significant qualities of mind, character, personality, and temperament. Blacks are lazy; whites are industrious; yellows are cunning; and the like.
3. Every member of a given race possesses the characteristics distinctive to that race—what is sometimes called the race's "essence." Sometimes race thinking allows for aberrant or untypical members not to possess the characteristics constituting the racial essence.
4. The race's essence of mind, character, and personality is grounded in biology.
5. The racial essence is passed from one generation to the next.

6. Races are generally also distinct in certain aspects of physical appearance. These somatic or phenotypic features are, therefore, indicators of the group's racial essence, its inner reality. For example, light skin and straight hair indicates initiative and inventiveness; dark skin and woolly hair indicates musicality and laziness.

7. Racial differences are fixed, innate, and unchangeable, because they are grounded in biology.

8. Races can be ranked in terms of superiority and inferiority generally or at least with regard to particular significant characteristics. This ranking should be and generally is reflected in the relations of power and status in society and civilizations.

9. The social order appropriately reflects, through its legal, institutional, and customary norms, the distinctness in nature between races by separating them as much as possible in occupational, social, personal, and public space. Segregation is "natural" and mixing is "unnatural," especially in regard to sexual and marital relations. When individuals of different races do interact, their interactions are to reflect the hierarchical order, the inferior group members showing deference to the superior.

Classic late nineteenth-century race involved both a vertical and a horizontal dimension. Horizontally, races were radically distinct from one another, and social distance and separation were meant to reflect this. Vertically, races were superior and inferior to one another, and the hierarchical social order was to reflect this as well.

This conception is the culmination of several centuries' development of the idea of race, a product of the interaction of economic, political, historical, social, and scientific factors. Yet it is not really coherent. No groups large enough to be "races" on this conception could possibly have the internal commonality, nor the comprehensive difference from other races, demanded by this view. Nor can somatic features plausibly be linked to the wide range of significant human characteristics involved in the view. Entire racial groups cannot be inherently "inferior" to entire other ones in any intelligible sense, though of course they can be treated as if they were [. . .].

[Part Two]

IS "RACE" A SOCIAL CONSTRUCTION? Recent academic writing frequently refers to race as a "social construct" or "social construction." This language can illuminate the meaning of "race," but only if it clearly and explicitly distinguishes between races, which do not exist, and racialized groups, which do. The statement "race is a social construction" does not draw that distinction, and can lead to obfuscation rather than illumination.

Several distinct meanings have been attached to the term "social construction." One is that the thing in question has been wrongly thought to be a product of "natural" (biological or physical) processes when it is in fact a product of social ones. Masculinity and femininity are frequently cited examples. Femininity in a given society involves not merely the possession of certain bodily organs and a particular chromosomal structure ("nature") but socially prescribed ways of behaving. This notion of social construction is sometimes but not necessarily conjoined with the view that only biological or physical entities or processes are "real" while social ones are not.

In the classic nineteenth-century sense races were purported to be natural rather than socially constructed; for they were understood as biological entities, in the same sense that the human species is. A racialized group, however, is socially constructed rather than natural, a group created by social and historical forces and treated as if it were a race.

A second meaning of "social construction" is that the thing in question is defined by social convention, and so is marked by an element of arbitrariness. Conventions of games, such as strikes, passed balls, and field positions in baseball, are examples. What makes something a strike is in a sense arbitrary. Baseball could have developed, or been "constructed," in such a way that four strikes instead of three counted as an out. In this sense strikes are indeed social constructs. But within the actual rules of baseball, it is not arbitrary that a particular pitched ball is a strike rather than a ball. Strikes are perfectly real; one simply has to understand the sort of convention-bound reality they possess.

An example of social construction more relevant to race is that of nations, which are historically contingent human creations that need not have existed or developed the particular character they have. The difference between baseball and nations is that everyone recognizes the conventional dimension of the former but not always the latter. Nations are sometimes talked or thought about as if they were natural human forms, primordial communities, created by God, destined to serve an historical mission, and the like. Rather, nations are, in Benedict Anderson's striking phrase, "imagined communities."[4] Because people can forget this, and especially because a "natural" view of nations provides fertile soil for virulent and destructive forms of nationalism, the idea of social construction can serve to remind us of the historically contingent character of nations. In this sense, a social-construction perspective is sometimes spoken of as "denaturalizing" that which is constructed.

Races are often spoken of as social constructions in this sense. But while there *are*, in fact, nations, there are *not* races. The groups we call "races" do not possess the features popular understanding attributes to races. In this sense "whites," "blacks," "Asians," and "Native Americans" are not races; they are racialized groups. By contrast, Nigeria, Mexico, and Thailand *are* nations.

Unlike races, racialized groups are real, and like nations they can provide a foundation for an appropriate and important social identity, for loyalty, for a sense of community and shared fate (though not a shared destiny), for sentiments of shame and pride. But as social creations they may wrongly be viewed as if they were natural, and they may encourage misplaced attachments, overblown and excessive loyalties, and disproportion in how one regards one's racialized identity in relation to other significant identities. Such distortions of racialized identities are likely to stem from wrongly thinking that one is not merely a member of a racialized group but of an actual race. But they are also possible in someone who is fully aware that her racial identity is socially and historically created and contingent.

Imagine, for example, an Asian-American who recognizes and accepts a racialized (not merely pan-ethnic) identity as "Asian"—seeing the source of that identity in the resentments, discrimination, and stereotyping to which her group is subject, not in characteristics inherent in her racial group. She may exaggerate the importance of this racialized identity in relation to her other identities—professor, Korean-American, parent, resident of Peoria, woman, lover of tennis. She may, for example, become blind to the fact that groups other than her own also suffer from discrimination and stereotyping. She may fail to recognize that despite differences she has much in common with other women professors.

MISUNDERSTANDINGS OF SOCIAL CONSTRUCTION   The idea of social construction has been subject to misunderstandings (often with some basis in the writings of its proponents) that bear clearing up if we are to make the best use of it in understanding "race." For one thing, "social construction" has sometimes been taken to imply that we could do away with what is socially constructed (genders, nations, racialized groups) if we so chose. Certainly, to recognize something as a human creation implies that it need not exist, at least in the form that it does, and thereby provides a basis for hope that we could live without various forms of injustice, oppression, and constraint attached to such creations. But to think we can simply jettison those creations is to fall prey to a kind of social voluntarism regarding social structures and identities. Racialized thinking is deeply embedded in our social existence; its constructedness notwithstanding, we may not be able to change these social forms without far-ranging and currently barely imaginable changes in familiar structures, such as an end to racial inequality and race-based social segregation.

A related misunderstanding of the import of social construction is that it is simply a form of labeling or categorizing: to be black is simply to be labeled or identified according to the rules that govern the practice of racial categorization. But this is like saying that to be a judge is simply to be a person whom society labels "judge." To be a judge is a good deal more; it involves being accorded authority to engage in certain behavior within certain institutional structures. Similarly, to *be* a racialized black person is not simply to be called "black." For racialization imposes certain ways of viewing the person who is called or self-identified as "black"—as having something fundamental and natural in common with other black people; as radically other than persons of different races; and as possessing certain humanly significant characteristics inherent in her racial nature.

If there are no races, it might seem natural to express this truth by saying that to be black is just to be called "black" by one's society, or to call oneself "black." But, consider the following incident: In 1977 two aspiring firefighters who were brothers identified themselves as "black" on a civil service exam. Under an affirmative action plan that admitted black aspirants with lower scores than whites to firefighter vacancies, the Malone brothers joined the force. They served for ten years. Then the fire commissioner noticed that they had been classified as black. They were promptly fired, but appealed, in a case that appeared before the Supreme Judicial Court of Massachusetts. All available evidence brought before the court led it to conclude that the Malones were white. Despite their claiming of the category "black," they seemed quite clearly to be white. They were members of the racialized group "white," despite claiming to be black, just as I am an American even if I go to the United Kingdom, affect a British accent, and attempt to pass myself off as British.

In the sense of a racialized group, the Malone brothers were white, not black; they were not merely identified or categorized as white. Still, racialized groups are social constructs, just as nations are; they are not natural, biological entities.

The social construction of race sometimes takes the form, "Biological races are not real, but social races are," or "Race is socially but not biologically real." If the social reality attributed to "race" involved decisively discarding the moral and conceptual trappings that attend popular understandings of it—as the idea of "racialized groups" is meant to do—I would not object to these expressions. Frequently, however, this social interpretation of race reimports all the associations of radical differentness among groups and commonality among all members of a group, excepting only the idea that characteristics of the group are grounded in their biology. At this point in our history, I think *any* conferring of reality on "race" is likely to carry these false and invidious associations. The term "racialized groups" is preferable as a way of acknowledging that some groups have been *created* by being treated as if they were races, while also acknowledging that "race" in its popular meaning is entirely false [. . .].

PETER WADE, *RACE AND ETHNICITY IN LATIN AMERICA*[5]

Race and ethnicity are not terms that have fixed referents. It is tempting to believe in a progressivist vision of social science that leads from ignorance towards truth—especially with the term race which, in earlier periods, was commonly used in evidently racist ways that are now known to be manifestly wrong. It seems obvious that post-war understandings of the term race are now "correct." But I argue that we have to see each term in the context of a history of ideas, of Western institutionalized knowledge (whether social or natural science) and of practices. Race and ethnicity are not terms that refer to some neutral way to a transparent reality of which social science gives us an ever more accurate picture; instead they are terms embedded in academic, popular and political discourses that are themselves a constitutive part of academic, popular and political relationships and practices [. . .].

Ethnicity

The term ethnicity is at once easier and more difficult: its history is shorter and less morally loaded, but it is also used more vaguely—sometimes as a less emotive term for race. The word ethnicity began in academic parlance and dates from the Second World War [. . .]. Ethnicity has often been used in place of race either because the very use of the word race has been thought to propagate racism by implying that biological races actually exist or because, tainted by its history, it simply "smelt bad."

But what does ethnicity mean? Banks collects a useful set of comments from anthropologists and concludes that ethnicity is "a collection of rather simplistic and obvious statements about boundaries, otherness, goals and achievements, being and identity, descent and classification, that has been constructed as much by the anthropologist as by the subject."[6] Ethnicity is a social construction that is centrally about identifications of difference and sameness, but the same could be said of race, gender and class—so where does the specificity of ethnicity lie, if anywhere? Some commentators remain vague on this point, but the general consensus is that ethnicity refers to "cultural" differences, whereas, as we saw above, race is said to refer to phenotypical differences—although some draw no real distinction between race and ethnicity. To give some substance to this rather bland definition, I will give some brief examples of how ethnicity has been understood.

Some early influential approaches emerged from the Manchester school of anthropology. Clyde Mitchell, for example, focused on the so-called Copper Belt mining towns of Northern Rhodesia (now part of Zambia). People from many different "tribes"—as anthropologists then tended to call them—congregated on these towns and Mitchell observed that "tribal" identities became more, rather than less, distinctive in an urban environment through opposition to each other. People categorized each other in terms of dress, speech, customs, appearance and so on. Ethnicity—as it was later to be called—was a way of categorizing complex cultural differences and thus defining for individuals who was who and how to behave towards them. In the Kalela dance, urban migrants expressed these differences in a jovial form: as they danced on rest days in these mining towns, men from each "tribe" caricatured the cultural traits of other groups and thus restated ethnic identities.[7]

Abner Cohen criticized these social classification approaches and took a line that has since been characterized as an "instrumentalist" or "resource mobilization" model. The basic argument was that people used aspects of culture to signal boundaries and create in-groups that tried to control some useful resource or political power. Thus Hausa migrants in the Yoruba town of Ibadan in Nigeria manipulated aspects of their culture—customs, values, myths, symbols—to create an ethnically identified in-group that controlled long-distance trade in cattle and kola nuts. For Cohen, ethnic groups were informal interest groups. This approach opposed the so-called "primordialist" perspective which implied that ethnic identity was just a basic feature of people's psychological make-up, a product of the way they classified people, for example.[8] A similar instrumentalist line was taken in the US by Glazer and Moynihan.[9]

This gives some idea of what ethnicity as discourse of cultural difference might mean, but it remains rather unspecific: in Britain, different classes are often thought to have particular cultural features, even if class is principally based on economic differences; men and women also differentiate each other by reference to speech, cultural behavior and so on. In this sense, ethnicity becomes an unsatisfactory residual analytic category: it includes all those forms of cultural categorization where there is no other primary discourse of differentiation, such as wealth, sex, age, phenotype, etc.

My own angle on this problem is that ethnicity is, of course, about cultural differentiation, but that it tends to use a language of *place* (rather than wealth, sex, or inherited phenotype). Cultural difference is spread over geographical space by virtue of the fact that social relations become concrete in spatialized form. This creates a cultural geography, or in Taussig's phrase, a moral topography.[10] People thus use location, or rather people's putative origin in certain places, to talk about difference and sameness. "Where are you from?" is thus the "ethnic question" *par excellence*. Of course, not all objective differences in location are important in terms of people's perceptions of cultural geography: as Barth pointed out many years ago, it is the people involved, not the analyst, who define what features constitute difference and sameness.[11]

This approach gives us a handle on a commonly noted aspect of ethnicity, the fact that ethnic identities are "nested" in a kind of Russian doll form. Rather than having a single and univocal ethnic identity, most people have multiple identities according to with whom they are interacting and in what context. Thus northerners and southerners in one country or region may differentiate themselves (in England, Italy, the US), but identify as the same *vis-à-vis* people from a different country (English versus Italians), yet identify with those people in the face of broader differences (Europeans or "Westerners" *versus* Africans).

The place perspective also helps to explain why "ethnicity" seems to have become a more common phenomenon in the modern world. Although people have doubtless always thought about difference in terms of place, and although people have migrated since the origins of the human species, it is reasonable to argue that with the onset of modernity and a global world—which, for argument's sake, I will say dates from the late fourteenth century and the Discoveries—people from different locations in their own cultural geographies have interacted with increasing intensity. The rise of nationalism from the late eighteenth century (in the US, then Latin America and Europe), the later phases of imperialism (for example, the carve-up of Africa) and postcolonial migrations (for example, from former colonies to former colonial nations) all instigated periods of intense re-definition of boundaries and of social collectivities in which the question of origin in a cultural geography as a defining feature of difference and sameness has become very salient. In this sense, then, as with race, ethnicity and ethnic categorizations are part of a particular history. To see ethnicity as a language of cultural geography is not a final objective definition, but reflects the importance of changing cultural geographies for people in the modern world.

Race and Ethnicity: Is There a Difference?

From the argument so far it may seem that race and ethnicity are distinct concepts. There are, however, two sets of reasons why some people might argue that they are the same. First, some people who do not effectively distinguish between race and ethnicity argue that race should be jettisoned as a term with too much invidious history; they prefer to talk about ethnic relations and ethnic minorities (or, less often, majorities—it is often forgotten that, for example, Anglo-Saxon North Americans are just as "ethnic" as Italian-Americans). A variant on this view argues that "ideas of 'race' may or may not form part of ethnic ideologies and their presence or absence does not seem to be a decisive factor." Anthias and Yuval-Davis do distinguish between race and ethnicity as modes of social categorization, but also see racism as the "discourse and practice of inferiorizing ethnic groups."[12] The second set of reasons is more complex and I will argue through it before returning to the first problem.

The dismantling of the biological concept of race and its general acceptance, at least in social sciences, as a social construction has brought about a recognition of the mutability of race—the comparison between North and Latin America discussed earlier is an example. Racial identities are now seen in somewhat the same way as ethnic identities: they are contextual, situational, multivocal. This view is an inevitable result of seeing races as social constructions, which by their nature must depend on shifting social relations, but more recently it also owes a lot to poststructuralist and postmodernist social theories [. . .].

It may be objected that racial identifications cannot be as flexible as this sort of view implies: social categories that use physical, bodily cues to assign identities do not seem that open to "decentering." There are two issues here. The first is that bodily cues can be used to mean various things: thus a certain skin tone and hair texture in the US might mean "black," whereas in Latin America it might mean *mulatto:* bodies themselves are socially constructed. In addition, bodies are not immutable: plastic surgery is the most obvious example, but hair-straightening, skin-lightening and sun-tanning are all ways of altering the body that can have an impact on racial identification—and Michael Jackson is only a recent example. The second issue is that anti-essentialism does not necessarily contest the apparent fixity of racial identifications: rather, the point is that the fact that someone is "black" or "white" or "indigenous" does not therefore say everything about that person. S/he may also be old/young, female/male, homosexual/heterosexual, rich/poor and so on: there are crosscutting identifications. Thus the point remains that racial identifications seem similar to ethnic identifications: both are partial, unstable, contextual, fragmentary [. . .].

Racial and ethnic identifications do, however, overlap, both analytically and in practice. At an abstract level, both race and ethnicity involve a discourse about origins and about the transmission of essences across generations. Racial identifications use aspects of phenotype as a cue for categorization, but these are seen as transmitted intergenerationally—through the "blood"—so that ancestral origin is important; likewise ethnicity is about origin in a cultural geography in which the culture of a place is absorbed by a person (almost "into the blood") from previous generations. On a more practical level, if ethnicity invokes location in a cultural geography, it may be the case that the phenotypical traits used in racial discourse are distributed across that geography: in Colombia, for example, "blacks" are located in certain parts of the country. Also, ethnic identifications may be made within a single racial category and vice versa, so that any individual can have both racial and ethnic identities.

DISCUSSION QUESTIONS

• According to Blum's nine-point typology of racial ideology in the nineteenth-century United States, what is a racial essence?

• What is the social construction of race, according to Blum?

• If ethnicity supposedly reflects one's culture or place of origin, how is it that Wade argues that it, like race, has come to be defined by an "in the blood" sort of essentialism?

• How does Wade's discussion of ethnicity as based on a sense of place or origin mirror Hall's description of the "old" ethnicity; by extension, how does Wade's argument parallel Hall's appeal to the "new" ethnicity?

NOTES

1. Cornel West, *Race Matters* (Boston: Beacon, 1993).

2. Jorge Cañizares Esguerra, "New Worlds, New Stars: Patriotic Astrology and the Invention of Indian and Creole Bodies in Colonial Spanish America 1600–1650," *The American Historical Review* 104 (February 1999): 33–68.

3. Lawrence Blum, *"I'm Not a Racist But . . .": The Moral Quandary of Race* (Ithaca: Cornell UP, 2002). Excerpt taken from 127–128, 156–160.

4. Benedict Anderson, *Imagined Communities: Reflections on the Origin and Spread of Nationalism* (London: Verso, 1991).

5. Peter Wade, *Race and Ethnicity in Latin America* (London: Pluto, 1997). Excerpt from 5, 16–21. Please note that this book was published in England; grammatical style may follow English rules.

6. Marcus Banks, *Ethnicity: Anthropological Constructions* (London: Routledge, 1996) 5.

7. Clyde Mitchell, *The Kalela Dance: Aspects of Social Relationships among Urban Africans in Northern Rhodesia* (Manchester: Manchester UP, 1956).

8. Abner Cohen, *Custom and Politics in Urban Africa: A Study of Hausa Migrants in Yoruba Town* (London: Routledge, 1969).

9. Nathan Glazer and Daniel Moynihan, eds., *Ethnicity: Theory and Experience* (Cambridge: Harvard UP, 1975).

10. Michael Taussig, *The Devil and Commodity Fetishism in South America* (Chapel Hill: U of North Carolina P, 1980).

11. Frederick Barth, ed., *Ethnic Groups and Boundaries: The Social Organisation of Cultural Difference* (London: George Allen & Unwin, 1969).

12. Floya Anthias and Nira Yuval-Davis, *Racialized Boundaries: Race, Nation, Gender, Colour and Class and the Anti-Racist Struggle* (London: Routledge, 1992).

Identity Construct #2: Class

As a concept, *class* is at once easy and difficult to comprehend, especially for Americans who tend to be ignorant of economic differentiation. For example, polls show that in 1940 fully 80 percent of Americans identified themselves as middle class, even though data revealed America's economic stratum to have been much more complex. While class would appear to be an objective condition based on one's wealth, semioticians view it as a construct no different from race, gender, nationality. It is an identity, the meaning of which varies in accordance with the particular discourses that went into its making at any given time and place.

In this chapter we provide some context for and then provide excerpts from a text by David Parker, a contemporary historian of Latin America, in order to examine two commonly held essentialist interpretations of class. The first contends that class position is a product of individual essence; the second holds that class consciousness springs from objective economic criteria. Parker challenges these essentialist arguments. He devotes his study mostly to the second interpretation, but it is necessary for us to understand the first to fully appreciate his argument.[1]

By definition, *class differentiation* implies that society allows its people to have unequal access to wealth. The question then becomes how society rationalizes that inequality. Prior to the Enlightenment and the French Revolution in the 1700s, Western society was divided into two classes: the aristocracy and everyone else, also commonly called the third estate. The third estate were typically rural workers, or peasants, who produced wealth that the aristocracy consumed. Such premodern societies were manifestly hierarchical and marked by a severe maldistribution of wealth. The peasants were poor and did manual labor their entire lives; the aristocracy was rich and never performed manual labor. Society defined aristocrats as meritorious people by virtue of the family line into which they were born. Peasants were believed to be born into to a lower order of people destined to toil. Fate determined one's position in life.

An aristocratically based society justified inequality through a form of essentialism, often identified as a bloodline. Aristocratic families were believed to possess a special essence that they passed down to their relatives. This essence distinguished them from the members of the third estate and justified their privileges. For this reason, class mobility was nonexistent. People were born, lived, and died as members of a particular class or estate, and so did their descendants.

Since humans are intelligent and complex, many people at the time recognized this system as an ideological project rather than an inalienable condition. Even so, these opponents of it remained in the minority, confronted by a powerful religious, legal, social, political, and economic norm that promoted differentiation based on birthright. One of the main challenges to this system came from a new economic sector that emerged steadily and slowly over the centuries. It was known as the bourgeoisie, literally the "town dwellers," and also occasionally called the middle class. They were not members of the aristocracy, and neither were they peasants. They lived in cities and engaged in commerce or early forms of factory production. In time, as the economy of the West gained in complexity and became more international, some members of the bourgeoisie became fabulously wealthy, surpassing most, if not all, of their aristocratic counterparts. Despite their wealth, the bourgeoisie remained legally and socially inferior to aristocrats purely by virtue of their birth.

Owing in part to the emergence of this amorphous middle sector, new philosophical ideas began to take hold that offered an alternative definition of human existence. These ideas, which would become the foundation of contemporary Western societies, were the core values of the Enlightenment—humans are born equal before the law and have the right to exchange goods and services in a free market, and government is subject to their will. These ideas, and many others like them, required decades, if not centuries to coalesce into solidified political programs, and the process goes on, as societies continue adjusting their lived reality to parallel these ideals. Most contemporary Westerners take for granted that status by birth is an antiquated principle rightly replaced by new ideas that better reflect the true state of human nature.

Today's Enlightenment-based societies, which include the United States, continue to exhibit class inequality, albeit in reduced extremes compared with premodern societies. However, these modern societies still need to rationalize inequality. Instead of basing it on birthright, they explain it as a product of naturally occurring differences between individual human beings. The idea is that a free society removes limits placed on individuals, freeing them to make of themselves as they wish, or at least as they are able according to capabilities. Our moral principles impel us to create safety nets for those who are physically or mentally incapable of looking after themselves, but beyond that we allow human beings to be whatever they are able to be. This is the foundation of the *meritocracy*, the idea that one's merits determine one's future, not birthright or bloodline.

Of course, for this system to operate as it is supposed to, there must be a "level playing field," as it is often called in contemporary political parlance. One person cannot have unfair advantages over another. Much contemporary political debate takes place over the degree to which we have created equal opportunity. Conservatives tend to argue that we have done so, whereas liberals tend to believe that we need to do more. Either way, both liberals and conservatives operate on the common foundation that with a level playing field one's class position will reflect one's natural capacity or, as it is sometimes called, one's God-given talents. They readily acknowledge that exceptions to the rule occur, that some people squander their God-given talents, while others who lack such gifts get lucky and rise above their likely station in life. But proponents of a meritocracy believe that in most cases "the cream rises to the top."

It would seem, then, that we have abandoned to the dustbin of history the notion of class essentialism. But have we? Semioticians argue that our contemporary justifications for inequality are not so different from those of our premodern ancestors. We disseminate resources based on the belief that some people are more deserving than others because of qualities they were born with, be it intelligence, determination, patience, or whatever other trait allows them to excel in life. Whereas the proponents of this system believe it is rooted in objective truths about human nature, semioticians see it as based on ideas (i.e., discursive constructs).

Semioticians are highly suspicious of modernist claims to equality, seeing them as facades for hierarchical power relations rooted in discursive constructs of race, gender, and nationality, among others. Take, for example, the case of John Edwards, the Democratic vice presidential candidate in the 2004 election. Edwards was born to a working-class family in a small town in South Carolina and, like his father, worked in a mill as a young man. But Edwards was also intelligent and driven. He became the first member of his family to attend college, eventually going on to have a long and lucrative career in law. Starting in the mid-1990s, he began a meteoric political career, serving first as senator from North Carolina and then launching his candidacy for president in 2004. Although his goal of being the Democratic candidate failed, he gained widespread support in the party and was selected by Senator John Kerry to serve as his running mate. Much of Edwards's political campaign revolved around his personal story and his hope that every American would have the opportunity to succeed as he did. While no one should begrudge Edwards his achievements or his heartfelt concern for others, semioticians might point out that some of the factors that allowed him to excel had more to do with discursive constructs than his own inner drive for success. For instance, had Edwards been black or female, his opportunities in life might have been circumscribed. He would have confronted discursively constituted meanings of what a lawyer or a politician is and what being black or female mean. Had he not been a white male, the likelihood that he would have been a vice presidential candidate is virtually nil. Closer examination of his biographical history might reveal other, more practical advantages, however seemingly inconsequential at the time, that allowed him to excel but would not have necessarily been available to someone else.

Semioticians challenge the idea that inequality should be justified by a belief in the existence of a unique, individual essence. They see this notion as identical to the idea of the rational Cartesian subject and challenge it as an idea rather than an ontology. They see the modern rational actor emerging at a particular moment in history, in a particular place, and for particular reasons. Modernists believed they had found the true nature of humanity, but semioticians argue that they have constructed the idea of the rational subject in accordance with their discursive norms, just as their premodern predecessors constructed ideas about human nature. Semioticians define human beings as discursively constructed entities whose identities and ideas are being constantly redefined. Therefore, rationalizations for social inequity based on the principle of an unyielding individual essence can only be dubious. Semioticians argue that the qualitative values we place on individual essences are saying much more about the discourses we use to define our world, rather than being an objective truth.

Essentialists also believe that class consciousness originates in objective economic criteria. Briefly, this approach posits that people who occupy a particular economic position in society will share common interests and that they will enter into the political arena collectively to defend those interests. In short, they share a class identity or class consciousness. Essentialists see economic classes as objective entities and the consciousness that emerges from them as based on the solid ground of fact, not the whimsical realm of human thought.

Many modernist theorists have analyzed history from this perspective. Some, like Adam Smith and David Ricaud, have supported capitalism, while others, like Karl Marx, envisioned a different form of utopia. We could focus on any one of these theorists to prove our point, but Marx arguably provides one of the clearest examples. His basic premise was that human history is driven by economic conditions. Within any given stage of it, the engine of change, that is, the force that will advance humanity into the next and higher stage of lived existence, will be an economic class, a group of people who share a common economic condition. In the feudal era, Marx's engine for change was the bourgeoisie, and in the capitalist era it is the proletariat (or working class). The assumption underlying Marx's ideas, and indeed those of most all modernist thinkers like him, is that members of a particular class naturally hold the same basic perspective. Out of this has emerged a long tradition in historical analysis of seeking out the existence of a particular class, either qualitatively or quantitatively, and then interpreting historical events from the perspective of the actions of that class.

David Parker dedicates his study of early twentieth-century Peru to this particular issue. Parker begins by focusing on a strike by urban shopkeepers in Lima, Peru's capital city, in 1919. Although Peru was familiar with work stoppages because of its active labor movement, this strike was different. It was instigated by upper-level employees who advocated for different types of benefits than their working-class counterparts, such as longer lunch breaks, more vacation time, and an eight-hour workday. If Parker had employed a classically essentialist approach, like that of Marx, he would have interpreted this revolt, and the following decade of middle-class political activism, as a prototypical example of economic conditions giving rise to a new social class that then entered politics to defend itself. From this perspective, what occurred in Peru had already happened elsewhere, and would be repeated many times over in other countries for roughly similar reasons. In short, Peru's middle class had been materially born, joining other middle classes throughout the world.

Parker is not a strict semiotician, but he brings recent developments in cultural theory to bear on this series of events in early twentieth-century Peru. He acknowledges that Peru's society was growing more diverse and that, statistically, more people were earning a living that put them somewhere between the richest and poorest of society. But Parker interprets the appearance of Peru's middle class as an act of social construction rather than an inevitable outgrowth of objective conditions. He accepts the argumentative threads in cultural theory which propose that members of any given economic stratum inhabit too many conflicting worlds of identity to be limited to the singular realm of class. In addition to their income or their possession of property, they are motivated by ethnicity, gender, family, region, nationality, neighborhood, and so forth. Because semioticians see all these identities as discursively constituted, they consider the members of Peru's middle class in the early twentieth century to have framed their world with multiple discursive lenses.

Therefore, Parker insists that Peru's middle class identity did not spring forth naturally from objective or material conditions, like a volcanic eruption resulting from changes in the earth's inner core. Instead, Peru's middle class was nothing more than an idea, cobbled together from a swirling mass of local and international discourses about what being middle class meant. Parker argues that to understand the emergence of Peru's middle class we must study the content of the relevant discursive threads and then determine how they coalesced in the minds of the people who voiced them in Peru's literary and political arena. Only then, Parker insists, will we be in position to appreciate how this notion of middle class identity impacted Peru's history.

DAVID PARKER, *THE IDEA OF THE MIDDLE CLASS*[2]

September 1919 was Lima's first citywide white-collar strike ever, and more important, it was the first time that any group of demonstrators had taken to the streets in the name of "the middle class," a concept virtually absent from the discourse of the previous century. Employees made it a point to emphasize that theirs was not the case of the proletariat but of the forgotten, long-suffering *clase media*. Underlying their rhetoric was an increasingly clear picture of what it meant to belong to that middle class, an assertion of what separated them from the workers below and from the aristocrats above [. . .].

The middle class is hardly a new topic for Latin Americanists. As early as 1958, John J. Johnson's *Political Change in Latin America* exploded the myth that the nations of Latin America had no middle classes to speak of.[3] Against the popular stereotype of a continent peopled only by landed oligarchs and impoverished masses, Johnson described a region in which large and growing "middle sectors" increasingly dominated public life. Among their political achievements were the promotion of economic nationalism and state-sponsored development, the rapid expansion of public education, the introduction of social welfare policies, and, perhaps most important, the impulse, albeit halting and imperfect, toward democratization and the broadening of the electorate. This image of progressive, reformist middle sectors had already appeared in earlier writings by Latin Americans, but Johnson's succinct formulation made a profound impression in both Americas and came to symbolize the vision of mesocratic reformism as one guiding theme of twentieth-century Latin American history [. . .].

If scholars of the 1960s and 1970s found in Latin America's middle class everything from modernizing democratic reformers to status-obsessed clients of the aristocracy to frustrated revolutionaries, what are we to do today as the very concept of class has come under increasing attack? Two major difficulties immediately come to mind. First, of course, is the problem of definition. What is the middle class? How is it possible to describe the class characteristics of groups as diverse as shopkeepers, lawyers, teachers, stockbrokers, medium-sized farmers, bureaucrats, and white-collar employees? Johnson deliberately used the term "sectors" rather than "class" in order to underline this heterogeneity, but his choice merely begged the question: If the middle sectors were too heterogeneous to be a class, could anything at all useful be said about them? The second, more basic problem arises from the temptation to conceptualize classes as concrete, conscious historical actors. Was there, to cite a well-known analogy, such a group as "the bourgeoisie" in eighteenth-century France and did it bring about the French Revolution? A generation of revisionist scholarship has answered in the negative. At the very least we must reject the idea that social classes speak with a single voice, act as a single individual, or play a single role in the shaping of historical destiny. Classes are, at the end of the day, abstractions that we reify at our peril. Splitting classes into "residual" and "emergent," "bourgeois" and "proletarianized," "old" and "new" cannot solve this fundamental epistemological problem.

In the case of Latin America, precious little seems to unite the millions of lives we tend to lump together statistically as middle-class. The closer one looks, the greater the differences appear: immigrant versus native born, white versus mestizo, salaried versus independent, public sector versus private sector, university-trained versus self-taught, urban versus rural. These distinctions create an enormous spectrum of living standards, consumption patterns, cultural tastes, social circles, economic interests, and political affiliations. If our social history is a study of daily life, then there can be no such thing as a single social history of the middle class, for Peru or for anywhere else. We would need a hundred different histories before a sufficiently complete picture emerged [. . .].

From whence did that palpable cultural reality, that widely shared understanding of what the middle class meant, arise? This book hopes to show that Peruvians' idea of the middle class was basically an invention of the early twentieth century. At that time, white-collar workers and other similar occupational groups chose to identify themselves explicitly as members of the middle class, in part to gain a sense of identity, but also to lend legitimacy to their fight for social legislation. [. . .] As people began to think and talk regularly about the middle class, and as those ideas increasingly influenced government policy, the Peruvian middle class was, in a sense, "made": tentatively and impermanently, but made nonetheless [. . .].

Th[e] relationship between structure and discourse has become a growing source of controversy, as poststructuralism and the "linguistic turn" of social history have simultaneously found favor and sparked opposition [. . .].

This book pays very close attention to the role of ideology in shaping how people interpret the world and, consequently, how they live their lives within it. Ideas do not merely reflect power, they are power. This recognition depends, however, upon three prior suppositions. First, "ideology" needs to be defined in the broadest possible manner. Far beyond explicitly political ideas, ideology extends to the entire universe of thoughts, perceptions, prejudices, stereotypes, habits, and language that form the essence of subjectivity. Ideology provides the organizing logic by which people comprehend an otherwise incomprehensible "reality"; it gives meaning to their surroundings, forms their sense of identity, and profoundly influences their actions. Second, ideology must be understood not as a hegemonic imposition from above but as a collective enterprise of construction, a dialogue in which a significant amount of conflict is taking place. Third, while admitting that ideology shapes history, we should never go so far as to think that it is the only force that shapes history.

A coherent study of "ideology" so broadly defined and so largely writ borders on the impossible. This book therefore limits its scope to class ideologies. It starts from one simple premise: classes, like other abstractions, are products of the mind. Because society is so extraordinarily complex, it can be described in an almost infinite number of ways; therefore, when people identify themselves as members of a particular social class, they are making profound ideological choices, rooted in a string of assumptions about the nature of society and their place in it. A class identity, no matter how deeply it seems to be rooted in material experience, requires a vision of what classes are and what one's own class looks like. What are a class's defining characteristics? Who belongs to a particular class and who does not? Who are its allies and who are its enemies? What does the class need, what does it deserve? None of these are simple questions, and there are no inevitably "right" answers. These ideas of class are invented constructs that serve ideological ends: they place people in an imaginary hierarchy, exalting some and stigmatizing others, and they negotiate the rules by which some people deem themselves better than the rest.

Ideas of class must compete for acceptance; they must appeal to those whom they would unite by explaining reality in a convincing way. Like all ideas, ideas of class have their producers and consumers. They may be created by intellectuals, by opinion makers in the media, or by potential leaders hoping to build a base of support. They are often propagated by "interest entrepreneurs" who invest their time and effort in organizing a specific group, a group to which they themselves may or may not personally belong. And while it might be possible in certain rare historical moments for ideas of class to spring up spontaneously—as when the violent repression of a strike engenders the camaraderie of the barricades—more typically they emerge and compete with little fanfare, in newspapers, in public debate, in conversation, and in the private thoughts of ordinary men and women.

In order to win acceptance, ideas of class must successfully appear to reflect everyday experience. They must be consistent with collective identities, the sense of "us" versus "them," that are being forged on a daily basis among people who carry out the same tasks, earn the same pay, and suffer the same indignities. Ideas of class must have resonance and explanatory power; they cannot simply be decreed from above. Beyond that, ideas are unlike any other product: the consumer of ideas transforms them in his or her own mind, constantly shaping and reshaping them until they mesh with preexisting attitudes and experiences. In other words, the generation of ideas is a uniquely collective enterprise, where consumers are at the same time producers. To that extent, but to that extent only, class identification arises from below as a reflection of shared experience.

Ideas of class face tremendous competition in the marketplace of ideas. There are opposing collective identities grounded in religion, gender, ethnicity, and so on, just as there are visions of society that deny altogether the existence of classes or class conflict. Even workers in evident struggle against oppression have often eschewed the rhetoric of class, choosing instead to define themselves simply as "the people." Ideas of class also compete among themselves. Centuries of social theory have generated a wide range of concepts and definitions, of which the Marxist division of society into bourgeoisie and proletariat, or the Aristotelian three-class model (upper, middle, and lower), are but two of the more influential. Ideas of class may draw upon previous ideological traditions of rank and hierarchy, as with seventeenth-century British conceptions of "better sorts," "middling sorts," and "common sorts," or they may be tied to the special legal privileges of a society of estates, as in pre-Revolutionary France or colonial Latin America. Beyond that, even apparently similar images of class can mask very different operating rules: people may perceive class membership as a function of income, occupation, race, education, family name, consumption, residence, or a combination of attributes.

Being ideological creations, ideas of class gain or lose currency as a result of ideological struggles. When some people deny that class barriers exist, or others contend that social inequalities reflect intrinsic differences in ability or character, their arguments serve an agenda. The same can be said for those who assert that class distinctions are purely arbitrary impositions, or that they are uniquely determined by the division of labor. Which ideas win out has much to do with who has the power to impose their vision over the competing voices of others. It is probably safe to say, moreover, that in most modern societies ideas propagated by the rich and powerful are more likely to gain the spotlight than the ideas of the poor and weak: the former are able to exercise influence through a variety of channels.

Yet the construction of ideology is by no means a unilateral process of imposition and acceptance, hegemony and socialization. Ideological battles are a dialogue—a dialogue between unequals, to be sure, but a dialogue nonetheless. Not only do subordinate groups frequently contest and reject those ideas with which they disagree, they also appropriate elements of the dominant discourse and use them in new ways to challenge accepted truths. Alternatively, the powerful regularly co-opt the arguments of the opposition, recasting those ideas in less dangerous terms, but at the same time increasing their legitimacy. This dialogue is almost always disorderly, inconclusive, and only partially understood by those involved. Ideological change comes piecemeal rather than in leaps and bounds. To further complicate matters, the dialogue is not two-sided, but multisided. Innumerable voices are clamoring to be heard; some succeed, others do not. The point is that ideology matters, and the conflict of ideas has a great deal of autonomy from the many other forms of conflict.

This dialogue of ideological competition is mediated by language. The words and concepts that exist to describe the existing order are essential building blocks of ideology: to manufacture consent, the powerful seek to create a world in which their vocabulary and their definitions are the only ones used. Because of this, literary critics have in recent years engaged in an active debate over whether language is really a transparent tool of expression, or if it is instead an opaque, immutable structure that is in itself an ideology, controlling or at least distorting the very ideas expressed. I side with the contention, typically attributed to Bakhtin, that language is neither of these: language is not a fully open system in which people can create any discourse they like, but neither is it a closed system that preempts people's abilities to say what they want to say. On the one hand, words come with a great deal of historical baggage. That baggage, made up of past meanings and usages, accepted definitions, and others' use of the same words, cannot easily be jettisoned or subverted. This is particularly true for emotive political words such as "freedom," "democracy," "equality," and "rights," but it is no less the case for the vocabulary employed to describe the social order. People are handed an already constituted language with which to work; the culturally understood meanings of existing signs place a limit on people's ability to signify new things. In other words, some ideas may be impossible to formulate because the words and concepts with which to express them do not exist.

But on the other hand, language is not a closed and immutable system. There is enormous diversity within the shared community of language, and even greater room for movement over time. Different people employ the same words with entirely distinct meanings and connotations, and those meanings can and do compete with one another. Old terms are appropriated and used in new ways. New meanings for old words and even entirely new words are invented on a regular basis. Concepts, vocabulary, and definitions also cross boundaries from one language to another: scholars of Latin America in particular have long understood the importance of ideological and linguistic borrowing, particularly from Europe and North America. As we will see, all of these mechanisms come into play in the case of ideas of class.

Finally, these symbolic struggles over language and ideology can and do concretely affect the course of social conflicts, their outcomes, even the winners and losers. Specifically, ideas and vocabularies of class contribute in absolutely concrete ways to the constitution of real historical actors. This assertion, while by no means original, is still controversial; the point is best made with examples. First of all, ideas of class delineate the fault lines of collective organization. Is the working class limited to manual workers, or does it include all who sell their labor for a wage? Does it include the unskilled occasional worker? The poorly paid clerical worker? The unemployed? Women? The character and scope of labor unions may vary enormously depending on how their members answer those questions. Second, ideas of class have an impact on the kinds of demands that groups make and the language in which they express those demands. A vision of the working class that includes factory foremen will be difficult to reconcile with demands to abolish foremen's special privileges; by the same token, an idea of the working class that includes office personnel will be incompatible with a rhetoric emphasizing workers' role as the producers of goods. Gendered ideas of work as inherently "manly" can lead unions to ignore or marginalize the demands of women, sometimes even in spite of their leaders' conscious intent.

Third, and perhaps most important, ideas of class are claims on society. The invented image of what a class looks like contains explicit arguments and implicit assumptions about what that class should look like, the rights it should enjoy, the duties it should fulfill to others, and the benefits it rightly deserves. Such claims are a crucial element of class struggles, for if they achieve legitimacy, they can inspire new laws or other equally tangible changes. To cite a classic example, debates over minimum wage legislations typically invoke competing definitions of an "acceptable" minimum living standard. Scientific pretensions aside, this definition ultimately hinges upon an idea of class par excellence; the socially and ideologically constructed image of what a worker should and should not be expected to consume [. . .].

To sum up, ideas of the middle class are by no means determined simply by the objective structures of occupation, income, or status. Not only do distinct images of class compete within any given society, but the outcomes of those struggles are likely to differ greatly from one place to the next. Each nation has its own unique history of economic development, racial and ethnic tension, social conflict, political competition, and ideological legitimation. We should hardly expect countries with such diverse experiences to arrive at identical or even similar visions of what the middle class is, where its boundaries lie, or what qualities it embodies. Thus, models of the middle class developed in Europe or North America are quite likely to be inapplicable in Latin America, a region with very different economic, demographic, political, social, legal, moral, religious, and cultural traditions. In its attempt to understand both the material and the ideological forces that shaped Peru's emerging middle class, this book hopes to shine a spotlight on how Latin America's unique cultural heritage, combined with its distinct economic and social structures, led to a process of class formation that diverged widely from the experience of the industrial, Anglo-Saxon West [. . .].

When those *empleados* first walked off the job in 1919, they could not have imagined the impact they would have on Peruvian society, yet their impact was arguably immense. All they wanted was an eight-hour day, higher salaries, and a longer lunch break, but in the pursuit of those goals they ended up achieving a great deal more: they invented a new conception of their social order, in which the *clase media* figured prominently.

Their vision employed the established stereotypes of a hierarchical society, ordered by family name, prestige, and "respectability," but recast those concepts into a modern explanation of why *empleados*, as born members of the middle class, needed and deserved certain exclusive benefits. Little by little the *empleados'* arguments, championed by representative organizations like the SEC, filtered into Peru's political discourse and captured public opinion to a degree that would have been hard to imagine even a decade earlier.[4]

In the mid-1920s, this idea of the middle class succeeded in inspiring precedent-setting social legislation, which gave new legal force to the traditional distinctions between manual workers (*obreros*) and nonmanual *empleados*. This *obrero-empleado* division, a central and enduring feature of Peruvian labor law, cannot be understood except as an outgrowth of the *empleados'* vision of a middle class defined by nonmanual work amid intrinsically, almost biologically, distinct from the working class. This caste-like idea of the middle class survived surprisingly intact through the 1930s and 1940s, and continued to inform Peruvian government policies on everything from unemployment relief to summer vacations. At the same time, the middle class became a significant ingredient of Peru's public debate, as emerging leaders and political movements, most notably the APRA Party of Víctor Raúl Haya de la Torre, adopted elements of the employees' rhetoric in their official platforms. Distinct and even contrary ideas of class never completely disappeared: APRA leaders sometimes talked about the middle class but at other times talked about "manual and intellectual workers," while Peruvian Communists promoted the belief that employees were destined to join the proletariat. Yet to a surprising degree the conception of the middle class that white-collar employees had created continued to set the agenda for subsequent discussion of the nature of Peruvian society. Ideas that were new and dangerous in the 1910s became the hackneyed clichés of the 1940s and 1950s, clichés that often still echo through the present.

DISCUSSION QUESTIONS

• In the process of talking about early twentieth-century Peru, Parker offers some broader theoretical comments. Two of the more revealing ones are: "Ideas do not merely reflect power, they are power," and "classes, like other abstractions, are products of the mind." What do these two comments mean? How does Parker show them to be relevant to Peru?

• How can semioticians define something so seemingly material and factual as class or wealth as merely an idea?

• Parker is obviously challenging prior conceptualizations of class. But he does not jettison them as useful intellectual concepts. As he puts it, "Is anything gained, therefore, by using the concept of class, specifically 'the middle class,' to tell the social history of clerks and bureaucrats in twentieth-century Peru? In my view the answer remains an emphatic yes." How can Parker say this? It may help you to think of the issue of race and consider classist thinking in the same way we suggested redefining race as racialist thinking.

• How does Parker's argument about language (as being neither entirely determinant or entirely malleable) reflect earlier arguments (e.g., Hall's) that seek to balance essentialist and semiotic interpretations?

NOTES

1. Patrick Joyce has played a key role in redefining class from a cultural theory perspective in *Class* (Oxford: Oxford UP, 1995) and *Visions of the People: Industrial England and the Question of Class, 1848–1914* (Cambridge: Cambridge UP, 1991).

2. David Parker, *The Idea of the Middle Class: White Collar Workers and Peruvian Society, 1900–1950* (University Park: Penn State UP, 1998). Excerpt comes from 2–3, 5–7, 9–14, 16–17, 20–21. As of 2007, David Parker was serving as an associate professor of history and the chair of undergraduate studies at Queen's University in Ontario, Canada.

3. John J. Johnson, *Political Change in Latin America: The Emergence of Middle Sectors* (Stanford: Stanford UP, 1958).

4. The SEC is the Sociedad de Empleados de Comercio (Commercial Employees Society).

CHAPTER 8

Identity Construct #3: Gender

"I get *race*, I can do *class*, *nation* is fine, but please don't take *gender* away from me!" This exclamation rang out as we entered our classroom one March afternoon. Indeed, gender may be one of the most challenging of all identity categories. We have found that while most students are willing to accept that race, class, and nation are discursively constructed, they resist the idea that gender, too, is a construct. Students are attached to their gender, more than to any other category, as crucial in defining their identity. Why does gender create such strong reactions and why is it such a core element of our modernist identities?

Almost all societies categorize their members fundamentally according to gender. Regardless of where we are from, we learn from an early age the appropriate behavior for our gender category. Indeed, the possibility that an infant's gender category might be mistaken has given rise to piercing at birth the ears of babies with female genitalia and making sure that babies with male genitalia never get near any color resembling pink. You may recall from our general introduction that, from an essentialist perspective, femininity and masculinity are intrinsic qualities that emanate from the gendered core of women and men. Essentialists believe that gender, like all of our other identity categories, is ontological, existing in and of itself prior to human interpretation and objectively observable as such. Many contemporary ideas about gender derive from this ontological stance.

We have used the way people cross their legs to illustrate that, to essentialists who believe that gender exists as a core trait of every human being, human behavior reflects an inner masculine or feminine soul. For this reason, when a man crosses his legs "like a lady," the degree of his so-called masculine essence can be questioned.

Semioticians agree with essentialists that people possess distinct girl parts and boy parts, if you will. Some have the ability to give birth. Testosterone courses through some bodies more than others. Neither essentialists nor semioticians challenge the idea that we are biologically different. Different so-called racial groups have biological differences in skin color, hair texture, facial features, and so forth. But semioticians want to address the meanings assigned to these biological differences as well as to study how those meanings have come to take on consequences in the way people are treated and how they interact. For instance, semiotics teaches us that the idea that women are maternal because they possess a uterus and that men are aggressive because they have bigger muscles and more testosterone is nothing more than an idea. In semiotic terms, the physical signifier *uterus* becomes attached to the signified *maternal* through arbitrary and conventional use, not because their relationship is intrinsically connected. Because society considers this relationship between the signifier and the signified natural, a woman who abandons her child will be considered particularly monstrous (i.e., a woman who is not a woman) while a father who does the same is considered, at worst, to be a louse or a dead-beat dad, but not an aberration to his sex category.

Our small liberal arts university in South Carolina provides two excellent examples of the way gender is both learned and practiced every day. In the 1950s, Furman University was moved from downtown Greenville to the foothills of Paris Mountain. It may not have been a coincidence that at the new campus all of the men's dormitories were located next to the hard sciences and athletic buildings, while the women's residence halls were nearest the lake, the music building, and the academic halls that housed humanities courses. The very design of the campus at once inculcated and practiced the ideological underpinnings of gender discourse in the 1950s. By stating that this was likely not a coincidence, we are not implying that it was a conspiracy on the part of architects, administrators, or teachers in order to manipulate the generation who would carry on these specific gender and educational agendas. On the contrary, it was simply logical that the planners map out the new campus in ways that made sense to them. What the semiotic model wants us to question is why this particular layout was seen as normal and proper.

In the late nineteenth century, as the women's movement gained strength in Western society in part because of the effects of the Industrial Revolution, empirical scientific experiments set out to prove what had been a staple of modernism: The brains of women are too delicate to withstand the rigors of intellectual thought, so women ought to be excluded from studying in fields other than the arts, as well as from even entering institutions of higher education. By the early twenty-first century, in a complete turnaround in events and in order to maintain a relative gender balance, Furman, as well as many other selective liberal arts institutions in the United States, must practice a sort of affirmative action for male students who are being out-numbered and outperformed by female students across all fields, including both the social and hard sciences.

A more contemporary example concerns the segregation of public rest-rooms in North America according to sex category. Sociologists have long pointed out that this segregation is a purely cultural arrangement, since women and men have relatively similar ways of eliminating their bodily waste and often share the same facilities at home. It is purely cultural also because separate facilities (urinals for men, grooming fixtures for women) are not provided in all places and spaces. The equipment which might suggest essential male and female natures varies across cultures and circumstances. While we were teaching the seminar from which this book is derived, for example, the hall leading to our classroom was undergoing renovation. The women's bathroom was turned into a men's bathroom when a piece of paper was taped to the door, directing users to "STOP! This restroom is now for MEN." This same space reverted just as easily back to a women's bathroom the next month when the flier was removed from the door. Each time, equipment was neither installed nor removed from the restroom. Toi-let segregation most often serves to confirm the illusion that separation of the sexes is a natural consequence of their biological differences. In fact, the act of dividing the sexes in this way contributes to the *production* of these differences.

Just as racialist and classist thinking has varied over time and space, so too has "genderist" thinking. Different cultures have different conceptions of gender roles, just as they have changed and evolved their gender norms over time. In sub-Saharan Africa, for example, women have historically worked in the fields; in Europe, cultural norms insist that they are not fit for such physically demanding labor.

Some feminists criticize postmodernism's move to decenter the subject and the author at the very historical moment when women are coming into their own right as individuals and writers. Just as colonized peoples helped to prompt postcolonial studies but also challenged the decentering of nationhood as they embarked on their own independence, academic fem-inism's insistence that the (male) canon be revised questioned the intellec-tual foundation upon which the idea of dead authorship was predicated. The existence of many differences of approach and opinion attests to what some have coined "feminisms" (plural, not singular). Women authors in much of the Spanish-speaking world, for example, argue convincingly that they have been marginalized by the dominant feminism hailing from the United States and France and that they have been effectively "ghettoized" by the patriarchal critical establishment that typically wields the label of feminism to separate their work from the mainstream canon. Many Hispanic women writers and directors refuse the feminist label, expressing their desire to be considered good artists, rather than good artists who are women. Essentialist genderists would regard the absence of a universal feminist subject as evidence that we are getting ever closer to rooting out failed theories and to finding out the truth about women. Semioticians, on the other hand, would point out that the lack of a feminist standard across space (cultures, nations, regions) and time (eras) attests to the impossibility of collective, as well as individual, essences.

The student's exclamation that begins this chapter was a reaction to the assigned readings for that day; excerpts of those readings by West and Zimmerman and Connell are included here. Lest we fall into the trap of equating gender studies with feminism and women's studies, we have included pieces that treat both of these issues, as well as others of concern to the field, namely transgender and masculine studies.

West and Zimmerman, who are professors of sociology at the University of California, Santa Cruz, and the University of California, Santa Barbara, respectively, study gender as performance and acknowledge differences between the sexes, but they deny that these differences are essential. Lawrence Blum and Peter Wade exposed race as a construct in Chapter 6 and replaced the term with the more appropriate *racialized groups.* West and Zimmerman use the term *sex category* to emphasize that male and female are cultural divisions that are both reflected and produced in the daily achievement of gender. These authors illustrate the way gender is achieved or defined on a daily basis with a case study of a transgendered person who at age seventeen had to learn how to display the appropriate markers associated with being a woman. West and Zimmerman emphasize the link between gender norms and power by exposing the moral grounds upon which norms are based. They also argue that gender is accomplished individually but that this individual accomplishment sustains, reproduces, and renders legitimate the institutions that society agrees upon.

In an excerpt from *The Science of Masculinity,* Connell, a professor of education at the University of Sydney, Australia, expresses skepticism about the social practice of gender. By examining both the history of gender studies—and in particular those dealing with masculinity—as well as contemporary gender research and practice, she argues that all are gendered enterprises in which the structures of discourse have only begun to be investigated. Like Stuart Hall, Connell rejects the extremism of both the essentialist and deconstructivist approaches and argues that one must ground oneself in a place, however temporary that may be, from which to begin a dialogue about gender. She locates that place, as Hall does, within a "process of identification"; in this case, a process of gender identification. Like Blum and Wade, who describe the historical trajectory of perceptions regarding racialized groups, Connell contextualizes the shifting modernist discourses of masculinity to expose gender as a construct that varies across time.

CANDACE WEST AND DON ZIMMERMAN, "DOING GENDER" [1]

We suggest at the outset that important but often overlooked distinctions should be observed among *sex, sex category,* and *gender. Sex* is a determination made through the application of socially agreed upon biological criteria for classifying persons as females or males. The criteria for classification can be genitalia at birth or chromosomal typing before birth, and they do not necessarily agree with one another. Placement in a *sex category* is achieved through application of the sex criteria, but in everyday life, categorization is established and sustained by the socially required identificatory displays that proclaim one's membership in one or the other category. In this sense, one's sex category presumes one's sex and stands as proxy for it in many situations, but sex and sex category can vary independently; that is, it is possible to claim membership in a sex category even when the sex criteria are lacking. *Gender,* in contrast, is the activity of managing situated conduct in light of normative conceptions of attitudes and activities appropriate for one's sex category. Gender activities emerge from and bolster claims to membership in a sex category [. . .].

Perspectives on Sex and Gender

In Western societies, the accepted cultural perspective on gender views women and men as naturally and unequivocally defined categories of being with distinctive psychological and behavioral propensities that can be predicted from their reproductive functions. Competent adult members of these societies see differences between the two as fundamental and enduring, and these differences are seemingly supported by the division of labor into women's and men's work and an often elaborate differentiation of feminine and masculine attitudes and behaviors that are prominent features of social organization. Things are the way they are by virtue of the fact that men are men and women are women—a division perceived to be natural and rooted in biology, producing in turn profound psychological, behavioral, and social consequences. The structural arrangements of a society are presumed to be responsive to these differences [. . .].

We argue that gender is not a set of traits, nor a variable, nor a role, but the product of social doings of some sort. What then is the social doing of gender? It is more than the continuous creation of the meaning of gender through human actions. We claim that gender itself is constituted through interaction. To develop the implications of our claim, we turn to Goffman's account of "gender display."[2] Our object here is to explore how gender might be exhibited or portrayed through interaction, and thus be seen as "natural," while it is being produced as a socially organized achievement [. . .].

Sex, Sex Category, and Gender

Garfinkel's case study of Agnes, a transsexual raised as a boy who adopted a female identity at age 17 and underwent a sex reassignment operation several years later, demonstrates how gender is created through interaction and at the same time structures interaction.[3] Agnes, whom Garfinkel characterized as a "practical methodologist," developed a number of procedures for passing as a "normal, natural female" both prior to and after her surgery. She had the practical task of managing the facts that she possessed male genitalia and that she lacked the social resources a girl's biography would presumably provide in everyday interaction. In short, she needed to display herself as a woman, simultaneously learning what it was to be a woman. Of necessity, this full-time pursuit took place at a time in her life when most people's gender would be well-accredited and routinized. Agnes had to consciously contrive what the vast majority of women do without thinking. She was not faking what real women do naturally. She was obliged to analyze and figure out how to act within socially structured circumstances and conceptions of femininity that women born with appropriate biological credentials take for granted early on. As in the case of others who must "pass," such as transvestites, Kabuki actors, or Dustin Hoffman's "Tootsie," Agnes's case makes visible what culture has made invisible—the accomplishment of gender.

Garfinkel's discussion of Agnes does not explicitly separate three analytically distinct, although empirically overlapping, concepts—sex, sex category, and gender.

Sex

Agnes did not possess the socially agreed upon biological criteria for classification as a member of the female *sex*. Still, Agnes regarded herself as a female, albeit a female with a penis, which a woman ought not to possess. The penis, she insisted, was a "mistake" in need of remedy.[4] Like other competent members of our culture, Agnes honored the notion that there are essential biological criteria that unequivocally distinguish females from males. However, if we move away from the common-sense viewpoint, we discover that the reliability of these criteria is not beyond question. Moreover, other cultures have acknowledged the existence of "cross-genders" and the possibility of more than two sexes.

More central to our argument is Kessler and McKenna's point that genitalia are conventionally hidden from public inspection in everyday life; yet we continue through our social rounds to "observe" a world of two naturally, normally sexed persons.[5] It is the *presumption* that essential criteria exist, and would or should be there if looked for, that provides the basis for sex categorization. Drawing on Garfinkel, Kessler and McKenna argued that "female" and "male" are cultural events—products of what they term the "gender attribution process"—rather than some collection of traits, behaviors, or even physical attributes. Illustratively, they cite the child who, viewing a picture of someone clad in a suit and a tie, contends, "It's a man, because he has a pee-pee."[6] Translation: "He must have a pee-pee [an essential characteristic] because I see the *insignia* of a suit and tie." Neither initial assignment (pronouncement at birth as a female or male) nor the actual existence of essential criteria for that assignment (possession of a clitoris and vagina or penis and testicles) has much—if anything—to do with the identification of sex category in everyday life. There, Kessler and McKenna note, we operate with a moral certainty of a world of two sexes. We do not think, "Most persons with penises are men, but some may not be" or "Most persons who dress as men have penises." Rather, we take it for granted that sex and sex category are congruent—that knowing the latter, we can deduce the rest.

Sex Categorization

Agnes's claim to the categorical status of female, which she sustained by appropriate identificatory displays and other characteristics, could be discredited before her transsexual operation if her possession of a penis became known and after by her surgically constructed genitalia. In this regard, Agnes had to be continually alert to actual or potential threats to the security of her sex category. Her problem was not so much living up to some prototype of essential femininity but preserving her categorization as female. This task was made easy for her by a very powerful resource, namely, the process of common-sense categorization in everyday life.

The categorization of members of society into indigenous categories, such as girl or boy, or woman or man, operates in a distinctively social way. The act of categorization does not involve a positive test, in the sense of a well-defined set of criteria that must be explicitly satisfied prior to making an identification. Rather, the application of membership categories relies on an "if-can" test in everyday interaction. This test stipulates that *if* people *can be seen* as members of relevant categories, *then categorize them that way.* That is, use the category that seems appropriate, except in the presence of discrepant information or obvious features that would rule out its use. This procedure is quite in keeping with the attitude of everyday life, in which we take appearances at face value unless we have special reason to doubt them. It should be added that it is precisely when we have special reason to doubt appearances that the issue of applying rigorous criteria arises, but it is rare, outside legal or bureaucratic contexts, to encounter insistence on positive tests.

Agnes's initial resource was the predisposition of those she encountered to take her appearance (her figure, clothing, hair style, and so on) as the undoubted appearance of a normal female. Her further resource was our cultural perspective on the properties of "natural, normally sexed persons." Garfinkel notes that in everyday life, we live in a world of two—and only two—sexes. This arrangement has a moral status in that we include ourselves and others in it as "essentially, originally, in the first place, always have been, always will be once and for all, in the final analysis, either 'male' or 'female.'"[7] [. . .]

Gender

Agnes attempted to be "120 percent female," that is, unquestionably in all ways and at all times feminine.[8] She thought she could protect herself from disclosure before and after surgical intervention by comporting herself in a feminine manner, but she also could have given herself away by overdoing her performance. Sex categorization and the accomplishment of gender are not the same. Agnes's categorization could be secure or suspect, but did not depend on whether or not she lived up to some ideal conception of femininity. Women can be seen as unfeminine, but that does not make them "unfemale." Agnes faced an ongoing task of *being* a woman—something beyond style of dress (an identificatory display) or allowing men to light her cigarette (a gender display). Her problem was to produce configurations of behavior that would be seen by others as normative gender behavior [. . .].

Gender and Accountability [. . .]

Although it is individuals who do gender, the enterprise is fundamentally interactional and institutional in character, because accountability is a feature of social relationships and its idiom is drawn from the institutional arena in which those relationships are enacted. If this is the case, can we ever *not* do gender? Insofar as a society is partitioned by "essential" differences between women and men and placement in a sex category is both relevant and enforced, doing gender is unavoidable [. . .].

Gender Power and Social Change [. . .]

But doing gender also renders the social arrangements based on sex category accountable as normal and natural, that is, legitimate ways of organizing social life. Differences between women and men that are created by this process can then be portrayed as fundamental and enduring dispositions. In this light, the institutional arrangements of a society can be seen as responsive to the differences, the social order being merely an accommodation to the natural order. Thus if, in doing gender, men are also doing dominance and women are doing deference, the resultant social order, which supposedly reflects "natural differences," is a powerful reinforcer and legitimator of hierarchical arrangements [. . .].

Gender is a powerful ideological device, which produces, reproduces, and legitimates the choices and limits that are predicated on sex category. An understanding of how gender is produced in social situations will afford clarification of the interactional scaffolding of social structure and the social control processes that sustain it.

R. W. CONNELL, *MASCULINITIES*[9]
Rival Knowledges

The concepts "masculine" and "feminine," Freud observed in a melancholy footnote, "are among the most confused that occur in science." In many practical situations the language of "masculine" and "feminine" raises few doubts. We base a great deal of talk and action on this contrast. But the same terms, on logical examination, waver like the Danube mist. They prove remarkably elusive and difficult to define.

Why should this be? In the course of this book I will suggest that the underlying reason is the character of gender itself, historically changing and politically fraught. Everyday life is an arena of gender politics, not an escape from it.

Gender terms are contested because the right to account for gender is claimed by conflicting discourses and systems of knowledge. We can see this in everyday situations as well as in high theory [. . .].

So the conflicting forms of knowledge about gender betray the presence of different practices addressing gender. To understand both everyday and scientific accounts of masculinity we cannot remain at the level of pure ideas, but must look at their practical bases.

For instance, common-sense knowledge of gender is by no means fixed. It is, rather, the rationale of the changing practices through which gender is "done" or "accomplished" in everyday life-practices revealed in elegant research by ethnomethodologists [. . .].

The different forms of knowledge do not stand on an equal footing. In most contexts, scientific claims have an undeniable edge [. . .].

This has shaped the development of ideas about masculinity through the twentieth century. All the leading discourses make some claim to be scientific, or to use scientific "findings," however grotesque the claim may be [. . .].

But the appeal to science plunges us into circularity. For it has been shown, in convincing historical detail, that natural science itself has a gendered character. Western science and technology are culturally masculinized. This is not just a question of personnel, though it is a fact that the great majority of scientists and technologists are men. The guiding metaphors of scientific research, the impersonality of its discourse, the structures of power and communication in science, the reproduction of its internal culture, all stem from the social position of dominant men in a gendered world. The dominance of science in discussions of masculinity thus reflects the position of masculinity (or specific masculinities) in the social relations of gender [. . .].

The Male Role

The first important attempt to create a social science of masculinity centered on the idea of a male sex role. Its origins go back to late nineteenth-century debates about sex difference, when resistance to women's emancipation was bolstered by a scientific doctrine of innate sex difference. Women's exclusion from universities, for instance, was justified by the claim that the feminine mind was too delicately poised to handle the rigors of academic work. The resulting mental disturbance would be bad for their capacities to be good wives and mothers. The first generation of women who did get into North American research universities not only violated this doctrine. They also questioned its presuppositions, by researching the differences in mental capacities between men and women. They found very few.

This scandalous result triggered an enormous volume of follow-up research, which has flowed from the 1890s to the 1990s. It has covered not only mental abilities but also emotions, attitudes, personality traits, interests, indeed everything that psychologists thought they could measure. There is a remarkable amount of "sex difference" research. It is technically fairly simple to do, and there is constant interest in its results.

That in itself is curious, for the results have not changed. Sex differences, on almost every psychological trait measured, are either non-existent or fairly small. Certainly they are much smaller than the differences in social situations that are commonly justified by the belief in psychological differences—such as unequal incomes, unequal responsibilities in child care and drastic differences in access to social power. When groups of studies are aggregated by the statistical technique of meta-analysis, it is more likely to be concluded that *some* sex differences in psychological characteristics do exist. But their modest size would hardly register them as important phenomena if we were not already culturally cured to exaggerate them [. . .].

Around the midcentury, sex difference research met up with a concept that seemed to explain its subject-matter in an up-to-date way, the concept of "social role." The meeting gave birth to the term "sex role," which in time passed into everyday speech.

The idea of a sex role is now so common that it is worth emphasizing its recent origin. The metaphor of human life as a drama is of course an old one—it was used by Shakespeare. But the use of "role" as a technical concept in the social sciences, as a serious way of explaining social behavior generally, dates only from the 1930s. It provided a handy way of linking the idea of a place in social structure with the idea of cultural norms. Through the efforts of a galaxy of anthropologists, sociologists and psychologists the concept, by the end of the 1950s, had joined the stock of conventional terms in social science [. . .].

Most often, sex roles are seen as the cultural elaboration of biological sex differences. But this is not necessary. The sophisticated statement of sex role theory made in the mid-1950s by Talcott Parsons in *Family, Socialization, and Interaction Process* takes another approach. Here the distinction between male and female sex roles is treated as a distinction between "instrumental" and "expressive" roles in the family considered as a small group. Thus gender is deduced from a general sociological law of the differentiation of functions in social groups [. . .].

When Pleck in 1981 published a comprehensive re-examination of the male role literature, *The Myth of Masculinity*, this relation between role and self was central. He criticized the "Male Sex Role Identity" paradigm (his name for functionalist sex role theory) above all for its assumption of concordance between norm and personality—the idea that conformity to sex role norms is what promotes psychological adjustment.

This criticism was highly effective. Pleck demonstrated how much is taken for granted by functionalist sex role discourse, and how little empirical support there is for its key ideas. Even more interesting, Pleck offered an almost Foucaultian argument that the rise of normative sex role theory was itself a form of gender politics. Historical changes in gender relations required a shift in the form of social control over men, from external to internal controls [. . .].

This is not to say the dramaturgical metaphor of role is entirely useless in understanding social situations. It is apt for situations where (a) there are well-defined scripts to perform, (b) there are clear audiences to perform to, and (c) the stakes are not too high (so it is feasible that some kind of performing is the main social activity going on). None of these conditions, as a rule, applies to gender relations. "Sex role" is basically an inappropriate metaphor for gender interactions. (One can, of course, think of specific situations in gender interaction where roles are definitely played. Ballroom dancing competitions spring to mind—as in the charming film *Strictly Ballroom*.)

In sex role theory, action (the role enactment) is linked to a structure defined by biological difference; the dichotomy of male and female—not to a structure defined by social relations. This leads to categoricalism, the reduction of gender to two homogenous categories, betrayed by the persistent blurring of sex differences with sex roles. Sex roles are defined as reciprocal; polarization is a necessary part of the concept. This leads to a misperception of social reality, exaggerating differences between men and women, while obscuring the structures of race, class and sexuality. It is telling that discussions of "the male sex role" have mostly ignored gay men and have had little to say about race and ethnicity [. . .].

The Social Organization of Masculinity [. . .]

"Masculinity" is not a coherent object about which a generalizing science can be produced. Yet we can have coherent knowledge about the issues raised in these attempts. If we broaden the angle of vision, we can see masculinity, not as an isolated object, but as an aspect of a larger structure [. . .].

Defining Masculinity

All societies have cultural accounts of gender, but not all have the concept "masculinity." In its modern usage the term assumes that one's behavior results from the type of person one is. That is to say, an unmasculine person would behave differently: being peaceable rather than violent, conciliatory rather than dominating, hardly able to kick a football, uninterested in sexual conquest, and so forth [. . .].

Definitions of masculinity have mostly taken our cultural standpoint for granted, but have followed different strategies to characterize the type of person who is masculine [. . .].

Essentialist definitions usually pick a feature that defines the core of the masculine, and hang an account of men's lives on that. Freud flirted with an essentialist definition when he equated masculinity with activity in contrast to feminine passivity—though he came to see that equation as oversimplified. Later authors' attempts to capture an essence of masculinity have been colorfully varied: risk-taking, responsibility, irresponsibility, aggression, Zeus energy . . . Perhaps the finest is the sociobiologist Lionel Tiger's idea that true maleness, underlying male bonding and war, is elicited by "hard and heavy phenomena." Many heavy metal rock fans would agree.

The weakness in the essentialist approach is obvious: the choice of the essence is quite arbitrary. Nothing obliges different essentialists to agree, and in fact they often do not. Claims about a universal basis of masculinity tell us more about the ethos of the claimant than about anything else [. . .].

Semiotic approaches abandon the level of personality and define masculinity through a system of symbolic difference in which masculine and feminine places are contrasted. Masculinity is, in effect, defined as not-femininity [. . .].

In the semiotic opposition of masculinity and femininity, masculinity is the unmarked term, the place of symbolic authority. The phallus is master-signifier, and femininity is symbolically defined by lack.

This definition of masculinity has been very effective in cultural analysis. It escapes the arbitrariness of essentialism and the paradoxes of positivist and normative definitions. It is, however, limited in its scope—unless one assumes, as some postmodern theorists do, that discourse is all we can talk about in social analysis. To grapple with the full range of issues about masculinity we need ways of talking about relationships of other kinds too: about gendered places in production and consumption, places in institutions and in natural environments, places in social and military struggles [. . .].

What can be generalized is the principle of connection. The idea that one symbol can only be understood within a connected system of symbols applies equally well in other spheres. No masculinity arises except in a system of gender relations.

Rather than attempting to define masculinity as an object (a natural character type, a behavioral average, a norm), we need to focus on the processes and relationships through which men and women conduct gendered lives. "Masculinity," to the extent the term can be briefly defined at all, is simultaneously a place in gender relations, the practices through which men and women engage that place in gender, and the effects of these practices in bodily experience, personality and culture [. . .].

The History of Masculinity

I have stressed that masculinities come into existence at particular times and places, and are always subject to change. Masculinities are, in a word, historical [. . .].

To understand the current pattern of masculinities we need to look back over the period in which it came into being. Since masculinities exists only in the context of a whole structure of gender relations, we need to locate it in the formation of the modern gender order as a whole—a process that has taken about four centuries. The local histories of masculinity recently published provide essential detail, but we need an argument of broader scope as well [. . .].

Transformations

The history of European/American masculinity over the last two hundred years can broadly be understood as the splitting of gentry masculinity, its gradual displacement by new hegemonic forms, and the emergence of an array of subordinated and marginalized masculinities. The reasons for these changes are immensely complex, but I would suggest that three are central: challenges to the gender order by women, the logic of the gendered accumulation process in industrial capitalism, and the power relations of empire.

The challenge from women is now well documented. The nineteenth century saw a historic change in gender politics, the emergence of feminism as a form of mass politics—a mobilization for women's rights, especially the suffrage, in public arenas. This was closely connected to the growth of the liberal state and its reliance on concepts of citizenship.

Yet women's challenges to the gender order were not confined to the suffrage movement, which had a limited reach. Gentry and middle-class women were active in reforms of morals and domestic customs in the early nineteenth century which sharply challenged the sexual prerogatives of gentry men. Working-class women contested their economic dependence on men as the factory system evolved. Middle-class women again challenged men's prerogatives through the temperance movement of the late nineteenth century. The conditions for the maintenance of patriarchy changed with these challenges, and the kind of masculinity which could be hegemonic changed in response [. . .].

DISCUSSION QUESTIONS

• Why do you think people find it so difficult to accept gender as a social construction, even if they willingly regard nation and class in that way?

• If transsexuality remains atypical, i.e., if it is not an issue for the vast majority of people in society, how are West and Zimmerman able to apply the case of Agnes to the broader discussion of semiotic versus essentialist notions of gender?

• Think back to our introduction on race in which we described the arguments against considering minority groups racist. Can similar arguments be made against considering women's groups sexist?

• In what ways are you a "dead actor" in terms of gender? In other words, in what ways are you gendered without necessarily having the conscious opportunity to make decisions about that?

• How is Connell's historical exploration of gender construction comparable to Blum's and Wade's historical explanation of racial/ethnic construction?

• Can you think of other ways in which a belief in gender essences reveals contradictory practices across time or place? We provided the example of women in sub-Saharan Africa who do field labor versus those in Europe who would not. Can you think of other such examples? One might be the rise and fall of the belief around the turn of the twentieth century in the medical condition known as female hysteria.

NOTES

1. Candace West and Don Zimmerman, "Doing Gender," ed. Judith Lorber and Susan Farrell, *The Social Construction of Gender* (Newbury Park: Sage, 1991). Excerpt taken from 14–16, 18–24, 32, 34.

2. Erving Goffman, *Interaction Ritual: Essays on Face-to-Face Behavior* (Garden City: Anchor, 1967) 47–95.

3. Harold Garfinkel, *Studies in Ethnomethodology* (Englewood Cliffs, NJ: Prentice-Hall, 1967) 118–140.

4. Garfinkel 126–127, 131–132.

5. Suzanne Kessler and Wendy McKenna, *Gender: An Ethnomethodological Approach* (New York: Wiley, 1978) 1–6.

6. Kessler 154.

7. Garfinkel 122–128.

8. Garfinkel 129.

9. R. W. Connell, *Masculinities* (Berkeley: U of California P, 1995). Excerpt taken from 3–7, 21–27, 67–71, 185–194.

Identity Construct #4: Nation

Whereas race, gender, and class offer essentialists something tangible when defining essence (skin color, sex organs, and economic standing), national identities are not quite so accommodating. The nation seems at once to be all around us, yet something we can not quite touch or see. Is it the government, the army, a legal code, patrimonial documents, art, language, or something else entirely? Where exactly does the nation reside? Despite the apparent challenge of answering these questions, the belief in national essence by nationalists and their celebration of it have defined human existence over the last two hundred years. With alarming regularity, millions of people have not only killed for their nations, they have willingly died for them.

The modern concept of the nation-state emerged in the wake of the French Revolution in 1789. The monarchies of the ancien régime were being swept aside by the new ideas of modern government and republics grounded in Enlightenment values. Whereas the ideological justifications for monarchy were the principles of God's will and of status by birth, the foundations for the new political order were individual liberties based on natural law and government by and for the people. At least in theory, nation-states were built on the notion that people first recognized themselves as individuals and then agreed to come together in a unified whole for the purpose of collectively administering their own lives. Admittedly, nation-states (then and now) often failed to live up to these ideals, if they even aspired to them, but, at least in principle, a nation-state was fundamentally different from the monarchical and aristocratic system of the past.

Modernist hermeneutics and its corresponding belief in national essence provided the necessary justification for creating the nation. A person who joined the nationalist project had to surrender some individual liberty in the name of the greater national good. In practical terms, deciding to do so might seem reasonable. After all, there is strength and opportunity in numbers and being part of a nation might be a better alternative to living in isolated villages or belonging to a small, remote community. But even if this practical incentive were the primary motive behind national unification, the nation-state is not necessarily or automatically the only way to satisfy the desire for self-defense through collective organization. Furthermore, the idea of the nation presents the pressing question of who is supposed to gather together with whom. Essentialists responded to these questions by appealing to national essence.

Hermeneutic nationalists believe in the existence of an ontological spirit that binds people together into the national unit. They believe that certain people share intrinsic nationalist traits which are almost like bloodlines, which they cannot deny, and which fundamentally determine who they are. And so, like scientists seeking out mathematical formulas for natural laws, hermeneutic nationalists sought out these traits. Naturally, they came up with many different and often-competing definitions, which varied geographically and changed over time. Some defined the nation in racial terms, others by language, religion, a shared historical experience, folk culture, architecture, or any number of other traits. Despite their differences in interpretation, national essentialists shared the common belief that the nation was an ontological truth. Subsequently, they believed that the national spirit or identity could be identified and brought to the light of day. Failure to create the nation-state and then to defend its existence was akin to violating natural law. And so, in the name of the nation-state, nationalists made war on monarchies, other nations, or isolationist groups within their national borders that they defined as hindering the righteous project of national consolidation.

Semioticians see that all this is a massive social construct and a classic example of modernity promoting something as an essential truth that is nothing more than an idea, though one that is not without its powerful purposes and effects. Semiotic thinkers argue that nations, like races, genders, and classes, are a product of society's ideas about itself and are determined by and reinforced in discursive practice.

From a semiotic interpretation, nations and monarchies don't look very different. Modern nationalists challenged the truth claims upon which monarchies justified their existence. Although the modernists never defined them as such, they basically saw monarchies as social constructions resting upon ideas whose adherents believed to be absolute truth (God's will and aristocratic birth). In contrast, modern nationalists believed they possessed the real truth of how people should organize themselves politically. But from a semiotic perspective, modernist nationalism is hardly different from its monarchist predecessor. Modern nations may no longer rely on kingly bloodlines to construct the illusion of national essence and cohesion, but they do rely on an admittedly abstract notion of ancestry. Nationalists believe that citizens share essences typically defined as intrinsic traits, such as integrity, goodness, bravery, treachery, evil, cowardice, etc., that began with the founding fathers and were passed down through the blood to future generations.

Two excerpts on this national issue, one hermeneutic, the other semiotic, are included in this chapter. The hermeneutic offering is by Arthur de Gobineau (1817–1882), a French diplomat and novelist who is regarded as one of the most prominent theorists of race and national identities in nineteenth-century Western civilization. His fame rests largely on his theory of *degeneration*. In 1854, Gobineau published *The Inequality of Human Races,* in which he attempts to prove the existence of a racial hierarchy. He does so by promoting a theory of degeneration in which race is collapsed into nation and both are inherited through bloodlines. According to Gobineau, degeneration is a nation's loss of "characteristic virtues" that eventually leads to the downfall of a society. This loss of character and value is a direct effect, he believes, of racial mixing. When a people occupies a foreign land and miscegenation results, the blood of the conquering race is tainted and weakened by foreign blood, which will dilute the nation's character and its innate power to conquer. His essentialist view is explicitly rooted in the belief that a nation's identity—its unique qualities and characteristics—is defined solely by the blood of its people, who have an inborn affinity with their own kind and a "secret repulsion from the crossing of blood."[1] Therefore, a nation's intrinsic value cannot be changed by circumstances, only by altering the blood.

In a contradictory moment in his argument, Gobineau asserts that if a nation is to take advantage of its innate power, it must conquer. This inevitably leads to racial mixing, which he has already theorized as the weakening of the nation and the cause of its eventual degeneration. Not all nations, however, have been endowed by nature with an ability to improve themselves by claiming new lands. Not surprisingly, Gobineau believes the "pure-blooded yellow and black races," two racialized groups with a long history of being persecuted, are inherently weak and incapable of conquest, while the white races were born to it. This ability to conquer is seen as the destiny of powerful nations, and it is also creates what Gobineau calls a "real nation." In other words, conquest is both the origin and destination of nations.

Gobineau's treatise does not rise out of a vacuum. The discourses of his era informed his essentialist presuppositions of a natural hierarchy of races, as well as of a world that can be broken down into racially pure and impure nations. His theories, in turn, helped to shape competing discourses. Although Gobineau's racial nation was just one variant within the hermeneutic discourse of defining national essence, it was a particularly powerful one, as evidenced by the fact that his theories acquired widespread recognition during the nineteenth century and gained a prominent place in Nazi ideology.

Latin America, too, was deeply influenced by racially derived notions of national identity, which predate Gobineau. Domingo Sarmiento's *Facundo: Civilization and Barbarism* (1845), is just one example.[2] Throughout most of Latin American history, race and nation have been almost inseparable as concepts. Even in the nationalist period of the first half of the twentieth century, when populist-oriented politicians and intellectuals articulated a new vision of the nation based on broader inclusiveness, race and racial identity were paramount, especially regarding the mestizo (a mix of Spanish and Indian). Sometimes this celebration of mixing, or *mestizaje* as it has come to be called, was overtly racial, as in the appeal by José Vasconcelos (1822–1959), a Mexican writer and politician, to the racially mixed person as the highest form of human existence, the new "cosmic race." Other times it was defined in more cultural terms. But in either case, the new mestizo nationalism excluded as often as it included because mestizo inevitably got conflated with a racial type that did not accord status to Indians or Africans. Not surprisingly, these newly imagined mestizo societies had a difficult time shaking their white supremacist heritage rooted in hermeneutic essentialism, and lighter skin color continued to be privileged.

In contrast, Louis Pérez approaches national identity as a competition of ideas rather than of bloodlines. In the introduction to his *On Becoming Cuban: Identity, Nationality, and Culture*, Pérez, who has an endowed professorship at the University of North Carolina at Chapel Hill and is a scholar of Cuban history, lays out the premises for a semiotic interpretation of national identity and applies it Cuba. Pérez immediately dispenses with the notion of origins and essences by defining national identity as "not . . . a fixed and immutable construct but rather [a] . . . cultural artifact . . . almost always in flux," a definition reminiscent of Hall's process of identification.[3] With specific regard to Cuban national identity, Pérez focuses on the interaction of the United States and Cuba from the 1850s to the 1950s and the process of "cultural inflection," whereby North American culture— Hollywood films, technological advancements, consumerism, etc.—shaped the ways Cubans came to view the world and themselves. In making the assertion that Cuban identity is located in large part outside of Cuba, Pérez rejects the conventional essentialist logic, as expressed by Gobineau, that national identity comes from the blood of its people. Instead, he says that the notion of national identity being formed in isolation is no longer tenable. In response to the perception in some circles that Cuba had surrendered its identity to its colossal neighbor to the north, Pérez examines contact between Cubans and North Americans as "it moved in both directions, often repeatedly back and forth, transformed and transforming."[4] He is not so naïve as to deny that dominant nations have greater capacity to shape cultural discourse, but he also notes that weaker nations participate in shaping the discourses of stronger ones. One illuminating example that Pérez offers in this regard involves the influences of Cuban music and dance on U.S. popular culture and, simultaneously, of Cubans' strategy of reselling for the North American market.

Pérez suggests that this unequal relation ultimately led to Cuban disenchantment with U.S. market culture and consumption. He asserts that the attraction to U.S. cultural hegemony later becomes the grounds for repulsion: "The power of U.S. hegemony was embedded in cultural forms that served as the principal means by which the North American presence was legitimized. It just happened that these forms also served as the means by which North American influences were contested and otherwise diminished or eliminated altogether."[5] According to Pérez, this disenchantment lead to Cuban support for populist/socialist leaders such as Fidel Castro.

ARTHUR DE GOBINEAU, *THE INEQUALITY OF HUMAN RACES*[6]
Chapter IV: The Meaning of the Word "Degeneration"; the Mixture of Racial Elements; How Societies Are Formed and Broken Up [. . .]

Bichat,[7] as we know, did not seek to discover the great mystery of existence by studying the human subject from the outside; the key to the riddle, he saw, lay within. Those who followed the same method, in our own subject, were traveling on the only road that really led to discoveries. Unfortunately, this excellent idea of theirs was the result of mere instinct; its logical implications were not carried very far, and it was shattered on the first difficulty. "Yes," they cried, "the cause of destruction lies hidden in the very vitals of the social organism; but what is this cause?" "Degeneration," was the answer; "nations die when they are composed of elements that have degen-erated." The answer was excellent, etymologically and otherwise. It only remained to define the meaning of "nation that has degenerated." This was the rock on which they foundered; a degenerate people meant, they said, "A people which through bad government, misuse of wealth, fanaticism, or irreligion, had lost the characteristic virtues of its ancestors." What a fall is there! Thus a people dies of its endemic diseases because it is degener-ate, and is degenerate because it dies. This circular argument merely proves that the science of social anatomy is in its infancy. I quite agree that soci-eties perish because they are degenerate, and for no other reason. This is the evil condition that makes them wholly unable to withstand the shock of the disasters that close in upon them; and when they can no longer endure the blows of adverse fortune, and have no power to raise their heads when the scourge has passed, then we have the sublime spectacle of a nation in agony. If it perish, it is because it has no longer the same vigor as it had of old in battling with the dangers of life; in a word, because it is degenerate. I repeat, the term is excellent; but we must explain it a little better, and give it a definite meaning. How and why is a nation's vigor lost? How does it degenerate? These are the questions which we must try to answer. Up to the present, men have been content with finding the word, without unveiling the reality that lies behind. This further step I shall now attempt to take.

The word *degenerate,* when applied to a people, means (as it ought to mean) that the people has no longer the same intrinsic value as it had before, because it has no longer the same blood in its veins, continual adulterations having gradually affected the quality of that blood. In other words, though the nation bears the name given by its founders, the name no longer con-notes the same race; in fact, the man of a decadent time, the degenerate man properly so called, is a different being, from the racial point of view, from the heroes of the great ages. I agree that he still keeps something of their essence; but the more he degenerates the more attenuated does this "something" be-come. The heterogeneous elements that henceforth prevail in him give him quite a different nationality—a very original one, no doubt, but such origi-nality is not to be envied. He is only a very distant kinsman of those he still calls his ancestors. He, and his civilization with him, will certainly die on the day when the primordial race-unit is so broken up and swamped by the influx of foreign elements, that its effective qualities have no longer a suf-ficient freedom of action. It will not, of course, absolutely disappear, but it will in practice be so beaten down and enfeebled, that its power will be felt less and less as time goes on. It is at this point that all the results of degenera-tion will appear, and the process may be considered complete.

If I manage to prove this proposition, I shall have given a meaning to the word "degeneration." By showing how the essential quality of a nation gradually alters, I shift the responsibility for its decadence, which thus becomes, in a way, less shameful, for it weighs no longer on the sons, but on the nephews, then on the cousins, then on collaterals more or less removed. And when I have shown by examples that great peoples, at the moment of their death, have only a very small and insignificant share in the blood of the founders, into whose inheritance they come, I shall thereby have explained clearly enough how it is possible for civilizations to fall—the reason being that they are no longer in the same hands [. . .].

The human species seems to have a very great difficulty in raising itself above a rudimentary type of organization; the transition to a more complex state is made only by those groups of tribes, that are eminently gifted. I may cite, in support of this, the actual condition of a large number of communities spread throughout the world. These backward tribes, especially the Polynesian negroes, the Samoyedes and others in the far north, and the majority of the African races, have never been able to shake themselves free from their impotence; they live side by side in complete independence of each other. The stronger massacre the weaker, the weaker try to move as far away as possible from the stronger. This sums up the political ideas of these embryo societies, which have lived on in their imperfect state, without possibility of improvement, as long as the human race itself. It may be said that these miserable savages are a very small part of the earth's population. Granted; but we must take account of all the similar peoples who have lived and disappeared. Their number is incalculable, and certainly includes the vast majority of the pure-blooded yellow and black races.

If then we are driven to admit that for a very large number of human beings it has been, and always will be, impossible to take even the first step towards civilization; if, again, we consider that these peoples are scattered over the whole face of the earth under the most varying conditions of climate and environment, that they live indifferently in the tropics, in the temperate zones, and in the Arctic circle, by sea, lake, and river, in the depths of the forest, in the grassy plains, in the arid deserts, we must conclude that a part of mankind, is in its own nature stricken with a paralysis, which makes it for ever unable to take even the first step towards civilization, since it cannot overcome the natural repugnance, felt by men and animals alike, to a crossing of blood.

Leaving these tribes, that are incapable of civilization, on one side, we come, in our journey upwards, to those which understand that if they wish to increase their power and prosperity, they are absolutely compelled, either by war or peaceful measures, to draw their neighbors within their sphere of influence. War is undoubtedly the simpler way of doing this. Accordingly, they go to war. But when the campaign is finished, and the craving for destruction is satisfied, some prisoners are left over; these prisoners become slaves, and as slaves, work for their masters. We have class distinctions at once, and an industrial system: the tribe has become a little people. This is a higher rung on the ladder of civilization, and is not necessarily passed by all the tribes which have been able to reach it; many remain at this stage in cheerful stagnation.

But there are others, more imaginative and energetic, whose ideas soar beyond mere brigandage. They manage to conquer a great territory, and assume rights of ownership not only over the inhabitants, but also over their land. From this moment a real nation has been formed. The two races often continue for a time to live side by side without mingling; and yet, as they become indispensable to each other, as a community of work and interest is gradually built up, as the pride and rancor of conquest begin to ebb away, as those below naturally tend to rise to the level of their masters, while the masters have a thousand reasons for allowing, or even for promoting, such a tendency, the mixture of blood finally takes place, the two races cease to be associated with distinct tribes, and become more and more fused into a single whole [. . .].

I think I am right in concluding from these examples, which cover all countries and ages, including our own, that the human race in all its branches has a secret repulsion from the crossing of blood, a repulsion which in many of the branches is invincible, and in others is only conquered to a slight extent [. . .].

Thus mankind lives in obedience to two laws, one of repulsion, the other of attraction; these act with different force on different peoples [. . .].

In the picture which I am presenting—and which in certain features is that of the Hindus, the Egyptians, the Persians and the Macedonians—two facts appear to me to stand out. The first is that a nation, which itself lacks vigor and power, is suddenly called upon to share a new and a better destiny—that of the strong masters into whose hands it has fallen; this was the case with the Anglo-Saxons, when they had been subdued by the Normans. The second fact is that a picked race of men, a sovereign people, with the usual strong propensities of such a people to cross its blood with another's, finds itself henceforth in close contact with a race whose inferiority is shown, not only by defeat, but also by the lack of the attributes that may be seen in the conquerors. From the very day when the conquest is accomplished and the fusion begins, there appears a noticeable change of quality in the blood of the masters. If there were no other modifying influence at the work, then—at the end of a number of years, which would vary according to the number of peoples that composed the original stock—we should be confronted with a new race, less powerful certainly than the better of its two ancestors, but still of considerable strength. It would have developed special qualities resulting from the actual mixture, and unknown to the communities from which it sprang. But the case is not generally so simple as this, and the intermingling of blood is not confined for long to the two constituent peoples.

The empire I have just been imagining is a powerful one; and its power is used to control its neighbors. I assume that there will be new conquests; and, every time, a current of fresh blood will be mingled with the main stream. Henceforth, as the nation grows, whether by war or treaty, its racial character changes more and more. It is rich, commercial, and civilized. The needs and the pleasures of other peoples find ample satisfaction in its capitals, its great towns, and its ports; while its myriad attractions cause many foreigners to make it their home. After a short time, we might truly say that a distinction of castes takes the place of the original distinction of races [. . .].

In every other place where there were really any castes at all, they ceased to exist at the moment when the chance of making a fortune, and of becoming famous by useful discoveries or social talents, became open to the whole world, without distinction of origin. But also, from that same day, the nation that was originally the active, conquering, and civilizing power began to disappear; its blood became merged in that of all the tributaries which it had attracted to its own stream.

Generally the dominating peoples begin by being far fewer in number than those they conquer; while, on the other hand, certain races that form the basis of the population in immense districts are extremely prolific—the Celts, for example, and the Slavs. This is yet another reason for the rapid disappearance of the conquering races. Again, their greater activity and the more personal part they take in the affairs of the State make them the chief mark for attack after a disastrous battle, a proscription, or a revolution [. . .].

A people may often go on living and working, and even growing in power, after the active, generating force of its life and glory has ceased to exist. Does this contradict what I have said above? Not at all; for while the blood of the civilizing race is gradually drained away by being parceled out among the peoples that are conquered or annexed, the impulse originally given to these peoples still persists. The institutions which the dead master had invented, the laws he had prescribed, the customs he had initiated—all these live after him. No doubt the customs, laws, and institutions have quite forgotten the spirit that informed their youth; they survive in dishonored old age, every day more sapless and rotten. But so long as even their shadows remain, the building stands, the body seems to have a soul, the pale ghost walks. When the original impulse has worked itself out, the last word has been said. Nothing remains; the civilization is dead.

I think I now have all the data necessary for grappling with the problem of the life and death of nations; and I can say positively that a people will never die, if it remains eternally composed of the same national elements. If the empire of Darius had, at the battle of Arbela, been able to fill its ranks with Persians, that is to say with real Aryans; if the Romans of the later Empire had had a Senate and an army of the same stock as that which existed at the time of the Fabii, their dominion would never have come to an end. So long as they kept the same purity of blood, the Persians and Romans would have lived and reigned [. . .].

But if, like the Greeks, and the Romans of the later Empire, the people has been absolutely drained of its original blood, and the qualities conferred by the blood, then the day of its defeat will be the day of its death. It has used up the time that heaven granted at its birth, for it has completely changed its race, and with its race its nature. It is therefore degenerate [. . .].

I have now given a meaning to the word degeneration; and so have been able to attack the problem of a nation's vitality. I must next proceed to prove what for the sake of clearness I have had to put forward as a mere hypothesis: namely, that there are real differences in the relative value of human races [. . .].

LOUIS PÉREZ, *ON BECOMING CUBAN*[8]

This is a study of the Cuban–North American connection, not in the form of these relations, but as a relationship: its multiple and multifaceted aspects examined as one vast, interrelated constellation of factors and forces. The particular focus of the book is the Cuban encounter with the United States and the ways that this encounter influenced the context in which Cuban identity and nationality acquired recognizable forms. What Cubans derived from this experience shaped how they came to understand their relations with North Americans, no less than the relations among themselves. Attention is given to the diverse circumstances under which Cubans sustained contact with North Americans and came to know them, how that familiarity contributed to the assumptions by which Cubans presumed to understand the world, how North American ways revealed themselves, and how these revelations shaped the people Cubans became [. . .].

Central to this discussion is the proposition of national identity not as a fixed and immutable construct but rather as cultural artifact, as contested— and contesting—representations often filled with contradictions and incoherencies, almost always in flux. This national identity constantly adjusts to and reconciles perceptions of reality with changing needs, and vice versa, with its own particular history, specifically a way to experience the meaning of inclusion of previously disparate constituencies within the notion of nationality. It is, as it were, a work in progress, in a state of continual development. This is identity as historically contingent, as both national expression and individual construction, possessing multiple forms, often simultaneously, sometimes successively; it is always changing with changing times: open not fixed, more a process than a product. In this sense, culture exists as a system of representation, signifying the practices and institutions from which nationality is derived and acted out [. . .].

Cubans early mastered the skills to negotiate their encounter with the North, which meant that they developed an extraordinary—but not unlimited—capacity to accommodate North American cultural forms in their midst. Cubans themselves introduced baseball to the island in the nineteenth century. Some of the most noteworthy Protestant inroads were registered by Cuban missionaries. These phenomena became even more pronounced in the twentieth century. Cuba was a country in which many citizens knew something about big-league baseball and professional boxing. Cubans participated eagerly in North American consumer culture and developed loyalties to U.S. brand names. They were unabashedly devoted to Hollywood, its movies and movie stars. In remote country stores it was common for rural consumers to have direct access to canned foods and ready-made clothing, as well as tools and farm equipment, manufactured in the United States, not as instruments of oppression, but as material goods eagerly adopted to improve daily life.

North Americans, in turn, in varying degrees throughout the twentieth century, appropriated and adapted elements of things Cuban in response to cultural transformations and commodity imperatives. Such negotiations took place in both Cuba and the United States, often as a result of tourism, typically by way of popular culture, most notably in the areas of music and dance. The resonance of U.S. hegemony was such, however, that Cubans reappropriated North American representations of "Cuban" as a strategy calculated to accommodate North American market forms.

North American hegemony was experienced mainly as a cultural inflection: culture served to condition the moral order in which power was ex-

ercised and encountered and, in the end, the way power was registered and
resisted. The vitality of North American forms was derived from their capacity to shape consciousness, to remake people by redefining the common
assumptions of their everyday life.

These were not efforts devised explicitly to control Cubans. On the
contrary, they were many of the same ways by which North Americans
themselves were formed. And therein lay the power of things and ways
North American. Due in part to historical circumstances and in part to
geography, Cubans happened to have been among the first people outside
the United States to come under the influence of North American material
culture.

The success of U.S. hegemony in Cuba was less a function of political
control and military domination than a cultural condition in which meaning and purpose were derived from North American normative systems.
U.S. influence expanded from within, usually in noncoercive forms, just
as often introduced by Cubans themselves as by North Americans. U.S.
culture spread rapidly across the island and emerged as one of the most accessible means by which to aspire to well-being and thus was a powerful
motivator in the acceptance of new social norms and new cognitive categories. This was the principal way that Cubans entered the postcolonial order,
the circumstances under which social institutions were formed and moral
hierarchies established, the means by which many citizens arranged the
terms of their familiarity with the world at large.

This is not to minimize the role of coercion and violence in defense of
the status quo. U.S. armed intervention occurred periodically. Political in-
termeddling was constant. Nor were these methods of social control and
political domination unimportant. Economic control and political power
served to obtain some measure of Cuban acquiescence, and could—and
did—act as powerful forces to secure Cuban emulation of what was increasingly becoming known as the "American way of life." [. . .]

These relationships endured varying degrees over the course of a century,
often in ways that ceased to be apprehended at all. They operated as a system
possessed of its own logic. Because that system lacked organization does
not mean that it was without order. The power of North American forms
resided expressly in their capacity to assume the appearance of normal and
ordinary, the ease with which their major elements could be appropriated,
and the degree to which these elements influenced the standards to which
Cuban men and women aspired to achieve self-definition and self-worth.
It is not clear that Cubans fully discerned the sources of their own formation. What is apparent, however, is that U.S. forms penetrated so deeply
through habitual usage and became so much a part of everyday life as to

be indistinguishable from what passed as commonplace, but most of all for what passed as Cuban [. . .].

DISCUSSION QUESTIONS

• Although Gobineau's theories may appear to be outdated, they continue to be embedded in contemporary discourse. Provide as many examples as you can regarding this assertion.

• Compare these two works. How would Pérez respond to Gobineau's idea of national identity?

• How does Pérez's argument on Cuban national identity resemble Hall's theory of contingency?

NOTES

1. Arthur de Gobineau, *The Inequality of Human Races*, trans. Adrian Collins (New York: Howard Fertig, 1967) 136 [originally published 1845].

2. Domingo Sarmiento, *Life in the Argentine Republic in the Days of Tyrants or, Civilization and Barbarism* (New York: Collier, 1966) 43.

3. Louis Pérez, *On Becoming Cuban: Identity, Nationality and Culture* (Chapel Hill: U of North Carolina P, 1999) 8.

4. Perez 6.

5. Perez 13.

6. De Gobineau, *The Inequality of Human Races.*

7. De Gobineau is referring to Francois Xavier Bichat (1771–1802), a French anatomist and physiologist, who worked so hard to advance the study of surgery and understandings of the human body that he compromised his own health and died at a young age. Nevertheless, he made numerous contributions to medical science.

8. Pérez, *On Becoming Cuban: Identity, Nationality and Culture.* Excerpt is from 5, 8, 10–11, 12–13.

Identity Construct #5: Latin America

This chapter is one of the most important parts of this introductory section on theory. It broadly describes the debates over what it means to be Latin American and offers a specific example of the difference between essentialistic and semiotic interpretations of identity. It includes excerpts from Gerald Martin, Leslie Bary, and Walter Mignolo, who describe themselves as scholars of cultural studies, though one is obviously a modernist and the other two are cultural theorists. Martin interprets Latin America from a more essentialist foundation and appeals to literary genres that he believes reveal its true identity. Bary adopts a more semiotic approach by citing authors who maintain a consistently critical stance and whose works expose discursive constructs. Mignolo's approach advances Bary's.

Martin, a professor at the University of Pittsburgh, specializes in twentieth-century Latin American narrative with an emphasis on the works of Miguel Angel Asturias and Gabriel García Márquez. *Journeys Through the Labyrinth*, the book from which the next selection is drawn, was published in 1989. It helped establish Martin as an authority on Latin American narrative and identity. Martin was also selected to write essays on Latin American narrative for the distinguished *Cambridge History of Latin America*. Our selection is drawn from Martin's opening chapter, in which he outlines his understanding of Latin American identity and then provides a summary of literary works that support his claim.

Martin begins by pointing out Latin America's unique position in the world. It has a legitimate claim to being Western because of its strong, historic ties to Europe. But it is also very non-Western in that a significant part of its demographic and cultural heritage comes from indigenous America and Africa. Latin American nations, therefore, have much in common with the United States and Canada. All of them were colonies of Europe that broke away in the late eighteenth or early nineteenth centuries to form independent republics based largely on Enlightenment principles. Latin America, however, remains distinct from its northern neighbors by having failed to achieve their unique levels of social development and economic growth. Thus, it is caught in a paradox: it is neither old nor new, and is at once Western and underdeveloped.

As a result, its "grand historical narratives," which are sort of Genesis stories, differentiate Latin America from the United States, Canada, and Europe. Martin sees these narratives as so widely accepted that they have become, as he calls them, "great cultural myths" or "foundational myths" that are essentially unbending in their constancy.

Martin takes the United States as the primary representative of the developed Western world. The narrative of its identity is based upon notions of its sustained economic development and its status as a world power. According to the myth, although the United States is a vast and diverse land populated by peoples from all over the world, it has accomplished the rare and difficult task of unifying its sense of self. In short, it has become "singular." The myth claims that, with notable but rare exceptions, the United States does not fight against itself, and its inhabitants have a collective understanding of the need to work together in order to achieve great things. The narrative does not clarify which came first, the singularity of identity or economic development. They are mutually reinforcing elements that collectively pushed the United States into its position of supremacy.

The narrative for Latin America revolves around duality, giving it a sort of split personality. Its myth portrays it as lacking a sense of unity or common purpose. It is broken up into many nations, and many of them are too small and too poor to compete in the international arena. Within each of them, people remain divided, lacking a sense of wholeness. This duality is often referred to as *mestizaje*, an expression meant to describe Latin America as an unresolved mixing of European (Spanish) and American (Indian) identities. Unable to resolve this dichotomy, Latin Americans at once embrace and reject each identity, inevitably leaving them bogged down in uncertainty and confusion.

Martin refers to these narratives as myths, so it might seem that he considers them to be discursive constructs, making his approach semiotic. If that were the case, he would first describe the myths in detail and then expose the falsified essentialisms upon which they are based. And Martin appears to adopt this approach in challenging the idea of U.S. singularity.

He points out that the myth conveniently ignores "racism, genocide, imperialism, the destruction of nature and the menace of the nuclear shadow."[1] Martin is astutely able to recognize the amnesia that commonly afflicts historical memory in the most modern societies of the West. They are quick to point out their advances and take credit for developing foundational ideas like liberty and individual rights but slow to recognize their own colossal failures, or to take responsibility for their role in creating some of history's greatest injustices. If he were to extend this analysis, Martin would question the accuracy of the idea of Latin America's duality. Rather than seeing Latin America as trapped in a quagmire of competing identities, he would have observed that this notion of duality tends to benefit those who have traditionally held power in Latin America—the elites of European descent who insist upon modeling their nations after the United States or Europe. He ultimately does not overturn these identity myths, however, and accepts them as generally accurate, notwithstanding his challenge to U.S. singularity.

Martin explores Latin American identity through the lenses of race, nation, class, and gender—conveniently identical to the categories we offer. By looking at the history of modern Latin America through these identities, Martin contends that it has been trapped in its duality and has struggled in vain to find its identity. He believes that modern Latin American literature is inundated with references to labyrinths and solitude. The labyrinth is essentially a metaphor for the struggle for modernity. To be trapped in a labyrinth is to be stuck in some form of premodernity. To escape the labyrinth is to achieve modernity and development. Being trapped in a labyrinth is to be alone, isolated, and insular, or to be suffering from solitude. To enter into modernity is to join the most advanced sectors of human existence, to become part of a broader collective whole that sees no limits to human potential and believes that human beings can overcome almost any obstacle. In Martin's words, "To overcome solitude [is to] attain some kind of collective unity and identity."[2] He claims that Europe left its labyrinth during the Renaissance (roughly 1500), which marks the beginning of modernity in Western history. Supposedly, the United States was freed from its labyrinth sometime in the late nineteenth century, when its identity shifted from an internally divided, former British colony to a unified world leader. Latin America, on the other hand, has yet to join them outside its labyrinth.

Martin admits that the modern West (the United States and Europe) reentered its labyrinth in the middle of the twentieth century because of the overwhelming devastation wrought by two world wars. In literature this second entrance was expressed in the discombobulating work of James

Joyce and Franz Kafka, among many others, with their rambling, circular, surreal, and often senseless narrative forms. But whereas some critics perceive this reentrance as the beginning of the postmodern age and the death of modernity, others like Martin see it as a temporary period of adjustment, when the modern West is working out its kinks, righting its listing ship. In contrast, a similar expression of disorientation in Latin American literature, the so-called Boom of magical realism in the 1960s and 1970s, is seen as an expression of Latin America's deep-seated dualism and its ongoing effort to exit its own labyrinth. In summary, Martin basically challenges his readers to ask why so many of Latin America's great writers, including Jorge Luis Borges, Octavio Paz, and Gabriel García Márquez, obsess about labyrinths and solitude unless Latin America truly suffers from an essence of duality and must continue searching for the way out.

An alternative perspective to Martin is provided by Leslie Bary, a professor of Spanish at the University of Louisiana who specializes in questions of identity construction and representations of *mestizaje* in Latin American literature. The selection from her work is drawn from a brief introduction that Bary wrote for a book not unlike this one in its structure and organization. There, Bary set the stage for eight selections of readings surveying modern Latin America history. They begin with Simón Bolívar's famous speech before the Congress of Angostura in 1819 and end with Rigoberta Menchú's testimonial, *I, Rigoberta Menchú*, which explores Indian life in the midst of Guatemala's civil war in the 1970s and 1980s. Also included are Domingo Sarmiento's *Facundo*, Andrés Bello's study of Spanish grammar in Latin America, José Enrique Rodó's *Ariel*, Jose Martí's *Our America*, and *The Cosmic Race* by José Vasconcelos. These are canonical literary texts for studying modern Latin America. Gerald Martin refers to most of them, and some are readings in this book.

Bary reads these texts from a semiotic perspective. She first challenges the notion of identity as an essence or constant, instead positing it as a construct that is always subject to change. More specifically, Bary defines identity as an "arena for struggle."[3] She means that we make our identities in the process of acting upon our preconceptions of them, not that our actions emerge from innate and ontological identities.

Bary's arena for struggle can be further clarified using politics as an example. Rather than being based on accurate or inaccurate understandings of peoples' true identities, politics and policymaking represent moments at which identities are made and given meaning. If a national government adopts a specific policy toward its Indians, for example, it is acting on ideas about Indian identity whether or not a consensus about those ideas exists or how explicitly they might be stated. If policy makers are operating from an essentialist perspective, they assume Indians to have an ontological identity and they believe their understanding of that identity is based on scientific fact. Their interpretation of Indian identity legitimizes their political program.

A semiotic interpretation would view policy-making initiatives as moments at which identity is given meaning. Certain policies and policy makers might advocate one identity, others would offer an alternative. Thus, politics is the arena in which people fight over the meanings of identity, and political contests represent moments when existing identities are either preserved or changed. The people involved in these political disputes usually are not consciously aware that their debates are about identity. As "dead authors" of political programs, they see themselves as fighting to make policy adhere to ontological truth. Bary illustrates the principle of dead authorship by pointing out that authors whose works advocate equality, like Mexico's José Vasconcelos or Brazil's Oswald de Andrade, often end up enhancing hierarchical structures.

For further clarification of Bary's argument, think back to David Parker's interpretation of class in Chapter 7. Parker challenged the traditional idea that class originates in material conditions and that *class politics* is a term that simply signifies people entering the political arena to defend these pre-existing class interests. Parker argues instead that class identities are made at the moment people enter into the political arena and begin to think of class as an objective concept. Thus, politics makes class, rather than class giving rise to a certain kind of politics. Bary makes the same argument about Latin American identity. It is made and defined by the authors who write about it or the policy makers who create policies based on their perception of it.

Bary does not address specifically the concepts of singularity and duality as Martin does. But applying Bary's interpretive approach to Martin certainly focuses attention on Martin's apparent failure to apply his critique of U.S. singularity to Latin American duality. From Bary's perspective, Martin's ability to see through the facade of U.S. singularity could have resulted in an interrogation of Latin America's duality. Perhaps Latin America isn't so dual, or at least those who argue for this duality should be subjected to deconstructive criticism so that their discursive positioning could be laid bare.

Whereas Martin appeals to authors whom he believes possess an accurate interpretation of Latin America's true identity, Bary looks to those who question the place from which truth claims about identity originate.

Specifically, Bary appeals to Brazilian essayist Angel Rama, Anglo-Irish academic Benedict Anderson, and Cuban anthropologist Fernando Ortiz. These authors introduced three theoretical concepts in the late 1970s and early 1980s that Bary uses to reread Latin American identity. Respectively, these concepts are the *lettered citizen*, *imagined communities*, and *transculturation*.

We will not define these three concepts at length, allowing Bary to do so. Briefly, Rama's discussion of the lettered citizen introduces the idea that people in positions of power possess a disproportionate ability to shape public opinion, but that simply because they are in power does not mean they hold the truth or that they are divorced from discursive influences any more than are people out of power. Anderson's notion of imagined communities contends that nations are cultural constructs rather than ontological essences. Ortiz's argument about transculturation asserts that elites and masses engage in a constant dialogue and that, despite the hegemonic power of the elites, masses inject themselves and their values into the system. Together, these three concepts allow for a different sort of textual analysis. For example, when reading a text like Sarmiento's *Facundo* or Martí's *Our America* we are encouraged to ask how authors construct Latin American identity rather than to what extent they possess knowledge of its true identity. Even if these three concepts do not mention discourse specifically, they invite us to question the discursive influences that shape an author's thinking.

Armed with these three concepts, Bary asks, Whose voice is being represented in the text? Who is speaking on behalf of whom? Which voices are being excluded when the voice in the text is being heard? If an author purports to speak on behalf of all of Latin America, who is still being left out? Do authors' particular views or arguments, even if they look egalitarian on the surface, actually exclude a minority or even a majority of the population? What is the discursive position of these authors? As you read, consider Bary's own words: "A key question is who directs the creation of culture and the production of cultural identity."[4]

An excerpt from Walter Mignolo, an Argentine-born scholar now teaching at Duke University, is also included in this chapter. Like Bary, Mignolo approaches the question of Latin American identity from a semiotic perspective. Rather than believing in the existence of a true and ontological Latin America, Mignolo believes that identities come into existence during the process of defining them. He advocates deconstructing identity claims in order to expose them as constructs. We have chosen Mignolo for a very specific reason: He gives voice to the so-called third way that typifies the

Latin American–based critique of European and U.S. cultural studies traditions, even though he is a well-known and distinguished professor at a prestigious North American university.

Mignolo critiques the notion of European or U.S. singularity by insisting that Western civilization, for all the benefits it has bestowed on the planet, has engaged in colonialism, racism, and genocide. He argues that it is necessary to look at Western civilization from the perspective of the "border," that is, from Latin America, Asia, or Africa, or those places that have been subjected to the darker side of U.S. and European history. This allows for "border thinking," Mignolo's term for a new philosophical tradition that draws upon Western and non-Western perspectives and recognizes the limits and possibilities of both. He also refers to this new way of thinking as "gnosis," a term borrowed from African philosophical traditions.

Reminiscent of Stuart Hall, Mignolo stresses the importance of place and of defining one's place as the starting point for discussing identity. He defines one's place as "local history." It is from the perspective of our local histories, our particular places, he argues, that we are in position to question the assumed truths of large-scale metanarratives—like Western civilization being the source of progress, liberty, and rationality in the world. Mignolo refers to metanarratives of Western superiority as "global designs" and contends that these designs are often imposed on Latin America. Mignolo looks at an alternative historical experience to question the presumed validity of global designs—the three hundred years of Spanish colonialism and the two hundred years of neocolonial endeavors by other European powers and the United States. Mignolo refers to this imperial history as "coloniality."

Like Hall, Mignolo does not privilege or essentialize local history. Instead he posits it as a useful position of criticism. To paraphrase Mignolo's general argument, the perspective of local history allows us to deconstruct global designs and come to a new position of knowledge which resides at the border of the global and the local, which draws upon both and privileges neither.

Mignolo acknowledges the tremendous influence and importance of the theories of postmodernism, poststructuralism, deconstruction, and world systems, among others, that are embodied in the works of Michel Foucault, Jacques Derrida, Jacques Lacan, Roland Barthes, and Immanuel Wallerstein. But he insists that these scholars and the intellectual positions they have spawned fail to take into account the experience of places like Latin America, which is on the border of the global. Therefore, he calls the cultural studies tradition a "Euro-centric critique of Euro-centrism." It is in this regard that Mignolo echoes the Latin Americanist critique of the so-called U.S. school of cultural studies that we have associated with scholars like Daniel Mato. Mignolo insists that his intellectual position resides with Latin American scholars in Latin America and Latino scholars in the United States, such as Enrigue Dussel, Anibel Quijano, Gloria Anzaldúa, and Norma Alarcón, among many others.

Mignolo's work is not commonly read by introductory audiences. He typically assumes that his readers possess much knowledge about both Latin America and theory. But we believe that this particular excerpt is accessible and we have included a number of our own explanatory footnotes in hopes of clarifying his complex terminology and concepts.

GERALD MARTIN, *JOURNEYS THROUGH THE LABYRINTH*[5]
Myth: Father Europe and Mother America Weave Their Labyrinth

Those who journey often over time through Latin American cultural history and its artistic expressions may come gradually to glimpse the outlines of "grand historical narrative" which is effectively the Continent's own dominant self-interpretation and which, in its persistence and coherence through the trajectory of such phenomena as the New Novel, can safely be said to have the dimensions and the relative stability of a great cultural myth [. . .].

The myth, Romantic in origin, Surrealist in focus, rebellious in orientation, is in essence about the relation of the New World to the Old. It tells of discovery and conquest, endlessly reproduced and repeated, and of desperate struggles, usually fruitless, to resist, rebel and liberate, to overcome solitude and attain some kind of collective unity and identity. And it shows how the people's dreams, utopias and occasional triumphs become internalized through folk memory and through art which, sometimes at least, can make itself the written record of that memory, and thus unite past, present and future at the level of representation.

In reality the Latin American myth is merely one version of the great master narrative of Western history: the road to freedom, progress and development through self-realization. Jorge Luis Borges notes in one of his fictions that "the generations of men, throughout recorded time, have always told and retold two stories—that of a lost ship which searches the Mediterranean seas for a dearly loved island, and that of a god who is crucified on Golgotha."[6] The word "men" has rarely been used more ambiguously than here. It includes, fallaciously, "non-Western men," and (as is usual) excludes, through invisibility, "Western women": it is, in short, an innocently imperialist and patriarchal discourse. Still, Borges's reference to the Odyssey and to the Bible, the two great historic transformers of the oral and the experiential into the scriptural and the discursive, is an exact enough encapsulation of a cultural tradition. These two narratives have indeed been essential sources for the metanarratives of Western development (as well as the usual Greek meaning, "meta" also signifies goal or objective in Spanish), currents flowing into the watershed of modernity, one of whose great expressions is Joyce's Ulysses (1922), which draws on both of them. When, after the illusions of the 1960s, the watershed was perceived to be a dam—man-made?—the era of Post-modernism was declared.

The United States, in the north of the New World, was able to carve out its own independent territory within the space of European—now Western—development, and could thus cultivate a self-satisfying foundational myth. Minorities fleeing from oppression had sailed the dangerous seas to freedom, set up small, democratic, God-fearing communities, and followed the sun and their own manifest destiny across a receding frontier from east to west, reluctantly defending themselves against wild animals and savage Indians to whom they had first offered the hand of friendship. Immigrants and their cultures could be simply aggregated to this scheme. One could say, then, changing our metaphors, that the capitalist prow cuts through the surface of reality, simplifying as it goes, but leaving the wash and spray of turmoil and confusion in its wake. Such an experience permits the repeated unfurling of the great myth of progress, the endless frontier, the one identity, the permanent march of capitalism, knowledge and freedom: "man's search to know his world and himself," to quote Daniel J. Boorstin.[7] The fact that this "triumph of the west," to cite another similarly enterprising history, has involved racism, genocide, imperialism, the destruction of nature and the menace of the nuclear shadow, is easy to ignore (except in Faulkner's South), especially since the space age allows the myth another dimension through its literally endless frontier. These are just bad dreams, to be exiled from the garden of a nation that likes to "feel good about itself."

Latin American experience allows no such happy simplicities. In Latin America at the time of the conquest there were not just nomadic Indians, but a complex tapestry of great civilizations (defined, of course, by their conquerors as great organized barbarisms) and smaller cultural groupings, which could not all be moved on or ignored, nor even easily liquidated: besides, the colonization was not a family or community activity but a great state enterprise carried out on behalf of the Crown through the Army and the Church, without ordinary laborers and very largely without women, other than voluntary or involuntary Indian collaborators like Cortés's mistress and interpreter, Malinche. It was said to be a liberation from ignorance, but this was difficult to believe even at the time: there were too many en-slaved survivors of the defeated for ideology to turn completely into myth. Moreover, since Independence in Latin America there has been a plurality of countries which have failed to become a United States of Middle and South America. Progress has been made, but usually for brief periods, errati-cally, sporadically, spasmodically: and hardly ever as a successful collective enterprise but through the efforts of individuals, often tyrants. There was not just one frontier; there were many different ones, sometimes within the fragmented nation states, sometimes across them. Nothing has ever been simple, unified and consistent, except through the ruthless will of some charismatic or authoritarian figure. Otherwise: improvization, intuition, inspiration, spontaneity; or lethargy, original sin, bad blood, sad tropics, sick people, a failure to assimilate and advance, sudden outbursts of vio-lence, devastating continental, national and individual solitude. They had been marooned, isolated, banished, exiled, forgotten, negated, cursed; they were in hell, purgatory, limbo, nowhere: in a state of inferiority, second-class, comic-opera figures, caricatures, mimic men. Could they not es-cape and progress? No, because they were in chaos, darkness, obscurity, unpredictability—unknown and unpredictable even to themselves. When the great liberator Simón Bolívar saw the collapse of his continental vision, he declared: "Those who serve a revolution plough the sea."[8] [. . .]

The complete myth rarely if ever appears—Miguel Angel Asturias's *Men of Maize* (*Hombres de maíz,* 1949) would be one exception—but usually partially, sometimes fragmentarily, and even momentarily, like a forest or a mountain glimpsed through the mist. The basic story is as follows:

Mother America, aboriginal, virgin, fertile, creative and productive—nature's muse—was violated by the Spaniard, the European outsider, cold, rationalistic and covetous, motivated by theories, not experience, by lust and power, not love and understanding. The product of this assault was the illegitimate Mestizo (of mixed blood), the Latin American culture hero. Its effect is felt to this day whenever Latin Americans gaze at the spectacle of their history and ponder their identity: for theirs is not an identity but a du-ality: Indian/Spaniard, female/male, America/Europe, country/city, matter/spirit, barbarism/civilization, nature/culture, and, perhaps most ironic in the context of Latin American fiction, speech/writing. What is the Latin American's origin? Native America in its multiple forms? Renaissance Spain (itself heir to Greece, Rome and Jesus)? Or the moment of violation in 1492? What is her/his future? A "return" to Native America? A "return" to European civilization? Or an acceptance of being for ever a member of a hybrid culture in a non-European continent?

Of course "Europe," including North America, the vanguard of scientific, technological and cultural progress, is still there, although any relation with it has always thus far required the perpetuation of a dependent, neocolonial status for a Latin America still considered new, young and underdeveloped after almost five hundred years. Native America is gone, though Bolívar's "La Patria Grande," now Guevara's socialist America, may still beckon. But Mestizo America, oscillating, crucified between the two poles, remains the constitutive reality. This is not a complementarity but a conflict, an opposition, the variable sign for a real contradiction which determines many others.

Some dualisms are universal and are manipulated—in different ways—by all human societies, usually to range them in interlinking hierarchies which justify the dominant epistemology and prevailing social status quo. The existence of males and females and of day and night, for example, underpins the way in which human beings think about reality and organize their culture. These two oppositions alone account for much of the basic content of mythical thought, as numerous contemporary anthropologists have shown. The key dualism in Latin American culture, however, is unmistakable and has a specific historic point of departure which happens to be a moment of cultural confrontation: between an already existing, known world of "Europe," and a new, recently "discovered" world named "America." Like the Romans before them, the Spanish imperialists defined that which was other as barbarous, and themselves as civilized, through a strategy which has certainly not outlived its usefulness even at this "Post-modern" finale to the twentieth century [. . .].

All these dualisms have journeyed inexorably throughout Latin American history and culture, along the forking paths of race, nation, class and gender, taking up ever new forms and combinations, slipping, superimposing, eliding, metamorphosing, yet somehow—as long as certain kinds of antagonism continue to exist—always reemerging over time in some new and unexpected guise. The myth we are tracing can exist wherever a "civilization" vanquishes a "barbarism" (it could have been written in England soon after the triumph of the Romans, or of William the Conqueror, or in Ireland at any time since the sixteenth century). But only in Latin America, because of the emergence of the Mestizo culture and the enduring nature of the historical contradictions involved in its creation, have these essentialist human, Western and continental dualisms been given the force to create such an enduring historical and literary myth, whose time is not yet past.

Since 1492 the Latin American Mestizo has been forced to abandon the sedentary communities of his native forebears and, dialectically negating the historical mission of crusaders, explorers and conquistadors, has taken to the road in search of his own cultural identity, national expression and continental liberation (heir to Ulysses, Theseus, Prometheus, Dante, Quetzalcoatl). This unended and perhaps endless journey through the labyrinth has woven the myth of Latin America behind it, and, finally, contradictorily, integrated it into the Western culture from which it continues to feel itself alienated. A succession of mainly masculine writers, seeking to impose themselves on the colonized territory of Latin American culture, have found themselves, rather like the Irishman James Joyce, having to retreat to higher ground and to enlist unexpected allies, including natives and women. This is why in Latin American fiction the story is so often inverted and heroic biographies are so frequently underpinned by a mythical origin in virgin, Indian America, and a utopian objective in "La Madre Revolución" and "La Patria Grande." [. . .]

History: The Quest for Identity and the Field of Forking Paths

Given the imposed dualism of Latin America's Mestizo culture, the concept of choices, crossroads, forking paths or alternative destinies is inscribed in the very origin of the new continent. Their persistence explains why it is that the greatest Latin American novels are not just the vehicles of speculation, experimentation or playfulness, but determined explorations of Latin American reality [. . .].

Culture: The Magic Labyrinth

I find myself in a conflict, between the desire to return the confidence you have placed in me and the difficulty of satisfying it, given both the lack of documents and books and my limited knowledge of a country as immense, varied and unknown as this New World. [SIMÓN BOLÍVAR, "THE JAMAICA LETTER," 1815]

It is unusual these days to pick one's way through a literary supplement without coming across some fictional or critical work based implicitly or explicitly upon the concept of the labyrinth. Umberto Eco's *Il pendolo di Foucault* (1988) is only the best known recent example of a novel structured around a paradigm which may, retrospectively, dominate our vision of twentieth-century narrative. In no literature, however, are images of labyrinths as persistent and pervasive as they have been in Latin American literature, not just recently but since the 1920s, and an astonishing number of works which do not even mention the concept nevertheless embody it in their structure or view of the world or both. Is it merely a fashion which has turned into a tradition? Or simply the influence of Jorge Luis Borges (1899–1986), author of the celebrated *Fictions* (*Ficciones*, 1944), who almost patented these concepts in elaborating his own conception of what reading, writing, thinking, and culture are? Or that of Octavio Paz (1914–1998), who has applied the concept archetypally to the question of Latin America's historical identity in his influential *Labyrinth of Solitude* (1950)?[9]

As we have seen, the colonial origin of "Latin" America left its people with a traumatic self-conception whose inherent dualism inevitably heightened the "natural" human tendency to think and advance by means of contrasts, differences, and opposites. Latin America's history can thus be interpreted in retrospect as a field of forking paths, to refashion Borges's influential metaphor ("The Garden of Forking Paths" is one of his best-known stories), with the choice between "Europe" and "America" inaugurating and preordaining a whole series of later choices as the determinants of race, nation, class and gender construct, reconstruct and deconstruct individual and collective identities.

Labyrinths and Mirrors

A labyrinth may be natural or man-made, above or below ground—the Ulyssean or Thesean variants—designed as a puzzle, entertainment, trap or prison. It may be real or imaginary, metaphor, symbol, or myth. It may be essentially symmetrical, or spiral, or have no discernible structure: its outer boundaries may likewise be of any shape. It may have a central focus, or several, which may or may not be at its topographical heart, which may give meaning to the whole, or rather to the journey or journeys which it implies, offers or demands. Most often, perhaps, one associates it with an underground quest, in the darkness, through spiralling corridors, in which one may easily get lost, downwards towards some intimidating centre; nocturnal, the space of our worst dreams but also the arena of our greatest triumphs and discoveries, including—perhaps above all—our identity and the meaning of our life. But then we find ourselves asking: is this an origin and purpose rediscovered or a name conquered for oneself? For Freud, and above all Jung, the labyrinth is, archetypally, uterine, symbolizing a simultaneous longing to return to the maternal origin and fear of regression to the preconscious world of chaos; or, more historically, the site of a journey from a dark, enveloping matriarchal consciousness into the light of knowledge and patriarchal civilization. Needless to say, the problem with this for either a colonized or feminine imagination is that all the signs may have to be reversed if liberation is to be achieved [. . .].

Europe's last labyrinthine moment had been the era of the romance at the end of the Middle Ages. Then, like Latin America after Independence, Europe had been unknown unto itself, and the novels of chivalry charted the quest of European consciousness towards its own reconciliation of individual and collective identity. That discovery coincided with the vanquishing of the East and the discovery of the New World of the West. In the period after the First World War, when Europe again entered a labyrinth—recorded in literature by Joyce and Kafka—from which it has not yet re-emerged, Latin America's historical experience had been inherently labyrinthine for a century, but without the mental tools to think around its contours and without, as yet, the consolation that Europe was in a similar predicament. On the contrary, Europe provided, albeit temporarily, such models of reason as were still available. Thus famous twentieth-century novels like Miguel Angel Asturias's *The President* (1946) or García Márquez's *One Hundred Years Of Solitude* (1967) portray the development of Latin America as a kind of tragicomic caricature of European history, or as a vicious circle, a repetitive nightmare in which the same sins and curses come to haunt the continent and its children through century after century—conquest, murder, violation, illegitimacy, and dictatorship—countered by the redemptive quest for legitimacy and identity and the struggle for liberation, inevitably involving a raising of consciousness, further repression from without and within, and a new round of disillusionment and despair. Little wonder, then, that the labyrinth has become a symbol of Latin American literature which may well stand ultimately for Latin American history itself. García Marquéz has chosen to entitle his new novel on the great Liberator Simón Bolívar "The General in his Labyrinth" ("El general en su laberinto," 1989).

Plots Thicken

Yet somehow there must be a way out. When that way out has been found, Latin Americans will know where they are, who they are, where they have come from and where they are going. They will have escaped from the labyrinth of solitude, have completed the quest for identity: they will be able to look at themselves in the mirror and see what is truly there. What does this involve? Above all, it involves exploration of their own Mestizo culture. As we have seen, the problem for a Latin American, more than for the members of any other major world culture, is that identity is not given: it has to be searched for, discovered or even invented. And it is always twice dual. The most cursory glance at Latin America's typical cultural expressions in the twentieth century would suggest that within each Latin American two mythical beings are always at war, an original Spaniard (or Portuguese, or Frenchman) and an original Indian (or Negro, especially in Brazil, Cuba and Haiti); and beyond this inner conflict, he and she are permanently crucified between their own, already dual America and the external world of Europe (and later North America). A Latin American must face the fact that s/he is both part of and the product of many cultures, but at least two: hence the proliferation of concepts like bi-culturalism, transculturation, the neo-baroque, or Magical Realism, as codes for the social reality and cultural expression of the colonized Mestizo continent—whose project, nonetheless, in the modem era, must surely be that of the truly multicultural and polylingual space.

This only very recently desired outcome—first visible in Asturias's *Men of Maize* (1949)—means choosing a future which is different from the past, maybe even a negation of the past. It means not seeking to impose oneself by violence, not conquering as a means of establishing identity, not repressing the other, weaker part of oneself; possibly even encouraging all the traditions of resistance and rebellion, seeking out the suppressed democratic, cooperative and ecological currents of the culture, seeking to fuse rather than split, to unite rather than separate, because America took the wrong road at the start and must take a different road in the future if the way is to be found. If this is done, the Latin American republics may be better placed to confront the world that is to come than other nations with a willed—rather than inherited—lust for progress through violence.

As we have seen, Latin American reality itself, by the 1920s, was already extraordinarily complicated—twenty separate nation states unified and divided by history and geography and by inextricably interwoven concepts of race, nation, class, gender, and culture. But the problems of decipherment were getting more formidable as they went along. As the Western world itself, in the age of modernity, entered its own twentieth-century maze, Latin Americans were obliged, more than ever before, to understand what we now call the "First" and "Second" Worlds of Europe and North America in order to understand themselves, which implied travelling simultaneously through two superimposed labyrinths without any guide to tell them how to read the signs. For the irresponsible this created an endless playground, a gigantic hall of mirrors in which all paths led to the truth—or none. For the committed avant-garde writer, however, who sought to combine political and aesthetic revolution in the age of cultural Modernism—Joyce and/or Kafka—the challenge was momentous.

As a matter of fact, things were even more complicated than this suggests. What critics complacently call "the labyrinth" (dissolving differences) or "labyrinths" (multiplying differences indefinitely) is really three—among many—different phenomena. First and last, it is an image of "life" (the Borgesian version), that is, the human condition, the eternal perplexity of what some American film-makers like to call "man," condemned to journey perpetually through a time and space odyssey towards death, without ever knowing why. But equally, as we have already seen—and in this case perhaps more decisively—it is also "history" (Paz's variant), however abstractly conceived, and in this instance the history of Latin America, of each of its individual republics and each of their individual inhabitants, and of the relation of each of these to each other and to the rest of the world. The literary debate about the relation of these two categories is interminable. My simple contention is that the greatest novels, in Latin America or elsewhere, attend simultaneously to both dimensions. The quest, then, is for identity, for the meaning of life, oneself, one's culture, nation, continent, in relation to others. The triumph is finding it, defining it, taking possession of it: liberating the labyrinth. The tensions between the verbs I have chosen are self-evident, derive from the dialectic of Latin American history, and help to explain the contradictory dynamism of recent Latin American writing.

LESLIE BARY, "THE SEARCH FOR CULTURAL IDENTITY"[10]
Politics and Culture

The central role given the concept of "culture" in the formation of modern Latin American society will be examined in this chapter. Our texts will demonstrate the importance in Latin American thought of the idea that the region's culture did not develop organically but was—or, according to some, must still be—specifically created. We will see how the imperative, inherited from colonial times, to seek "civilization" and cultural knowledge outside the Latin American continent (an imperative that marks, for instance, the Argentine writer and statesman Domingo Faustino Sarmiento's Facundo), gives way to a complex search for native cultural models. Peruvian intellectuals and political leaders such as Teodoro Valcárcel, Victor Raúl de la Torre, and José Carlos Mariátegui created native models based on Indianness and designed to restore the Indian's place at the center of society. But the most recurrent conceptualization of Latin American identity, of which José Martí and José Vasconcelos are among the best known exponents, posits racial mixture and cultural hybridization as the true bases of Latin American civilization since the beginnings of European colonization [. . .].

Postcolonial intellectuals often theorize autonomous identities for their societies by asserting a radical difference from the culture of their former colonizers, attempting to recover the difference effaced as the "native" culture was suppressed and subjected to European "reason" through the colonial process. This endeavor is always complex because of the changes colonization makes in the structure of "native" society. It is especially difficult in Latin America because the great variety of cultures brought into contact there during the long colonial period formed a heterogeneous culture. The large-scale decimation of indigenous populations and their displacement from the center of society, along with complex patterns of immigration and miscegenation, made it difficult to differentiate between "native" and "foreign." Paradoxically enough, the post-Independence leaders who first framed the debates on national culture were largely members of white, European-educated, colonial elites, who sought the culture they termed "civilization" in European (and particularly French) models. Cultural identity, then, does not emerge as a given, preexisting "essence" but as an arena for struggle. The concept of identity itself needs constant redefinition as the terms that contribute to it—gender, race, class, nation, continent—come into conflict and shift in relation to one another.

Unity and Diversity

The search for cultural identity and the struggle for political and economic autonomy functioned jointly in the endeavor of post-Independence Latin American nations to take control of their own futures. As is well known, however, the post-Independence era brought a continued European economic hegemony and increasing political and economic influence from the United States. In the realm of high culture, many Latin American artists and intellectuals still looked to European models, even after Europe's economic power waned. In response to this lingering legacy of colonialism, the concept of cultural union has often been invoked, even long after Independence was formalized. José Enrique Rodó's essay *Ariel* (1900) was ground-breaking in that it affirmed not only the uniqueness but also the value of Latin American culture. In the 1920s the poet Oswald de Andrade insisted in his *Manifesto Pau-Brasil* ("Brazilwood Manifesto") and *Manifesto Antropófago* ("Cannibal's Manifesto") that his native Brazilian culture is different from, but as valid and as rich as, the European; and Vasconcelos asserted that, since so many cultures have come together in America, it is here that civilization will culminate.

The unity that such nationalist projects presuppose is real, but the imperative to unity elides "an interior diversity which is a more precise definition of the continent." In a context where cultural identity is linked in so many ways to political power, a key question is who directs the creation of culture and the production of cultural identity. Because the Latin American man of letters is, from Independence to the present day, so often also a man of state, the formulations of identity that have gained the greatest measure of power are closely tied to the social reproduction of the elites. In Brazil and Mexico especially, and in other countries as well, cultural identity now often means identification with an officialized national culture. Even such an oppositional construction of culture as Roberto Fernández Retamar's "Calibán" (1971), written in part to contest the elitist implications of Rodó's *Ariel*, supposes a Latin American unanimity which, although it may be necessary as a strategic position, also elides the question of intracontinental difference.

Nevertheless, marginalized social groups affirm particular identities which, in some cases, subvert the ideology of the modern nation-state. In the twentieth century, figures such as the black Cuban poet Nicolás Guillén and the Guatemalan Indian leader Rigoberta Menchú insist on particular minority cultural identities as bases for political action and historical consciousness. These struggles, internal to the nation and continent, although often overshadowed by the search for a cohesive national and continental identity, are increasingly visible today.

Three Theoretical Concepts

We have been discussing the relationship between culture and political power, the production of culture and cultural identity, and the hybrid nature of "Latin American culture." The recurrence of these topics in debates on cultural identity has given rise to the creation of three theoretical concepts, which are now commonly used to ground discussion of modem Latin American culture and society. These are the *lettered city, imagined communities*, and *transculturation*.

In his book on the social role of the Latin American intellectual, *La ciudad letrada* (1984), Angel Rama develops the concept of the "lettered city" to elucidate the relationship between culture and power structures on the continent from the colony to the twentieth century. Briefly, the lettered city is the urban group composed of educated elites who wield pens to execute the will of viceroys and later, postcolonial rulers. According to Rama, it is this group that determines and enforces society's official order. Rama is careful to emphasize the gap between the "lettered" and "real" city, thus underlining the artificiality or the nonorganic nature of the order imposed by the lettered city and revealing the *letrados'* project as the actual production of society, as opposed to the interpretation and codification of an already existing one. One example of the power of this lettered vision is nineteenth- and twentieth-century *indigenista* narrative, which attempts to depict the reality of indigenous peoples to an urban reading public. Written by non-Indians, this type of narrative often corresponds closely to contemporary government policy and anthropological discourse on the Indian. As such, it is very different from, for instance, the real-life testimony of Menchú.

The concept of the lettered city is important as a reminder of the close ties between notions of culture and relations of power and between intellectuals and the state, and of the central role that intellectuals played in shaping post-Independence society and educating the public to identify with their vision. An 1868 essay on national literature by the Mexican novelist and poet Ignacio Altamirano is brilliantly illustrative of this. Altamirano writes that "novels are undoubtedly the genre the public likes best. . . . They are the artifice through which today's best thinkers are reaching the masses with doctrines and ideas that would otherwise be difficult to impart."

Benedict Anderson's study of nationalism, *Imagined Communities* (1983), can help us to see in a more general way how, in fact, the public was brought to identify with the nation. Anderson argues that the modern nation-state (in Latin America and elsewhere) is precisely not an organic but an "imagined" community. By this he means that the consciousness of shared identity and common discourse grounded in that identity which are the bases of nationalist feeling are specifically created, both by historical forces such as the development of print culture, and by ideological interventions such as José de San Martín's 1821 decree that, when Peru's independence had been won from Spain, Native Americans should no longer be called Indians or natives but Peruvians. Anderson emphasizes that identification with a nation cannot be opposed to identification with a "truer" community. Rather, all communities are "imagined," and "communities are to be distinguished, not by their supposed falsity or genuineness, but by the *style* in which they are imagined."

The choice of a style in which to imagine the post-Independence communities was far from obvious, given the heterogeneity of the continent's population and the variety of its cultural roots. The desire for difference from Europe led some nineteenth-century thinkers to see the question of identity in terms of originality. "Aspire to independence of thought," warns the writer and educator Andrés Bello in an 1848 article against the imitation of European philosophies. "Our civilization too will be judged by its works, and if it is seen to copy Europe in a servile manner, what opinion of us will European thinkers have?"

Understandable though it is after centuries of colonialism and in light of the prestige that French thought had in the early days of Independence, this anxiety of imitation is tied to a cultural debate framed in terms of the dichotomies America and Europe, tradition and modernization, and regional and cosmopolitan or "universal" culture. In contrast, thinkers such as Bolívar and Martí abandon the search for a pure (underived) originality, locating "Latin Americanness" instead in the concept of cultural hybridity. "The blood of our citizens is different; let us mix it to unify it," says Bolívar. Martí proudly emphasizes the heterogeneous origins of what he called, in a now-famous phrase, "our half-breed [mestizo] America," and affirms that the diverse continent possesses a "continental soul" and raises its voice in a "hymn of oneness." Yet the concept of hybridization does not resolve the question of cultural identity; it merely points out the arena in which the issue may most fruitfully be discussed. Both Bolívar and Martí assume, for instance, that the hybrid space must be a unified one, and they imply that the process of hybridization must be directed from above.

The concept of transculturation introduced by the Cuban anthropologist Fernando Ortiz provides a much clearer analysis of cultural hybridization. Ortiz argues that, although Latin American intellectuals and elite classes may have attempted to derive their thought from Europe's models and to imitate its cultural forms, Latin America as a whole is something other than a replica of Europe. Most important, he views crosscultural contact and the formation of hybrid cultures as an interactive process in which pressure is exerted from below as well as from above.

Ortiz proposed the term as a more accurate description than "acculturation" of the passage from one culture to another. "Transculturation" refers not only to the acquisition of a new culture but also to the partial loss of a preceding one and, importantly, the activity of the subjects of this process, whom Ortiz's model views not simply as receivers of culture but as creators of new cultural phenomena. It is an ongoing process that engages continuing foreign influence, received either directly or mediated through the capital cities (which have the closest connections to such influence, and in which national policy is made), and the selective appropriation, modification, and assimilation of such influence to a preexisting culture, which does not simply fade away but exerts its own influence on the culture received.

Because of its dynamism—its ability to account for and make use of conflict—the concept of transculturation permits us to see hybrid cultures as something more than a repetition of previous ones, reorganized in the form of harmonious syntheses, homogenizing "melting pots" or aggregate "mosaics." This is especially important since some of the best-known presentations of cultural heterogeneity posit it as a new and utopian unity (the "we Mexicans" of Vasconcelos's *La raza cósmica* or the "we Brazilians" of Andrade's poetic and cultural manifestos), which often functions to enhance state power and, hence, the hegemony of the elites.

WALTER MIGNOLO, *LOCAL HISTORIES, GLOBAL DESIGNS*[11]

I

Thinking from the colonial difference implies thinking from an other place, imagining an other language, arguing from an other logic. The canonical thinkers of the Western canon can no longer provide a starting point for the epistemology that the colonial difference requires. Let me add a new scenario. In Chapter 2 I distinguished postmodern from post-Occidental thinking as a critique of modernity from the interior borders (postmodernism) and from the exterior borders of the modern/colonial world (post-Occidentalism).[12] This observation could be extended to deconstruction (which I explore in Chapter 1) and to world system analysis, which is implied in several of my arguments but is never directly addressed.[13] World system analysis is indeed a critique of Eurocentrism, but a Eurocentric critique of Eurocentrism, like postmodern theories and deconstruction are.[14] In his presidential address to the Fourteenth World Congress of Sociology, [Immanuel] Wallerstein identified six challenges to the social sciences, with four of them more directed in particular to sociology.[15] Two of the challenges are relevant to my argument. One comes from the external borders of the world/colonial system (Abdel-Malek 1981) and could be added to the many instances on which I build my argument.[16] I would like to devote a paragraph here to the challenge of feminist theory. Evelyn Fox Keller, trained as a mathematical biophysicist, Donna J. Haraway, trained as a hominid biologist, and Vandana Shiva, trained in theoretical physics are Wallerstein's examples.[17] There is a remarkable difference between the epistemological critique one encounters in Fox Keller and Donna Haraway—on the one hand, and on Vandana Shiva, on the other. As Wallerstein himself observes, "Vandana Shiva's critique is focused less on scientific methods proper than on the political implications that are drawn from science's position in the cultural hierarchy. She speaks as a woman of the South [i.e., developing world], and thus her critique rejoins that of Abdel-Malek."[18] That is, Abdel-Malek and Vandana Shiva are critiquing epistemology in the social and natural sciences, from the colonial epistemic difference and the experience of subaltern knowledges.[19] Let me complement Wallerstein's examples, which he doesn't push to the limits, with one of my own: Paula Moya's criticism

of postmodern feminist perspective (and, more specifically, of Donna Haraway's appropriation of Chicana's discourse) from a Chicana perspective:

> Within the field of U.S. literary and cultural studies, the institutional-
> ization of a discourse of postmodernism has spawned an approach to
> difference that ironically erases the distinctiveness and relationality
> of difference itself. Typically, postmodernist theorists either internal-
> ize difference so that the individual is herself seen as "fragmented" and
> "contradictory" [. . .] or they attempt to "subvert" difference by show-
> ing that "difference" is merely a discursive illusion. [. . .] In either case,
> postmodernists reinscribe, albeit unintentionally; a kind of universaliz-
> ing sameness (we are all marginal now!) that their celebration of
> "difference" had tried so hard to avoid.[20]

Moya complements her own observation with one from Linda Alcoff, where
she observes that "the rising influence of postmodernism has had a noticeable debilitating effect on the project of empowering women as knowledge
producers, producing a flurry of critical attacks on unproblematized accounts of experience and on identity politics." And Moya adds to this observation that "such critical attacks have served, in conventional theoretical
wisdom, to delegitimize *all* accounts of experience, and to undermine *all*
forms of identity politics—unproblematized or not."[21] I am aligning these
examples with those of Vandana Shiva and Abdel-Malek as far as they are
generated from the colonial difference. Postmodern criticism of modernity
as well as world system analysis is generated from the interior borders of the
system—that is, they provide a Eurocentric critique of Eurocentrism. The
colonial epistemic difference is located some place else, not in the interior-
ity of modernity defined by its imperial conflicts and self-critiqued from a
postmodern perspective. On the contrary, the epistemic colonial difference
emerges in the *exteriority* of the modern/colonial world, and in that particular form of exteriority that comprises the Chicano/as and Latino/as in the
United States a consequence of the national conflicts between Mexico and
the United States, in 1848 and of the imperial conflicts between the United
States and Spain in 1898.[22] However, what is important to underline here is
that the feminist challenges to modern epistemology are as follows: while
postmodern feminists show the limits of "masculine epistemology,"[23]
women of color and Third World feminism[24] show the limits also of "white
epistemology;" of which postmodern feminism critics remain prisoner,[25] as
Moya's critique of Haraway suggests.[26] In Wallerstein's perception, the two
challenges to the social sciences I mention here fall short in understanding

the colonial difference. He perceives the gender critique to epistemology, not its racial component. In the case of Abdel-Malek, Wallerstein perceives a different notion of time beyond the limits of the world system, but he fails to see that Abdel-Malek's elaboration of the differences in the conceptualization of time is, indeed, ingrained in the colonial epistemic difference. *It is the colonial epistemic difference that calls for border thinking.*

II

"As a European, I am especially proud of two breakthroughs for which Europe is responsible, and which seem to be of decisive importance for the future: the formulation of the project of modern science in the seventeenth century; and the promulgation of the ideal of democracy. Europeans live at the intersection of at least two different systems of values—scientific rationality on one side, and collective behavior rationality on the other. This polarity imposed by historical evolution could not but lead to some stress which was to be felt in much European thought. It is of great importance, particularly at present, that we reach a better harmony between the different rationalities involved in sciences, democracy and civilization." So suggests Ilya Prigogine (1986).[27]

If I were European, I would also be proud of *Radio Tarifa,* a musical ensemble from southern Spain whose great impact and creativity reside in the style in which the musicians articulate Spanish with Arabic music memories and stretch themselves from the fourteenth century to today; across the Mediterranean and across the Atlantic. They provide a powerful music whose power emanates from the quality of the musicians, of course, but also and perhaps mainly from the remapping of the colonial difference and transcending it through border thinking. This kind of cultural production is no less relevant for the future of planetary democratic diversity that will no longer rely on the values and credos of the local concept of "democracy" launched in eighteenth-century Europe. The "good" thinking on just social organizations coming from all social knowledges, past and present, South and North, East and West, are as important as the legacies of the European Enlightenment. The same can be said about science. The future of planetary knowledge requires transcending the colonial difference, the pride in the belief in the privilege of some geohistorical locations without looking at the historical conditions making them possible. Transcending the epistemological colonial difference, having in border thinking one way to pursue it, is of the essence once we understand that the splendors of Western sciences go together with its miseries. There is something beyond the dialectics of the Enlightenment that Walter Benjamin thought us to be proud of and that the other members of the Frankfurt School (Adorno, Horkheimmer) had difficulty in understanding.[28] That "something" is a dimension of knowledge beyond the logic of science and the dialectic of the Enlightenment. In the case of Benjamin (but also of Adorno and Horkheimmer), it was the experience of the imperial (internal) difference as it was lived and endured by Jewish communities in the rearticulation of racial-religious differences in the sixteenth century, at the inception of Occidentalism as the imaginary of the modern/colonial world.

The link between knowledge and geohistorical locations was one of the main concerns of this book. As someone who grew up and was educated in Latin America, who had no choice but to internalize the fact that the Americas are a by-product of the modern/colonial world, I recognize, of course, the contribution of science. However, I cannot be proud of it in the same way that Prigogine is because I am not European. And that is another version of Chakrabarty's dilemma.[29] Science, Prigogine is telling me, is not a human achievement but a European one. I suspect, however, that the question is not the distinction in the intelligence of European men who invented science, but the favorable conditions under which they did so. Such conditions were, in large measure, due to the emergence of the Americas in the colonial horizon of modernity, the forced labor of slaves and Amerindians that produced the gold and silver of the American mines and the cotton, sugar, and coffee from the Caribbean that made possible the economical takeoff of Europe and the conditions for intellectual production. I cannot celebrate Prigogine's European pride without thinking of the darker side of the Renaissance and the Enlightenment.[30] But I am certainly proud of the achievement of the "human species" and world civilizations, from ancient to contemporary China; from ancient Mesoamerica and the Andes to contemporary Latin America; from modern to contemporary Europe; from the Muslim world south of the Mediterranean to the complex civilization of India. Regarding the ideals of democracy, I am concerned with the fact that the universal proclamation of democracy was blind to the local histories in which that very proclamation was taking place in relation to almost three hundred years of colonialism and the constitution of the modern/colonial world system. I am concerned in general, about the legitimization of social truth that is not predicated on the responsibilities of those who made the predicament, but on some transcendental value that was supposed to be independent of those who invoked it. Democracy, we all know, was invoked by Pinochet to justify the military coup that dethroned Salvador Allende; was invoked by Stalin on the name of socialism; was constantly named by presidents Ronald Reagan and George Bush as the imponderable spirit that keeps Western civilization alive.

Blindness is not a feature that can be attributed to those living and making local histories engendering and enacting global designs as universal models. Perhaps one of the most salient features of the late eighteenth century in western Europe was the fact that it was projected from hegemonic local histories and embraced by subaltern ones as a model to be imitated. The confluence of the industrial revolution in England with the social revolution in France, together with the powerful philosophical contribution of Kant, Hegel, and Marx, became a desirable model for others, including rising nation-states (e.g., in the Americas), imperial states in decay (e.g., Spain), nations peripheral to the modern/colonial world (e.g., the North Atlantic world), and countries that joined in the standards of civilization at the end of the nineteenth (e.g., China and Japan). Spain is an interesting case for my argument. I would like to quote Leopoldo Zea's description of the situation of Spain at the turn of the eighteenth century vis-à-vis the global order and the interior conflict and borders of the modern/colonial world:

> The first half of the nineteenth century witnessed a constant struggle for liberalism in Spain, which, though repressed again and again, sought to change her into a modern nation. It was a version of liberalism perpetually battling the forces of theocratic Spain and the interests of Western Europe that were turning Spain into a new economic colony for the profit of the West. The liberal struggled in vain to establish a national bourgeoisie, a middle class which, as in Western Europe [e.g., France, England, Germany, Holland], would contribute greatly to the new Spanish nation. [. . .]
>
> What liberalism could no longer do was to carry out the necessary social, political, and economic reforms to transform Spain into a modern nation. In Spain, as in Spanish America during the same period, old privileges remained in force and prevented the establishment of a middle class that might have acted as a springboard for the nation's progress.[31]

There is more to it, however, as Philip Silver has shown in his analysis of Spanish romanticism and intellectuals and their reaction to Napoleon's invasion of Spain at the beginning of the nineteenth century.[32] The Spanish were caught in a double bind: they envisioned a modernization of Spain following (and imitating) the northern (French and English) model, but they could not of course endorse Napoleon's invasion. The decision to imitate and to bring Spain at the level of France was their decision, not Napoleon's. Thus caught in between a foreign invasion and the theocratic forces of Spain's past, Spanish intellectuals at the beginning of the nineteenth century faced a different dilemma than Spanish American postcolonial intellectuals during the same period.

Esteban Echeverría, a postindependence ideologue in Argentina, bought into the same idea and embraced "democracy" as defined in France. He did not spend much time either in thinking about the colonial difference and how it shaped the local histories of France in Europe and Argentina in Spanish America nor to the two hundred years of imperial conflicts in the North Atlantic that preceded the French Revolution. Born and educated in Latin America, I am concerned with the ideological presuppositions of Prigogine's remarks in which the colonial difference is once more reproduced, the colonial side of modernity obscured, and the contribution of other local histories around the planet ignored. Asians, Africans, and (Latin) Americans shall not feel less proud than Prigogine for having made it this far in the history of the universe, of life on earth. However, the imaginary of the modern/colonial world is such that Prigogine's remarks are made out of a "natural" belief and as a "natural" development of universal history.[33] Cosmopolitanism cannot be achieved by insisting on continental pride forged by the history of the modern/colonial world system. Nativism or regionalism from the center is as pernicious as nativism or regionalism from the periphery. Border thinking, as an intellectual and political project, calls attention to the fact that achievements located in Europe (and, not in Africa, Asia, or [Latin] America) are a historical consequence of the formation and transformation of the modern/colonial world. I shall not repeat here what crossed the Atlantic from east to west while the general belief was that civilization was west to east. Neither shall I mention again the slave trade, paradoxically following the same geographical direction as the spread of civilization, from East to West.

The epistemological potential of border thinking is to contribute to Dussel's call to move beyond Eurocentrism, recognizing the achievements and revealing the conditions for the geopolitics of knowledge in the modern/colonial world—recognizing and revealing the coloniality of power imbedded in the geopolitic of knowledge.[34] As someone who was educated and lived in (Latin) America half of his present life span and relocated in (Anglo) America, after a three-year intermission in France, I am proud (echoing Prigogine) of the Haitian Revolution. I am proud because it showed the limits of liberal democracy a few years after its very promulgation and was locally based on the experiences of a "new" European order in which France, England,

Holland, and Germany were displacing and replacing previous imperial orders. More recently, almost two hundred years after the Haitian Revolution and its "natural" failure,[35] the Zapatistas [in Chiapas State in southern Mexico] are again showing the limits of democracy in its regional eighteenth-century definition and recasting it based on the five hundred years of particular local histories in the Americas.[36] "Democracy" was taken off the domain of global designs and reconverted to the needs of Chiapas's local history where indigenous and Western wisdom interact—where the colonial difference is being addressed and border thinking enacted. Government of the people, by the people, for the people has next to it today another dictum: "To rule and at the same time obeying."[37] If "democracy" as a word is the place of encounter from Pinochet to the Zapatistas and to Prigogine, one should not waste time trying to define it by finding its universal (or perhaps transcendental) meaning. Instead, one could think of putting all the people and communities claiming democracy in a domain of interaction where social organization will be made out of the decisions and understandings of all of them. The management of democracy by those who hold power and the right interpretation of the word will not solve the problem of democratic societies held together by the persuasive language and seduction of arms. New ways of thinking are required that, transcending the colonial difference, could be built on the borders of competing cosmologies whose current articulation is due in no small part to the coloniality of power imbedded in the making of the modern/colonial world [. . .].

IV

Since colonial discourse established itself in the constant and charged construction of hierarchical oppositions, deconstructing colonial discourse is indeed a necessary task. There is, however, another related task that goes beyond the analysis and deconstruction of colonial discourse and the principle of Western metaphysics underlining it. I am referring here to the colonial difference, the intersection between Western metaphysics and the multiple non-Western principles governing modes of thinking of local histories that have been entering in contact and conflict with Western thoughts in the past five hundred years in the Americas, and in the past two hundred years in India from where Garg thinks and projects the culture of transience.[38] The Sun and the Moon, in Amerindian categories of thought are not opposite, contrary, or contradictory; they are complementary. To extend deconstruction beyond Western metaphysics or to assume that there is nothing else than Western metaphysics will be a move similar to colonizing global designs under the belief of the pretense of the improvement of humanity if we can make them all like us. Grammatology and deconstruction have vis-à-vis the colonial experience the same limitations as Marxism vis-à-vis race and indigenous communities in the colonized world: the colonial difference is invisible to them.[39] Decolonization should be thought of as complementary to deconstruction and border thinking, complementary to the "double séance" within the experience and sensibilities of the coloniality of power.[40]

Double consciousness, double critique, an other tongue, an other thinking, new mestiza consciousness, Creolization, transculturation, and culture of transience become the needed categories to undo the subalternization of knowledge and to look for ways of thinking beyond the categories of Western thought from metaphysics to philosophy to science.[41] The projects of Edward Said, Gayatri Spivak, and Homi Bhabha, in the past twenty years, have been instrumental for a critique of subalternization of knowledge. Said showed through Michel Foucault the construction of the Orient as a discursive formation; Bhabha described through Lacan the hybridity and the third space of colonial discourse; Spivak pushed the deconstruction of colonial discourse through Derrida.[42] However, beyond these conceptual genealogies where the postcolonial emerges, piggybacking on postmodern or poststructuralist theories, there were also emerging in a parallel fashion similar manifestations of border thinking, which I have explored in this book, attached to particular *places* resulting from and produced by local modern/colonial histories. My own conceptualization, in this book, followed the move made by Said, Bhabha, and Spivak, but is based on the work of Wallerstein, an (Anglo) American sociologist rather than French philosophers or psychoanalysts. But I have also departed from Wallerstein by introducing the colonial difference and the coloniality of power and thus linking my work with that of Anibal Quijano in Peru and Enrique Dussel in Argentina and Mexico, both active since the late 1960s and early 1970s—about the same years that Wallerstein, Foucault, Derrida, and Lacan were producing their intellectual impact.[43] One of the reasons, and not a trivial one, of my decision to follow Wallerstein and then move to Quijano and Dussel was my need to go beyond the eighteenth century and the Enlightenment, which is the reference and starting point of poststructuralist and early postcolonial theorizing. I needed the sixteenth century and the Renaissance, the emergence of the Americas in the colonial horizon of modernity, a local history out of which Quijano, Dussel, Anzaldúa, and myself (among many others, of course) are made.[44] What I needed to argue for was a way of thinking in and from the borders of the colonial differences in the modern/colonial world: the borders between enacting and desiring global designs; the borders between transforming received global designs into local projects; the borders between subaltern and hegemonic knowledges reart-iculated from the perspective of the subalterns.

Where is then border thinking located, in terms disciplines? Philosophy, because I claimed gnoseology, epistemology, and hermeneutics? Sociology, because I located it in the external borders of the modern/colonial world? History, because my argument was built historically and from the perspec-tive of coloniality? Anthropology, because I dealt with issues that have been the province of anthropology, which is the closer discipline to the colonial difference? Cultural studies, because it is none of the above? I would say that the transdisciplinary dimension of border thinking is cultural critique in the precise sense that Stuart Hall defines cultural studies, as trans-disciplinary and trans-national: "In a sense, if there is anything to be learnt from British cultural studies, it's the insistence that cultural studies is always about the articulation—in different context of course—between culture and power. I am speaking in terms of the epistemological formation of the field, not in the sense of practicing cultural studies."[45]

V

There are indeed remarkable differences between Western civilization, Oc-cidentalism, and modern/colonial world system. Western civilization is neither a synonym for Occidentalism, nor for modern/colonial world sys-tem. Western civilization is supposed to be something "grounded" in Greek history as is also Western metaphysics. This reading, implicit in the Renais-sance, became explicit in the Enlightenment. Occidentalism is basically the master metaphor of colonial discourse since the sixteenth century and spe-cifically in relation to the inclusion of the Americas as part and margin of the West. It is an ambiguous metaphor in the sense that from the sixteenth century up to the Enlightenment, America has had an ambiguous role in colonial discourse. On the one hand it was portrayed and conceived as the daughter and inheritor of Europe, thus its future. On the other, as daughter and inheritor, it occupied a subaltern position in the geopolitics of knowl-edge and in the coloniality of power: the Americas, from the point of view of European intellectuals and until post–World War II, was the subaltern same. There is certainly another parallel story here, which is the relocation of the Americas (Spanish and Anglo) after 1848 and 1898. But this process seemed to have been bypassed (perhaps with the exception of Tocqueville) by the European intelligentsia. The situation was further complicated by the fact that in the rearticulation of the geopolitics of colonial power, Amerindians and Afro-Americans, with all their diversity in the Americas, were left out of the picture of an updated Occidentalism.

Western civilization was not (could not have been) yet conceived as a cultural entity in the fifteenth century. There Christendom was located in something as ill-defined as Europe (Tawantinsuyu or Anahuac were ill-defined at the same time), the land of Western Christians (in a sense, the land of Japhet).[46] On the other hand *it was precisely the imaginary of the modern/colonial world that began to build on the idea of Western civilization without which there would not (could not) have been a modern/colonial world system.* Thus the imaginary of the modern/colonial world was the location for the grounding of the very idea of Western civilization. *I call Occidentalism, then, the Western version of Western civilization (its own self-description) ingrained in the imaginary of the modern/colonial world.* The idea of Western civilization, Western metaphysics, Western logocentrism, and the like is a consequence and necessity of the modern/colonial world as the modern/colonial world was articulated in the growing imaginary of Western civilization, and so on. It is indeed interesting to note that Derrida's *De la grammatologie [On Grammatology]* (1967) left blank the moment in which the very idea of Western civilization and Western metaphysics became the seeds of the overarching imaginary of the modern/colonial world system.

De la grammatologie (1967) has three exerges: one from ancient times and the writing of the people (*l'écriture du peuple* [EP]), the second from Rousseau, and the third from Hegel. There is nothing in between in this diagram of universal history from ancient Greece to modern France and Germany—nothing in between and nothing on the side, in the space of parallel geohistorical configurations, from the east to the northwest of the Mediterranean; from the Indian to the Pacific Ocean; from the Mediterranean to the Atlantic in the sixteenth century. Now I am not suggesting that this frame shall be corrected in the name of the truth of universal history. I am just saying that for Derrida, Rousseau and Hegel are the references of "modern" times, whereas for Quijano, Dussel, Marmon Silko, and myself, universal history has a different reference: the five hundred years summarized in Marmon Silko's historical map (see my introduction).[47] This is one of the silenced, paralleled, and interconnected histories left on the side because of the blindness to the colonial difference.

And certainly there is more, much more. From the perspective of China and Japan there are other histories and variegated perspectives on the colonial difference. But the colonial difference is there, hiding most of the time the interaction of China and Japan with the modern/colonial (North Atlantic) world. There is also the history of Islam and the Arabic countries after the sixteenth century articulating a zone of violent conflicts. And, of course, it is not just the "history" I am talking about here. I am talking about "knowledges" hidden under the reproduction of Western civilization and Western metaphysics. All those stories are tangential to Western metaphysics; Western metaphysics is tangential to them. The coloniality of power and the colonial difference are what link them in problematic and conflictive ways. If they are outside of Western metaphysics, such a statement could only be meaningful from the hegemony of the coloniality of power, not from the local histories for which Western metaphysics is not a totality but a global design. It is precisely the coming into being of a historical and critical consciousness of both the global scope of Western metaphysics as an instrument of colonization (from religion to reason), and the knowledges subalternized by it, that brings to the foreground the awareness of the borders and of border thinking. There is nothing outside of totality, of course, but totality is always projected from a given local history. Therefore, there is nothing outside the totality of a given local history other than other local histories perhaps producing either alternative totalities or an alternative to totality. A nonontological cosmology, as Amerindian's cosmologies illustrate from the sixteenth to the end of the twentieth century, is an alternative to Western ontological cosmology as the grounding of totality (be it Christian faith or secular reason). The interesting aspect of all of this is how such imaginary, which is part of the history of the modern/colonial world system itself, justified economic decisions, public policy designs and implementations, wars and other forms of control, exploitation, and the management of peoples [. . .].

VIII

Once upon a time I was convinced that there is no such a thing as "inside and outside."[48] I still hear today such a statement, in which I no longer believe. I am not saying, of course, that "there are" inside and outside, but that neither of such proposition holds water and that both are supported by the same epistemological presupposition: that a referential assertion can be made regarding the world and that assertions can be judged by their true referential value. I understand that the assertion "there is no such a thing like inside and outside" has another admonition. The question is not whether such a "thing" exists or doesn't exist. To say that "there is an inside and outside" is as absurd as to say that there is not. For who can tell us really which one is true beyond God? On the other hand, both propositions—as I just stated them—are supported in a very questionable principle: that it is possible to assert what really is or is not. What I do seriously believe is that what "is" is someone asserting what there "is." The undeniable fact is the assertion itself, whether or not the content of the assertion corresponds to what the assertion asserts. I do believe, consequently, that the glass is indeed half full as it is half empty.

However, there is another caution to the assertion that "there is no such a thing as inside and outside." What the proposition asserts is that we should eliminate dichotomies from our vocabulary. And in this principle I do believe, since colonial discourse was one of the most powerful strategies in the imaginary of the modern/colonial world system for producing dichotomies that justified the will to power. Historically, that is that. It is fine with me to assert that there is no inside and outside, out there in the world. It is fine for me to eliminate dichotomies, or at least to try. What is more difficult to achieve is forgetting or eliminating the historical dichotomies that colonial discourse and epistemology imposed upon the world by inventing colonial differences.

I am not so much interested here in a logical as I am in pursuing a historical argument. If you talk about interior and exterior borders (e.g., exteriority) in the modern/colonial world system, you are in some ways presupposing that there is indeed an outside and an inside. If you assert, furthermore, that "Occident" is the overarching metaphor of the modern/colonial world imaginary, you are somewhat asserting that "Occident" defines the interior while you are also presupposing that there is an exterior, whatever that exterior may be. Of course, you can say that the "totality" is the sum of the interior and the exterior of the system and, therefore, there is no outside of the totality. That is fine, but it is historically dangerous and irrelevant. Historically, and in the modern/colonial world, the borders have been set by the coloniality of power versus colonial difference.

Historically, and in the frame of the modern/colonial world system, I hear today assertions equivalent to the logico metaphysical "there is no outside and inside." It so happens that such an assertion is pronounced by colleagues who are clearly placing themselves "inside" and, by so doing, being oblivious to the "outside." I have heard, on the other hand, colleagues (more clearly colleagues in some corner of the Third World) who do believe in the inside/outside distinctions. Now, one could explain this fact by saying that, it is unfortunate, but they are theoretically behind, underdeveloped, as they do not know yet that the last discovery in the humanities in the metropolitan research centers is that truly there is no such thing as inside and outside. It would be nice to have such an explanation, except that it counters the facts. Colleagues in the Third World asserting vehemently the distinction between inside and outside (which is made in the form of center and periphery, or center and margin, or First and Third World) are the ones who are most theoretically sophisticated and "developed." I also know colleagues in the Third World who will no doubt emphatically assert that there is no inside and outside. It may be that they are the less theoretically sophisticated and the most intellectually colonized, repeating and rehearsing dominant propositions coming from an academic avant-garde intelligentsia, and responding to local histories "interior" to the modern/colonial world.

Inside and outside, center and periphery are double metaphors that are more telling about the loci of enunciation than to the ontology of the world. There are and there aren't inside and outside, center and periphery. What really is is the saying of agents affirming or denying these oppositions within the coloniality of power, the subalternization of knowledge, and the colonial difference. The last horizon of border thinking is not only working toward a critique of colonial categories; it is also working toward redressing the subalternization of knowledges and the coloniality of power. It also points toward a new way of thinking in which dichotomies can be replaced by the complementarity of apparently contradictory terms. Border thinking could open up the doors to an other tongue, an other thinking, an other logic superseding the long history of the modern/colonial world, the coloniality of power, the subalternization of knowledges and the colonial difference.

DISCUSSION QUESTIONS

• What does Martin mean by singular and dual identities? And why is the United States singular and Latin America dual?

• We have argued that Martin adopts an essentialist approach by accepting Latin America as having a dual identity. After reading Martin's ideas in his own words, is it possible that his position is ambiguous, and that he is simply revealing what Latin American authors have argued rather than advocating a specific position?

• What role does Martin see literature playing in the issue of identity? Does it simply reveal or does it actively construct identity?

• Does Bary ever try to define Latin America?

• Bary and Martin mention many of the same authors. How do their interpretations differ?

• Bary mentions some authors that Martin does not, such as Rigoberta Menchú and the Cuban poet Nicolás Guillén. How do Bary's references to these authors challenge Martin's essentialism?

• Neither Bary nor any of the authors to whom Bary appeals mention the concept of discourse. So, how is Bary's interpretive approach semiotic rather than essentialist? How does it encourage us to reread texts by looking for discursive influence?

• How does Mignolo use the issue of gender to critique cultural theory and promote his argument for a critical-theory perspective that lies "outside" Western civilization, or the "modernity/coloniality" enterprise? Do you see the resemblance between Mignolo's use of gender and the example of gender we used in the introduction to this book to show how cultural theory's decentering of the self might disempower women, even though, ironically, feminist criticism was a powerful impetus behind its development?

• How would Mignolo respond to Martin and Bary? Pay particular attention to the authors' examination of the relationship between discourse and power.

• What concrete examples of Mignolo's theories have we already presented? Think for instance of examples within contemporary U.S. academia given by Daniel Mato as cited in our introduction. What examples can you come up with on your own?

• How does Mignolo's proposal of "border thinking" represent a sort of third way between essentialist hermeneutics and radical cultural-theory decentering? How does his perspective acknowledge the gains of the West as well as its flaws without taking a singularly defensive stance of Latin America? Think of Mignolo's statement that "nativism or regionalism from the center is as pernicious as nativism or regionalism from the periphery." Think also of another one of his statements: "I do believe, consequently, that the glass is indeed half full as it is half empty."

• How does Mignolo draw upon the specific and concrete historical experience of Latin America to develop his concept of "border thinking" and its critique of Western society's colonialist framework? Think of his repeated references to slavery, the colonial era in Latin America, the Haitian revolution, and so forth.

• How is the scientific revolution of the seventeenth century related to the colonial experience? In what ways does Mignolo critique the scientific revolution? Describe how Mignolo's argument represents a challenge to the discourse of the scientific revolution, the way the scientific revolution is still presented today, and the way this affects how the West views the developing world.

NOTES

1. Gerald Martin, *Journeys Through the Labyrinth: Latin American Fiction in the Twentieth Century* (London: Verso, 1989) 10.

2. Martin 9.

3. Leslie Bary, "The Search for Cultural Identity: Concepts," ed. John

Chasteen and Joseph Tulchin, *Problems in Latin American History: A Reader* (Wilmington: Scholarly Resources, 1994) 170.

4. Bary 171.

5. Excerpt is drawn from 8–13, 25–29.

6. Jorge Luis Borges, "The Gospel According to Mark," trans. N. T. de Giovanni, *Doctor Brodie's Report* (London: Allen Lane, 1974) 19.

7. Daniel J. Boorstin, *The Discoverers: A History of Man's Search to Know His World and Himself* (New York: Random House, 1983).

8. Simón Bolívar, "Letter to General Flores," trans. Gerald Martin, *Doctrina del Libertador* (Caracas: Ayacucho, 1976) 321.

9. Martin's book was published nine years before Paz's death, so we have added this information.

10. This excerpt is drawn from 169–174.

11. Walter Mignolo, *Local Histories/Global Design: Coloniality, Subaltern Knowledges and Border Thinking* (Princeton: Princeton UP, 2000). This excerpt is from 313–319, 326–329, 337–338. He is the William H. Wannamaker Professor of Literature and Romance Studies at Duke University. See his Web page at <http://fds.duke.edu/db/aas/Romance/faculty/wmignolo>.

12. The issue of interior and exterior lay at the center of Mignolo's argumentative framework. What is interior is from within Western civilization; what is exterior, from areas located outside the so-called borders of the West, like Latin America, Africa, or Asia. Mignolo insists that modern Western civilization cannot be understood without taking into account its history of colonialism (both the initial phase starting in the late 1400s and that starting in the late 1880s) and all its attendant horrors, such as slavery and forced labor. He uses the term *modern/colonial* to describe this linked history of colonialism and modernity. He will also use Occidentalism to express the same idea, and post-Occidentalism to define recent theoretical perspectives, such as his own, which acknowledge the relationship between colonialism and modernity. Ultimately, Mignolo will challenge the validity of this dichotomy between interior and exterior as part of his search for an alternative kind of border thinking that acknowledges the benefits and failures of both the West and the non-West.

13. "World system" refers to the argumentative framework put forth by the North American sociologist Immanuel Wallerstein in the 1970s and 1980s. Wallerstein developed a model for interpreting world history that placed colonialism and European/North American imperial activities at the center of the story. He argued that Western development was made possible by exploiting the natural and human resources of Latin America, Africa, and Asia. In other words, development and underdevelopment in world history are causally related. Mignolo draws upon Wallerstein's arguments, but then goes beyond them because he believes Wallerstein did not incorporate an argumentative perspective from the periphery. Wallerstein criticized Western civilization from within Western civilization, whereas Mignolo is looking for an alterative perspective. See Immanuel Wallerstein, *The Modern World System: Capitalist Agriculture and the Origins of the European World-Economy in the Sixteenth Century* (New York: Academic,

1974); *The Modern World System II: Mercantilism and the Consolidation of the European World-Economy, 1600–1750* (London: Academic, 1980); and *The Modern World System III: The Second Era of Great Expansion of the Capitalist World-Economy, 1730–1840s* (London: Academic, 1989).

14. Mignolo cites one of Wallerstein's later works here: "Eurocentrism and Its Avatars: The Dilemmas of Social Science," *New Left Review* 226 (1997): 93–107.

15. Immanuel Wallerstein, "The Heritage of Sociology, the Promise of Social Science," Presidential address, XIVth World Congress of Sociology, Montreal, 26 July 1998.

16. Anouar Abdel-Malek, *Social Dialectics*, vol. 1: *Civilizations and Social Theory* (London: Macmillan, 1981).

17. Vandana Shiva, ed., *Biodiversity Conservation: Whose Resource? Whose Knowledge?* (New Delhi: Indian National Trust for Art and Cultural Heritage, 1994); Vandana Shiva and M. Mies, eds., *Ecofeminism* (New Delhi: Kaly for Women, 1993); Immanuel Wallerstein, "The Rise and Future Demise of World-Systems Analysis," *Review* 21:1 (1998): 103–112.

18. Wallerstein, "Rise and Future Demise," 42.

19. The term *subaltern* draws upon theories that emerged in the 1980s and 1990s, largely from India. Subaltern refers to those people excluded from or repressed by the centers of power, such as the billions of impoverished people living in Latin America, Africa, and Asia whose lives have been largely controlled by Western economic and political systems, colonialism, and slavery. It often refers to the system of neoliberal globalism. *Subaltern* is also used in more local settings, for example, to refer to workers in a factory struggling against their bosses or members of a poor village struggling against governmental authorities. For a specific, albeit advanced, discussion of subaltern studies in Latin America, see Ileana Rodríguez, ed., *The Latin American Subaltern Studies Reader* (Durham: Duke UP, 2001).

20. Paula Moya, "Postmodernism, 'Realism,' and the Politics of Identity: Cherríe Moraga and Chicana Feminism," ed. Chandra Talpade Mohanty and M. J. Alexander, *Feminist Genealogies, Colonial Legacies, Democratic Futures* (New York: Routledge, 1997) 125–150. The extract is from 126.

21. Moya 27; Linda Alcoff, "The Elimination of Experience in Feminist Theory," paper presented at the Women's Studies Symposium, Cornell University, 3 Feb. 1995.

22. Mignolo consistently revisits 1848 and 1898 as dates that defined the relations of power in the Western Hemisphere. The first refers to the end of the U.S.-Mexican War (1846–1848), which resulted in the annexation by the United States of large portions of Mexican national territory, now much of the Southwest. In 1898 the United States defeated Spain in the Spanish-American War and assumed control of its last colonial possessions, Cuba and Puerto Rico, the Philippines, and Guam. The defeat of Spain is often thought of as the moment the United States emerged as a dominant military power. Mignolo also refers here to Chicanos (Mexican Americans) and other Latinos who, he says, represent a sort of exterior perspective. He is arguing that certain minority groups in the United States are "subalternized," like people

living in Latin America, Africa, or Asia. They experience the power and repression of a society dominated by a Western-centric (Occidentalist) framework that effectively excludes them from the centers of power (the interior).

23. Sandra Harding, *Is Science Multicultural? Postcolonialism, Feminisms, and Epistemologies* (Bloomington: Indiana UP, 1998).

24. T. Mohanty, A. Russo, and L. Torres, eds., *Third World Women and the Politics of Feminism* (Bloomington: Indiana UP, 1991).

25. Harding, *Is Science Multicultural*; Donna Haraway, *ModestWitness@ FemaleMan_Meets_OncoMouse: Feminism and Technoscience* (New York: Routledge, 1998).

26. Moya.

27. Ilya Prigogine, "Science, Civilization and Democracy: Values, Systems, Structures and Affinities," *Futures* 18:4 (1986): 493–507.

28. The Frankfurt school refers to the group of scholars associated with the Frankfurt Institute for Social Research in Germany, which opened in 1924. Many of the earliest members of the school are also some of its most widely recognized figures, including Max Horkheimer, Theodor Adorno, Herbert Marcuse, Erich Fromm, and Walter Benjamin. In the post-WWII era, the Frankfurt school is most commonly associated with the work of Jürgen Habermas. In its initial stages, the work emerging from the school tended to be Marxist in orientation but often with highly sophisticated rereadings and reinterpretations of Marxist theory. In later years, Habermas addressed the issue of postmodernism, and although he often seemed to embrace many of its basic tenets, he remained solidly situated in a modernist framework, contending that modernity could indeed achieve its objective of bettering the human condition. Mignolo is critiquing the Frankfurt scholars for failing to take into account the central issue of colonialism in their intellectual endeavors. He says that they remained wedded to looking at Western civilization from within and that whatever criticisms they directed against Western civilization were based on its repression of internal minorities, like Jewish people.

29. Dipesh Chakrabarty, "Provincializing Europe: Postcoloniality and the Critique of History: Who Speaks for 'Indian' Pasts?" *Representations* 37 (1992): 1–26.

30. Mignolo is referring here to the title of his book, *The Darker Side of the Renaissance: Literacy, Territoriality and Colonization* (Ann Arbor: U of Michigan P, 1995).

31. Leopoldo Zea, *The Role of the Americas in History* (1957; Westfield, NJ: Rowman & Littlefield, 1992), 129.

32. Philip Silver, *Ruin and Restitution: Reinterpreting Romanticism in Spain* (Nashville, TN: Vanderbilt UP, 1997) 3–41.

33. Mignolo uses *imaginary* to refer to Western civilization's sense of itself. By "the imaginary of the modern/colonial world," Mignolo means that colonialism has played a central role in providing Western society's sense of its own identity. By "natural belief" and "universal history" he means that Western society has used modernist/scientific principles to promote its definitions of self and others (i.e., the developing countries). The West

therefore claims its vision of the world to be undeniably true, thus justifying its actions in the world and imposing a powerful discursive framework, or metanarrative, of Western progress upon non-Western regions. Mignolo immediately challenges this Western self-identity as failing to acknowledge the repressive horrors that define colonialism and slavery.

34. Mignolo's repeated appeals to Dussel refer to the Argentine/Mexican scholar Enrique Dussel (1934–), who has challenged Western civilization's sense of modernity and self-identity. One of the more readily available and accessible examples of Dussel's work in English is "Eurocentrism and Modernity (Introduction to the Frankfurt Lectures)," ed. John Beverley, José Oviedo, and Michael Aronna, *The Postmodernism Debate in Latin America* (Durham: Duke UP, 1995) 65–76.

35. Michel-Rolph Trouillot, *Silencing the Past: Power and the Production of History* (Boston: Beacon Press, 1995).

36. Here Mignolo is referring to the Zapatista uprising in Mexico's southern state of Chiapas. The uprising began in January 1994 when the rebels, mostly Mayan Indians, occupied a half-dozen cities in San Cristóbal de las Casas. Since then, the Mexican government has surrounded Zapatista strongholds and launched a low-intensity warfare that relies on local conflicts and paramilitary attacks to try to drain support away from the Zapatista cause. The Zapatistas have responded by further entrenching themselves in autonomous municipalities and demanding to be left alone by the government. Available studies on the Zapatistas and the uprising are becoming quite extensive, but one that provides a historical overview is Nicholas Higgins, *Understanding the Chiapas Rebellion: Modernist Visions and the Invisible Indian* (Austin: U of Texas P, 2004).

37. Here Mignolo is referring to brief studies of Chiapas by Dussel and himself. Enrique Dussel, "Ethical Sense of the 1994 Maya Rebellion in Chiapas," *Journal of Hispano-Latino-Theology* 2:3 (1995): 41–56; Walter Mignolo, "The Zapatista's Theoretical Revolution: Its Epistemic, Ethic and Historical Consequences," Keynote address to the 31st CEMERS conference, "Comparative Colonialisms: Preindustrial Colonial Intersections in Global Perspectives," 31 Oct.–1 Nov. 1997.

38. Pulin Garg and Indira Parikh, *Crossroads of Culture: A Study in the Culture of Transience* (New Delhi: Sage, 1995).

39. *Grammatology* refers to Jacques Derrida's poststructuralist approach to language, also known as deconstruction. Derrida published *Of Grammatology* in 1967. Mignolo is arguing that postmodernists/poststructuralists like Derrida have ignored the colonial reality in formulating their theories, similar to the way Karl Marx subsumed issues of ethnicity to that of class.

40. *Double séance* basically refers to Derrida's strategy of deconstruction, and the cultural theory argument that a piece of writing often operates at multiple levels, containing many hidden, discursively constituted meanings. Mignolo is arguing that colonialism rests upon binary oppositions/ hierarchies, such as white supremacy and the superiority of Western civilization over all others, that often go unspoken. In other words, Western writers and policy makers simply assume them to be true and therefore do

not feel the need to necessarily acknowledge the issues repeatedly. This was the basic premise of Edward Said's argument in *Orientalism*.

41. Mignolo is using this amalgamation of terms to draw upon a variety of intellectual traditions that he sees as challenging standard Western-centric ideology. When he calls for the undoing of "the subalternization of knowledge," he is not opposing those people he previously defined as subaltern, i.e., Latin Americans, Africans, and Asians. He wants to overturn the hierarchical intellectual systems that define ideas coming out of subaltern regions as being lesser than those emerging from the metropolitan (i.e., Western) centers.

42. Bhabha refers to Homi Bhabha (1949–), the Indian scholar who is identified as a key intellectual figure in the field of postcolonialism. He has spent most of his professional life in England and the United States. See his *Nation and Narration* (New York: Routledge, 1990) and *The Location of Culture* (New York: Routledge, 1994). Gayatri Spivak (1942–) is another Indian-born scholar who also has spent most of her professional life in the United States and written extensively in cultural theory and post-colonialism. She is one of the founding figures of subaltern studies. See Donna Landry and Gerald MacLean, eds., *The Spivak Reader* (New York: Routledge, 1996).

43. Anibal Quijano is a professor of sociology at SUNY Binghamton, where Immanuel Wallerstein has spent much of his professional career. Quijano was educated in Chile and Peru and has spent most of her professional life in Latin American universities.

44. Gloria Evangelia Anzaldúa (1942–2004), was a Chicana lesbian, feminist theorist, poet, and writer. Her *Borderlands/La Frontera: The New Mestiza* (San Francisco: Spinsters/Aunt Lute, 1987) combines poetry, memoir, and historical analysis. Anzaldúa is a foundational figure in the development of *mestiza* consciousness and the notion of borderland studies.

45. D. Morley and K. H. Chen, (eds.), *Stuart Hall: Critical Dialogues in Cultural Studies* (New York: Routledge, 1992) 395.

46. The Tawantinsuyu and Anahuac are indigenous peoples in Peru.

47. Leslie Marmon Silko, (1948–) is a Native American writer born and raised on a New Mexican Indian reservation. Marmon Silko's map that Mignolo refers to appears in the front of the book from which this excerpt is drawn (p. 25). It is a sort of spatial redrawing of the U.S.-Mexican border that takes into account its complex, multiethnic history.

48. This is where Mignolo returns to the issue of interior and exterior. Mignolo is addressing the complexity of his desire to break down such dichotomies in order to create a more genuinely egalitarian space where Westerners and non-Westerners can exchange ideas in an open environment. Yet, he also recognizes the reality that unequal opportunities define the difference between the developed West and the underdeveloped non-West.

PART III

Reading(s)

CHAPTER II

Civilized Folk Defeat the Barbarians:
The Liberal Nation

The excerpt in this chapter is by Domingo Faustino Sarmiento, who exemplifies the lettered citizen in Latin America. Sarmiento served as president of Argentina in the mid-nineteenth century and was one of Latin America's most important writers. His renowned work, *Facundo: civilización y barbarie* (*Facundo: Civilization and Barbarism*), motivated generations of politicians and remains influential today. In fact, so canonical is *Facundo* that Sarmiento has achieved that rare status of transcending nationality and becoming a de facto citizen of all Latin America.

Born in 1811 in San Juan, Argentina, Sarmiento grew up on the frontier between Argentina and Chile. Largely self-taught, he became involved in Argentina's tumultuous political scene as a young man in the late 1820s. At the time, the emerging nation of Argentina was divided between Unitarians and Federalists. The Unitarians were based in Buenos Aires and espoused liberal programs rooted in the ideals of the European Enlightenment. But because they were positioned in Argentina's main port they adopted a political stance that was conservative, defending the colonial era tradition of a strong central government. The Federalists were based in Argentina's interior provinces; aside from the issue of governing structures, they were deeply conservative. Refusing to bow to Buenos Aires, they espoused a decentralized form of government.

Although Sarmiento was from the interior, his disposition toward liberalism led him to the Unitarian side.[1] By the age of twenty, he was forced into exile in Chile. He returned briefly to Argentina to open a school and publish a politically oriented newspaper, only to be imprisoned and exiled once again in 1835. During his second exile he traveled to the United States,

Europe, and North Africa, studying the educational system of each place. When he returned to Chile in 1845 he wrote *Civilización y barbarie* as a series of newspaper articles. Designed as a biography of the fictional rural strongman Juan Facundo Quiroga, the book was an extended polemic against Argentina's federalist regime of Juan Manuel de Rosas. Upon the demise of Rosas in 1852, Sarmiento returned to Argentina and entered politics, serving as a governor and ambassador to the United States. He was elected president in 1868. During his political life he strove to implement liberal policies that he and his fellow Unitarians believed would build Argentina into a world power. Sarmiento often looked to the United States as a model for applying Enlightenment ideals in the Americas. Upon his death in 1888 he was serving as director of schools in Buenos Aires.

Sarmiento's *Facundo* stands out as one of the most influential treatises on nation building in modern Latin American literary history. In fact, many scholars regard it as a work of international importance, arguing that it helped define the largely European-centered Romantic nationalism of the early and the mid-nineteenth century. In *Facundo*, Sarmiento tells his native Argentina that it has two options, civilization or barbarism. He locates civilization in Argentina's urban areas, especially Buenos Aires, which was filled with educated citizens who sought to emulate Europe and North America. Not surprisingly, Sarmiento's civilization also tends to have white skin. The alternative, barbarism, is rooted in Argentina's rural areas and is exemplified by the treacherous Facundo, a caudillo (strongman). For Sarmiento, Facundo represents everything wrong with Argentina—a lack of education, insularity, and regressive economic and social views. Sarmiento's barbarism also tends to have dark skin. Sarmiento believes the choice is obvious: Argentina must choose civilization and expend all necessary energy to defeat the forces of barbarism.

Facundo is a deeply essentialist work. In juxtaposing civilization and barbarism, Sarmiento believes he captures the essence of Argentina's identity. He does not see himself inventing either alternative, but simply revealing their existence and advocating one over the other. Most of Sarmiento's readers over the past one hundred fifty years have interpreted *Facundo* from an equally essentialistic perspective. Much of the debate over the book—and it has been extensive—concerns whether readers agree with Sarmiento's description of Argentina. While some embraced his appeal to civilization, others turned to the "barbarians." A smaller number of readers rejected his dichotomy altogether and offered an alternative approach. Regardless of their differences, all these essentialist readers agreed with Sarmiento on one key point: Argentina, like any other nation, possessed an objective, ontological identity.

Semioticians reject these debates and approach *Facundo* from an alternative perspective. They argue that Sarmiento's civilization/barbarism dichotomy was a discursive construct that invented Argentina's and, by extension, Latin America's identity rather than revealed it. They do not ask whether the civilization/barbarism dichotomy is accurate but from what sources it originated as an idea. These theorists take particular interest in Sarmiento's portrayal of Argentina's gauchos, the semi-itinerant cowboys who inhabited Argentina's vast interior plains. Renowned for knife wielding, horsemanship, and herding the wild cattle that roamed Argentina's plains, the gaucho was about as close as Argentina came to an indigenous culture outside of its small Indian populations. Sarmiento dedicates the first third of his book to a demographic and geographic survey of Argentina, which includes an extended description of the gaucho. The study of the caudillo Facundo consumes the remaining two-thirds.

Seminomadic, lacking in formal education, and racially mixed, gauchos were the author's nemesis. Sarmiento portrays them as "half-breeds" driven by passion rather than intellect.[2] They represented the type of mindless people who allowed caudillos like Facundo to rise to power. While Sarmiento believed in the rehabilitative powers of education, he was also highly practical. He desired to uplift the impoverished masses in Argentina but placed priority on the need to promote civilization at all costs. Thus, the gaucho ultimately had to be exterminated. Sarmiento wrote in a letter in 1861: "Do not try to economize the blood of gauchos. It is a fertilizer, like the blood of animals from the slaughterhouse, that must be made useful to the country."[3]

But Sarmiento's hatred for the gaucho placed a potentially dismantling paradox at the center of his argument. How could he at once espouse the destruction of an indigenous culture while promoting Argentina's distinct national identity? How could he promote the United States and Europe as models for Argentina's future while simultaneously promoting Argentina as a unique and viable nation? *Facundo* is an attempt to resolve these contradictions. The gauchos would be remembered in song and lore, incorporated into the collective memory of Argentines across the ages, but eradicated as living, breathing people.

Semioticians find Sarmiento's compromise revealing and see it as a classic example of a text speaking against itself. Instead of *Facundo* resolving its own paradox, it is trapped inside itself. Instead of revealing Argentina's unique essence, *Facundo* offers a distillation of racialist and nationalist discourses that were swirling throughout intellectual and political circles both at home and abroad. In particular, they see Sarmiento's nationalism as prototypical of romanticism. At its core, romanticism struggled with this same conflict between uniqueness and homogeneity, celebrating the individuality of citizens while calling upon them to surrender to the sacredness of their national project, and hailing national uniqueness while recognizing the need to incorporate foreign models.

Essentialists situate *Facundo* in the Romantic tradition in order to substantiate their interpretations. So, if the Romantics were right (or wrong), then perhaps Sarmiento was as well. Semioticians, on the other hand, see *Facundo*'s debt to romanticism as part of a discursive framework that constructed ideas in the mind of its author. While not ignoring Sarmiento's astounding intellectual capacity, they see him as a "dead" author and political actor who envisioned Argentina through a dizzying storm of discourse. In time, Sarmiento's civilization/barbarism dichotomy would become its own discourse, a sort of metanarrative about Latin American nation building that would influence generations of thinkers and policy makers. But before we look at Sarmiento's impact on his progeny, we should read his own words from *Facundo*.

DOMINGO SARMIENTO, *FACUNDO* [4]
Physical Aspect of the Argentine Republic: Its Effect on the People

The Continent of America ends at the south in a point, with the Strait of Magellan at its southern extremity. Upon the west, the Chilean Andes run parallel to the coast at a short distance from the Pacific. Between that range of mountains and the Atlantic is a country whose boundary follows the River Plata up the course of the Uruguay into the interior, which was formerly known as the United Provinces of the River Plata, but where blood is still shed to determine whether its name shall be the Argentine Republic or the Argentine Confederation. On the north lie Paraguay, the Gran Chaco, and Bolivia, its assumed boundaries.

The vast tract which occupies its extremities is altogether uninhabited, and possesses navigable rivers as yet unfurrowed even by a frail canoe. Its own extent is the evil from which the Argentine Republic suffers; the desert encompasses it on every side and penetrates its very heart; wastes containing no human dwelling, are, generally speaking, the unmistakable boundaries between its several provinces. Immensity is the universal characteristic of the country: the plains, the woods, the rivers, are all immense; and the horizon is always undefined, always lost in haze and delicate vapors which forbid the eye to mark the point in the distant perspective, where the land ends and the sky begins. On the south and on the north are savages ever on the watch, who take advantage of the moonlight nights to fall like packs of hyenas upon the herds in their pastures, and upon the defenseless settlements. When the solitary caravan of wagons, as it sluggishly traverses the pampas, halts for a short period of rest, the men in charge of it, grouped around their scanty fire, turn their eyes mechanically toward the south upon the faintest whisper of the wind among the dry grass, and gaze into the deep darkness of the night, in search of the sinister visages of the savage horde, which, at any moment, approaching unperceived, may surprise them. If no sound reaches their ears, if their sight fails to pierce the gloomy veil which covers the silent wilderness, they direct their eyes, before entirely dismissing their apprehensions, to the ears of any horse standing in the firelight, to see if they are pricked up or turned carelessly backwards. Then they resume their interrupted conation, or put into their mouths the half-scorched pieces of dried beef on which they subsist. When not fearful of the approach of the savage, the plainsman has equal cause to dread keen eyes of the tiger, or the viper beneath his feet. This constant insecurity of life outside the towns, in my opinion, stamps upon the Argentine character a certain stoical resignation to death by violence, which is regarded as one of the inevitable probabilities of existence. Perhaps this is the reason they inflict death or submit to it with so much indifference, why such events make no deep or lasting impression upon the survivors.

The inhabited portion of this country—a country unusually favored by nature, and embracing all varieties of climes—may be divided into three sections possessing distinct characteristics, which cause differences of character among the inhabitants, growing out of the necessity of their adapting themselves to the physical conditions which surround them.

In the north, an extensive forest, reaching to the Chaco, covers with its impenetrable mass of boughs a space whose extent would seem incredible if there could be any marvel too great for the colossal types of Nature in America.

In the central zone, lying parallel to the former, the plain and the forest long contend with each other for the possession of the soil; the trees prevail for some distance, but gradually dwindle into stunted and thorny bushes, only reappearing in belts of forest along the banks of the streams, until finally in the south, the victory remains with the plain, which displays its smooth, velvet-like surface unbounded and unbroken. It is an image of the sea upon the land; the earth as it appears upon the map—the earth yet waiting for the command to bring forth every herb yielding seed after its kind. We may indicate, as a noteworthy feature in the configuration of this country, the aggregation of navigable rivers, which come together in the east, from all points of the horizon, to form the Plata by their union, and thus worthily to present their mighty tribute to the Ocean, which receives it, not without visible marks of disturbance and respect. But these immense canals, excavated by the careful hand of Nature, introduce no change into the national customs. The sons of the Spanish adventurers who colonized the country hate to travel by water, feeling themselves imprisoned when within the narrow limits of a boat or a pinnace. When their path is crossed by a great river, they strip themselves unconcernedly, prepare their horses for swimming, and plunging in, make for some island visible in the distance, where horse and horseman take breath, and by thus continuing their course from isle to isle, finally affect their crossing.

Thus is the greatest blessing which Providence bestows upon any people disdained by the Argentine gaucho, who regards it rather as an obstacle opposed to his movements, than as the most powerful means of facilitating them; thus the fountain of national growth, the origin of the early celebrity of Egypt, the cause of Holland's greatness, and of the rapid development of North America, the navigation of rivers, or the use of canals, remains a latent power, unappreciated by the inhabitants of the banks of the Bermejo, Pilcomayo, Parana, and Paraguay. A few small vessels, manned by Italians and adventurers, sail up stream from the Plata, but after ascending a few leagues, even this navigation entirely ceases. The instinct of the sailor, which the Saxon colonists of the north possess in so high a degree, was not bestowed upon the Spaniard. Another spirit is needed to stir these arteries in which a nation's lifeblood now lies stagnant. Of all these rivers which should bear civilization, power, and wealth, to the most hidden recesses of the continent, and make of Santa Fé, Entre Rios, Corrientes, Cordova, Saltas, Tucuman, and Jujui, rich and populous states, the Plata alone, which at last unites them all, bestows its benefits upon the inhabitants of its banks. At its mouth stand two cities, Montevideo and Buenos Ayres, which at present reap alternately the advantages of their enviable position. Buenos Ayres is destined to be some day the most gigantic city of either America. Under a benignant climate, mistress of the navigation of a hundred rivers flowing past her feet, covering a vast area, and surrounded by inland provinces which know no other outlet for their products, she would ere now have become the Babylon of America, if the spirit of the Pampa had not breathed upon her, and left undeveloped the rich offerings which the rivers and provinces should unceasingly bring. She is the only city in the vast Argentine territory which is in communication with European nations; she alone can avail herself of the advantages of foreign commerce; she alone has power and revenue. Vainly have the provinces asked to receive through her, civilization, industry, and European population; a senseless colonial policy made her deaf to these cries. But the provinces had their revenge when they sent to her in Rosas the climax of their own barbarism.

Heavily enough have those who uttered it, paid for the saying, "The Argentine Republic ends at the Arroyo del Medio." It now reaches from the Andes to the sea, while barbarism and violence have sunk Buenos Ayres below the level of the provinces. We ought not to complain of Buenos Ayres that she is great and will be greater, for this is her destiny. This would be to complain of Providence and call upon it to alter physical outlines. This being impossible, let us accept as well done what has been done by the Master's hand. Let us rather blame the ignorance of that brutal power which makes the gifts lavished by Nature upon an erring people of no avail for itself or for the provinces. Buenos Ayres, instead of sending to the interior, light, wealth, and prosperity, sends only chains, exterminating hordes, and petty subaltern tyrants. She, too, takes her revenge for the evil inflicted upon her by the provinces when they prepared for her a Rosas!

I have indicated the circumstance that the position of Buenos Ayres favors monopoly, in order to show that the configuration of the country so tends to centralization and consolidation, that even if Rosas had uttered his cry of "Confederation or Death!" in good faith, he would have ended with the consolidated system which is now established. Our desire, however, should be for union in civilization, and in liberty, while there has been given us only union in barbarism and in slavery. But a time will come when business will take its legitimate course. What now concerns us to know is that the progress of civilization must culminate only in Buenos Ayres; the pampa is a very bad medium of transmission and distribution through the provinces, and we are now about to see what is the result of this condition of things.

But above all the peculiarities of special portions of the country, there predominates one general, uniform, and constant character. Whether the soil is covered with the luxuriant and colossal vegetation of the tropics, or stunted, thorny, and unsightly shrubs bear witness to the scanty moisture which sustains them; or whether finally the pampa displays its open and monotonous level, the surface of the country is generally flat and unbroken—the mountain groups of San Luis and Cordova in the centre, and some projecting spurs of the Andes toward the north, being scarcely an interruption to this boundless continuity [. . .].

The people who inhabit these extensive districts belong to two different races, the Spanish and the native; the combination of which form a series of imperceptible gradations. The pure Spanish race predominates in the rural districts of Cordova and San Luis, where it is common to meet young shepherdesses fair and rosy, and as beautiful as the belles of a capital could wish to be. In Santiago del Estero, the bulk of rural population still speaks the Quichua dialect, which plainly shows its Indian origin. The country people of Corrientes use a very pretty Spanish dialect. "Dame, general, una chiripá," said his soldiers to Lavalle. The Andalusian soldier may still be recognized in the rural districts of Buenos Ayres; and in the city foreign surnames are the most numerous. The negro race, by this time nearly extinct (except in Buenos Ayres), has left, in its zambos and mulattoes, a link which connects civilized man with the denizen of the woods. This race mostly inhabiting cities, has a tendency to become civilized, and possesses talent and the finest instincts of progress.

With these reservations, a homogeneous whole has resulted from the fusion of the three above-named families. It is characterized by love of idleness and incapacity for industry, except when education and the exigencies of a social position succeed in spurring it out of its customary pace. To a great extent, this unfortunate result is owing to the incorporation of the native tribes, affected by the process of colonization. The American aborigines live in idleness, and show themselves incapable, even under compulsion, of hard and protracted labor. This suggested the idea of introducing negroes into America, which has produced such fatal results. But the Spanish race has not shown itself more energetic than the aborigines, when it has been left to its own instincts in the wilds of America. Pity and shame are excited by the comparison of one of the German or Scotch colonies in the southern part of Buenos Ayres and some towns of the interior of the Argentine Republic; in the former the cottages are painted, the front-yards always neatly kept and adorned with flowers and pretty shrubs; the furniture simple but complete; copper or tin utensils always bright and clean; nicely curtained beds; and the occupants of the dwelling are always industriously at work. Some such families have retired to enjoy the conveniences of city life, with great fortunes gained by their previous labors in milking their cows, and making butter and cheese. The town inhabited by natives of the country, presents a picture entirely the reverse. There, dirty and ragged children live, with a menagerie of dogs; there, men lie about in utter idleness; neglect and poverty prevail everywhere; a table and some baskets are the only furniture of wretched huts remarkable for their general aspect of barbarism and carelessness [. . .].

The Argentine cities, like almost all the cities of South America, have an appearance of regularity. Their streets are laid out at right angles, and their population scattered over a wide surface, except in Cordova, which occupies a narrow and confined position, and presents all the appearance of a European city, the resemblance being increased by the multitude of towers and domes attached to its numerous and magnificent churches. All civilization, whether native, Spanish, or European, centres in the cities, where are to be found the manufactories, the shops, the schools and colleges, and other characteristics of civilized nations. Elegance of style, articles of luxury, dress-coats, and frock-coats, with other European garments, occupy their appropriate place in these towns. I mention these small matters designedly. It is sometimes the case that the only city of a pastoral province is its capital, and occasionally the land is uncultivated up to its very streets. The encircling desert besets such cities at a greater or less distance, and bears heavily upon them, and they are thus small oases of civilization surrounded by an untilled plain, hundreds of square miles in extent, the surface of which is but rarely interrupted by any settlement of consequence.

The cities of Buenos Ayres and Cordova have succeeded better than the others in establishing about them subordinate towns to serve as new foci of civilization and municipal interests; a fact which deserves notice. The inhabitants of the city wear the European dress, live in a civilized manner, and possess laws, ideas of progress, means of instruction, some municipal organization, regular forms of government, etc. Beyond the precincts of the city everything assumes a new aspect; the country people wear a different dress, which I will call South American, as it is common to all districts; their habits of life are different, their wants peculiar and limited. The people composing these two distinct forms of society, do not seem to belong to the same nation. Moreover, the countryman, far from attempting to imitate the customs of the city, rejects with disdain its luxury and refinement; and it is unsafe for the costume of the city people, their coats, their cloaks, their saddles, or anything European, to show themselves in the country. Everything civilized which the city contains is blockaded there, proscribed beyond its limits; and any one who should dare to appear in the rural districts in a frock-coat, for example, or mounted on an English saddle, would bring ridicule and brutal assaults upon himself [. . .].

A fact which explains many of the social phenomena of nations deserves a passing notice. The natural peculiarities of any region give rise to customs and practices of a corresponding peculiarity, so that where the same circumstances reappear, we find the same means of controlling them invented by different nations.

From these general customs and tastes are developed remarkable peculiarities, which will hereafter embellish the national dramas and romances, and give them an original shade of color. I propose at present only to notice a few of these special developments, in order to complete the idea of the customs of the country, and so to explain subsequently the nature, causes, and effects of its civil wars.

The Rastreador

The most conspicuous and extraordinary of the occupations to be described, is that of the Rastreador, or track-finder. All the gauchos of the interior are Rastreadores. In such extensive plains, where paths and lines of travel cross each other in all directions, and where the pastures in which the herds feed are unfenced, it is necessary often to follow the tracks of an animal, and to distinguish them among a thousand others, and to know whether it was going at an easy or a rapid pace, at liberty or led, laden or carrying no weight.

The Rastreador proper is a grave, circumspect personage, whose declarations are considered conclusive evidence in the inferior courts. Consciousness of the knowledge he possesses gives him a certain reserved and mysterious dignity. Every one treats him with respect; the poor man because he fears to offend one who might injure him by a slander or an accusation; and the proprietor because of the possible value of his testimony.

The Baqueano, or Path-finder

Next to the Rastreador comes the Baqueano, a personage of distinction, and one who controls the fate of individuals and of provinces. The Baqueano is a grave and reserved gaucho, who knows every span of twenty thousand square leagues of plain, wood, and mountain! He is the most thorough topographer, the only map which a general consults in directing the movements of his campaign. The Baqueano is always at his side. Modest and mute as a garden-wall, he is in possession of every secret of the campaign; the fate of the army, the issue of a battle, the conquest of a province, all depend upon him. The Baqueano almost always discharges his duty with fidelity, but the general does not place full confidence in him.

If the Baqueano belongs to the pampa, where no roads exist, and a traveler asks him to show the way straight to a place fifty leagues off, he pauses a moment, reconnoiters the horizon, examines the ground, fixes his eyes upon some point, and gallops off straight as an arrow, until he changes his course for reasons known only to himself, and keeps up his gallop day and night till he arrives at the place named.

The Gaucho Outlaw

The example of this type of character, to be found in certain places, is an outlaw, a squatter, a kind of misanthrope. He is Cooper's Hawkeye or Trapper, with all the knowledge of the wilderness possessed by the latter; and with all his aversion to the settlements of the whites, but without his natural morality or his friendly relations with the savages. The name of gaucho outlaw is not applied to him wholly as an uncomplimentary epithet. The law has been for many years in pursuit of him. His name is dreaded—spoken under the breath, but not in hate, and almost respectfully. He is a mysterious personage; his abode is the pampa; his lodgings are the thistle fields; he lives on partridges and hedgehogs, and whenever he is disposed to regale himself upon a tongue, he lassos a cow, throws her without assistance, kills her, takes his favorite morsel, and leaves the rest for the carrion birds.

The Cantor (The Minstrel)

And now we have the idealization of this life of resistance, civilization, barbarism, and danger. The gaucho Cantor corresponds to the singer, bard, or troubadour of the Middle Ages, and moves in the same scenes, amidst the struggles of the cities with provincial feudalism, between the life which is passing away and the new life gradually arising. The Cantor goes from one settlement to another "de tapera en galpon," singing the deeds of the heroes of the pampa whom the law persecutes, the lament of the widow whose sons have been taken off by the Indians in a recent raid, the defeat and death of the brave Ranch, the final overthrow of Facundo Quiroga, and the fate of Santos Perez [. . .].

Two distinct forms of civilization meet upon a common ground in the Argentine Republic: one, still in its infancy, which, ignorant of that so far above it, goes on repeating the crude efforts of the Middle Ages; the other, disregarding what lies at its feet, while it strives to realize in itself the latest results of European civilization; the nineteenth and twelfth centuries dwell together—one inside the cities, the other without them [. . .].

To conclude, the original poetry of the minstrel is clumsy, monotonous, and irregular, when he resigns himself to the inspiration of the moment. It is occupied rather with narration than with the expression of feeling, and is replete with imagery relating to the open country, to the horse, and to the scenes of the wilderness, which makes it metaphorical and grandiose [. . .].

The life of the Argentine country people as I have exhibited it is not a mere accident; it is the order of things, a characteristic, normal, and in my judgment unparalleled system of association and in itself affords a full explanation of our revolution. Before 1810, two distinct, rival, and incompatible forms of society, two differing kinds of civilization existed in the Argentine Republic: one being Spanish, European, and cultivated, the other barbarous, American, and almost wholly of native growth [. . .].

DISCUSSION QUESTIONS

• What impact does the success of other civilizations (France, Rome, etc.) have on Sarmiento's description of Argentina?

• How does this selection of *Facundo* make clear Sarmiento's appeal to other nations as models for Argentina, while simultaneously calling upon Argentina to promote its own individuality?

• In what way does this selection from *Facundo* reveal Sarmiento's racialist foundations?

• Romantics often focused on a nation's landscape as an expression of its uniqueness. Sarmiento identified Argentina's vast rural expanses as the home of barbarism. Is there a parallel between Sarmiento's portrayal of Argentina's natural landscape and its gauchos?

NOTES

1. Liberalism refers to the ideology emerging out of the Enlightenment and the French Revolution, among other key events in history. Most liberal ideologues advocated laissez-faire capitalism, individual liberty, freedom of worship and a decentralized, federalist government. Of course, the meaning of liberalism varied significantly from one region to the next, and the extent to which liberal political leaders implemented their ideologies in actual practice varied significantly as well. In Latin America, liberalism was a principal motive behind the independence movements in the early 1800s. After an initial success, however, liberals failed to maintain control and their ideological perspective was rivaled by older, conservative approaches which advocated retaining elements of the colonial era. Economic opportunities brought on by the second Industrial Revolution in the latter part of the nineteenth century promoted the liberal's vision of social change. They rode the economic wave into power all across the continent. Arguably, they have remained in power in some form or fashion throughout most of the continent to this day—socialist Cuba being one of the exceptions. Today, neoliberal policies have pushed liberalism to a new global level.

2. Domingo Sarmiento, *Life in the Argentine Republic in the Days of Tyrants or, Civilization and Barbarism* (New York: Collier, 1966) 43. (This translator of *Facundo: civilización y barbarie* used *Life in the Argentine Republic* as the title, as did other translators.)

3. Letter from Sarmiento to Bartolomé Mitre, 1861, quoted in John Charles Chasteen, *Born in Blood and Fire: A Concise History of Latin America* (New York: Norton, 2001) 169.

4. Sarmiento, *Life in the Argentine Republic.* The excerpt is from 25–33, 40, 44–45, 47–52, 58.

CHAPTER 12

Civilized Folk Marry the Barbarians:
The Nationalist Nation

INTRODUCTION TO *DOÑA BÁRBARA*
BY RÓMULO GALLEGOS[1]

Rómulo Gallegos has much in common with Domingo Sarmiento. Both were men of letters who became presidents of their respective countries, and both left an intellectual legacy of continental proportions. The literary works for which they are most famous, *Facundo* by Sarmiento and *Doña Bárbara* by Gallegos, had similar objectives of defining and celebrating their nation's essence. But the vision of the nation which Gallegos promoted shifted notably from that of Sarmiento's generation of nineteenth-century liberals. Whereas Sarmiento called for the destruction of barbarism, leaving only a nostalgic reminder, Gallegos sought a fusion between society's so-called barbarian and civilized elements. This goal was indicative of his generation's nationalist vision of a transformative union between ruling elites and popular masses.

Rómulo Gallegos (1884–1969) was born into a humble family in Caracas, Venezuela. He discovered a passion for writing at an early age and published his first essay, "*Lo que somos*" ("What We Are") at the age of nineteen. He considered studying law but decided to pursue his love of writing. He co-founded a weekly magazine and established himself as an essayist. He published his first novel, *El último solar,* in 1920, helping to solidify his literary reputation. In addition to writing, Gallegos worked as a schoolteacher and principal between 1912 and 1930.

Throughout much of his adult life, specifically between 1908 and 1935, Venezuela was under the control of an oligarchic dictatorship run by Juan Vicente Gómez. A classic caudillo from Venezuela's mountainous interior, Gómez rose steadily in the political ranks and eventually became president by overthrowing the man who had nurtured his career. Ironically, Gómez allied himself with elites and intellectuals who viewed Venezuela through a European and racialized lens. They supported Gómez out of a belief that Venezuela needed an authoritarian regime to control the masses. To its credit, the Gómez regime successfully centralized the national government and put an end to Venezuela's long history of internecine conflict between rival caudillo bands. This stability was facilitated by the government's exploitation of petroleum reserves in a joint venture with Great Britain.

In the 1920s, however, a growing nationalist and populist movement began to challenge the Gómez dictatorship, accusing it of corruption, nepotism, and selling the country out to foreigners. The annual Week of the Student celebration in 1928 turned into a mass protest against the regime. So decisive were these protests that they established an opposition that dubbed itself the Generation of '28.

Inspired by those protests, Gallegos wrote *Doña Bárbara* in 1929 as a critique of the Gómez government. Ironically, Gómez liked the novel, perhaps because Gallegos avoided the sensitive issue of oil and because the novel was well-received throughout Latin America. Gómez nominated Gallegos to be a senator, but Gallegos declined the offer, choosing to go into voluntary exile in Spain rather than compromise his political beliefs.

Following the death of Gómez from natural causes in 1935, Gallegos returned to Venezuela and was appointed minister of education. In 1945 he supported a coup d'état that brought Rómulo Betancourt to power. Then, during the election to select Betancourt's successor, Gallegos was chosen as the candidate of Acción Democrática (Democratic Action), a multiclass party founded in 1941 that drew support from a mixture of workers, peasants, and the middle class. Gallegos won the election in 1947 with a great majority of the popular vote, becoming the first freely elected president of Venezuela. Although short-lived, his government made gains in education and health care. The military, however, saw his policies as radically excessive and ousted Gallegos in a bloodless coup. He fled to Cuba in 1948 and later went to Mexico before returning in 1958 to Venezuela, where he remained until his death in 1969.

The story of *Doña Bárbara* revolves around a conflict between two characters, Santos Luzardo and Doña Bárbara. The novel opens as Luzardo, a refined lawyer from Caracas, is returning to his birthplace, the family's hacienda in Venezuela's interior plains. His initial intent is to sell the property, but upon arriving he discovers the region to be dominated by Doña Bárbara, a local caudillo boss, who has consolidated land and built up a cattle empire through a series of illegal and underhanded dealings. Not the least of her disreputable actions has been raiding cattle and stealing land from Altamira, as the Luzardo family property is called. Furthermore, she has allied herself with another greedy resident, a North American landowner and property speculator named Señor Danger. Inspired by the combination of an innate bond to his rural origins and a stubborn refusal to surrender to Bárbara's machinations, Luzardo decides to defend his property, and in the process civilize the rural hinterlands.

One of Bárbara's devious tactics to accumulate power is to seduce wealthy men, and then, once she has their confidence, to betray them and seize their riches. One of her victims is Lorenzo Barquero, Luzardo's cousin, who was also once a prosperous lawyer from the city and owner of La Barquereña, the property adjacent to Altamira. But now he is a shell of a man, living in a dilapidated hut on the dismal remains of his former lands, a victim of Bárbara's and Danger's machinations. The parallels between Barquero and Luzardo are obvious and serve as a warning of the dangers that Luzardo faces in daring to tangle with the "ogress of the plains." Barquero and Bárbara have a daughter named Marisela, whom Bárbara has abandoned. She lives with Baquero on the fringes of Bárbara's property. By the time Luzardo arrives, Marisela has grown into a young woman whose potential for beauty and vibrancy is evident, but who remains little more than a feral element of nature.

At first, the prospect of subduing Doña Bárbara seems insurmountable. Her reputation alone is enough to scare away most challengers. She supposedly possesses magical powers granted to her by a supernatural ally, known simply as her "partner," presumably a demon of some sort. But Luzardo works diligently in the name of civilization, and slowly but steadily makes progress against Bárbara's dark forces. Emblematic of his eventual success is the fact that Bárbara herself begins to feel yearnings for Luzardo and his civilizing mission. In time Luzardo is victorious. He restores his lands, educates Marisela, and sends Bárbara and Danger into oblivion.

Following in the footsteps of Sarmiento's civilization/barbarism dichotomy, Gallegos envisions Venezuela's identity to be divided between the wild plains and the civilized city. This duality provides a constant conflict that must be resolved in order for Venezuela to survive and progress. Throughout the novel, Gallegos demonstrates his belief in Luzardo's civilizing mission, as evidenced by the names Gallegos chooses for him. Santos means sainthood and Luzardo (from *luz*, "light") refers to the Enlightenment, whereas Doña Bárbara obviously evokes barbarianism, and Señor Danger represents the power of foreign oil companies or the threat of U.S. intervention.

Altamira means high view or forward looking, whereas Bárbara's land is simply called El Miedo (fear).

But the crux of the argument made by Gallegos is not simply that Luzardo's vanquishing of Bárbara implies a corresponding victory of civilization over barbarism. Rather, in order to win, Luzardo must merge civilization with barbarism to create a more unified and powerful whole. This union is most clearly expressed in his marriage to Marisela. Although he educated her and thereby symbolically civilized her, Luzardo also surrenders to her more seminatural influence upon his life, allowing himself to be changed in the process. In this regard, the novel is what literary critic Doris Sommer calls a "foundational fiction," in which two characters (Santos Luzardo and Marisela) represent conflicting ideologies (civilization and barbarism) and their marriage results in the union of the differing views, thus resolving a national conflict. Just as Sarmiento saw something uniquely Argentine in the nation's land and people, Gallegos sees something of Venezuela's essential spirit residing in the lands and people of the plains. To simply cast that aside in favor of the urban, European-oriented, civilized side of urban Venezuela would be to lose part of one's soul. Only when these two sides render themselves united will Venezuela achieve its full and lasting potential as a nation.

Essentialist readings of *Doña Bárbara* either agree or disagree with Gallegos's vision of a nationalistic, anti-imperialist future for Venezuela and his corresponding definition of the nation's true essence. Many people have agreed with Gallegos over the past decades, particularly in Venezuela, where *Doña Bárbara* remains mandatory reading in schools. Literary critics might also celebrate Gallegos's attempts to complicate his characters' motivations. Doña Bárbara's turn to barbarism, for example, is dated to her rape as a young woman by a group of brutal men who also killed Hasdrubal, the one man who had inspired earnest passion in her.

Semiotic readings of the novel acknowledge its canonical success but reveal the many discursive constructions running through it. They point out that although the author's fusion of barbarism and civilization was trendsetting, it also reinforced accepted notions of essence and hierarchy. For example, civilization remains male, whereas barbarianism is female. While Santos Luzardo is depicted as better off as a result of his embrace of Marisela's rural essence, his domain remains that of the rational, political, public world, whereas Marisela's remains domestic and private. By portraying Bárbara as a witch acting in concert with a spiritual familiar, Gallegos inscribes a discursive tradition that is centuries old of depicting women as weaker-willed than men and thus more susceptible to the wiles of dark spiritual forces.

Doña Bárbara offers semioticians the opportunity to demonstrate dead authorship. For example, Gómez liked the novel even though Gallegos intended it as a criticism of his government. And the film version made in Mexico in 1943 had the ironic effect of turning María Félix, the actress who played Doña Bárbara into a sort of feminist hero because she was the first woman in Mexican cinema to wear pants, or to wield a whip.

As they do with the nationalism in Sarmiento's *Facundo*, semiotic readings of Gallegos recognize the spiritualism and neoromanticism that influenced his ideas of the nation. Whether Gallegos realized it or not, he cast Venezuela's identity according to discursive patterns typical of Latin American nationalistic authors in the nineteenth and early twentieth centuries. Thus, a semiotician might suggest that the novel reveals more about the intellectual patterns of these early twentieth-century nationalists than it does about Venezuela.

Doña Bárbara is a long work (roughly five hundred pages). What follows are five brief excerpts dedicated mostly to character development. In order, the excerpts depict Santos Luzardo, Doña Bárbara, Señor Danger, Lorenzo Barquero, and Marisela.

RÓMULO GALLEGOS, *DOÑA BÁRBARA*[2]
[On Santos Luzardo]

The sudden transplantation from the midst of the Plain, rude, yet full of intense, character-forming emotional life, to the smooth, lulling atmosphere of the city existence between four walls in the society of a mother broken by terror, produced a peculiar slumber of his [Santos Luzardo's] faculties. He had been a boy of spirit, keenly intelligent, full of high courage; the pride of his father, who enjoyed watching him break a wild horse or retrieve himself with dexterity and assurance from amidst the constantly recurring dangers of the cattleman's life; a worthy representative of the fearless race that had furnished more than one epic with its centaur and the Plain with many a lord. His mother, with another concept of life, had placed so many hopes in him when she heard him express ideas revealing a subtle and reflective mind; he now became dull and procrastinating, and changed into a misanthrope.

But in the end, the city conquered the exiled soul of Santos Luzardo. Coming to himself after the sorceress nostalgia had lost her power, he realized that he was in his nineteenth year and not much richer in knowledge than he had been when he first came from the Arauca [the plains]. He resolved to make up for the time he had lost, and plunged eagerly into his studies.

Despite the reasons she had for loathing Altamira, Doña Ascunción [Santos's mother] had not been willing to sell the ranch. Her soul was the robust, unchangeable soul of the Plainsman, for whom there is nothing like his native soil, and although she had no thought of returning to the Arauca country, neither had she considered breaking the bond which joined her to it, especially as the ranch, managed by a loyal and honest overseer, brought her an excellent income.

"Let Santos sell it when I die," she used to say. But when she was dying, she said to him:

"Don't sell Altamira as long as you can avoid it."

And Santos kept it, out of respect for his mother's last wish, and because the income made it easy for him to cover the expenses of his temperate existence. Otherwise, he would have had no struggle in parting with the land. His native soil had no attraction for him, neither Altamira nor all the rest of it, since in losing his feeling that he was a part of that territory, he had lost all feeling for his fatherland. Urban life and intellectual habits had barred from this spirit all urge toward the free and savage life of the ranch. At the same time, however, they had produced an aspiration which that city itself could not permanently satisfy. Caracas, with all its excellencies, was far from being that ideal city, intricate and perfect as a mind, in which all movement becomes converted into ideas, and every reaction bears the seal of conscious efficiency. And as this idea seemed to be realized only in the aged civilization of Europe, he embraced the plan of permanently expatriating himself as soon as he had completed his studies at the university.

But as no one wanted to make himself Doña Bárbara's neighbor, and moreover, the revolutions had impoverished the Plain, he spent considerable time trying to find a purchaser.

On the journey, before the spectacle of the deserted Plains, he thought of doing many things: settling on the ranch to struggle against the enemy; defending his own property and his neighbors', outraged by the chiefs of the country, of whom Doña Bárbara was but one of many; struggling against nature herself, against the unhealthful conditions which were wiping out the race of Plainsmen, against the alternate floods and droughts which fought over the land all during the year, against the desert which shut off the Plain from civilization.

These, however, were not yet plans, but thoughts, the soliloquies of a man reasoning; and an optimistic mood would be succeeded immediately by pessimism.

"To carry all this out," thought Santos, "needs something more than the will to do it. What good will it do to put an end to the authority of Doña

Bárbara? It will just reappear under another name. The really necessary thing is to change the circumstances that lead to these evils, to populate the country. But before you populate, you must have sanitation, and before you have sanitation, you have to populate. It's a vicious circle."

But a single incident, his meeting with the Wizard and the words of the riverman warning him against crossing the path of the dread Doña Bárbara, had roused his impulse to struggle. It was the same aggressiveness which had ruined the Luzardos; but here it was subordinated to an ideal. To struggle against Doña Bárbara, symbol of the times, was not only to free Altamira, but to destroy the forces which were holding back the Plain. And he decided to throw himself into the task, with the impulsiveness of the Cunavicheros, men of a vigorous race, and also with the ideals of a civilized man, in which they had been lacking [. . .].

[On Doña Bárbara]

As for the tales of her powers as a sorceress, neither was all here the mere fancy of the Plainsman. She really believed herself endowed with super-natural powers, and often spoke of a "Partner," who had saved her life one night by blowing out the lamp to wake her just as a peon paid to assassinate her was entering her room, and who had appeared since then to counsel her in difficult situations or to acquaint her with such distant or future happen-ings as might interest her. She said that he was the Nazarene of Achaguas himself, but she called him simply and naturally "my Partner"—and from this arose the legend of her compact with the devil.

Whether god or tutelary demon, it was all the same to her, for religion and witchcraft, incantations and prayers were in her mind all changed and confounded into a single mass of superstition; so that scapulars and the amulets of Indian medicine men hung on her breast in perfect harmony, and the mantel of the room where the "Partner" appeared was occupied by holy pictures, crosses of blessed palm, alligators' teeth, flints, *curvinata* stones, and fetishes from the native settlements, all sharing the same votive lamp.

In the matter of love, the ogress was no longer the wild mixture of lust and hatred. Her appetites were strangled by her greed, and the last fibers of femininity in her being were atrophied by the habits of the virago—she personally directed the labor of the peons, tossed the lasso, and could bring down a bull out in the open as well as her most skillful cowboy. She was never without her lance-head dagger and her revolver, nor did she carry them in her belt as a mere threat. If reasons of pure expediency—such as the need of a docile henchman, or in the case of Balbino Paiba, of a personal representative in the enemy camp—moved her to be generous with her caresses, she was no more as a man who takes than as a woman who gives. A deep disdain for men had replaced her implacable hatred of them.

In spite of this sort of life and the fact that she was over forty, she was still an alluring woman, and if she was entirely lacking in womanly delicacy, the imposing appearance of this Amazon put, in exchange, the stamp of originality on her beauty: there was something about her at once wild, beautiful, and terrible.

Such was the notorious Doña Bárbara: a compound of lust, superstition, greed, and cruelty, with a pathetic little remnant in her bitter heart of something pure and sad—the memory of Hasdrubal, and the frustrated love which could have made her a good woman. But even this took on the characteristics of a barbarous cult demanding human sacrifice. The memory of Hasdrubal always came to her when she encountered a man who was a worthy prey [. . .].

[On Señor Danger]

He was a great mass of muscles under a reddish skin, with a pair of very blue eyes and hair the color of flax.

He had come to the Arauca some years before with a rifle slung over his shoulder as a hunter of tigers and alligators. The country pleased him because it was as savage as his own soul, a good land to conquer, inhabited by people he considered inferior because they did not have light hair and blue eyes. Notwithstanding the rifle, it was generally believed that he had come to establish a ranch and bring in new ideas, so many hopes were placed in him and he was cordially received. But he had contented himself with placing four corner-posts in land belonging to somebody else, without asking permission to do so, and throwing over them a palm-thatch roof; and once this cabin was built, he hung up his hammock and rifle, lay down, lighted his pipe, stretched his arms, swelling the powerful muscles, and exclaimed: "All right. Now I'm at home." [. . .]

[On Lorenzo Barquero and the properties]

But Lorenzo Barquero's rights did more than pass from the hands of one usurper to those of another. The only earnings he saw from his land were the bottles of whisky Señor Danger sent him upon his return from San Fernando or Caracas, with a good supply of his chosen beverage, or the flagons of the latter Señor Danger had sent from the El Miedo commissary, and that without paying a cent to Doña Bárbara for them.

In return for this the foreigner enriched himself by smuggling cattle at pleasure. The remains of the old La Barquereña were scarcely more than a lot of savannah crossed by a creek, dry in winter, called The Lick, whose salty banks attracted the cattle belonging to neighboring reaches. Numerous herds were always to be seen there licking the creek bed, and thanks to this it was very easy to capture unbranded herds within the limits of the piece of land, which did not attain to the size required by law for the common right to unmarked herds wandering over the prairie. Señor Danger, however, found it easy to vault over legal obstacles and seize his neighbor's cattle, for the Luzardo overseers were always corruptible and the owner of El Miedo did not dare to protest.

Interpreting this as a sign of definite declaration of war on Santos Luzardo, Balbino Paiba had planned the Altamira fires in the hope of recovering his mistress' lost favors, executing in advance the designs he attributed to her, and gave the carrying out of the plan to the surviving Mondragon brothers, who were again lodged in the house at Macanillal and were the only people in El Miedo who obeyed his orders.[3] But as he kept his responsibility a secret, on account of that "god help the man who dares to touch Santos Luzardo," Doña Bárbara, in her turn, interpreted the conflagrations which had razed Altamira as the work of the "powers" assisting her, especially as the destruction of the fence Luzardo expected to put an end to her outrages had been no more than the realization of her own desire. And thus she became calm, perfectly confident that all the other barriers separating her from the man she wanted would fall at the proper time, and that when she wished him to, he would come to give himself up with alacrity [. . .].

[On Marisela]

Santos concluded, pleased at the happy results of her alternating rude and docile naturalness, and seeing Marisela as a personification of the soul of the Plainsman, open as the prairie and improved by every experience.

But in addition to giving him the incomparable satisfaction of successful accomplishment, Marisela made the house a happy place for him and brought in the necessity of personal orderliness. When she arrived at Altamira, it was no longer the dirty bat-roost Santos had settled in a few days before, for he had seen to the whitewashing of the walls, spattered with the filth of the loathsome creatures, and the scrubbing of the floors, covered with a hard coating of clay brought in on the peons' feet for unknown years; but it was still a house without a woman. As to material things, there was no one to stitch and mend; his meals were served by a peon. Spiritually, and most important for Luzardo, there was the lack of any control, the liberty to go around any way he pleased, the fact that it did not matter if the peons' obscene speeches disturbed the silence, or if he neglected his appearance or forgot his little refinements.

Now, on the contrary, it was necessary to return from the rough toil of pursuing and herding cattle with a bunch of flowers for the young lady of the house, to change his clothing, get rid of the rank odor of horses and cattle clinging to his skin, and sit down to table to give an example of good manners and maintain an agreeable, carefully regulated conversation.

Thus, while Santos was polishing away her rusticity, Marisela served him as a defense against the adaptation of the roughness of his environment, the irresistible force with which the wild, simple life of the desert puts its seal on anyone who abandons himself to it [. . .].

But there was something else, something not included in his reflections, but in his soul, nevertheless, changing the feelings of this civilized man, overcoming all obstacles; there was Marisela, who seemed the spirit of the Plain, of its ingenuous, restless soul, wild as the *paraguatán* flower that perfumes the thicket and sweetens the honey of the wild bees.

DISCUSSION QUESTIONS

• How do the portrayals of civilization and barbarity by Sarmiento and Gallegos differ? How are they similar? How do they reflect their respective historical contexts?

• In what way do Doña Bárbara and Marisela offer contrasting images of women? In what way does Gallegos make clear that one of them should be encouraged as a foundation of the new nation and the other destroyed as a threat?

• Since Santos has lived both in the city and on the plains, does he represent the plains or the city or both? Why is this issue so critical to Gallegos's image of the nation? It might help you to again consider how he differs from Sarmiento's representations of the city and the pampas.

INTRODUCTION TO DORIS SOMMER'S *FOUNDATIONAL FICTIONS*

In her 1991 book, *Foundational Fictions: The National Romances of Latin America*, Doris Sommer reveals a trend among Latin American authors in the nineteenth and early twentieth century to write romance novels that serve nationalist ends. *Doña Bárbara* is one of those novels, and the next excerpt offers Sommer's analysis of it. In brief, she reveals that Gallegos was a "dead" author and that his creation of *Doña Bárbara* was rooted in a broader discourse of foundational fiction.

Sommer, the Ira Jewell Williams professor of Romance Languages and Literatures at Harvard University, defines the Latin American romance novel as a love story set in an allegorical frame. Typically, it consists of two star-crossed lovers who symbolize rival segments of society (races, regions, political parties, classes, and so forth). The story revolves around their efforts to overcome the obstacles before them and to satisfy their love. As the protagonists in the story, they instill partisan feelings on the part of the reader, who hopes that society will change so that they can live together happily ever after. Sommer calls this genre a foundational fiction because the successful resolution to the relational conflict creates, or "founds," a new society or nation, in which the protagonists and, more important, their progeny can thrive and forge new paths as new citizens. The novel becomes a virtual manual or guidebook to nation-building projects, and its wide acceptance allows the book to rise into the literary canon as patriotic literature.

Independence from Spain provided the impetus for foundational fictions, as the new Latin American republics, fraught with internal divisions, lacked cohesive identities beyond being former Spanish colonies. The new republican leaders took it upon themselves to define the nation's new identity, which in their minds meant defining the essence or spirit that inspired independence and nationalism to begin with. Like *Facundo*, many of the early unification motifs were rooted in white supremacy and hailed civilization over barbarism. But even someone like Sarmiento, who called for the gaucho's demise, was affected by the foundational fiction discourse. In appealing to the memory of the gaucho, he was creating a sort of Romantic union between barbarianism and civilization.

Latin America's foundational fictions resemble romance novels in French and British literature, but they differ in telling ways. French and British romances are tragic, extramarital, and unproductive. They typically involve love that is unrequited because of social impediments and love triangles. Latin American romances revolve around a couple. Although the lovers may face external challenges, they overcome hurdles to achieve fulfillment that predicts future success. Also, Latin American romances promote miscegenation as the solution, if not the goal, whereas European romances rarely address the issue or use it as an insurmountable obstacle. The reasons for these differences are potentially quite vast, but one explanation is that French and British national identities were well-established by the mid-nineteenth century, so romance novels did not need to service their construction.

Regardless of the explanation for these differences, simply noting their existence allows us to recall Hall's argument about place, or the Latin American–based theories of local knowledge. The authors of Latin American romance novels operate within a broad sea of discourses about romance and nationalism, but they are also coming from a distinct place, with particular needs and conceptualizations. Thus, their novels or the broader, foundational fiction discursive genre in which those novels are participating, will moderate or alter global frameworks to the needs of their localities. Sommer's arguments about foundational fictions provide an excellent opportunity to see how discourses shape perception while being affected by the human conduits through which they operate. As we said in the introduction, all of us participate in discursive production and transmission, even though we are not at all aware of it. While no one necessarily controls discourse, involvement in it has the potential to alter it.

One of Sommer's primary contributions to our understanding of Gallegos is her demonstration that he participated in a larger Latin American discourse of using heterosexual love to legitimize the state's power. Whether or not Gallegos was aware of that larger pool of writers and romance novels is irrelevant. What is crucial is that his foundational fiction reveals the ways that discourse speaks through Gallegos. His national project was just one of many being written in the nineteenth century.

Sommer begins this excerpt by examining how Gallegos's life and historical era informed his nationalist project. This is a good opportunity to see how someone conducting literary analysis practices Stuart Hall's approach to identity. Sommer identifies Gallegos's place and uses it as a basis to understand where he was situated when he wrote *Doña Bárbara*.

As you read, keep in mind that the most challenging part of the excerpt is her explanation of "semantic bleeding." Sommer uses this term to credit a text for offering nuanced appreciations of complex issues, such as the arbitrary nature of language in a legal system, the distinction between right and wrong, and the definition of civilization and barbarism. Nevertheless, *Doña Bárbara* remains a deeply essentialistic work in which Gallegos insists on the importance of a system that draws clear lines between these complex differences. In this way the novel asserts the need to establish truth. Order, however arbitrary it may be, is restored through the legal system. It is the legal system that, in turn, restores land to Santos Luzardo and allows him to marry Marisela. In the end, national consolidation and the state's authority are achieved nonviolently through Marisela and Santos's love and their desire to procreate and populate the vast, empty lands.

One of the recurrent features of Latin America's foundational fiction novels is that, for all their attempts at forging a new society, the hero is almost always a white, propertied male, and a quintessential member of the lettered society. The writing elite, while willing to envision and build a new society, is unwilling to give up its position of privilege. This can be attributed, in part, to the fact that readers in the nineteenth century were primarily bourgeois. In this way we can see that foundational fictions exhibit some typically modernist hierarchies.

DORIS SOMMER, *FOUNDATIONAL FICTIONS*[4]

Rómulo Gallegos became Venezuela's first freely elected president as the culmination of his career as educator and novelist. Before much direct involvement in politics, Gallegos published his best-known novel, *Doña Bárbara* (1929) during a trip to Spain, almost as if he were smuggling the book out. It responded to a series of events that led up to the 1928 riots, incited by some of Gallegos's best students, against Juan Vicente Gómez. The dictator tried to silence the students with a paternal warning; continued demonstrations would bring harsher measures. His patriarchal authoritarian style of address had generally secured a proper reception, counting on a paradoxical combination of traditional respect for caudillos—who dared to subdue regional interests to national cohesiveness—and the modern military-communications technology that guaranteed obedience. For an elite class that would have preferred to share his power, this became especially irritating in 1927 while foreign companies were extracting oil from Lake Maracaibo. Venezuelans might finally have looked forward to the enormous sums of money needed to develop their own industries, as well as to build schools, provide good housing, create jobs. But very little money went to local businessmen or to reform, an oversight that lead Gallegos's students to make public accusations and demands. [. . .] But when Gómez insisted that Gallegos finally take sides by appointing him as senator for the State of Apure, the gentle but ethical man saw no way but out. He followed his students into exile, returning in 1936 as the father of that new generation. [. . .] Long before they came home, the exiled intellectuals took up the novel as the narrative projection of their future victory [. . .].

Published after his disciples had already left Venezuela, at the nadir of oppositional activity, *Doña Bárbara* is Gallegos's fantasy of return and repair. It proposes a double emancipation, from an internal tyrant and her external ally; that is, from the local boss, Bárbara (Gómez), and her North American accomplice, Mr. Danger (oil industry). The failure of any internal resistance

during the Gómez years must have made anything short of emancipation
seem wholly impractical to Gallegos. There could be no Romantic project
of hegemonic alliances if the enemy refused to negotiate. Nor could Rivera's
hallucinations have seemed to the point, blurring the instrumental oppositions between heroes and villains, or between a metaphorized land and
the metonymized husband who might repossess her.[5] Gallegos reinscribes
those oppositions with a vengeance in *Doña Bárbara*. Neither love across
enemy lines nor a self-critical respect for unconquerable terrain were ter-
ribly promising for a man who had just lost his country to a usurping "barbarian." The question of whether or not the country should be controlled
might have seemed irresponsible to the exiles who raged against the control
of Gómez and foreign interests. Instead they asked how best to repossess
the national patrimony.

Gallegos stages that reconquest as a tale of triumphant civilization, in
the person of aptly named Santos Luzardo, who has come home to the llano
after graduating from law school in Caracas. His first intention was merely
to sell the family ranch and to spend the earnings in Europe. But the llano
makes claims on its rightful master, and Santos stays to put his ranch in
order. In the process he must subdue the barbarous woman who has been
rustling his cattle and seizing his land. Her very identity as a domineering
woman is a signal for censure, a rhetorical trespassing of populism's gendered code. Gallegos makes her the "personification" (21; 29) of the seductive land and of lawless usurpations, an oxymoronic obstacle to Santos's
demand for legally binding terms.[6] She justifies her territorial trespassing
with a partial reading of the law; but Santos, in his drive for progress, insists
on turning the page and winning his claim (107–108; 176–177). Meanwhile,
his newly fenced-in property adds newly diversified dairy products to the
original meat and hides, and production develops with factory efficiency.
Borders, fences, frontiers are civilization's first requirements, the kind of
writing that refuses to risk barbarous misreadings (86; 137). Undecidability
was precisely the semiotic transgression that gave seductive charm to the
llano—with its hallucinatory circle of receding mirages—and to Bárbara's
exorbitant sexuality, her "imposing appearance of Amazon [*marimacho*]
put [. . .] the stamp of originality on her beauty: there was something about
her at once wild, beautiful, and terrible" (31; 45–46).

With his land, Santos also reins in Bárbara's wild daughter, Marisela.
Abandoned at birth by her mother, Marisela had been living in a swampy
no-man's-land between Bárbara's treacherously expansive *Miedo* (Fear)
and Santos's reconstructive *Altamira* (high view). She lived there with her
father, Lorenzo Barquero, Luzardo's feuding cousin. This drunken ruin

of a man, since Bárbara despoiled and abandoned him, had been Santos's childhood idol. Santos hopes to save him from that liminal space, as he saves Marisela from Mr. Danger, Bárbara's lascivious associate. But Barquero is finally lost to drink, and to the despair of his own empty eloquence. Marisela, though, has by now acquired the civilized contours of the perfect wife.

To acquire the necessary shape and tone, Marisela had first to learn how to groom herself, and especially how to speak standard Spanish, like a city girl. Her regional, traditional language, that which distinguishes her as a llanera, is corrected in this cultural improvement or whitening. It is an ironic, perhaps self-defeating victory for the hero who learned to love his country because he learned to love his particular region (20; 26). But to follow his elite, hegemonic lead means that Marisela must learn an elite and self-consciously regulated code, to banish the undisciplined grunts and cries that amount to a linguistic pathology. And Santos's teacherly promises of improvement are his most effective seductions, as if educator Gallegos were pointing to his own political seductiveness [. . .].

For good reason, this novel has been read as a fairy tale, the story of Prince Charming who searches out the princess (land) that he is destined to husband and arouses her with his irresistible touch. One unmistakable reason is Gallegos's title for Part I, Chapter 11, in which Santos meets Marisela; he calls it "Sleeping Beauty." But the story could just as well be read as a morality play. Civilization conquers barbarism. The holy light (Santos Luzardo) of modern Reason banishes the archaic darkness of barbarous black magic, one source of his antagonist's power. The naturally public sphere of man replaces the obscenely personalized dominion of woman, returning her—through her daughter—to a more modest and procreative domestic space. An elite intelligentsia puts Venezuelan productivity first, instead of preferring alliances with local tradition or with foreign allies. However one reads it, *Doña Bárbara* respects a far more binary code than that of most nineteenth-century national novels [. . .].

By the time Gallegos published his founding fiction, Venezuela was certainly a different place from the newly established nations, and some reformers were cautious about particular kinds of liberty. It had generations of experience and disappointment with the kind of liberal participation in the world market that some earlier writers were hoping to achieve. With Independence in 1810, the cocoa it had been exporting to other Spanish colonies began to bring foreign exchange. But decades of civil war devastated many of the groves, while the North Atlantic market began to prefer coffee. So coffee is what Venezuela produced, for a market whose ups and downs sent political tremors through the country. Venezuela also had a century's worth of political experience behind her. An Independence movement, led by her own Simón Bolívar, was followed, as in many new Latin American nations, by civil wars between centralists and advocates for a loose federation. The wars ended, as they did in Argentina, only when a provincial caudillo took over the capital in 1830 and began a long and relatively stable dictatorship. The problem in Venezuela (and elsewhere) was that conflict did not end there; caudillos, usually from the llano, continued to raise personal armies and to destabilize the government. Well into Gallegos's youth, Venezuelan history showed a pattern of implacable dictatorships alternating with impractical and short-term regimes.

In 1909 the intellectuals of Gallegos's generation saw hope for a change when a young military man named Juan Vicente Gómez replaced the conservative president Castro. [. . .] Gómez turned out to be as ruthless a dictator as Venezuela had known, but more effective. And the populist response echoed the emancipatory demands of early nineteenth-century revolutionary Independence movements. But by now, after the experience of long civil wars following the wars of Independence, it was clear that freedom without stability leads back to (neocolonial) bondage [. . .].

One wonders if Gallegos admired him too; he certainly admits fascination for the dictator's incarnation into "the appealing body of a woman" (literally, her "appetizing flesh"). Gómez is said to have reciprocated by approving enthusiastically of *Doña Bárbara*, which, he said, "Venezuelan writers should imitate instead of getting involved in those goddamn revolutions." Gallegos and his critics also acknowledge that Santos, the civilizing "citizen," has something to learn about self-defense and necessary violence (I would add passion) from Bárbara before he can replace her. This is certainly a plausible reading; and it easily resolves the apparently bad fit between the year of the novel and its economic focus. As a critic of Gómez, Gallegos was exposing him as a barbarous caudillo, a formidable but vincible obstacle to prosperity and reform [. . .].

It is even possible that the historical guilt goes deeper and further back than the civil wars. Perhaps it extends to the beginnings of Venezuelan history, when white men started the process of modernizing or Europeanizing the colony. That meant first violating or exterminating the Indians, just as half-Indian Bárbara had been raped by others and was being removed by Santos. My speculation about Santos's unspoken guilt, or his uneasiness about the possibility that he and his forebears are implicated in the chain of usurpations on the llano, shares some ground with Roberto González Echevarría's reading of the novel's dilemma. He points out that the litigation over land with Doña Bárbara is not only an occasion for doubting the very legitimacy of law, if, that is, legitimacy is grounded in natural, genealogical rights. This is the vexed moral issue of Santo's legal victory, his lawyerly maneuvering through fine print. In order to win, he is forced to contemplate all the guilt-provoking issues raised above, by contemplating the judicial history of entitlement. It began with the indefensible conquest of the land from the indigenous, natural masters, by his "centaur" of a grandfather Evaristo Luzardo. If genealogical rights were the grounding legal rights, then Santos has no more right to the land than does Bárbara, perhaps less, since the mestiza can claim an immemorial genealogical grounding on her mother's side. But, as González Echevarría points out, the incommensurability between Evaristo's initial violence and the later law doesn't stop Santos from pressing his claim; this produces a moral and semantic undecidability that makes this novel precociously modern. Too self-interested to confess the contradiction between moral right and legal rights, Santos is not the persona for Gallegos on this analysis. Instead it is Lorenzo Barquero, the once-brilliant law student who dropped out of everything once he saw through the fiction of all language; one cannot use it without lying, and one cannot be human without using it [. . .].

Sensitive to the semantic bleeding between words like *right* and *wrong,* *civilization* and *barbarism,* *national* and *foreign,* *male* and *female,* Gallegos insists (where Rivera desists) on damming up the leak system of oppositions, because he is convinced that a system (of grammar, phonetics, law) is superior to systematic anarchy. However fictitious and arbitrary, rules are codifiable, generalizable, and therefore generally binding in a way that produces a society. "Although the law does not provide for fines or penalties or arrests," Santos retorts to Bárbara's refusal to comply, "it is binding *per se.* It obliges everyone to fulfill it, purely and simply" (107–108; 176–177) [. . .].

Gallegos is surely reinscribing the excess and dissemination, putting his finger on the wound of language from which meaning continues to ooze every time he tries to stem the flow, every time he stages the binding and suturing of meaning against the vagaries of roaming cattle, people, and popular speech. But he nonetheless continues to act out/on his control, staging it to some—perhaps—temporary effect. The lessons, the branding, and the whole system of arbitrary proprietary oppositions so nervously repeated throughout the novel all resonate, of course, with the scene of assigning ultimate possessive meaning, the morally equivocal legal arbitration of the land. And read in the context of the shock waves and insistent sutures this confrontation sends through the book, the scene is the occasion for settling moral ambiguity by fiat. When Santos forces the issue, the authority in town settles the question of property with a legal-speech act: "the laws must be fulfilled just because, otherwise they wouldn't be laws, that is, orders from the Government" (107; 177–178). Thanks to this kind of tautological voluntarism, Santos accepts that his entitlement is merely legal fiction; yet he accepts it all the same as constitutive of a modern order. And he is willing to consider the fiction foundational because, in this self-serving tautology, it promises to found something. If law is merely simulacrum for the right to possess, it nevertheless can stabilize the irrational dissemination that Bárbara puts into motion (her androgynous eroticism, her scattered cattle and boundless borders). The simulacrum can become a horizon for future representations; it can domesticate the llano's mirages by fencing in the land, by writing clearly. Truth, in other words, need not be the immutable given that Barquero demanded; it can be a procreative assumption. Although Santos may have no real genealogical claims, the legal fiction allows him to make generative claims, like the ones made in romantic founding novels. And like the language of love and politics in those dialectical romances, Santos's legal language has no a priori grounding; instead it lays the ground for productive relationships.

The analogy is hardly fortuitous. Marriage, after all, is a fiction, a contract that can be read as an allegory of the Law of the Llano. It makes no genealogical claims to legitimacy, since marriage partners need hardly be blood relatives; but it does make a promise of productivity. And Santos's projected marriage to Marisela both repeats and makes possible, in a familiarly dialectical way, the legal fiction aimed at populating the desert [. . .].

But this is to dwell on the difficulty of establishing historical legitimacy, the very problem the future-looking contract can displace. Legitimation here is not retrospective but proleptic, through the resourceful management and the procreative marriage the legal fictions project. By contrast, Bárbara's equally fictional claim on the land promises to found very little. Maternity for her was an infuriating victory of men who reproduce themselves on women; and management was left to traditional terror (28; 40). Santos plans to populate the llano with legitimate children; Bárbara doesn't. This practical difference allows us to sense a shift from the moral to the legal questions this novel raises, from personal claims to patriotic duty, from genealogical rights to the generative responsibility of fathering the fatherland. It is a responsibility that Gallegos and Santos can translate imperfectly but pragmatically into the transparently constructed but nonetheless effective difference between better or worse for civilization, for or against the necessary fictions that will ground productivity and prosperity.

DISCUSSION QUESTIONS

• How does Sommer's idea of foundational fiction expose Gallegos as a "dead author"?

• Although Sommer never calls foundational fiction a discourse per se, why is it clear from her reading that it is possible to do so?

• According to Sommer, how does Marisela's education reflect the values that Gallegos was hoping to impose on his nation?

• What does Sommer mean when she refers to Santos's historical guilt and how does Gallegos resolve this guilt?

INTRODUCTION TO JOSÉ MARTÍ'S "OUR AMERICA"

"Our America" has had such a profound impact on modern Latin America that it is easy to forget its brevity (ten pages) and the fact that José Martí wrote thousands more pages in his life. Perhaps its conciseness partly explains "Our America"'s lasting influence. With an economy of words, Martí called upon Latin Americans to be united in common cause, proud of their heritage, and free from foreign control. The general nature of Martí's petition gives it almost universal appeal, allowing opposing political factions to draw upon it. The Cuban government under Castro promotes Martí as a national hero, while Cuban exiles in south Florida appeal to him in their quest to overthrow Castro. In twentieth-century Latin American history, Martí and "Our America" are ubiquitous.

Born in Havana, Cuba in 1853, Martí began his lifelong journey of political activism at an early age. Cuba at that time was still a Spanish colony, one of the only possessions Spain retained after the wave of independence movements in the early 1800s. Martí was the firstborn son of a sergeant in the Spanish army in Cuba and an immigrant mother from the Canary Islands. In 1862, at the age of nine, he traveled through the province of Matanzas in eastern Cuba and observed slavery firsthand. As his first exposure to extreme social injustice, this experience affected him for life. Martí initially sought comfort in poetry, as it allowed him to express his feelings without activism or violence, but eventually he focused his attentions on Cuban independence from Spain and became more active. The combination of his writings and activism resulted in his arrest and deportation to Spain in 1869 at the young age of sixteen.

While in Spain, Martí enrolled in law school in Madrid and also worked as a journalist. He eventually began working with other Cubans and sympathetic Spaniards who shared his belief in the cause of Cuban independence. Martí

FIGURE 12.1   *Lenin and Martí in Cuba depicted in a mural. 1991. Photograph by Erik Ching*

made a name for himself as a poet and essayist, and even though he believed the United States to be a future threat to Latin American autonomy, he respected its accomplishments. In 1880 he moved to New York. He lived in the United States off and on for the next fifteen years. During that time he traveled throughout the eastern seaboard, spending most of his time in either New York or Florida. All the while he was constantly active in promoting the cause of Cuban independence.

Martí believed that independence for Cuba had to occur sooner rather than later because the longer the campaign lasted the more likely it would lead to the rise of authoritarian leadership or U.S. intervention. Thus, he began translating his philosophical dialogues into militant action. Often using south Florida as a base of operations, Martí helped organize armed groups to fight for independence in Cuba. He died in battle against Spanish forces in eastern Cuba in 1895. Had Martí lived to see the withdrawal of Spain from Cuba in 1898, he no doubt would have been disheartened but not surprised by the almost colonial seizure of his native land by the United States immediately thereafter.

Written and published in 1891, "Our America" is a call to arms that reads like a declaration of independence. Although Cuba served as Martí's primary frame of reference, "Our America," as the title makes clear, targets a broader audience. It calls upon all Americans (i.e., Latin Americans) to come together in the cause of national (continental or Ibero-American) development and to resist foreign aggression, especially the growing neocolonial power of the United States.

"Our America" is framed by the same civilization/barbarism dichotomy that defines Sarmiento's *Facundo* and Gallegos's *Doña Bárbara*. But Martí distinguishes himself from these authors in a decisive way. Instead of vanquishing barbarism, as Sarmiento does, or reconciling it with civilization, like Gallegos, Martí proposes that it be the foundation of America's future society. Martí actually moves away from civilization and barbarism and favors a language that emphasizes local origins versus foreign influence. As Martí put it, "The struggle is not between civilization and barbarity, but between false erudition and Nature."[7] By "false erudition" Martí means ideas or programs originating in foreign lands that are directed by foreigners and/or their local lackeys. By "Nature" he refers to homegrown ideas and leaders that are organic to the Americas and not imported. Martí purposefully capitalizes the word because he believes it is the foundation upon which America should be built.

Despite its brevity, "Our America" roots its political agenda in historical context. Whereas authors had argued and others would continue to argue that America was trapped in its duality between mother America and father Europe, Martí rejects the notion that the two aspects of American history (the indigenous and the colonial) are irreconcilable. Rather, out of their combined history emerges America's distinctiveness. In this way, "Our America" offers a classic nationalistic program by seeking out that which is supposedly original to the land and emphasizing it as the spirit or soul upon which the new nation should be built. Of course, Martí advocates for a continental nation, a Pan-America, rather than numerous individual nations, but the concept remains the same. The uniqueness of a land and its history is to be emphasized and drawn upon. In Martí's words, "Government must originate in the country. The spirit of government must be that of the country. . . . Good government is nothing more than the balance of a country's natural elements."[8]

Martí uses the dichotomy of mother America and father Europe to define the new natural leaders of America. The "sons of Our America," should not be "ashamed of the mother who reared them, because she wears an Indian apron," nor should they disown their mother because she is sick and on her deathbed. Instead, the natural leader should "tend his mother and nurse her in her illness." These "sons of Our America," Martí writes, "will be saved by its Indians."[9]

With this acute awareness of America's demographic diversity, the legacy of Europe, Africa, and Native America, Martí offers a remarkably forward-looking position on race. "There are no races," he writes; thus, "there can be no racial animosity."[10] With these few words, Martí envisioned a future different from that of almost all previous authors. If race is irrelevant and all people are truly born equal, then America's supposedly barbarian side should be neither destroyed (as in Sarmiento) nor simply tolerated (as in Gallegos), but rather embraced as foundational.

"Our America" is obviously a very progressive work. It challenged many essentialisms of the day, and it would be decades before its propositions became more commonplace. Notably in this regard, we position Martí after Gallegos, although "Our America" was written four decades before *Doña Bárbara*.

Despite its advanced ideas, "Our America" is still a product of its time, remaining rooted in essentialisms. A semiotic reading exposes the discursive influence upon Martí's conceptualizations of race, class, gender, and nation and predicts the ways in which "Our America," once it entered into the literary canon, would go on to propagate these discourses in future writings. In short, "Our America" can be read against itself.

Concerning race, for example, Martí describes the new Americans with their "white" heads and "mottled" bodies.[11] While Martí acknowledges the ethnic pluralism of the Americas and calls upon an undiscriminating embrace of this diversity, he links the intellectual side of America's future to Europe and white-skinned people and the corporeal side to Indians and Africans. This idea builds upon a cornerstone of racialist essentialism, the idea that darker-skinned people are driven less by intellect and more by passion or sensuality.

Martí also limits the new American leader (the "natural" man) to being urban and non-Indian, presumably white or at least mestizo. For instance, he writes that "in the Indian republics, the governors are learning Indian."[12] This passage celebrates the local orientation of the new American leader and the ethnic merging that will be America's future. But it also reveals a vision of government, particularly in those nations with Indian majorities, led by non-Indians. His text envisions America still led by elite, lettered citizens.

In an example of the collapsing of race and class essentialisms, Martí refers to the "uncultured masses" as "lazy and timid in the realm of intelligence."[13] The entire premise of "Our America" is based upon a belief in the nation (Pan-America) as an essence, not a construct. Martí also calls upon the new American leaders to be "real men."[14] He uses this rhetorical flourish to challenge the new leadership to have nationalistic pride, but he does so through a traditional appeal to manhood, which not only excludes women but also draws in the entire discursive history of masculinity and femininity.

"Our America" is an excellent illustration of the operation of discourse. It shows how a text that challenges old ideas can inadvertently rely upon old discursive assumptions and advance these discourses under the guise of new and revolutionary thinking. Certainly, old discourses were altered by Martí's ideas and contributions. But that is precisely how discourses operate. They are stable and long-lasting, yet flexible and adaptable. They affect the way authors view the world without their conscious knowledge; authors, in turn, affect discourses inadvertently while fulfilling their roles as propagators. Neither discourses nor authors are fully in control. We can see this dynamic in Martí's own words.

JOSÉ MARTÍ, "OUR AMERICA"[15]

Those carpenter's sons who are ashamed that their fathers are carpenters! Those born in America who are ashamed of the mother who reared them, because she wears an Indian apron; and those scoundrels who disown their sick mother, abandoning her on her sickbed! Then who is a real man? He who stays with his mother and nurses her in her illness, or he who puts her to work out of sight, and lives at her expense on decadent lands, sporting fancy neckties, cursing the womb that carried him, displaying the sign of the traitor on the back of his paper frock coat? These sons of Our America, which will be saved by its Indians and is growing better; these deserters who take up arms in the armies of a North America that drowns its Indians in blood and is growing worse! These delicate creatures who are men but are unwilling to do men's work! The Washington who made this land for them, did he not go to live with the English, at a time when he saw them fighting against his own country. These unbelievers in honor who drag that honor over foreign soil like their counterparts in the French Revolution with their dancing, their affectations, their drawling speech!

For in what lands can men take more pride than in our long-suffering American republics, raised up among the silent Indian masses by the bleeding arms of a hundred apostles, to the sounds of battle between the book and the processional candle? Never in history have such advanced and united nations been forged in so short a time from such disorganized elements. The presumptuous man feels that the earth was made to serve as his pedestal because he happens to have a facile pen or colorful speech, and he accuses his native land of being worthless and beyond redemption because its virgin jungles fail to provide him with a constant means of traveling the world, driving Persian ponies and lavishing champagne like a tycoon. The incapacity does not lie with the emerging country in quest of suitable forms and a utilitarian greatness; it lies rather with those who attempt to rule nations of a unique and violent character by means of laws inherited from four centuries of freedom in the United States and nineteen centuries of monarchy in France. A decree by Hamilton does not halt the charge of the plainsman's horse. A phrase by Sieyès does nothing to quicken the stagnant blood of the Indian race. To govern well, one must see things as they are. And the able governor in America is not the one who knows how to govern the Germans or the French; he must know the elements that make up his own country, and how to bring them together, using methods and institutions originating within the country, to reach that desirable state where each man can attain self-realization and all may enjoy the abundance that Nature has bestowed in everyone in the nation to enrich with their toil and defend with their lives. Government must originate in the country. The spirit of government must be that of the country. Its structure must conform to rules appropriate to the country. Good government is nothing more than the balance of the country's natural elements.

That is why in America the imported book has been conquered by the natural man. Natural men have conquered learned and artificial men. The native half-breed has conquered the exotic Creole. The struggle is not between civilization and barbarity, but between false erudition and Nature. The natural man is good, and he respects and rewards superior intelligence as long as his humility is not turned against him, or he is not offended by being disregarded—something the natural man never forgives, prepared as he is to forcibly regain the respect of whoever has wounded his pride or threatened his interests. It is by conforming with these disdained native elements that the tyrants of America have climbed to power, and have fallen as soon as they betrayed them. Republics have paid with oppression for their inability to recognize the true elements of their countries, to derive from them the right kind of government, and to govern accordingly. In a new nation a government means a creator.

In nations composed of both cultured and uncultured elements, the uncultured will govern because it is their habit to attack and resolve doubts with their fists in cases where the cultured have failed in the art of governing. The uncultured masses are lazy and timid in the realm of intelligence, and they want to be governed well. But if the government hurts them, they shake it off and govern themselves. How can the universities produce governors if not a single university in America teaches the rudiments of the art of government, the analysis of elements peculiar to the peoples of America? The young go out into the world wearing Yankee or French spectacles, hoping to govern a people they do not know. In the political race entrance should be denied to those who are ignorant of the rudiments of politics. The prize in literary contests should not go for the best ode, but for the best study of the political factors of one's country. Newspapers, universities and schools should encourage the study of the country's pertinent components. To know them is sufficient, without mincing words; for whoever brushes aside even a part of the truth, whether through intention or oversight, is doomed to fall. The truth he lacks thrives on negligence, and brings down whatever is built without it. It is easier to resolve our problem knowing its components than to resolve it without knowing them. Along comes the natural man, strong and indignant, and he topples all the justice accumulated from books because he has not been governed in accordance with the obvious needs of the country. Knowing is what counts. To know one's country and govern it with that knowledge is the only way to free it from tyranny. The European university must bow to the American university. The history of America, from the Incas to the present, must be taught in clear detail and to the letter, even if the archons of Greece are overlooked. Our Greece must take priority over the Greece which is not ours. We need it more. Nationalist statesmen must replace foreign statesmen. Let the world be grafted onto our republics, but the trunk must be our own. And the vanquished pedant hold his tongue, for there are no lands in which a man may take greater pride than in our long-suffering American republics.

With the rosary as our guide, our heads white and our bodies mottled, both Indians and Creoles, we fearlessly entered the world of nations [. . .].

Nations stand up and greet one another. "What are we?" is the mutual question, and little by little they furnish answers. When a problem arises in Cojímar, they do not seek its solution in Danzig. The frock coats are still French, but thought begins to be American. The youth of America are rolling up their sleeves, digging their hands in the dough, and making it rise with the sweat of their brows. They realize that there is too much imitation, and that creation holds the key to salvation. "Create" is the password of this generation. The wine is made from plantain, but even if it turns sour, it is our own wine! That a country's form of government must be in keeping with its natural elements is self-evident. Absolute ideas must take relative forms if they are not to fail because of an error in form. Freedom, to be viable, has to be sincere and complete. If a Republic refuses to open its arms to all, and move ahead with all, it dies. The tiger within sneaks in through the crack; so does the tiger from without [. . .].

The scorn of our formidable neighbor, who does not know us, is Our America's greatest danger. And since the day of the visit is near, it is imperative that our neighbor knows us, and soon, so that it will not scorn us. Through ignorance it might even come to lay hands on us. Once it does know us, it will remove its hands out of respect. One must have faith in the best in men and distrust the worst. One must allow the best to be shown so that it reveals and prevails over the worst. Nations should have a pillory for whoever stirs up useless hatred, and another for whoever fails to tell them the truth in time.

There can be no racial animosity, because there are no races. The theorist and feeble thinkers string together and warm over the bookshelf races which the well-disposed observer and the fair-minded traveler vainly seek in the justice of Nature where man's universal identity springs forth from triumphant love and the turbulent hunger for life. The soul, equal and eternal, emanates from bodies of different shapes and colors. Whoever foments and spreads antagonism and hatred between the races, sins against humanity. But as nations take shape among other different nations, there is a condensation of vital and individual characteristics of thought and habit, expansion and conquest, vanity and greed which could—from the latent state of national concern, and in the period of internal disorder, or the rapidity with which the country's character has been accumulating—be turned into a serious threat for the weak and isolated neighboring countries, declared by the strong country to be inferior and perishable. The thought is father to the deed. And one must not attribute, through a provincial antipathy, a fatal and inborn wickedness to the continent's fair-skinned nation simply because it does not speak our language, nor see the world as we see it, nor resemble us in its political defects, so different from ours, nor favorably regard the excitable, dark-skinned people, or look charitably, from its still uncertain eminence, upon those less favored by history, who climb the road of republicanism by heroic stages [. . .].

DISCUSSION QUESTIONS

• In addition to the examples provided in the introduction to Martí, can you find other places in the text where he relies on traditional essences of race, class, gender, or nation?

• Martí is a product of a European and U.S. education. Why would he then make such an anti-imperialist argument as that in "Our America"?

• Although Angel Rama's concept of the lettered citizen was not available to Martí in 1891, does "Our America" challenge the traditional dominance of the lettered citizen by appealing to the natural man as the new American leader? Or, does the image of the natural leader simply cast the lettered citizen in a new, American image?

• Imagine a society structured along the lines of "Our America." Would it be any different for so-called uncultured people?

NOTES

1. Sources consulted for this introduction were Joanne Hershfield, *Mexican Cinema/Mexican Woman: 1940–1950* (Tucson: U of Arizona P, 1996); Julie Skurski, "The Ambiguities of Authenticity in Latin America: Doña Bárbara and the Construction of National Identity," ed. Geof Eley and R. Suny, *Becoming National: A Reader* (New York: Oxford UP, 1996) 371–402; and Doris Sommer, *Foundational Fictions: The National Romances of Latin America* (Berkeley: U of California P, 1991) 272–289.

2. Rómulo Gallegos, *Doña Bárbara* (New York: Peter Smith, 1948), originally published in Barcelona by Editorial Araluce in 1929. These excerpts are from 23–29, 44–46, 139–140, 145, 185–186, 209–210, 297.

3. Paiba is one of Doña Bárbara's henchmen, and this sentence refers to his setting fire to a portion of Luzardo's property. He did so without direct orders from Doña Bárbara, who at this point is still assessing her strategy toward Luzardo.

4. This excerpt is drawn from the chapter called "Love of Country: Populism's Revised Romance in *La Vorágine* and *Doña Bárbara*," 272–279, 281, 284–289.

5. Sommer is referring to José Eustancio Rivera, author of *La Vorágine* (1924).

6. The page numbers in parentheses refer to the 1948 publication of *Doña Bárbara*.

7. José Martí, "Our America," ed. Deborah Shnookal and Mirta Muñiz, *José Martí Reader: Writings on the Americas* (Melbourne: Ocean, 2001) 113.

8. Martí 113.

9. Martí 112.

10. Martí 119.

11. Martí 115.

12. Martí 118.

13. Martí 114.

14. Martí 112.

15. This excerpt is from 111–120.

Film Foray: The Three Caballeros

When World War II was looming in Europe and Asia, the United States, under President Franklin Delano Roosevelt, introduced a plan it called its Good Neighbor policy. It was an attempt to secure Latin American allegiances and hemispheric unity as a protection against foreign invasion, as well as to boost export revenue in the economically depressed years following the stock market crash of 1929. In this climate, film was thought to play an important role in shaping popular belief. Between 1941 and 1943, Walt Disney and his staff were contracted by Nelson Rockefeller, director of the Office of Inter-American Affairs, and his assistant, John Hay Whitney, head of the motion picture section, to travel to Latin America in anticipation of creating animated films that would demonstrate that the United States understood Latin America and was offering its southern neighbor democracy and friendship in lieu of aggression and occupation.

Of course, the epistemological flaw in this idea was that, despite the apparent focus on Latin America, the spotlight remained squarely on the United States, though it seemed ready to view the Latin American "other" through new lenses. Presumably, the new disposition by the U.S. government in commissioning these films could be traced to its desire to put a great deal of distance between itself and the typical movie portrayal of Hispanics. In those films, Hispanics were seen as lazy ignoramuses or cunningly dangerous bandits and Latin America itself was a beautiful, light-skinned woman, as willing and ready for the taking as a banana from United Fruit Company, the monopolistic U.S. fruit exporter. However, despite the different characters, settings, media forms, or objectives, the treatment of race, class, gender, and nation in those films continued to fall in line with dominant North American discourses on Latin America. Of the many animated films produced between 1941 and 1945 from the material collected during Disney's three trips south of the border, the 1945 release of *The Three Caballeros* clearly demonstrates that the United States was using the same old prescription in the lenses through which it viewed Latin America.

This half-animated film begins with the typically clumsy Donald Duck receiving from his Latin American friends three birthday presents, which subsequently frame the movie into three parts. In a cinematographically reflexive move, the first gift that Donald opens turns out to be a movie projector. He tangles himself up in the projector's screen and ends up projecting the film on his hind feathers. Then the film "teaches" him through voice-over narrative about his feathered relatives to the south. One of them, Pablo the Penguin, succeeds in finding a way out of what he deems his miserable icy abode in the South Pole to a tropical island (part of the Galapagos) where he is decked out in shades and swimming trunks and ends up sweating in a hammock while a slow but willing, native turtle serves him cold drinks. This film within a film continues with an almost wholly didactic, Disney-esque taxonomy of bird species of Latin America. It ends with the exploitation of a magical bird-donkey who is put to work winning a race for birds. The bird-donkey wins the race but is disqualified when he is discovered and converted back into a mere donkey with wings.

In the second and third sequences of *The Three Caballeros*, animation using technology that would eventually allow the success of *Who Framed Roger Rabbit?* combines with live action as two other caballeros, the Brazilian parrot Joe Carioca and the Mexican rooster Panchito, make their appearances along with three famous Latin American actresses, the Brazilian Aurora Miranda, and Mexicans Carmen Molina and Dora Luz. In these sections, Donald's feathered friends show him their countries by way of picture books that come to life. In scenes reminiscent of Lewis Carroll's *Through the Looking-Glass*, Donald and the others enter into these animated frames and become participants in scenes of women dancing, singing, and frolicking as they are pursued by male admirers. Donald's emblematic clumsiness becomes sexualized in his own relentless pursuit of the beauties of Latin America, as the film departs from conventional Disney patterns of apparent sexlessness.

In "Don (Juanito) Duck and the Imperial Patriarchal Unconscious," Julianne Burton, a professor of Latin(o) American visual media at the University of California, Santa Barbara, articulates the "death" of the Disney filmmakers of *The Three Caballeros*. She shows that the film doubles back on its stated objectives of reimagining a relationship with Latin America; instead, it fortifies the patriarchal and imperialist approach.[1] In the section of her study called "Ten Perverse Propositions on Desire in Disney," Burton asserts that in an effort to present Latin America as a desirable place—through beautifully packaged presents that Donald receives from his cousins, parrot Joe Carioca and Panchito the rooster—the filmmakers succeed only in offering hegemony in exchange for the gifts of limitless desire for a beautiful land and beautiful ladies. Latin America is cast as female spectacle to serve and entertain the male United States, which is cast as the inept, nonthreatening Donald Duck.

Sexual props and images abound throughout. Joe Carioca's umbrella and cigar are transformed into two pistols, matching Panchito the Rooster's own pair. A dancing cowgirl is suddenly surrounded by phallic cacti and cracking whips. Interspersed among disembodied, kissing lips, a flaccid elephant trunk becomes erect and splashes water in Donald's face, animated flowers swallow and dizzy him, and a telescope lengthens and stiffens in Donald's hands as he ogles bathing beauties on Acapulco beach.

Even if we assume, as Burton does, that the makers of the film had no intention of infusing an animated film about Latin America with images of passion considered essential to this "other" culture, the sexual innuendo that underscores Donald's relationship with Latin America reveals the "'collective unconscious' of that culture-industry-cum-empire known as Walt Disney Productions."[2] Thus, regardless of the intentions of the filmmakers to imagine a new and improved version of hemispheric relations, the meaning created by the movie presents no challenge to former narratives. Instead, the film reinforces the status of the United States as hegemonic center while maintaining Latin America at the margins, all within a discursive community of neo-empire.

JULIANNE BURTON, "DON (JUANITO) DUCK AND THE IMPERIAL PATRIARCHAL DISCOURSE"[3]
Ten Perverse Propositions on Desire in Disney

FIRST PROPOSITION: LATIN AMERICA AS A WARTIME TOONTOWN   In *Roger Rabbit,* Toontown is a zone of marginality inhabited by the vulnerable and the victimized, literally "an/other world"/"an/Other's world" to be entered only with wariness and dread and seldom escaped intact. For the writers and animators of *The Three Caballeros,* Latin America is the 1940s equivalent of "Toontown," the seductive-repulsive zone of spectacular excess and excessive spectacle. In the sections depicting Brazil and Mexico, reason gives way to passion, order to disorder and incoherence, the logic of experience to the chaos of nightmare. It is this impression/projection of Latin-ness which unleashes both Donald's and Disney's libido. The Latin is rendered synonymous with license and licentiousness. The projection onto the other of what we most fear/reject/suppress/desire within ourselves lies at the root of the film's indulgence in excess—an excess which is, in this case, specifically, relentlessly sexual.

Certainly, I would be treading shaky ground if I were to attempt to (psycho) analyze the animators, but the uncharacteristic excess which erupts most overpoweringly in the final segment begins to seem somewhat less unfathomable once one tries to reconstruct the atmosphere at Disney Studios in the last years of the Great War. As noted above, financial losses occasioned layoffs and strikes which in 1941 reduced the workforce by half. By the end of that year, the Studios had turned into the most extensive "war plant" in Hollywood, housing mountains of munitions, quartering antiaircraft troops, providing overflow office space for Lockheed personnel. By 1943, fully 94 percent of the footage produced at the studios was war-related. Disney had become a government contractor on a massive scale. The restrictions on costs and equipment applied to the other studios did not apply to Disney because animation was exempted. It is not difficult to imagine, in this context of dreary war work, how the license implicit in the "surprise package" of *The Three Caballeros* project might have unleashed creative juices which had been stored too long under pressure.

SECOND PROPOSITION: SPECTACULAR PACKAGING   *The Three Caballeros* packages Latin America (or, more accurately, depicts Latin America as packaging itself) as pure spectacle. Each gift is an artifact of and for visualization: a movie projector and film, a pop-up book, a portfolio of scenes from various regions of Mexico. Parts II and III begin by emphasizing the spectacle of the Latin American landscape (ideally populated by singing, dancing natives) and ultimately progress to "bodyscape"—the spectacle of the playful, alluring, receptive Latin female.

THIRD PROPOSITION: AN ALLEGORY OF COLONIALISM   *The Three Caballeros* offers an allegory of (neo-) colonialism: every story packaged here is a narrative of conquest or of enslavement. In the first narrative from Part I, Pablo Penguin sets out from the south pole to find "the isle of his dreams." Having resourcefully overcome numerous comic setbacks, he finally reaches the Galapagos, where he is last seen tanning himself in a hammock while a tray-bearing tortoise brings him one iced drink after another. (It comes as no surprise that the narrative of this hapless indigene's enslavement has been conveniently omitted.) In the first segment's closing narrative, Gauchito captures and enslaves the donkey-bird because the instant he stumbles upon the creature, he immediately perceives that he "must be worth a fortune!"

FOURTH PROPOSITION: HIERARCHIES OF THE WILLING-AND-WAITING-TO-BE-CONQUERED   The chronology of conquest in *The Three Caballeros* recapitulates a hierarchy that goes from claiming territory (Pablo's tropical isle) to capturing and taming the local fauna (Gauchito's flying donkey) to Donald's designs on the female homo sapiens. Each rung in this hierarchy is represented as simply waiting to be taken; Donald's conquests fail not because his targets aren't willing but because he is not able.

FIFTH PROPOSITION: DONALD'S UN–DON JUANLY INEPTITUDE AS SOP TO THE EXCESSIVE MACHISMO OF HIS AVIAN ACCOMPLICES   If Donald's conquest is displaced (from geography onto the female body), it is also disguised or "de-fused" by his ineptitude, his failure to consummate his desires. The mechanisms of geopolitical and sexual conquest here enjoy a convenient congruence. Anxious to allay potential fears that this "neighborly" North American presence will be too potent, too overpowering, the filmmakers place the brunt of the film's humor on the sheer ludicrousness of Donald Duck as Don Juan—his impotence, his childish polymorphousness or, in baldest Lacanian terms, his lack of the phallus.

The *charra* sequence, part of the climactic second half of the Mexican segment, makes Donald's phallic inadequacy most glaringly apparent. Dressed in a feminized version of a traditionally male costume and carrying a riding crop, the phallic woman (Carmen Molina) stomps her high boots in a self-confident *zapateo.* She is surrounded by a phalanx of dancing cacti which, as they deploy and metamorphosize, alternately squash, obscure, fragment and otherwise overpower Donald. At the end of the sequence, Donald runs through a forest of elongated cacti, their prominent appendages dangling high above him, in futile pursuit of Carmen Molina who has herself "congealed" into a cactus before he can reach her. Green, the color of lust for the Latins and envy for the gringos, dominates the sequence. The imagery of inadequacy has seldom been more overdetermined.

In marked contrast to Donald, Joe Carioca and Panchito are more generously equipped. Each comes armed with a pair of phallic objects: a cigar and umbrella in the parrot's case (in the Mexican sequence, the umbrella more than once turns into a machine gun); and a pair of pistols liberally deployed in the case of the rooster, whose species itself is—needless to say—an emblem of male sexual prowess.

As recently as 1982, a film historian wrote apropos of this film that Donald Duck's "camaraderie with the caballeros from Brazil and Mexico symbolized the idea of hemispheric unity."[4] In fact, this male camaraderie provides a thin pretext for (and eventually a major impediment to) Donald's real interest, the (hetero)sexual pursuit of "priddy girls" of uniformly pale complexion. Donald's feathered companions are first potential rivals, later indomitable restrainers and disrupters. The Disney team apparently felt the need to reassure their Latin American counterparts that they need feel no threat to their sexual hegemony from this North American neighbor who, for all his quacking up and cracking up, is clearly incapable of shacking up.

SIXTH PROPOSITION: DOÑA JUANITA? The ultimate reassurance regarding Donald's nonthreatening nature is the recurrent feminization which he undergoes immediately after his attempts to "connect" with the objects of his desire—a desire no less fickle for all its obsessive intensity. Donald's surrogate femaleness at key moments is undermined by visual puns that verge on the subliminal but compel an embarrassing blatancy on the part of anyone wishing to describe them. (Oh well. Here goes.)

Seconds prior to the conclusion of both the Brazilian and the Mexican sequences, Donald is literally swept off his feet by a stream of ejaculate. His concluding appearance in the Brazilian sequence comes when he tries to imitate Aurora Miranda, whose compelling gestures "animate" her cartooned surroundings, making buildings and plazas pulse to a samba beat. In response to Donald's pathetic attempt at mimesis, a fountain shaped like an elephant's head extends is flaccid trunk into a rigid horizontal pipe and proceeds to overpower Donald with its spray.

In the frenetic "climax" of the Mexican sequence, which also ends the film, Joe Carioca and Panchito combat Donald in a mock bull-fight. The inept Donald has trouble maneuvering the bull armature which, with the instantaneousness of nightmare, he suddenly inhabits. His assailants are considerably more agile: Pancho goads him with red flags and wisecracks while Joe sets a cluster of firecrackers alight on his tail and then skewers him with a pair of pokers. After his ejection (ejaculation?) from the make-believe bull, which magically and terrifyingly continues to rampage unaided, Donald redirects his combative fury away from its original target (the "friends" who have so persistently thwarted his amorous efforts) and toward this emblem of masculinity, charging the bull head-on as Panchito sings in ironic voice-over, "like brother to brother/we're all for each other . . ." The trail of spewing fireworks in the Mexican finale rockets Donald skyward; embracing this stream, he then slides back "down to earth." The film's concluding frames show Donald in one of his many feminized poses, draped head to foot in a Mexican serape and protectively flanked by his two cohorts [. . .].

NINTH PROPOSITION: ILLUSORY RECIPROCITIES AND OTHER DECEPTIVE WAYS OF SEEING EYE TO EYE   The notion of reciprocity is deceptively evoked in the opening frames of the film when Donald, who has opened the first of his birthday gifts from Latin America to find a movie projector and screen, subjects the strip of celluloid to the close scrutiny of his naked eye. Cut to a point-of-view closeup of one of the frames, which animates: Pablo Penguin turns his telescope toward Donald/the camera/the viewer; its huge concentric circularity, a remote eye at its center, dominates the frame. This brief sequence embodies what might be called the "myth of the reciprocal gaze." The Other who gazes back at the gazer in fact "sees" nothing, since a figure imprinted on a single frame of celluloid cannot be either animate or sensate—except of course in a cartoon, and in a cartoon-within-a-cartoon.

But *were* Pablo Penguin to *see* the one who is seeing him (Donald Duck), he would arguably be merely mirroring himself. The Antarctic penguin is a notably "de-culturated" choice, a paradoxical bird if there ever was one: so terrestrial that he seems to be the antithesis of the avian; so southerly that he conveys the quintessence of northerliness. The "rare bird" given pride of place in the film's order of presentation is thus not in fact "one of them" but quite transparently "one of us." The further we travel, the more we stay at home—or some such paradoxical platitude—seems to be the subtextual invocation here.

Furthermore, Pablo's successful colonization of tropical America is rendered innocent because he comes from an ephemeral "nowhere." Without any attachment to terra firma, he simply cuts his igloo free from the icepack when he wants to navigate north to the tropics, and the ice floe which anchored him to his Antarctic community becomes the vehicle for his solitary migration. Similarly, he lacks the avian "ethno/specificity" conveyed by the coloration, symbolic accoutrements, and richly genuine accents of both Panchito and Joe Carioca. (To his credit, Disney insisted on native voices for these roles.) Even the frenetic Carmen Miranda-esque "song" of the mischievous and disruptive aracuan bird, who appears at "random" moments in parts I and II, connotes a cultural embeddedness of which Pablo is utterly devoid. Pablo has no voice at all: Sterling "Doc" Holloway, the vibrato-voiced narrator of *Peter and the Wolf,* is called in to tell his story for him in voice-over.

TENTH PROPOSITION: PREFIGURATIONS OF THINGS TO COME Illusory reciprocity constitutes the very core of this film. As we've seen, the production of meanings in *The Three Caballeros* is both explicit and veiled, brazen and coy. Much of the film's fascinatingly devious elusiveness derives from the intricacy of its reversals, from deceptive reciprocities in which there is no real exchange, or in which what is exchanged is not what has been promised. Anthony Wilden, writing in *System and Structure* on logical typing and the triangulation of binary oppositions, notes how the apparent symmetry of the binary pair is often governed by an "invisible" third term which converts difference into hierarchy.[5] In this case, the "third term" between the North American and the South American may be the neocolonizing ambition of the former.

A film which reportedly set out to be an offering of friendship toward Latin America adopts the reverse as its core premise. Latin America fetes Donald Duck, showering him with birthday gifts and hosting his visits to Bahia and Mexico, much as, in relation to the film's production, Latin Americans hosted Disney and his team and much as, in relation to the film's reception, Latin America was offered up as ready host to Donald Duck's successors, the American tourists. The perverse dialectic of economic aid, which rewards the donor while impoverishing the recipient, is replicated (one is almost tempted to say prophesied) here.

Disney's "gift" of intercultural understanding turns out to be the act of packaging Latin America for enhanced North-American consumption. The unspoken pact which makes that package possible rests upon the equation of cultural expression with femininity and cultural exchange with heterosexual conquest, and upon the positing of a shared assumption between conqueror and conqueree: that the female of the species is a willing target of appropriation.

To its enduring credit, *The Three Caballeros* does utilize Latin American music, accents, performers, locales, artifacts, and modes of cultural expression more extensively than any previous Hollywood film. Disney's quest for cultural authenticity was to that extent both sincere and successful. The results are often dazzling, even by today's elevated technical standards. But all these good intentions cannot mask the discomforting evidence which hides just below the comic frenzy: all cultural reciprocities are not created equal.

DISCUSSION QUESTIONS

• Explain and support the argument that *The Three Caballeros* is a U.S. version of an international foundational fiction, i.e., that the union of potentially oppositional sides is metaphorical for a broader political and/or diplomatic project.

- What discourses of gender, race, and nation are present in the phrase cited by Burton: All "'priddy girls' of uniformly pale complexion?"

- Why is Donald Duck as an inept (and animated) predator such an effective symbol for the ostensible change in U.S. policy toward Latin America? How would this film be different if another Disney character, such as the savvy Mickey Mouse, were chosen to represent the United States instead of Donald Duck? How does this choice of character bolster Burton's interpretation of the film?

- Burton interprets *The Three Caballeros* as presenting multiple sexual innuendos and containing scenes with seemingly obvious sexual overtones. She suggests that these images were not the conscious intent of the authors and reflect a broader sexualization of Latin America that is typical of an imperializing ethos. Is it possible that this is not the case and that it is just Burton and a few academics like her who see those images and thus interpret in a way that says more about themselves than about the film or what it represents? How would Burton, or perhaps Edward Said (author of *Orientalism*), respond to that question?

NOTES

1. Julianne Burton, "Don (Juanito) Duck and the Imperial Patriarchal Unconscious: Disney Studios, the Good Neighbor Policy, and the Packaging of Latin America," ed. Andrew Parker, *Nationalism and Sexualities* (New York: Routledge, 1992) 23.

2. Burton 24.

3. For a seminal study of Disney and discourse, see Ariel Dorfman and Armand Mattelart, *How to Read Donald Duck: Imperialist Ideology in the Disney Comic*, trans. David Kunzle (New York: International General, 1974). The excerpt is from Burton 32–38.

4. Richard Shale, *Donald Duck Joins Up: The Walt Disney Studios During World War II* (Ann Arbor: UMI Research Press, 1987) 107

5. Anthony Wilden, *System and Structure: Essays in Communication and Exchange* (London: Tavistock, 1980) xxxiii–xxxv.

The Socialist Utopia: Che Guevara and the Cuban Revolution

ANALYZING *THE MOTORCYCLE DIARIES*

Whether through the publication of Karl Marx's writings in the nineteenth century, the victory of the Russian Revolution in 1917, the formation of Communist parties throughout the Western Hemisphere in the 1920s and 1930s, or the onset of the cold war in the late 1940s, Communism has deeply impacted the history of Latin America and the rest of the world. But arguably it was not until the victory of the Cuban Revolution in 1959 that Communism began to define day-to-day life in Latin America. When Fidel Castro and his ragtag guerrilla army descended from the mountains of eastern Cuba and took control of the national government in Havana in January 1959, the future of socialism in Latin America suddenly became less of a dream (or nightmare) and more of a real possibility.

One of those people in the mountains with Castro was a young, obscure Argentine doctor named Ernesto "Che" Guevara. Today, he is arguably the most widely recognized Latin American figure in the world and the person most commonly associated with socialist revolution in Latin America. Many people today, especially youth, might know nothing more about Che than that his image is ubiquitous on T-shirts, a black figure set against a red background—a handsome, dashing, beret-adorned face with eyes gazing off into unknown utopian horizons. But regardless of how he is recognized or remembered, Che has unquestionably achieved the rare and immortal status of an icon.

We are interested in Che to the extent that he can stand as a symbol of the era of revolutionary socialism in Latin America, roughly the thirty-year period between 1960 and 1990. By subjecting his legend to semiotic analysis, we will illustrate the way in which discourses are present in the

FIGURE 14.1 *Marchers commemorating the twenty-fifth anniversary of the assassination of Archbishop Oscar Romero hold aloft a banner bearing Che's image. San Salvador, El Salvador, April 2, 2005. Photograph by Erik Ching*

socialist project. Of course, we are aware that something as grand and diverse as socialism in Latin America cannot be confined to the history of one man. But we believe Che is a good and accessible representative of the broader issues raised by this decisive phase in modern Latin America.

FIGURE 14.2 *The sign says, "We want you to be like Che—Fidel." Santa Clara, Cuba, 2004. Photograph by Scott McPherson*

Socialism, which is closely linked to Communism, purports to defend the little guys, the poor workers who have nothing to offer but their labor power, who toil day after day for the rich owners and still barely make enough to survive. Regardless of the horrendous things done in the name of socialism (e.g., by Stalin and Pol Pot), at its most basic level the ideal is that everyone has a right to enjoy the products of society's collective labor. Perhaps it is not surprising that Latin America would witness a sweeping wave of support for socialism. Historically, its societies have been marked by extreme maldistributions of wealth, and its governments have traditionally defended the haves against the have-nots.

Socialism's heyday in Latin America began with the Cuban Revolution in 1959 and ended more or less with the collapse of the Soviet Union in 1989. During that era, almost every government in Latin America was challenged by the political left, either in the form of a guerrilla army, a political party, or some combination of the two. Even if the success of these movements was marginal (fewer than half a dozen rose to national power, and most of them only briefly), socialism nevertheless inspired the hopes of millions.

Socialism in Latin America gained currency in the wake of the failure of nationalist populism in the first half of the twentieth century. Populist heroes like Juan and Eva Perón in Argentina (1946–1955; 1973–1974), Getúlio

Vargas in Brazil (1930–1945; 1950–1954), Raúl Haya de la Torre in Peru (1978–1979), and Jacobo Arbenz in Guatemala (1950–1954), and the various leaders of the Mexican Revolution (1910–1940) promised to change government to defend the lives and interests of poor people. Indeed, many of these populists made impressive gains. But on balance, major problems remained. By the 1960s, poverty was still a continental blight, and the populists, some of whom turned toward fascism, had failed to stave off the machinations of oppressive military dictatorships, which began sweeping into power. It was during the critical transition phase of the 1950s that Che Guevara gained his political consciousness and eventually embraced socialism.

Guevara was born to a prosperous, middle-class family in Argentina in 1928. He suffered from extreme asthma during childhood (and throughout his life). Asthma, it is said, sparked his interest in becoming a doctor. He entered the University of Buenos Aires in 1948 to study medicine. In the midst of his studies, Che embarked on two major trips that exposed him to Latin America's widespread poverty. The first came in 1950 when he rode alone on a moped for four thousand miles throughout northern Argentina. The second and now more famous trip was in 1951 and 1952 when, in the company of a biochemist friend, Guevara traveled throughout South America, first on motorcycle, then by hitchhiking and on foot. After returning to Buenos Aires to complete his studies, Guevara left Argentina again, this time for Bolivia and Guatemala. There he witnessed the mobilization following the Bolivian Revolution in 1952, and the U.S.-supported overthrow of the reformist Arbenz government in Guatemala in 1954.

From Guatemala, Che went to Mexico where he met Fidel Castro. Castro had been recently released from a Cuban prison where he was held for revolutionary activities. He and Che became fast friends, sharing general visions of an alternative future for Latin America. Castro invited Che to join his guerrilla band that landed on the coast of Cuba aboard the *Granma* in 1956. Of the eighty-one guerrillas who boarded the boat, only twelve survived the Cuban military's attacks and made it to the Sierra Maestra; Che and Castro were among those twelve. Che then fought alongside Castro for three years and became a revolutionary commander.

Che held various high-ranking posts in the new Cuban government, most notably minister of industry. At that time he was still a relatively unknown figure in international circles, but his reputation grew rapidly as he began to travel as a diplomatic representative of the Cuban government. He promoted guerrilla warfare and advocated a new, idealized form of socialism. In 1965 Che resigned his post in the Cuban government and returned to the life of an international revolutionary. He went to central Africa but failed to incite a successful movement. In 1966 he traveled to Bolivia, where he tried to initiate the first of many revolutionary fronts throughout Latin America. In 1967 he was hunted down and shot by the Bolivian military.

Throughout his abbreviated life and his many travels, Che was a fastidious diarist. At least four of his diaries have been published as books, including those from his trip in 1951–1952 (the so-called *Motorcycle Diaries*), his time fighting in Cuba between 1957 and 1959, in Africa in 1965, and in Bolivia in 1966–1967. Che also authored a definitive treatise on revolutionary militancy, *On Guerrilla Warfare*. In our attempt here to gain insight into the thinking of a socialist revolutionary, any one of these texts would provide ample opportunities for analysis. But we will focus on *The Motorcycle Diaries*, in part because of its accessibility, but also because the release in 2004 of a major motion picture starring the young Mexican actor Gael García Bernal, promises to make the story of the *Diaries* one of the more readily recognized aspects of Che's life.[1]

Among Che scholars, it is becoming fairly well-accepted that his eight-month, eight-thousand-mile journey throughout South America in 1951 and 1952 was a pivotal moment in his political evolution. Che himself accepted that the trip had changed him. As he says in the prologue to the published version of the *Diaries*, which he wrote years later, "Wandering around 'our America with a capital A' has changed me more than I thought. . . . I now leave you with myself, the man I once was."[2] By his own admission, he began the trip as a privileged member of the bourgeoisie, but the realities of Latin America seeped into his consciousness and his political perspective was on the way to being overhauled. He and his traveling companion became, in his words, "shadows of our former aristocratic selves."[3]

We were unable to gain permission to reprint excerpts from the *Diaries*, perhaps because of the heightened exposure the movie gave the published diary at the time of this writing. But a summary description of the *Diaries* here will be sufficient to offer a semiotic interpretation. It will also set the stage for a reading on Che by Alma Guillermoprieto and for two film analyses we have written and included here—one of the film based on the *Diaries* and the other of *Soy Cuba* (*I Am Cuba*), which was made in Cuba shortly after the triumph of the revolution.

During the eight-month odyssey in 1951–1952, Guevara traveled with Alberto Granado, a doctor then twenty-nine years old, who owned the motorcycle called La Poderosa II (The Powerful II) on which they began their journey.[4] Guevara and Granado began their trip in Córdoba, Argentina, one of Argentina's interior cities located roughly eight hundred miles northwest of Buenos Aires. They first headed southeast to Argentina's Atlantic coast and then turned west across Argentina and the Andes Mountains into Chile. La Poderosa broke down shortly after they arrived in Chile, forcing them to travel by foot, boat, or bus. They hitchhiked much of the way. In Chile, they turned north and worked their way steadily through Peru, Ecuador, and Colombia, ending up in Venezuela, where Guevara and Granado parted ways. Guevara caught a ride on a cargo plane to Argentina that went through Miami. When the plane landed in Miami, the pilot discovered the need for a major repair. Penniless, Guevara ended up spending an unexpected and difficult month there until the plane was fixed.

The Motorcycle Diaries is surprisingly brief, consisting of less than 150 pages, with most entries covering not more than two of those. The majority of the entries are brief descriptions of the journey, of places they stay or people they meet. Guevara offers a few philosophical insights and political commentaries, but these are the exceptions and most do not appear until late in their journey. If a person were to read the *Diaries* casually, without concern for deep analysis, it would appear to be a description of a rambunctious road trip by a couple of young university students looking for adventure. In the opening entry, Guevara says that the inspiration for the trip was little more than exasperation with the mundane realities of school and work. "I was restless too," he writes, "mainly because I was a dreamer and a free spirit; I was fed up with medical school, hospitals and exams . . . all we could see was the dusty road ahead and us on our bike devouring kilometers in the flight northward" (13). For the North American reader, the *Diaries* evokes images of the classic American road trip, akin to Jack Kerouac's *On the Road*, or any story of young people hitting the road during summer vacation, guided by little more than a sense of adventure.

Guevara tells of some hardships that he and Granado faced, such as mechanical failures and inadequate food, shelter, and money. But for the most part, the *Diaries* depicts a pair of happy-go-lucky travelers who flirt with women, see new and interesting sights, and con people for food and drink. For example, in describing his thoughts about their plan to travel to Easter Island off the coast of Chile, Guevara writes, "This wonderful place where the weather is ideal, the women ideal, the food ideal, the work ideal (in its blissful non-existence). Who cares if we stay there a year, who cares about studying, work, family, etc.?"[5] This seems hardly the stuff of a future guerrilla warrior.

A closer reading of the *Diaries*, however, reveals an underlying narrative of growing political consciousness. For example, in the same entry as his whimsical ruminations about Easter Island, Guevara tells the story of visiting an elderly woman who suffers from asthma. He found her living

in a squalid state, and his sense of helplessness caused him to turn on the
system that would allow such suffering.

> It is in cases like this, when a doctor knows he is powerless in such
> circumstances, that he longs for change; a change which would pre-
> vent the injustice of a system in which until a month ago this poor old
> woman had had to earn her living as a waitress, wheezing and panting
> but facing life with dignity. In these circumstances people in poor fami-
> lies who can't pay their way are surrounded by an atmosphere of barely
> disguised acrimony; they stop being father, mother, sister or brother and
> become a purely negative factor in the struggle for life. . . . How long
> this present order, based on an absurd idea of caste, will last I can't say,
> but it's time governments spent less time publicizing their own virtues
> and more money, much more money, funding socially useful projects.[6]

This is not yet Che's revolutionary call to arms. Such thoughts could have
been offered by any reformer who believes in capitalism but wants increased
state spending and aid to the poor. Nonetheless, Che's awareness is taking
shape. It is not until the latter third of the *Diaries* that explicit politics becomes more common. An afterthought, which Che apparently wrote after
returning to Argentina, contains one of his earliest and most romanticized
commitments to the life of a revolutionary:

> I now knew that when the great guiding spirit cleaves humanity into
> two antagonistic halves, I will be with the people. And I know it
> because I see it imprinted on the night that I, the eclectic dissector of
> doctrines and psychoanalyst of dogmas, howling like a man possessed,
> will assail the barricades and trenches, will stain my weapon with
> blood and, consumed with rage, will slaughter any enemy I lay hands
> on. And then, as if an immense weariness were consuming my recent
> exhilaration, I see myself being sacrificed to the authentic revolution,
> the great leveller of individual will, pronouncing the exemplary *mea
> culpa*. I feel my nostrils dilate, savoring the acrid smell of gunpowder
> and blood, of the enemy's death; I brace my body, ready for combat, and
> prepare myself to be a sacred precinct within which the bestial howl of
> the victorious proletariat can resound with new vigor and hope.[7]

This entry eerily predicts Che's death in Bolivia in 1967. Trapped in a gulch
by the Bolivian army, he and his few remaining comrades tried to fight
their way to freedom. Most of them were killed, and Che was wounded and

captured. He was brought to a nearby town where he was left on the floor of a schoolhouse overnight, bleeding and in pain. The following morning, a low-ranking officer entered the room and shot Che to death. When Guevara wrote the afterword entry, he was still just Ernesto Guevara, an unknown young medical student from Córdoba, Argentina. But it suggests the revolutionary life upon which he would embark and which would turn him into Che, which is Argentine slang for "guy" or "friend"—the name Guevara adopted as a sort of leveling appeal to the everyday person. Even if this afterword were excluded, *The Motorcycle Diaries* shows the steady politicization of a young man. Guevara may have been aware of social injustice prior to his journey, but not until after his return did he know that his life would somehow be dedicated to eradicating it.

As a committed socialist, an adherent of Marxism-Leninism, and a modernist, Che believed wholeheartedly in an ontological reality, and he subsequently viewed the world through an essentialistic or hermeneutic lens. Therefore, an equally essentialist or hermeneutic reading of his life and writings would share his belief in an objective world and would then either agree or disagree with his interpretation of it. Most leftist essentialists are inclined to agree with Che. They view *The Motorcycle Diaries* as a formative stage in the evolution of his thinking, when the objective reality of Latin America led him to see the light of Marxism-Leninism. Modernist essentialists who are procapitalism and anti-Communist disagree with Che and say that his interpretation of the world was wrong, or at least that his chosen method to solve its problems was misguided.

Semioticians, of course, do not concern themselves with whether Che was right or wrong. They look for the discursive constitution of his thinking. One semiotic approach to Che begins by defining him as a lettered citizen. Che, like any other good socialist, saw himself as a man of the people and a defender of the proletariat. Thus, in his eyes he was the antithesis—even the sworn enemy—of elite intellectuals, the lettered citizens like Sarmiento or Gallegos. In fact, Che and many socialist leaders like him did resemble lettered citizens. They thought they knew what was best for other people, especially for the uneducated proletarian masses. They believed they possessed enlightened knowledge that would improve society and that people should agree with them and accept their leadership. Che's realm of knowledge was guerrilla warfare and Marxist-Leninist dialectical materialism. In fact, part of the reason he was invited to join the Cuban Revolution as an Argentine was because of his abilities and training as a doctor. His knowledge certainly looked different than that of Sarmiento's liberal positivism, but both Che and Sarmiento promoted their platforms in similar ways, as a medicine that society needed and that was best delivered by their skilled hands. Che's and Sarmiento's respective medicines might have tasted differently, but they were based upon similar modernistic, scientifically based truth claims. In semiotic terms their origins reside in the same discursive pool.

Another semiotic approach to Che questions his authorial position (think back here to Leslie Bary in Chapter 10). To put it bluntly, Che was a wealthy white heterosexual male, and thus it is reasonable to question the extent to which his views were constituted by racialized, elite, heterosexual, and patriarchal discourses. The *Diaries* offers some clues. It reveals a young man quick to objectify women and criticize men who are homosexual or seem effeminate. The *Diaries* also demonstrates a persistent tendency toward racial essentialism, such as when Che writes, "The black is indolent and fanciful, he spends his money on frivolity and drink; the European comes from a tradition of working and saving which follows him to this corner of America and drives him to get ahead."[8]

From yet another semiotic perspective, the *Diaries* reveals Che's reliance upon intellectual traditions that contradict his eventual conversion to socialism. One of these is mestizo nationalism. He proudly refers to a speech he delivered in honor of his Peruvian host in which he recalls having said, "We are one single mestizo race with remarkable ethnographical similarities, from Mexico down to the Magellan Straits. And so, in an attempt to break free from all narrow-minded provincialism, I propose a toast to Peru and to a United America."[9] Che was obviously trying to thank his generous host and create a sense of common bond, but in defining Latin America as mestizo, he entered into the discursive trap set by *mestizaje*, which excludes anyone who does not fit its homogenizing criteria, such as Indians and Africans or any other person who chooses to live life outside the collectively accepted meaning of mestizo.

Indianism (a romantic idealization of the purity of indigenous communities, akin to ideas of the noble savage) is another seemingly contradictory intellectual tradition that reappears frequently in the *Diaries*. Che devoted a surprisingly large portion of his entries to describing Indians and ancient Indian ruins.

While in Cuzco, Peru, Che hailed the lasting presence of Incan temples that the Spanish used as foundations for their new churches:

> The temples to Inti were razed to their foundations or their walls
> used to build the churches of the new religion. The cathedral was
> constructed on the remains of the great palace, while the walls of the

FIGURE 14.3   *A main structure at the ruins of Monte Albán in central Mexico, 2004. It is the kind of pre-Hispanic archeological site that inspired the young Che Guevara during his journey. Photograph by Scott McPherson*

> Temple of the Sun served a base for the Church of Santo Domingo, a lesson and a punishment from the proud conqueror. And yet, the heart of America, trembling with indignation, still twitches the docile back of the Andes every now and then, sending huge shock waves up to the surface. The dome of proud Santo Domingo has come crashing down three times to the roar of broken bones and its walls have tottered, cracked and fallen too. But the foundation they were built on, the grey stone block of the Temple of the Sun, remain impervious, and however great the disaster befalling the usurper, not one of its huge rocks shifts.[10]

These observations can be seen as nothing more than the musings of an impressed tourist. But something deeper is also at work. Whether or not Che was aware of it, his attention to Latin America's Indian past was typical of nationalists living in the middle of the twentieth century who sought to bring dark-skinned masses and light-skinned elites together. Writers, artists, and politicians all began to celebrate their nation's Indian heritage, evoking a powerful neoromanticism that sought out their nation's uniqueness. Variations on this theme are evident in Jose Martí's celebration of the natural man and the rescue of barbarism by Gallegos in *Doña Bárbara*. A form of Indianism also contributed to the rise of magical realism, as we will see shortly in Elena Garro's story, "It's the Fault of the Tlaxcaltecas." Che's inspired descriptions of Indians and Indian ruins could easily have been met with favor by adherents of nationalism, even though Che himself was suspicious of nationalism at the time and eventually rejected the idea of nations in favor of revolutionary internationalism.

The Motorcycle Diaries was written by a young man whose future as a revolutionary was still unknown. We should be careful not to extrapolate too much from it, either about Che in later life or about the broader whole of socialism in Latin America. Even though Che's life was cut short, he might have changed his views as he grew older. The Che Guevara who implemented policy in Cuba and tried to foment revolutionary fronts in Africa and Bolivia might have been quite different from the young Ernesto Guevara who hitchhiked around the Andes and was impressed by the sights.

Nevertheless, we have tried to demonstrate in our semiotic reading of *The Motorcycle Diaries* that this formative moment in Che Guevara's life was profoundly inundated by discourses. To the extent that Che retained these ideas—or even if he changed them radically in later life—we can begin to intuit the discursive frameworks that went into the socialist project in Latin America. This will be more evident in our analyses of *The Motorcycle Diaries* and *Soy Cuba* that follow and the reading by Alma Guillermoprieto.

FILM ANALYSIS: *THE MOTORCYCLE DIARIES*

The Motorcycle Diaries, a film based upon the diaries of both Che and Granado—*With Che Through Latin America*—was released in U.S. theaters in September 2004. Directed by Walter Salles (who also made *Behind the Sun* and *Central Station*) and starring Gael García Bernal as Che Guevara, the film stays mostly true to the events and chronology of Che's journey as depicted in the published version of his diary. But the notable aspect of the film is the way it reads Che uncritically as a heroic figure and how it uses the visual medium to achieve that goal.

The narrative objective of the film is to show that the journey with Alberto Granado was pivotal in giving rise to Che's revolutionary consciousness as he witnessed suffering and injustice across the continent. That message is not necessarily obvious in Che's diaries. We have noted that the most explicit reference to this revolutionary effect came in an epilogue that Che apparently penned long after the trip's conclusion. But to maintain a semblance of narrative drive, the film placed this consciousness-raising process more at the center of the film, even making it the pivotal moment near the film's end.

FIGURE 14.4 *Granado watches the young Che transform himself into a leader in* The Motorcycle Diaries

The moment in question was Che's and Granado's visit to a leper colony in the Peruvian rain forest. There they find a committed core of doctors and nuns caring for a few hundred people suffering from leprosy, which in those days was a serious and incurable disease that necessitated living in segregated colonies far from the centers of society. The lepers live on one side of a river and their medical caretakers on the other. Che and Granado immediately begin challenging this hierarchy and separation by refusing to wear gloves when they meet the patients and disobeying rules about the segregation. Although they were at the colony for only three weeks, Che manages in that time to undermine many aspects of the segregation and soon has the two sides playing soccer with one another and building a sense of collective identity.

On his last night at the colony, which also happened to be his birthday, Che insists, in his most explicit demonstration of his commitment to uniting the two sides of the river, that he wants to spend the night on the other side of the river with the lepers. Unable to find a boat to take him across the river, he decides to ignore his asthma and the strong currents and swim across the chasm, a feat that supposedly no one had ever accomplished. His arrival on the other side is greeted with great applause by the lepers, who are ecstatic to receive him. The next morning, as Che and Granado get ready to leave, the film uses poignant imagery of fog and earth tones to express the sadness that the lepers feel as Che goes away. In an important framing device that cannot be achieved in Che's diary, the film focuses in on their faces to allow their expressions to reveal longing for Che and regard for his leadership. This framing device is used repeatedly throughout the scenes in the leper colony, where the lepers become reminiscent of people witnessing a miracle in religious paintings.

The analogy to Che's eventual life as a revolutionary leader in this scene is obvious. He throws aside concern for his own well-being out of an inherent embrace of the masses and their suffering. They, in turn, are drawn to him and become the malleable force that he will lead to a better future through revolution and mass activism. This same message is delivered in another scene on the night of his birthday, just before he crosses the river. Che offers a toast of thanks to doctors and nuns at the colony and delivers the brief speech in which he calls for Pan-Americanism and a brighter future with diminished suffering. The camera immediately shifts to the faces of those listening, whose expressions reveal a deep regard for Che. The camera hones in on Granado's face, which reveals amazement verging on anguish. Until that moment, Granado knew Che as a deeply decent but carefree and apolitical young medical student. Suddenly, Che became an eloquent leader of men. Granado's look seems to be one of revelatory awakening and wonderment but also fear of what this might mean for Che's future.

Another curious realignment by the film revolves around Che and Granado's womanizing and conniving. The *Diaries* portrays these less-than-ideal character traits as constant features of the two wanderer's travels, but the movie downplays such behavior as solely Granado's. Guevara is depicted as devoted to his girlfriend and honest to a fault: a counterpart to Granado's relentless pursuit of beauties and to free rides acquired through manipulation. In the one instance where Guevara does flirt with a woman, he is so drunkenly inept that he fails to achieve his objective. This scene allows the spectator to grant Che leniency. The woman looks like Che's girlfriend, and their resemblance makes the viewer empathize with Che and his commitment to her. Moreover, the woman he flirts with is more aggressive than Che, whose inebriated state makes him appear more careless than conniving. This attempt by the film to smooth over the complexity in Che's personality, coupled with the protracted scenes of him overcoming life-threatening asthma attacks, leads the viewer to honor Che and celebrate him.

Finally, a distinct cinematic device draws the viewer closer to Che. Black-and-white images of the faces of poor Latin Americans appear recurrently throughout the film, but especially at the end. As the viewer is asked to

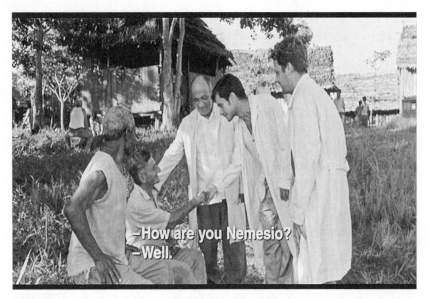

FIGURE 14.5 *Che shakes hands with lepers without wearing gloves in* The Motorcycle Diaries

linger on the images of these people who look directly back, the apparent intent is to show their humanity, to turn them into real people whose lined faces, modest clothing, and graying hair make the viewer sympathetic with their daily struggle for survival. The imagery, especially the use of black-and-white film, reminds us of *Soy Cuba* and its drawn-out scenes of people and places intended to capture Cuba's national essence. Similarly, these portraits in *The Motorcycle Diaries* seem to be saying that the humble people depicted in them are the soul of Latin America and that Che is on their side. It is not coincidental that the final image is that of the face of a Communist whom Che and Granado encountered while in Chile's northern desert and who told his tale of suffering and abuse at the hands of greedy capitalists and their defenders in the government and military. The determined look on this man's face begs the obvious question as to how long it will be before some great person comes along to lead them to a brighter future. That someone, of course, is Che Guevara.

INTRODUCTION TO ALMA GUILLERMOPRIETO'S "THE HARSH ANGEL"

Alma Guillermoprieto is one of Latin America's foremost essayists, journalists, and memoirists. She was one of the millions of Latin Americans

FIGURE 14.6 *An asthmatic Che pulls the weight of his own image.* Asthma *(oil on canvas) by Cuban artist Alexis Esquivel (ca. 2000)*

whose political consciousness was weaned on the image and myth of Che Guevara. Her personally decisive political moment seems to have been the massacre at Tlatelolco in Mexico in 1968. As a young journalist covering the student protests against Mexico's hosting of the Olympics in that year, Guillermoprieto bore witness to the Mexican government's brutal repression of the protests, in which the army killed at least three hundred people and wounded many hundreds more. Like so many young, politicized adults in Latin America at that time, Guillermoprieto found at least some resonance in Che's revolutionary critique of the existing social hierarchy, in which power mongers rule governments and even populist regimes seem to be little more than excuses for perpetuating hierarchy. Guillermoprieto did not join a revolutionary movement, but as a journalist and essayist she served as an intellectual conscience of her generation's questioning of the status quo.

Guillermoprieto is not a postmodernist per se, but her reading of Che's life and the Che legend functions semiotically. In a manner highly reminiscent of cultural studies deconstructionism, Guillermoprieto "looks into the margins" of Che's life to see behind the public persona. Even though she never uses *discourse* to describe her interpretation of Che, she shows how Che was constituted by social values of which he was not aware and which may not have been in accordance with his socialist idealism and revolutionary legend. Guillermoprieto shows that patriarchal manhood played a significant role in shaping Che's sense of self and his interpretation of his surroundings.

Her rendering of Che's life draws us back to Stuart Hall's argument about identity as an unsettled space that emerges "between a number of intersecting discourses."[11] Guillermoprieto shows us how Che's sense of self was constructed and how his life was a narrative, a series of narratives actually, that he told himself and that other people told about him. In Hall's words, "We tell ourselves stories of the parts of our roots in order to come into contact, creatively with it."[12] And so Guillermoprieto reveals to us the place, or space from which Che originated, the discursive localities that went into making him the man he thought he was and the man he had no idea he was.

While her reading of Che might come across as critical, it is not a hatchet job by a onetime member of the flock who has lost her faith. Guillermoprieto finds Che to be, not surprisingly, a real person, a complex man with merits and faults. But most important, she finds a man whose identity was made and remade by himself, the people around him, and the storytellers who came after him. In that regard, Che represents any other person. If he had lived, he might have rejected cultural studies, but he also might have found solace in the idea that his life, as a narrative construct, was discursively linked to everyone else's in the world. In this way, he could hardly have been more a man of the people.

ALMA GUILLERMOPRIETO, "THE HARSH ANGEL"[13]

Che was the century's first Latin American: an astonishing fact, given that hundreds of millions of people in the hemisphere are joined by the same language, the same Iberian culture, the same religion, the same monstrously deformed class system, the same traditions of violence and rancor. Despite those essential bonds, Latin America's twenty-one nations lived in determined isolation and a common mistrust until Che came along and, through his acts, proclaimed himself a citizen of them all. He was an artist of scorn, heaping it on the sanctimonious, the officiously bureaucratic, the unimaginatively conformist, who whispered eagerly that the way things were was the best way that could be arranged. He was a living banner, determined to renounce all the temptations of power and to change the world by example.

And he was a fanatic, consumed by restlessness and a frighteningly abstract hatred, who in the end recognized only one moral value as supreme: the willingness to be slaughtered for a cause.

Another astonishing fact is that so many members of my generation, who were just coming of age at the time of his death, wanted to be like him, and to obey him, even while we knew so little about him. It was only after he was hunted down by Bolivian army forces, on October 8, 1967, and the unforgettable picture of his corpse—emaciated torso, tousled hair, and liquid, vacant eyes—was displayed on the front pages of newspapers around the world that Che became familiar to young people. It was in death that he became known [. . .].

Ernesto Guevara de la Serna was born in Argentina in 1928, the son of an intellectually curious, high-strung mother and a debonair, womanizing father who ran through his wife's fortune and never quite managed to get any of his own business schemes off the ground. The couple fought constantly, and the father slept sometimes on the living-room sofa, sometimes in another house. At the age of two, Ernestito, the firstborn and favorite of the Guevaras's children (they had five), developed asthma, and for long stretches throughout his childhood he was bedridden. Spurred on by his mother, Celia, he became a precocious and methodical reader and a stoic patient. As with Teddy Roosevelt, physical hardship and endurance became a habit, and Ernesto seems never to have succumbed to the invalid's temptation to engage in complaint and self-indulgence.

In adolescence, and at least partly as a response to his handicap, Ernesto emerged as a full-fledged macho, having his way with the family maids (once literally behind the back of his favorite and very straitlaced aunt, who was then sitting primly at the dining-room table); refusing at the age of fifteen to attend a protest demonstration because he did not have a revolver; making it a point of pride never to bathe. (His upper-middle-class schoolmates remember his nickname, Chancho, or Pig, not so much because it was ugly as because he was so proud of it.) Before his machismo destroyed him, it served him well: it tempered his will and spurred him to become an athlete—one who, despite the crippling asthma, always made a point of outracing, outkicking, and outhiking his less exigent peers. (Machismo also gave him style: in the midst of his physical exploits, he would stop and suck on his inhaler for a few moments, or give himself a quick adrenaline injection through his clothes, and then return to the field.)

At twenty-two, when he was studying medicine in Buenos Aires, he discovered that the life of a wanderer suited him. Interrupting his studies, he left home and motorbiked alone through northern Argentina. The following year, he and his best friend embarked on an eight-month hitchhiking adventure: it took them through northern Argentina again and then on to Chile, Peru, Colombia, Venezuela, and, finally, the United States. He was already a disciplined diarist, and a few years later, when he was no longer signing himself "Pig" but, rather, "Che," he took his notes from that trip and turned them into a book. It was translated into English in 1995 and became a brisk seller for the British publishing house Verso, under the title *The Motorcycle Diaries*.

The diarist is an idealistic young medical student who has chosen his profession as a way of doing good in the world but otherwise does not think much about politics. The living conditions of the people he travels among shock him, but he is just as susceptible to the wonder of Machu Picchu [. . .].

By his own account, this jolly and enthusiastic young man was buried forever at the expedition's close [. . .].

We do know that his discovery of the revolutionary faith transformed him, as a writer, into a hopeless termagant. And we know something more remarkable: that the words he wrote were not simply a young man's posturing; for, from the time of his final departure from Argentina the following year, 1953, to the moment of his death in 1967, the asthmatic, footloose, irreverent diarist sought to become the iron-willed avenger of his prophecy. Another idealistic and enterprising young man, upon being confronted with the poverty, racism, and injustice that Guevara sees and records in *The Motorcycle Diaries* might have strengthened his commitment to medicine, or thought of ways to give Latin America's poor the weapon of literacy. For reasons that even the most ambitious biographer can only speculate on—rage against his father, love of humanity—Guevara decided instead to spend his life creating Che, the harsh angel.

Guevara remained a pilgrim for another three years, waiting for a cause to find him. During that time, he floated northward again, read Marx and Lenin, and decided that he was a Marxist. In Bolivia in 1953, he was a skeptical witness of Víctor Paz Estenssoro's populist revolution, whose limited—but hardly insignificant—achievements included the liberation of the Indian peasantry from virtual fiefdom and the establishment of universal suffrage. For his part, Guevara never considered any alternatives to violence and radicalism, and perhaps it is true that in the Latin America of those years it required more self-delusion to be a moderate reformer than to be a utopian revolutionary. At any rate, a nine-month stay in Guatemala was cut short by the 1954 coup against the reformist government of Jacobo Arbenz—a coup sponsored by the Central Intelligence Agency. This monumentally stupid event not only set Guatemala on the road to decades of bloodshed but confirmed Che's conviction that in politics only those will-ing to shed blood make a difference.

In late 1954, Guevara arrived in Mexico, and he spent two years there that would have been listless and inconsequential but for two events. He made an unhappy marriage to a Peruvian radical he had first met in Guate-mala, Hilda Gadea, and he had a child with her. (Guevara and women is a nasty subject. Anderson, ever attentive to his subject's sex life, quotes from Guevara's unpublished diary on the courtship: "Hilda declared her love in epistolary and practical form. I was with a lot of asthma, if not I might have fucked her. [. . .] The little letter she left me upon leaving is very good, too bad she is so ugly.")[14] And he met Fidel Castro, who arrived in Mexico in 1955, fresh from a two-year imprisonment in Cuba following his disastrous assault on the Moncada army barracks.

There is no record of Ernesto Guevara's ever before, or subsequently, ex-pressing unrestrained admiration for a fellow being. Fidel, with his natu-ral bonhomie, energy, and boundless faith in his own leadership, was the exception. The chemistry was mutual: Fidel trusted him, relied on him, and, on the evidence, loved him more than any of his other comrades, with the possible exception of Celia Sánchez (Fidel's closest companion until her death, in 1980). Guevara's relationship to love, whether it involved his parents, his comrades, or his women, was uneasy, but his love of Fidel was wholehearted and transforming, because it opened the path to the life he was seeking. Within hours of their first meeting, Guevara signed on as a medic for Fidel's harebrained plan to land an expedition on the eastern end of Cuba and start an insurrection against the dictator Fulgencio Batista.

In November of 1956, the creaky yacht *Granma* set sail from Veracruz, bound for Cuba and glory. By then, the Argentine Guevara, who, like all his countrymen, interjected the word *che*—roughly, "man" or "you"—at least once in every sentence (as in "Hey, *che*, is that the way to clean a rifle, *che?*"), had been rebaptized. He would be, forevermore, *el Che*—the Argentine. It was a term that underlined not only affection and respect his comrades felt for him but also their intense awareness of his differentness, his permanent standing as a foreigner in the revolution he had adopted as his own.

He was keenly aware of his outsider status as he sailed for Cuba. Other portents must have been harder for him to see. There was his medical train-ing, for example, which had drilled into him the universality of the prin-ciple of the scientific cure (that is, that penicillin, say, will get rid of pneu-monia in both a French peasant and a Mexican socialite). A central flaw in his thinking for the rest of his life was to assume that what he learned about guerrilla warfare in the process of overthrowing Batista amounted to a prescription—a necessary remedy for every form of social disease. Another flaw was that he was inescapably committed to a certain definition of virility and to the code of conduct it implied: a macho definition, not unusual among Latin Americans of his generation. As a result, he found it unbearably humiliating ever to lose face, back down, admit defeat. He could not see that Sancho Panza might be as heroic as Quixote. And he was as blind to nuances of character as he was tone-deaf: for all the painful insights into his own nature that he reveals in his diaries, and for all his astute observations in them on landscape, warfare, and political dynamics, there are no credible portraits of his fellowmen. There are only revolutionaries, who are full of virtue, and counterrevolutionaries, who are worthless.

The next chapter in Che's life coincides with one of the century's most startling military triumphs. Having landed as disastrously as was to be expected on Cuba's shores, Che, Fidel Castro, Fidel's brother Raúl Castro, and a handful of others survived Batista's ferocious assault and went on to forge the beginnings of a revolutionary army in the Sierra Maestra. By 1958, Che's military intuition and daring, his organizational skills, and his outstanding personal bravery had won him the undisputed title of Comandante and a leading role in the revolution. Sharing his life with Cubans, who have always held ablutions and nattiness to be almost supreme virtues, Guevara still refused to bathe, or even tie his shoelaces, but now that he was Che, his odorous aura was part of a mystique. He was roughing it in the great outdoors, planning strategy with Fidel, sharing his camp cot with a stunning *mulata*, risking his life and proving his manhood on a daily basis. His days, as he narrates them in *Reminiscences of the Cuban Revolutionary War* (again, reworked pages from his diary turned into a book), read blissfully like an adventure out of *Boys' Life*. [. . .] Happiness and the desire for it—"the need to live"—were, in a revolutionary, symptoms of weakness.

Che's life following the revolution's triumph was a slow accretion of wreckage, and it is in the narration of this collapse that *Compañero*, Jorge Castañeda's beautiful and passionate biography, is most lucid.[15] We turn the pages hoping that the trouble will end soon, that Guevara may be spared, or spare himself, if not from failure, then from ludicrous defeat; if not from hideous physical suffering, then from death; if not from death, then from ignominy. But Castañeda is as unflinching as his hero: he has searched CIA records and the recollections of Guevara's closest comrades in order to pry away layers of after-the-fact justifications and embellishments of the Che legend. In the process, he makes Ernesto Guevara understandable at last, and his predicament deeply moving.

Castañeda's Che is a man who could not bear the natural ambivalence of the world and found relief from it (and, curiously, from the torment of asthma) only in the unequivocal rigors of battle and radicalism. Appointed first to the National Agrarian Reform Institute and then to head the Central Bank in Fidel's revolutionary regime, he was, like so many other battle heroes before and after him, flummoxed by the day-to-day realities of governance. Why should Cuba have a monetary policy that sought to placate imperialism? Why was it necessary to compensate exploiters and oppressors for their sugarcane haciendas instead of merely expropriating the land for *el pueblo*? Why corrupt workers by offering them more money to work harder? Che nearly killed himself accumulating "volunteer work hours" of his own, cutting cane and stacking sacks of sugar after the grueling hours he put in at his desk, in order to prove that moral incentives could beat lucre as a stimulus to productivity. He may have begun to suspect toward the end of his stay in Cuba that other mortals liked to put their free time to a different use. He certainly believed that the Revolution's leadership was tacking dangerously toward pragmatism. "The New Man"—a new type of human being that the Revolution was to manufacture—was not being turned out swiftly enough.

Che was unable to deal with his disapproval of the course that Fidel was taking and his simultaneous love for the man; with his disillusionment with the Soviet Union and the self-satisfaction of the burgeoning Cuban bureaucracy; with the palace intrigues of the new regime (particularly those of Fidel's brother Raúl); and, probably, with the gnawing awareness of his own failings as a peacetime revolutionary. It seems reasonable to interpret his decision to leave Cuba as Castañeda does—as the result of his need to get away from so much internal conflict. (In the course of explaining this decision, Castañeda provides an extraordinary account of the ins and outs of Cuban state policy, Cuban-Soviet relations, and Castro's dealings with the United States.) Che was leaving behind a second wife, six children, his comrades, his years of happiness, and the revolution he had helped give birth to; none of these were enough to convince him that he belonged.

Guevara's original intention was to return to his homeland and start a guerrilla movement there. A 1965 expedition to the Congo, where various armed factions were still wrestling for power long after the overthrow and murder of Patrice Lumumba, and his last stand in Bolivia, Castañeda writes, followed improbably from Fidel's anxious efforts to keep Che away from Argentina, where he was sure to be detected and murdered by Latin America's most efficient security forces. Castro seems to have felt that the Congo would be a safer place, and the question of whether it was a more intelligent choice doesn't seem to have been addressed either by him or by the man he was trying to protect. (In Cairo, Jon Lee Anderson notes, Gamal Abdel Nasser warned Che not to be militarily involved in Africa, because there he would be "like Tarzan, a white man among blacks, leading and protecting them.")

As things turned out, the Congo episode was a farce, so absurd that Cuban authorities kept secret Che's rueful draft for a book on it—until recently, that is, when one of his new biographers, Paco Ignacio Taibo, was able to study the original manuscript. Guevara was abandoned from the beginning by Congolese military leaders, such as Laurent Kabila, who had initially welcomed his offer of help. He was plagued by dysentery and was subject to fits of uncontrollable anger, and emerged from seven months in the jungle forty pounds lighter, sick, and severely depressed. If he had ever considered a decision to cut bait and return to Cuba, that option was canceled weeks before the Congo expedition's rout. On October 5, 1965, Fidel Castro, pressed on all sides to explain Che's disappearance from Cuba and unable to recognize that the African adventure was about to collapse, decided to make public Che's farewell letter to him: "I will say once again that the only way that Cuba can be held responsible for my actions is in its example. If my time should come under other skies, my last thought will be for this people, and especially for you."

Guevara was sitting in a miserable campsite on the shores of Lake Tanganyika, bored, frustrated, and in mourning for his mother, when he was told that Fidel had publicized the letter. The news hit him like an explosion. "Shit-eaters!" he said, pacing back and forth in the mud. "They are imbeciles, idiots."

Guevara's final trek began at this moment, because once his farewell to Fidel was made public, as Castañeda writes, "his bridges were effectively burned. Given his temperament, there was now no way he could return to Cuba, even temporarily. The idea of a public deception was unacceptable to him: once he had said he was leaving, he could not go back." He could not bear to lose face.

A few months later, having taken full and bitter stock of his situation, he made the decision to set up a guerrilla base—intended as a training camp, really—in southern Bolivia, near the border with Argentina. From there, he convinced himself, he would ultimately be able to spark the revolutionary flame in Argentina and, from there, throughout the world.

He knew, of course, that his death would fan that flame. One wonders if he had any sense in the final awful weeks of how badly things would end, not just for him but for everyone involved in the ubiquitous attempts at armed radical revolution that followed upon his death. [. . .]

Guevara was born in Latin America's hour of the hero. So many of our leaders have been so corrupt, and the range of allowed and possible public activity has been so narrow, and injustice has cried out so piercingly to the heavens, that only a hero could answer the call, and only a heroic mode of life could seem worthy. Guevara stood out against the inflamed horizon of his time, alone and unique.

There is, however, a problem with the heroic figure (as the Cubans, who kept Che's diaries and documents secret all this while, perceived), and that is that the hero can have no faults, and is answerable, as Che was, only to his own exalted sense of honor. This picture of the hero is still satisfying to large numbers of Latin Americans who are not in a position to exact an accounting from their leaders but do, on the other hand, demand that their leaders act grandly and provoke fervor and states of rapture, as the dead Che now does. But the living Che was not the perfect hero for his time and place: he demanded that others follow his impossible example, and never understood how to combine what he wanted with what was achievable. It remains forever a matter of debate whether Che's life and example speeded the advent of the present era, in which there are no perfect causes, and where men like him are more than ever out of place.

DISCUSSION QUESTIONS

- What identity issues or discourses does Guillermoprieto identify as defining Guevara's personality and his political and ideological orientations?
- How does Guillermoprieto, in so many words, portray Guevara to be a "dead author" and how does this transform our reading of *The Motorcycle Diaries*?
- According to Guevara, what are the qualities of a good revolutionary? How does this reveal Guevara's own essentialist interpretation of the world?
- Given the opportunity, how would Guillermoprieto critique the film version of *The Motorcycle Diaries*?

FILM ANALYSIS: *SOY CUBA/YA KUBA (I AM CUBA)*

Soy Cuba/Ya Kuba, set in prerevolutionary Havana, attempts to legitimize further the Cuban Revolution that had triumphed over the U.S.-backed dictatorship of Fulgencio Batista five years earlier. The film was directed and photographed in 1964 by the acclaimed Russian filmmaking team of

Mikhail Kalatozov and Sergei Urusevsky. In 1958 they won the top prize at Cannes with *The Cranes are Flying*. *Soy Cuba* was coscripted by the Russian poet Yevgeny Yevtushenko and the Cuban novelist Enrique Piñeda Barnet. The film is typically both praised as an aesthetic and cinematographic achievement and denounced as anti-American propaganda. The task of the semiotician, however, is not to pass judgment on the film but to examine the discourse that speaks through the text, which is often disparate from the intentions of the filmmakers. *Soy Cuba* is a particularly stark case of this latter phenomenon. Despite the film's anticapitalist stance in legitimizing socialism for Cuba and for the world, it was criticized by Castro as counterrevolutionary and censured in Cuba and the Soviet Union. It was rescued from cultural oblivion in the capitalist West—first in 1992 by the Telluride Film Festival for a tribute to Kalatozov, and later in 1995 by Francis Ford Coppola and Martin Scorsese who, with Milestone Films, restored and re-released it with English subtitles (thereby, in a sense, entering it into the capitalist canon).

All of this provides evidence that *Soy Cuba* inadvertently challenges its own pro-socialist pretensions. Our contention is that because the film is deeply rooted in an appeal to Cuban essence, it runs the risk of opposing socialism's ideology of universalism. Moreover, we argue that its unwitting engagement with patriarchal presuppositions is at odds with the revolution's professed commitment to gender equity. Finally, the film's intention to portray the failure of religion in the characters' lives inadvertently conveys the sense that prerevolutionary Cubans were devout Catholics who were subsequently denied the right to religious practice. This presents a dangerous assertion, since Cuba was officially declared an atheistic state after the revolution when religious practice purportedly became a nonissue for most Cubans, rather than being severely restricted by the new government.

Filming of the movie began in 1962, just two weeks after the Cuban missile crisis and three years after Fidel Castro came to power. It comprises four principal stories that define Batista's Cuba through the hardships and injustices suffered by the Cuban people at the hands of their dictator and the U.S. capitalists who pull his strings for their own gain. Each story promotes the seeds of resistance that will eventually become a popular revolution toppling the dictatorial regime. A female narrator links the stories by reciting Yevtushenko's poetry in a mournful but firm voice-over and repeating the title refrain, "Soy Cuba," to signal the end of one defining episode and usher in the next. From the young Havana couple whose future together is ruined by poverty, repression, and imperialism to the sugar farmer who torches his own house and cane fields in rebellion against the United Fruit Company that is about to evict him, to the university students who are murdered for protesting and plotting against the government, to the simple peasant who is driven from his home by Batista's air raids and is welcomed by Castro and Che into the rebel army, the film strives to locate the island's national identity in the moment of popular rebellion. Not unlike *Facundo* and *Doña Bárbara*, *Soy Cuba* locates national identity in the supposedly unique land and peoples of the nation, privileging the individual (Cuba) over the whole (the global worker).

We will focus only on the first of the four narratives in the film, partly for brevity but also for clarity, because it offers explicit examples of the text working against itself. This is the story of René, a fruit vendor who clandestinely but actively supports the revolution, and María, a girl from the slums who hides the fact that she prostitutes herself to survive.

From its opening scenes, the film establishes Cuba as a glamorous playground for wealthy (particularly male) North Americans. Stunningly vanguard cinematography combines with omniscient narration in revealing the film's intention to expose the glaring disjuncture between the poverty of Cuba's citizens and the commodification of the nation and its people, first by Spanish conquerors and then by U.S. businessmen and tourists. As the initial images invite the spectator to peer into rural Cuba from a bird's-eye camera angle (what has come to be known as the "helicopter shot"), a melancholy voice-over narrates the arrival of Christopher Columbus to, in his words, the "most beautiful land ever seen by human eyes." While the camera pauses on a large white cross made enormous and imposing by a low-angle shot, the narrator addresses Columbus with a painfully ironic "Gracias, Sr. Colon" (*Colon* is Spanish for Columbus). The camera then descends to water level on a river to witness the honest and tranquil labor of Afro-Cuban mothers and workers and then abruptly cuts to distorting and uncomfortable closeups of musicians blaring North American swing music while beautiful (and white-skinned) hotel guests drink, lounge, gaze, and bathe poolside. Even the Cuban beauty pageant contestants that the camera seems to caress and follow into the pool and under water are as light-skinned as the guests, suggesting that beauty will be defined as a reflection of the tourist market. As the complexity of the river water is replaced with the shallow transparency of the water in the pool, melancholy tranquility is juxtaposed with flashy superficiality representing the immoral and egotistical behavior which, in pursuit of conspicuous indulgence, exploits Cuba and its people. In this way the film reminds us of the forgotten Cuban whose hard work supports this lighthearted merriment and whose poverty is a direct consequence of it.

Once we are introduced to the protagonists in the film (René and María), we notice an intention to portray, once again, a distinct reality operating just beneath a seemingly joyous surface. René strolls the streets, singing as he delivers his goods. María accompanies him. Dressed in a virginal white scarf tied around her head, she represents an ideal image of innocence and prudence. But when René tells her that he wants to marry her in the gleaming white cathedral that looms over them, and that María will wear a white dress, she looks away dejectedly. René interprets her reaction as in keeping with the innocent impression she gives and says, "You've never kissed anyone before, have you?" This is the first indication we have of some forthcoming trouble in paradise.

A theme that will repeatedly play itself out through the rest of the film concerns the ways North Americans treat Cuba as their own private paradise, but in doing so create a living nightmare for the Cuban people. When his friends pretend to buy fruit from him, René reaches just below the surface of his basket to reveal papers which he passes to them and which we can assume are plans regarding the revolution. René and María are Afro-Cubans, but these friends look European. Their lighter skin, as well as their dress, suggest they belong to a higher rung of Cuban society. Details like these underscore the ideals of the revolution—the leveling of hierarchy and the pursuit of equal opportunity for all regardless of class or race—a discourse that graphically demonstrates blacks and whites, the poor and the middle class banding together to effect change. María, however, becomes immediately marginal to this revolutionary endeavor for stating her fear of the dealings that take place between René and his accomplices, and this provides an initial glimpse of the patriarchal discourse that we will see confirmed in the film's conclusion.

This scene concludes as René, whose cart is notably inscribed "Angel," professes his love for María by offering her a symbolic tangerine: "Te quiero María . . . María. . . ." he says. María walks away and out of the frame, and the film cuts to a nightclub decorated with bamboo poles hanging from the ceiling. María exchanges her virginal scarf for a tight dress and a large crucifix necklace, and René's voice from the last frame still echoes offscreen, calling her name. With this juxtaposition we leave the serene streets of Havana, where René and María are each hiding information from each other, to enter the claustrophobic, labyrinthine, and soon-to-be frenetic space of the nightclub. Close-ups of an Afro-Cuban singer passionately yet sorrowfully belting out "Loco Amor," ("Crazy Love") while becoming obscured by and entangled in a maze of hanging bamboo poles, again underscore a sense of imprisonment and labyrinth. Given that all of the women to whom he directs his song are prostitutes for the North Americans who frequent the club, the film suggests that love is neither what the North American male tourists are looking for nor what the Cuban prostitutes can afford to desire.

Indeed, soon afterward we hear a trio of clubbing North Americans order up prostitutes as if they are ordering food with their daiquiris: "I'll take that tasty morsel," and "I'll have that dish." One of them is reluctant to partake and admonishes his compatriots for their indecent behavior, saying "I never touch stuff like that." They call him a prude, and he is "awarded" María/Betty (the name she assumes when in the club) in a game in which the names of prostitutes are drawn from a hat. He then easily becomes consumed with possessing both her and the crucifix around her neck.

From the moment she walks into the nightclub, "Betty" is sullen and refuses almost all conversation and anything offered to her, such as a light for her cigarette, befitting her reluctance to prostitute herself. When she is pulled onto the dance floor and subsequently thrown between all three North Americans—symbolic of Cuba's domination by the United States— the scene turns into something akin to a house of horrors as the wide-angle lens rapidly pans across the faces of the admiring people around her, disfiguring them. Maria hears the beat of an African drum, interrupting and distorting the swing music playing for the crowd and triggering a "primitive" response in her. Giving in to the ethnic rhythm supposedly natural to her, María dances frenetically to it while clutching her head, as a presumably Afro-Cuban essence surges out of her in a protest against having to sell her soul to whites. This exaltation of the unique, essential qualities of Cubans to heighten the sense of their exploitation contributes unwittingly to the film's opposition to the message of socialism: the proletariat is universally exploited by the bourgeoisie.

At the end of the night, the North American tourist insists on going home with María/Betty. A taxi drops them off where the paved roads end in the shantytown that is María's neighborhood, and they must hop from stone to stone over what the viewer can presume to be stagnant sewage to make their way through a labyrinth of shacks where electricity lines resemble fallen and distorted crucifixes, emphasizing once again the perverse role of the church in Cubans' lives.

Working against this deliberate message of exploitation by imperialists who have commodified all that is Cuba, including the religion imposed upon it by Spanish conquerors, however, is the way the film unconsciously cues the spectator to recognize that the innocence with which René regards María is simply a product of his own naiveté and that the symbol of martyrdom she wears like a trophy around her neck heightens María's hypocrisy.

FIGURE 14.7 *René stands over María/Betty after discovering her with the North American in* Soy Cuba

While René's secrecy contributes to the progress of the revolution, María's undermines it.

Once María is inside her one-room shack, her innocence is further debunked as she takes off her crucifix necklace. The spectator is made to despise the expressionless North American tourist who attempts to put it back over María's neck and then ignores her suffering as she throws it to the ground and begins to cry, demonstrating her physical anguish over what she is about to do. In this way the film gives the viewer mixed messages. It clearly wants us to hold the North American accountable and to sympathize with María, yet it has already placed part of the burden of blame on her for feigning innocence in her deception of our hero, René.

Cut to the next morning. While María lies sleeping in a martyred position (each arm outstretched as if in a crucifixion), the North American tourist is dressed and, in symbolic explanation of what happened during the night, is eating the tangerine that was a figurative gift of love from René the day before. He awakens María and then ignores her refusal to sell him her crucifix, one of her only valuables, by simply laying extra money on the bed. As the tourist starts to leave, René enters the shack singing happily and carrying a stalk of bananas, which he lies down in symbolic phallic defeat when he sees María in bed and then attempts to cover her naked body with the white bed linens.

He glares at the stranger and then stares angrily at María and her client, assessing the situation. When the full impact of what has happened hits him, his fury grows and he walks slowly toward María. Then he approaches the North American menacingly but backs off and continues to scowl at María. The tourist takes this opportunity to leave, with a jolly "Goodbye, Betty!" As he exits the shack, he polishes off the rest of the tangerine and tosses the peel to the ground as easily as he discards María/Betty and any conscious thought of his contribution to Cuba's socioeconomic woes. Meantime, René spits the typical U.S. name she is using back at María— "Betty?!"—and, without waiting for any explanation, abandons her, while she shivers in shame.

What is highly relevant in this final sequence is the discursive shift that has evidently occurred, the seeds of which have been planted along the way. The U.S. tourist is held explicitly accountable for his ignorant hedonism. After leaving María's shack, he is caught up in the maze of the shantytown where Afro-Cuban mothers, children, and elderly people stare out at him blankly or implore him for money from behind bamboo poles like those in the bar, which are also reproduced in miniature in the canary cages hanging above their heads. The omniscient female narrator chides him: "Why are you running away? You came to have fun—go ahead, have fun! Isn't this a happy picture? Don't avert your eyes. Look!" Nevertheless, the character who is ultimately and inadvertently blamed by the film is María.

FIGURE 14.8 *A dejected René leaves María/Betty in* Soy Cuba

The spectator is poised to identify with René, the idealist revolutionary in love with María, as well as to sympathize with María/Betty's exploitation, which is parallel to Cuba's exploitation, first by Spanish conquerors and proselytizers and then by North American capitalists. When René storms indignantly out of her shack, the implication is that María, as a Cuban accomplice to U.S. imperialism, is worse than the North American, since she not only sabotages Cuba but does so as a traitor to her own people and especially to Cuban men. Thus, the film reveals the way in which the revolution is unwittingly gendered. It asks the spectator to sympathize with the victimized Cuba, personified in María. Once she loses her virginity, however, María is outside the revolution. The film seems to forget that she has no choice in the matter, and the class issues that frame the rest of the film curiously cease to apply here. María is ultimately reduced to being a loose and deceptive woman who deserves to be abandoned by René. The film thus contradicts itself by defining María first and foremost as a woman, not as a poor person. In so doing, it reinforces the notion that a discourse (patriarchy, in this case) can seep into a film text that ostensibly advocates gender, class, and racial equality.

The film makes an overt attempt to delegitimize Catholicism's value in Cuba by portraying Cubans' religious faith as a belief in hollow dogma that serves to further the injustices they suffer. Nevertheless, this attempt proves counterproductive because what remains with the spectator is the strong presence of the faith that was strictly prohibited after the revolution.

To the extent that *Soy Cuba* strives to capture a unique Cuban essence in its attempt to promote Castro's socialist revolution, it embarks upon a nationalist discourse that undermines socialism's tenet of a unified essence for the global proletariat.

DISCUSSION QUESTIONS

• How do the discourses operating in the film cut across the filmmakers' intentions?

• The first of the four episodes of *Soy Cuba* recalls the connection between landscape and bodyscape that Julianne Burton emphasizes as the broader sexualization of Latin America in *The Three Caballeros*. Can you think of other ways in which Burton's argument that female Latin America is cast as spectacle and as a willing subject for male North American consumption play out in this film?

• Keep in mind what is being portrayed regarding our four identity categories and the visual and aural means by which the film puts forth that portrayal. Where does the film situate itself discursively, despite its intentions? The title of the film, *Soy Cuba*, is repeated in a voice-over narration throughout the film. Who is the "I" (*Soy*) of Cuba? Is there a specific character(s) in the film who embodies the nation of Cuba? Is it always the same character or does it change during the course of the film? Who/ what else is Cuba? What does this representation of Cuba include and, consequently, exclude? How does this in turn fit into what is included or excluded in the portrayal of the Cuban Revolution? When attempting to answer these questions, consider the ways in which national identity intersects with gender, class, and race identity.

• Why is it significant that the film has a sizable Soviet presence in its production? In what way might this film say more about the lens through which Russians view Cuba than about the film's explicit subject, Cuba itself?

• We offer a description of *Soy Cuba* without additional analyses from other scholars. When you have the opportunity to see the first vignette of *Soy Cuba*, can you see the presence in our analysis of a discourse that we might not be aware of? The successive interpreters of Said's *Orientalism*, for example, are themselves subjected to critical theory readings. For this exercise, keep in mind graph 2.3 in the introductory chapter.

• In what ways is the representation of women in the film similar to Che's relationship with women as described by Alma Guillermoprieto? What do these two examples suggest to us about the role of gender in the Cuban Revolution and later in the revolutionary government?

NOTES

1. This is a reading of Ernesto "Che" Guevara, *The Motorcycle Diaries: A Journey Around South America*, trans. Ann Wright (London: Verso, 1996).
2. Guevara 12.
3. Guevara 49.
4. As of 2004, Granado was alive and living in Cuba. He recently traveled to Brazil for a premiere of the movie that is based on the *Diaries*. Larry Rohter, "Che Today? More Easy Rider Than Revolutionary," *New York Times*, 26 May 2004: A4.
5. Guevara 51.
6. Guevara 52.
7. Guevara 152.
8. Guevara 148.
9. Guevara 135.
10. Guevara 90.
11. Stuart Hall, "Ethnicity: Identity and Difference," ed. Geof Eley and R. Suny, *Becoming National: A Reader* (New York: Oxford UP, 1996) 339.

12. Hall 348.

13. Alma Guillermoprieto, *Looking for History: Dispatches from Latin America* (New York: Pantheon, 2001). This excerpt is from 73–83, 85–86.

14. Jon Lee Anderson, *Che Guevara: A Revolutionary Life* (New York: Grove, 1997).

15. Jorge Castañeda, *Compañero: The Life and Death of Che Guevara* (New York: Knopf, 1997).

Boom Goes the Literature: Magical Realism as the True Latin America?

"La culpa es de los Tlaxcaltecas" ("It's the Fault of the Tlaxcaltecas"), by the Mexican author Elena Garro, is a short story written in the magical realist style. Garro wrote the story in the early 1960s, just as magical realism was beginning to be consolidated into a genre of international proportions. Even though Garro's work was not accepted as a leading voice in this movement, her style was on the cutting edge of it. "It's the Fault of the Tlaxcaltecas" is no exception.

Born in Mexico in 1920, Elena Garro traveled far beyond her nation's borders. She lived in many countries, and in each one she took up political and social issues dear to her. She embarked on many different career tracks, including choreographer, playwright, and news reporter, but she is best remembered for her fiction, which broke through many boundaries and prejudices faced by female writers in Latin America. Perhaps it is for that reason that her work was disparaged throughout much of her life. After marrying Octavio Paz, the Mexican poet and philosopher, Garro went to Spain and joined other Latin American intellectuals in support of the Republicans in the Spanish Civil War (1935–1939). Upon returning to Mexico, she worked as a reporter for a while before leaving again for New York. From there she went to Europe to join Paz and the community of artists living in exile in Paris. In the 1960s Paz and Garro's relationship ended while he was serving as ambassador to Japan. In 1968 Garro left Mexico as an exile because the government accused her of participating in the 1968 student rebellions. When she returned in 1991, she finally received recognition for her writing and has since come to be regarded as one of Mexico's great writers of the twentieth century. She died in Mexico in 1998.[1]

Magical realism, as we mentioned in the introduction to the book, is a literary style that rose to prominence in Latin America in the 1960s and 1970s.[2] Also known as the Boom, because its authors gained international acclaim for their work, magical realism blurs the lines between reality and fantasy. Along with the narration of fantastical events as if they were everyday occurrences, the genre is typified by a narrative that moves back and forth in time and/or space, often with little or no warning, leaving the reader with a sense of confusion.

Most Boom authors leaned to the political left and defended the popular masses against reigning military and elitist governments. The style and subject matter of their writings often advance the perspective of marginalized and silenced peoples. Their incorporation of Indian themes leads them to emphasize the magical elements of their culture. Indian religions were based on a belief in a closer and more constant link between the spiritual and material worlds than some versions of Christianity. Accordingly, magical realist authors see themselves approaching a deeper and truer sense of Latin American identity. They refuse to glean identities from the developed West and consider themselves literary orphans who celebrate Latin America's distinctiveness.

The focus of the short story reprinted in this chapter is Doña Marina, or La Malinche, as she is often called, one of Mexico's most central and highly contested national figures. She was an indigenous woman held as a slave by Tabascan Indians. Their leader gave her and nineteen other young women to the Spanish conquistadors. La Malinche became an interpreter for the Spanish leader Hernán Cortés and played a vital role in the Spaniards' military success. She also became Cortés's mistress and gave birth to his child, who is often identified as the first mestizo or Mexican child.

As a character, La Malinche is heavily debated in Mexican history. Throughout much of the twentieth century, as nationalist arguments have held sway, she has been identified as a traitor to Mexico and the symbol of many of its current identity problems. One of the greatest contributors to this master narrative of Mexican identity was Garro's husband, Octavio Paz. In *The Labyrinth of Solitude,* his renowned account of Mexican identity, Paz defines Doña Marina as a whore mother who engenders an entire race of bastard mestizo children—contemporary Mexicans. While winning over many supporters, Paz's arguments have also inspired many detractors, such as Elena Garro. As the title of her story suggests, the Tlaxcaltecas, an indigenous group tired of paying tribute to the Aztec empire, joined the Spaniards and provided them with thousands of warriors who proved critical to the Spanish conquest of the Aztec capital of Tenochtitlán. From that perspective, the Spanish victory occurred for many complex reasons.

Garro's story revolves around the character of Laura, an upper-class, twentieth-century woman who tells her experiences to her indigenous servant, Nacha. During the course of the story, Laura travels back to Tenochtitlán three times in 1520, during the fall of the Aztec empire. There she visits a man (actually, her cousin and her husband) whom she loves. With each visit she grows more and more resentful of her twentieth-century husband, Pablo, a well-established mestizo. The theme of betrayal is present throughout the story, and in the end Laura flees the present to return to her indigenous past. Laura symbolizes La Malinche as she tries to determine who is responsible for the problems each respective era is facing.

Just as Laura has to navigate a complicated web of gender expectations, so did Garro herself. Boom authors were almost universally male, and they did not regard her as a peer, even though she befriended many of them, including Jorge Luis Borges and César Vallejo, during her time in Paris. Octavio Paz articulated the ideological foundations for their disregard in *The Labyrinth of Solitude:*

> Women are inferior beings because, in submitting, they open themselves up. Their inferiority is constitutional and resides in their sex, their submissiveness, which is a wound that never heals. . . . Like almost all other people, the Mexican considers women to be an instrument, sometimes of masculine desires, sometimes of the ends assigned to her by her morality, society, and the law. It must be admitted that she never has been asked to consent to these ends and that she participates in their realization only passively as a "repository" for certain values.[3]

Garro at once challenged and surrendered to these gender norms. She was known for referring to her own writing as a hobby while calling Paz's works masterpieces. Yet, she also challenged the male-dominated realm of Boom literature and the tradition in which the interpretation of La Malinche—as either the mother of Mexico or a traitor to the nation—rests with vocal males. In "It's the Fault of the Tlaxcaltecas" Garro allows her female protagonist to choose her own cultural identities. Whereas Paz insists that Mexican men believe that they cannot share their secrets without risking a "lessening of manliness," Laura tells her entire story to Nacha with an openness that directly defies Paz's warning.[4] Showing a more liberal sense of women's sexuality, Garro fills her story with erotic descriptions of the cousin-husband.

Garro's narrative breaks with tradition, but these breaks are often countered by the class and gender issues that she leaves unchallenged. Garro uses an upper-class spokesperson, but her ideal audience is indigenous, like Nacha. Unlike other Boom authors, however, she does not claim to represent an indigenous perspective, even though she celebrates Mexico's indigenous past by having her character prefer it to the mestizo present, from which both Laura and Nacha disappear by the end of the story.

Semiotic critics of magical realism argue that Boom authors succeeded in part because they reaffirm for Western readers the West's hegemony, pushing Latin America further into its peripheral position of the Other. They claim that magical realism fixes the identity of Indians and marginalized people as nonlinear, nonscientific, and superstitious, in stark contrast to the West's self-definition as progressive and rational. Perhaps most important, authors in the Boom remain lettered citizens. They are highly educated men who live abroad and often hold political positions. Although they purport to speak on behalf of impoverished masses, they themselves, for the most part, have not lived the realities of that life; they dictate Latin America's identity from far away. Even if she was not accepted as a peer among this group, Garro shared many characteristics with male lettered citizens, thus situating her at once outside and inside the center.

ELENA GARRO, "IT'S THE FAULT OF THE TLAXCALTECAS" [5]

Nacha heard them calling at the kitchen door and froze. When they insisted, she opened it reluctantly and looked out into the night. Laura appeared with a finger over her lips in a sign of silence. She was still wearing the white suit, burnt and soiled with dirt and blood.

"Señora!" whispered Nacha . . .

"Nachita, give me some coffee . . . I'm cold."

"Señora, the señor will kill you. We had already given you up for dead."

"For dead?"

Laura stared in amazement at the white tiles, drew her feet up on the chair, clasped her knees and became pensive. Nacha put the water on to boil for coffee and looked sideways at her mistress; she couldn't think of anything else to say. Laura rested her head on her knees, she seemed very sad.

"You know, Nacha? It's the fault of the Tlaxcaltecas."

Nacha didn't answer, preferring to stare at the water that wasn't boiling

"Don't you agree, Nacha?"

"Yes, señora."

"I am like them: a traitor," Laura said mournfully. "And you, Nachita, are you a traitor?"

She looked at her expectantly. If Nacha shared her disloyalty, she would understand her, and Laura needed someone to understand her that night.

"Yes, I too am a traitor, señora Laurita."

"You know, Nachita? Now I know why we have so many accidents on the infamous road to Guanajuato. At Thousand Peaks we ran out of gas. Margarita was scared because it was already getting dark. A trucker gave us enough to get to Morelia. At Cuitzeo, when crossing the white bridge, the car stopped suddenly. Margarita got upset with me, you know how empty roads and Indians' eyes frighten her. When a car full of tourists came by, she went to the pueblo to look for a mechanic and I stayed in the middle of the white bridge that crosses the dried lake with a bottom of white stones. The light was very white and the bridge, the stones and the automobile began to float in it. Then the light broke into many pieces until it became a thousand points and began to spin until it was fixed like a picture. Time had taken a complete turn, like when you look at a postcard and then turn it over to see what's written on back. That was how I came to the lake of Cuitzeo, to the other girl that I was. Light produces these catastrophes, when the sun turns white and one is at the center of its rays. Thoughts also become a thousand points, and you suffer vertigo. In that moment, I saw the texture of my white dress and in that instant I heard his steps.[6] I wasn't surprised. I looked up and I saw him coming. In that instant, I also remembered the magnitude of my treason; I was afraid and tried to run away. But time closed in on me. It became rare and dying, and I couldn't move from the seat of the automobile. 'Some day you will find yourself faced with your actions changed into solid stone like that one,' they told me as a child when showing me the image of some god, I don't remember which one now. One forgets, right Nachita? But only for a while. Back then, the words also seemed to me like stone, but like crystalline and fluid rock. The stone would solidify at the end of each word, to remain written forever in time. Weren't those the words of your elders?"

Nacha reflected for a few moments, then convinced, she agreed.

"So they were, señora Laurita."

"The terrible thing is, I discovered in that instant that all the unbelievable is real. There he came, moving along the edge of the bridge, with his skin burned by the sun and the weight of defeat over his naked shoulders. His steps rang like dried leaves. His eyes were brilliant. From far away their black spark reached me and I saw his black hair waving in the blind light of our meeting. Before I could avoid it, he was in front of my eyes. He stopped, grabbed the door of the car and looked at me. He had a cut in his left hand, his hair was full of dust, and from the wound on his shoulder dripped blood so red that it seemed black. He didn't say anything to me. But I knew that he was running, defeated. He tried to tell me that I deserved to die, and at the same time he told me that my death would bring about his own. He was wounded, badly hurt, in search of me.

"It's the fault of the Tlaxcaltecas," I told him.

"He turned and looked at the sky. Afterwards, his eyes rested on mine once again.

" 'What have you been up to?' he asked with his profound voice. I couldn't tell him that I had married, because I am married to him. There are things you just can't say, you know that, Nachita.

" 'And the others?' I asked him.

" 'Those who came out alive are in the same situation as I am.' I saw that each word hurt his tongue and I stopped talking, thinking of the shame of my treason.

" 'You already know that I am afraid and that's why I betray . . .'

" 'I already know,' he answered and hung his head. He has known me since childhood, Nacha. His father and mine were brothers and we were cousins. He always loved me, at least he said that, and so everyone believed it. On the bridge I was ashamed. The blood flowed onto his chest. I took out a handkerchief from my purse and without a word, I began to wipe it off. I always loved him, too, Nachita, because he is the opposite of me: he is not afraid and he is not a traitor. He took my hand and looked at me.

" 'It's very faded, it looks like one of their hands,' he told me.

" 'It's been awhile since I've been in the sun.' He lowered his eyes and dropped my hand. We stood that way, in silence, listening to the blood run over his chest. He never reproached me, knowing well of what I'm capable. But the little threads of his blood wrote on his chest that his heart continued to hold my words and my body. There I found out Nachita, that time and love are one and the same.

" 'You have always had the most precious place in my heart,' he said. He looked down at the ground covered with dried stones. With one of them he drew two parallel lines that he extended until they joined and became only one.

" 'This is you and I,' he said without raising his eyes. I, Nachita, remained silent.

" 'It won't be long before time runs out and we are only one . . . that's why I have come looking for you.' I had forgotten, Nacha, that when time runs out, the two of us must remain one in the other in order to enter in real time converted into one. When he told me this, I looked in his eyes. Before,

I would have dared to look into them only when he made love to me, but now, as I already told you, I have learned not to respect the eyes of a man. It is also true that I didn't want to watch what was happening around me . . . I am really a coward. I remembered the screams and I listened again: shrill, blazing in the middle of the morning. I also heard the blows of the stone and I saw them whizzing over my head. He kneeled in front of me and crossed his arms over my head to make me a little roof.

" 'This is the end of man,' I said.

" 'I will return at night, wait for me,' he whispered. He grabbed his shield and looked at me from far above.

" 'It won't be long before we are one,' he added with his usual politeness.

"When he left, I heard once again the shouts of combat and I left, running in the shower of stones, and I lost myself on the way to the stalled car on the bridge of the Lake of Cuitzeo.[7]

" 'What happened? Are you hurt?' Margarita shouted at me when I came. Frightened, she touched the blood on my white dress and pointed out the blood on my lips and the dirt that had fallen in my hair. From another car, the mechanic from Cuitzeo looked at me with his dead eyes.

" 'Those savage Indians! A woman shouldn't be left alone!' he said when jumping from his car supposedly to help me.

"At dusk we arrived in Mexico City. How it had changed, Nachita, I almost couldn't believe it! At noon the warriors were still there, and now not even a trace. Nor was there any rubble left. We went through silent and sad Zócalo; there was nothing left of the other plaza, nothing![8] Margarita looked at me suspiciously. When we came to the house, you greeted us: Do you remember?"

Nacha nodded. It was certainly true that only two short months ago señora Laurita and her mother-in-law had left to visit Guanajuato. The night that she had returned, Josefina the maid and she, Nacha, had noticed blood on the dress and the absent eyes of the señora, but Margarita, the older señora indicated that they should be quiet. She seemed very worried.

Señora Margarita, his mother, had already told him what happened and she made a sign as if to say: "Be quiet! Have pity on her!" Señora Laurita didn't answer: she stroked her lips and smiled knowingly. Then the señor spoke again of President López Mateos.

"The way things are, Nachita, I had never noticed how much Pablo bored me until that night!" commented the señora, clasping her knees affectionately and suddenly admitting this to Josefina and to Nachita.

The cook crossed her arms and nodded. "Ever since I entered this house, the furniture, the vases and the mirrors overwhelmed me and left me sadder than I already was. How many days, how many years will I still have to wait for my cousin to come for me? I told myself this and regretted my treason. When we were eating dinner I noticed that Pablo didn't speak with words but with letters. And I started to count them while I watched his thick mouth and his dead eye. Suddenly he was quiet. You know that he forgets everything. He sat with his arms down. 'This new husband doesn't have a memory and doesn't know more than daily things.'

" 'You have a troubled and confused husband,' he told me, looking again at the stains on my dress. My poor mother-in-law grew flustered and since we were drinking coffee, she got up to play a twist.

" 'To cheer you up,' she told us with a fake smile, because she saw the fight coming.

"We remained quiet. The house filled with noises. I looked at Pablo. He reminds me of . . . and I didn't dare to say his name for fear that he would read my thoughts. It's true that he is like him, Nacha. Both of them enjoy water and cool houses. Both look at the sky in the afternoon and they have black hair and white teeth. But Pablo speaks in short bursts, gets furious for no reason and constantly asks: 'What are you thinking about?' My cousin husband doesn't say or do any of that."

"It's true! It's true that the señor is a pain in the ass!" said Nacha with disgust.

Laura sighed and looked at her cook with relief. At least she had her as a confidante.

"During the night, while Pablo kissed me, I would repeat to myself: 'When will he come for me?' And I almost cried at the memory of the blood from his shoulder wound. Neither could I forget his arms crossed over my head to shelter me. At the same time I was afraid that Pablo would notice that my cousin had kissed me in the morning. But no one noticed anything, and if it hadn't been for Josefina who frightened me in the morning, Pablo never would have known."

Nachita agreed. It was Josefina with her love of scandal who was to blame for it all. She, Nacha, had warned her: "Shut up! Keep quiet, for the love of God. There's probably a good reason why they didn't hear our shouts!" But, of course, Josefina had hardly entered the master bedroom with the breakfast tray when she let loose what should have been kept quiet.

"Señora, last night a man was spying through the window of your room! Nacha and I screamed and screamed!"

"We heard nothing," the señor said surprised.

"It's him!" cried the señora without thinking.

"Who is 'him'?" asked the señor, looking at the señora as if he were going to kill her. At least this is what Josefina said afterwards.

Terrified, the señora put her hand over her mouth and when the señor asked the same question over, each time with more anger, she responded: "The Indian . . . the Indian that followed me from Cuitzeo to Mexico City."

That was how Josefina found out about the Indian and that was how she told it to Nachita.

"We have to call the police immediately!" shouted the señor.

Josefina showed him the window through which the stranger had been peering and Pablo examined it carefully: on the sill were traces of almost fresh blood.

"He's wounded," said the señor, preoccupied. He walked into the bedroom and stopped in front of his wife.

"It was an Indian, señor," Josefina corroborated Laura's words.

Pablo saw the white suit thrown over a chair and he seized it viciously.

"Can you explain to me the origin of these stains?"

The señora remained silent, looking at the bloodstains over the breast of her suit, and the señor struck the dresser with a fist. Then he walked over to the señora and gave her a hard slap. This is what Josefina saw and heard.

"His looks are savage and his conduct is as incoherent as his words. It is not my fault that he accepted defeat," said Laura with disdain.

"That's right," agreed Nachita.

After all, what could the señor complain about? From a mile away, it was obvious that Laura was too good for him.

"I fell in love with Pablo on a highway during one minute in which he reminded me of someone I knew, but whom I'd forgotten. Later, at times, I would recall that instant in which it seemed he would change into that other whom he resembled. But it wasn't true. Immediately he became absurd, without memory, and he only repeated the gestures of all of the men of Mexico City. How did you expect me not to realize the deceit? When he gets angry he doesn't let me go out. As you well know! How many times does he pick a fight in cinemas and restaurants? You know it, Nachita. On the other hand, my cousin husband never, but never, gets angry at a woman."

Nacha knew that what the señora told her now was true, because of that morning when Josefina appeared in the kitchen frightened and crying, "Wake up señora Margarita, the señor is beating the señora!" She, Nacha, ran to the room of the older señora.

The presence of his mother calmed señor Pablo. Margarita remained very surprised to hear of the incident of the Indian because she had not seen him in the Lake of Cuitzeo, she had only seen the blood that we could all see.

"You know, Nachita, what I was thinking that morning? What if he had seen me last night when Pablo kissed me? And I wanted to cry. In that moment I remembered that when a man and woman love each other and don't have children, they are condemned to become one. That is what my other father used to tell me whenever I brought him water and he stared at the door behind which my cousin and I slept. Everything that my other father had told me is coming true now. From the pillow I heard the words of Pablo and Margarita and they were nothing but nonsense. 'I'm going to look for him,' I told myself. 'But where?' Much later, when you came to my room to ask what we should have for dinner, a thought came to my head: 'To the café Tacuba!'[9] And I didn't even know that restaurant, Nachita, I only knew it by name."

Nacha remembered the señora as if she were seeing her right now, putting on her white dress stained with blood, the same one she was wearing this moment in the kitchen.

"For God's sake, Laura, don't put on that dress!" said her mother-in-law. But she paid her no mind. To cover the stains, she put on a white sweater over it, buttoned to the neck, and she went out in the street without saying good-bye.

"There was nobody at the café Tacuba. It's a very sad place, Nachita. A waiter came up to me. 'What can I get you?' I didn't want anything, but I had to order something. 'A cocada.' My cousin and I ate coconuts as kids . . . In the café a clock kept the time. 'In all the cities there are clocks that keep time, it must be slipping away. When there is only a transparent layer remaining, he will come and the two drawn lines will become only one and I will live in the most precious part of his heart.' That is what I told myself while I ate the cocada.

" 'What time is it?' I asked the waiter.

" 'Twelve o'clock, señorita.'

" 'Pablo comes at one,' I told myself. 'If I tell a taxi to take the beltway home, I can still wait a bit longer.' But I didn't wait and I went out into the street. The sun was silver-plated, my thoughts became a brilliant powder and there was no present, past or future.[10] On the sidewalk my cousin stood in front of me, his eyes were sad, he stared at me for a long time.

" 'What have you been up to?' he asked me with his profound voice.

" 'I was waiting for you.'

"He stood still like a panther. I saw his black hair and the red wound on his shoulder.

" 'Weren't you afraid of being here alone?'

"The stones and cries began whizzing around us and I felt something burning behind me.

" 'Don't look,' he told me.

"He knelt on one knee and with his fingers smothered my dress that had begun to burn. I saw his grieving eyes.

"'Take me away from here!' I shouted with all my might because I remembered that I was in front of my father's house, that the house was burning and that behind me my parents and my brothers and sisters lay dead. I saw everything reflected in his eyes while he had one knee on the ground smothering my dress. I let myself fall over him so he would hold me in his arms. With his warm hand he covered my eyes.

"'This is the end of man' I told him with my eyes beneath his hand.

"'Don't look at it!'

"He held me against his heart. I heard it like thunder rolling over the mountains. How much longer before time would stop and I could hear it forever? My tears refreshed his hand that burned in the fire of the city. The shouts and the stones drew closer to us, but I was safe against his chest.

"'Sleep with me . . .' he said in a very low voice.

"'Did you see me last night?' I asked.

"'I saw you.'

"We slept in the light of the morning, in the heat of the fire. When we awakened, he stood up and grabbed his shield.

"'Hide until dawn. I will come for you.'

"He left running, his naked legs moving swiftly . . . and I escaped again, Nachita, because I was afraid by myself." [11]

Josefina came down later tripping over the stairs. "Señora, the señor and señora Margarita are at the police station!"

Laura stared at her in surprise, silent.

"Where did you go, señora?"

"I went to the café Tacuba."

"But that was two days ago."

Josefina was carrying the *Latest News*. She read it out loud: "The señora Aldama is still missing. It is believed that the sinister individual with an indigenous appearance who followed her from Cuitzeo is a madman. The police are investigating in the states of Michoacán and Guanajuato."

Señora Laurita wrenched the newspaper from Josefina's hands and tore it up angrily. Then she went to her room. Nacha and Josefina followed her, it was better to not leave her alone. They saw her throw herself over her bed and dream with her eyes wide open. The two had the same thought and they told each other later on in the kitchen: "It seems to me that señora Laurita is in love." When the señor arrived, they were still in the bedroom of their mistress.

"Laura!" he cried. He rushed to the bed and took his wife in his arms.

"Love of my life!" sobbed the señor.

Señora Laurita seemed moved for a few seconds.

"Señor!" shouted Josefina. "The señora's dress has been scorched."

Nacha looked at her disapprovingly. The señor scrutinized the señora's dress and legs.

"It's true . . . even the soles of her shoes are burnt. My love, what happened? Where were you?"

"At the café Tacuba," answered the señora composedly.

Señora Margarita wrung her hands and drew close to her daughter-in-law.

"We already know that the day before yesterday you were there and that you ate a cocada. And then?"

"Then I took a taxi and I came home on the beltway."

Nacha lowered her eyes, Josefina opened her mouth as if to say something and señora Margarita bit her lip. Pablo, on the other hand, seized his wife by the shoulders and shook her forcefully.

"Stop playing the fool! Where were you for two days? . . . Why is your dress burned?"

"Burned? But he smothered it." Laura blurted out.

"Him? . . . That disgusting Indian?" Pablo shook her again in his fury.

"He found me at the door of the café Tacuba," cried the señora, frightened to death.

"I never thought you were so low!" said the señor, and he pushed her back on the bed.

"Tell us who he is," asked her mother-in-law, softening the voice.

"It's true, isn't it Nachita, that I couldn't tell them he was my husband?" Laura sought her cook's approval.

Nacha commended the discretion of her employer, and remembered that day at noon that, she, distressed by the condition of her mistress, had suggested: "Perhaps the Indian of Cuitzeo is a witch."

But señora Margarita turned on her with glaring eyes and responded almost screaming: "A witch? You mean an assassin!"

Afterwards, they would not let señora Laurita leave the house for many days. The señor ordered that the windows and doors of the house be guarded. The cook and the maid checked in on the señora continually. Nacha refrained from expressing her opinion on the matter or from speaking about peculiar incidents. But, who could silence Josefina?

"Señor, at dawn the Indian was at the window again," she announced while bringing in the breakfast tray.

The señor rushed to the window and found more evidence of fresh blood. The señora began to cry.

"Poor thing! . . . poor thing!" she said between sobs.

It was that afternoon when the señor arrived with a doctor. From then on, the doctor returned every evening.

"He asked me about my childhood, about my mother and my father. But, I, Nachita, didn't know which childhood, nor which father nor which mother he wanted to know about. That's why I told him about the conquest of Mexico. You understand me, don't you?" asked Laura peering over the yellow saucepans.

"Yes, señora . . ." And Nachita, nervous, scrutinized the garden through the kitchen window. The night barely let one see among its shadows. She remembered the señor's loss of appetite at dinner and the afflicted expression of his mother.

"Mama, Laura told the doctor the *History* of Bernal Díaz del Castillo. She says that it's the only thing that interests her."

Señora Margarita dropped her fork.

"My poor child, your wife is insane!"

"She speaks only of the fall of the great Tenochtitlán," added Pablo in a gloomy tone.

Two days earlier, the doctor, señora Margarita and Pablo decided that Laura's depression was increasing with her isolation. She should have contact with the outside world and face her responsibilities. From that day on, the señor ordered a car to take his wife to Chapultepec for short strolls. The señora would leave accompanied by her mother-in-law and the chauffeur had orders to watch her closely. But the air from the eucalyptus trees didn't improve her health, because as soon as she returned to the house, señora Laurita would lock herself in her room to read *The Conquest of Mexico* by Bernal Díaz.

One morning señora Margarita returned from Chapultepec alone and disheartened.

"That crazy woman escaped!" she shouted in a thunderous voice as soon as she entered the house.

"Imagine, Nacha, I sat down on the usual bench and I told myself: 'He won't forgive me. A man can forgive one, two, three, four betrayals, but not a permanent betrayal.' This thought made me very sad. It was hot out and Margarita bought a vanilla ice cream; I didn't want any, so she sat in the automobile to eat it. I noticed that she was as bored with me as I was with her. I don't like her being constantly watched and I tried to look at other things so I wouldn't see her eating her cone and watching me. I saw the gray moss that hung from the pines and I don't know why, but the morning became as sad as those trees. 'The trees and I have seen the same catastrophes,' I told myself. Along the empty street the hours strolled alone. I was like the hours, alone on an empty street. My husband had contemplated my eternal betrayal through the window and had abandoned me on that street made of things which did not exist. I remembered the smell of the leaves of corn and the whispered rumor of his steps. 'That is how he walked with the rhythm of dried leaves when the wind of February carries them over the stones. I never used to have to turn my head to know that he was there watching me from behind' . . . I was thinking these sad thoughts when I heard the sun slip away and the dry leaves began to stir.[12] I felt his breath on my back, then he was in front of me, I saw his bare feet in front of mine. He had a scratch on his knee. I raised my eyes and found myself beneath his. We stood for a long time without speaking. Out of respect I waited for his words.

"'What have you been up to?' he said.

"I saw that he didn't stir and that he seemed sadder than before.

"'I was waiting for you,' I answered.

"'The last day is coming . . .'

"It seemed to me that his voice came from the bottom of time. Blood continued to flow from his shoulder. I was filled with shame, lowered my eyes, opened my purse and took out a handkerchief to wipe his chest. Then I put it away. He stood still, watching me.

"'Let's go to the exit of Tacuba . . . There are many betrayals . . .'

"He took my hand and we walked among the people, who were yelling and whimpering. There were many dead floating in the water of the canals. There were women sitting in the grass watching them float. The stench was everywhere and the children ran crying from one end to the other, having lost their parents. I watched everything without wanting to see it. The smashed canoes carried nothing but sadness. My husband sat me beneath a broken tree. He put one knee on the ground and attentively watched the events around us. He wasn't afraid. Afterwards he looked at me.[13]

"'I know you're a traitor and that you have affection for me. The good grows together with the bad.'

"I could hardly hear him over the children's cries. They came from far away, but they were so strong that they ruptured the light of the day. It seemed like it was the last time they would cry.

"'It's the children,' he told me.

"'This is the end of man,' I repeated, because I could think of nothing else to say.

"He put his hands over my ears and then held me against his chest.

"'As a traitor I met you and as such I loved you [. . .]. Wait for me here.'

"He looked at me and left to fight with the hope of avoiding defeat. I remained huddled up. I tried not to see the fleeing people to avoid temptation, and I tried not to see the bodies that floated in the water to avoid the tears. I began to count the small fruit that hung from the broken branches: they were dry and when I touched them with my fingers the red rinds fell from them. I don't know why that seemed a bad omen, but I preferred to look at the sky, which began to grow dark. First it became brown, then it began to take on the color of those drowned in the canals. I sat there remembering the colors of other afternoons. But the afternoon became bruised, swelling, as if suddenly it was going to burst and I realized that time was up. If my cousin didn't return, what would become of me? Perhaps he was already dead in battle. His fate no longer mattered to me and I left that place as fast as I could, pursued by my own fear. 'When he arrives and looks for me . . .'[14] I didn't have time to finish my thought because I found myself in the twilight of Mexico City. 'Margarita must have finished her vanilla ice cream and Pablo must be very mad.' A taxi took me home on the beltway. And do you know, Nachita, that the beltways were those canals infested with cadavers?[15] That is why I arrived so sad . . . Now, Nachita, don't tell the señor that I spent the night with my husband."

Nachita settled her hand over her lilac skirt.

"Señor Pablo has already been gone ten days to Acapulco. He became very weak during the weeks of the investigation," explained Nachita with satisfaction.

Laura looked at her without surprise and sighed with relief.

"The one who is up there is señora Margarita," added Nacha, raising her eyes to the kitchen ceiling.

Laura clasped her knees and looked out the windows at the roses erased by the nocturnal shadows and at the lights to the neighboring windows that were beginning to go out.

Nachita poured salt over the back of her hand and ate it as if it were candy.

"So many coyotes! The pack is excited!" she said with a voice full of salt.[16]

Laura sat still, listening a few moments. "Damned animals, you should have seen them this afternoon," she said.

"As long as they don't obstruct the señor's travel or make him take the wrong road," commented Nacha, afraid.[17]

"If he's never been afraid of them, why should he be afraid of them tonight?" asked Laura, irritated.

Nacha drew close to her employer to emphasize the sudden intimacy established between them. "They are weaker than the Tlaxcaltecas," she told her in a low voice.

The two women sat quietly. Nacha devoured little by little another small mound of salt. Laura listened worriedly to the howls of the coyotes that filled the night. It was Nacha who saw him coming and who opened the window.

"Señora . . . He has come for you," she whispered to her in a voice so low that only Laura could hear it.

Afterwards, when Laura had already left with him forever, Nachita washed the blood from the window and chased off the coyotes, who came in to her century, a century ended in just that instant. Nacha checked with her ancient eyes in order to see if everything was in order: she washed the coffee cup, threw the cigarette butts stained with lipstick into the waste can, set the coffee pot in the cupboard and turned out the light.

"I say that señora Laurita was not from this time, nor was she meant for the señor," she said in the morning, when she carried breakfast to señora Margarita.

"I no longer feel at home in the Aldama house. I am going to look for another job. I told Josefina." And when the maid wasn't looking, Nacha left without even collecting her pay.

DISCUSSION QUESTIONS

- How does Garro's story typify magical realist literary structures?
- To what class does Laura belong and how does that determine which women possess voice and agency?
- Considering Garro's social status, political activism, and eventual exile, how does she figure into Angel Rama's concept of the lettered citizen? Does Garro successfully give a voice to the nonlettered citizen?
- In the story, Laura's cousin-husband makes a reference to the whitening of Laura. Is this suggested as a cultural improvement? How is it reflective of discourse speaking through Garro's text?
- How might Garro's story be considered a foundational fiction? Recall Sommer's notion of a foundational fiction as a union between characters symbolizing two oppositional sides, which serves as a metaphor for nation building.
- How does Garro's construction of women and indigenous people differ from and/or resemble that of Sarmiento and Gallegos (as well as that of Octavio Paz—from what you have learned of him from our introduction)?

NOTES

1. Biographical information on Garro can be found in Angel Flores, *Spanish American Authors: The Twentieth Century* (New York: Wilson,

1992). See also the online version of *El Universal*, a Mexican newspaper, <*http://www.eluniversal.com.mx/pls/impreso/noticia.html?id_nota 5240963&tabla5notas*> and another online site dedicated to Mexican literary culture, <*http://www.eluniversal.com.mx/pls/impreso/noticia.html? id_nota=240963&tabla=notas*>.

2. For a brief description of magical realism, see Zamora Faris, ed., *Magical Realism: Theory, History, Community* (Durham: Duke UP, 1995).

3. Octavio Paz, *The Labyrinth of Solitude: Life and Thought in Mexico*, trans. Lysander Kemp (New York: Grove, 1961) 30, 36.

4. Paz 30.

5. Elena Garro, "It's the Fault of the Tlaxcaltecas," trans. Patricia Wahl, *RIF/T: An Electronic Space for Poetry, Prose and Poetics*, ed. Kenneth Sherwood and Loss Pequeño Glazier, version 2.1, winter 1994, originally accessed on 16 December 2002 <http://wings.buffalo.edu/epc/rift/rift02/ wahl0201.html>.

6. This is the first moment that Laura travels back in time to the sixteenth century.

7. Here Laura returns to the present on the outskirts of Mexico City.

8. The zócalo is a roughly four-square block plaza at the center of Mexico City. It was also the center of Tenochitlán.

9. Café Tacuba has been a café in the center of Mexico City since 1912. It is famous for serving traditional Mexican dishes.

10. This is the second time Laura travels back in time to the sixteenth century.

11. Here Laura returns to the twentieth century.

12. This is the third time Laura travels back to the sixteenth century.

13. This is a description of the fall of the Aztec capital of Tenochitlán to the Spaniards.

14. Here Laura returns to the present for the third time.

15. The beltways of Mexico City were built over the Aztec water canals.

16. In this sentence, the past and the present coexist, as there are no coyotes in present-day Mexico City.

17. Nacha's reference to the señor has changed, and she is referring here to Laura's indigenous cousin-husband, instead of to Pablo.

Film Foray: Como agua para chocolate
(Like Water for Chocolate)

Como agua para chocolate, a novel by Laura Esquivel, is a story of forbidden love. In 1991 it was made into a movie by Alfonso Arau, her husband at the time, a year after its publication. Esquivel also wrote the screenplay. The story revolves around a romance involving Tita and Pedro, the main characters. Their love affair simmers constantly throughout the story, but especially in the magical way in which Tita infuses her emotions into the food she prepares for Pedro. In consuming her meals, Pedro ingests Tita's passion for him as they bide their time waiting for the day when they can consummate their love. Once the film demonstrated its strong box office clout in Mexico and the United States, initial lukewarm reviews by Mexican critics gave way to ten Ariel awards (Mexico's Oscar) in 1992 from the Mexican Film Academy. A full-on advertising campaign by Miramax accompanied distribution of the film in the United States. The marketing scheme began with posters praising its achievement as the most successful foreign language film ever, as if profits were the only proof of cinematographic merit. After sixty-three consecutive weeks in theaters the film had grossed more than $20 million. Copies of the novel were sold at movie theaters, persuading Mexican restaurants across the United States to recreate the dishes made in the film. They also staged "seductive recipe" contests with trips to Mexico as prizes. At a party celebrating the film, Claudette Maille, the actress who played Gertrudis, recreated her most memorable scene by being carried off naked on horseback, this time along the West Side Highway in New York City, while all those in attendance were treated to a banquet identical to the wedding feast prepared by Tita and her indigenous servants.

The two articles excerpted in this chapter attempt to provide an explanation for the unprecedented success of *Como agua para chocolate*. Barbara Tenenbaum, a specialist on the culture of Mexico from the Hispanic division of the Library of Congress, sets out to prove that the film captures the essence of Mexico and thus manages to please audiences on either side of the border, despite what she believes are their intrinsic differences in the way they experience love, life, and death. Harmony Wu, a lecturer at Emerson College in the Department of Visual and Media Arts, examines the film's accolades, marketing, and profits for what they reveal about U.S. perceptions regarding Mexicanness (and by extension, Latinness). She also looks at the influence the film has had in the United States and elsewhere in shaping and reinforcing these perceptions as truths.

We could say that Barbara Tenenbaum is to Gerald Martin as Harmony Wu is to Leslie Bary. In our introductions to Chapter 10, we stated that Martin bases his interpretation of Latin America on a more essentialist foundation and cites literary genres that he believes reveal its true identity. We also said that Bary adopts a more semiotic approach by citing authors whose works expose discursive constructs. In a similar way, Wu exposes *Como agua para chocolate*'s discursively constituted definition of Mexican essence as magical other, which is sold to and consumed by Mexicans, the United States, and the rest of the world. Meanwhile, Tenenbaum demonstrates that she has unconsciously consumed and been consumed by these very constructs and advances them as truths of Mexican identity.

The film is set in 1910 at the start of the Mexican Revolution. Mama Elena, one of its key characters, has assumed control over the family ranch upon the death of her husband. He had a heart attack when he learned that Gertrudis, one of his three daughters, is the illegitimate offspring of an affair between Mama Elena and a mulatto. When Nacha, the indigenous servant who serves as the family's cook and surrogate mother to Tita, the youngest daughter, prophecies that the first boy who sets eyes on Tita will fall in love with her, Mama Elena decides to resurrect a family tradition abandoned long ago. She declares that Tita will never marry since she will be responsible for taking care of her until her death. When Nacha's prophecy comes true and Pedro asks Tita to marry him, Mama Elena offers her daughter Rosaura instead. Pedro accepts the offer as a way to remain near Tita.

From this moment, Tita, about whom it is said that she cried so much in her mother's womb that her dried birth water "yielded a forty-pound sack of salt," becomes the focus of the magical realism in the film. Tita is unknowingly able to express her desire for Pedro by magically incorporating it into the food she prepares. In the scene most emblematic of this power, Tita uses rose petals from a bouquet given to her by Pedro in honor of completing one year as head cook to create a rose petal sauce for the quail she is preparing, altering a pre-Hispanic recipe of Nacha's. The film explains that with each bite, Tita enters Pedro's body, and it is clear that the impact is tremendous. But the character who actually acts out the passion of the rose-petal sauce is Tita's sister Gertrudis. When Pedro exclaims that the dish is "the nectar of the gods," Gertrudis becomes so aroused that she feels forced to run to the bathhouse to cool off with a shower. Instead, she sets the structure on fire, and as she flees naked from the blaze, she is plucked from the flames by a *Villista* (a revolutionary) on horseback who has smelled her burning rose petal passion from miles away, thereby incorporating Gertrudis into the revolution.

Months pass and Mama Elena does everything in her power to keep Tita and Pedro apart. She even sends Pedro, Rosaura, and their baby son, whom Tita has been nursing because Rosaura is too weak and incapable of doing so and because Tita "can't stand to see anyone go hungry," across the border to live. Tragically, the son dies soon afterward. Hearing this news, Tita goes mad and is left mute. Mama Elena then sends her across the border to a sanatorium to be cured by the North American doctor John Brown, as "there is no place at the ranch for lunatics." Tita regains her health under Dr. Brown's care but remains mute until Chencha, another family servant, arrives at the sanatorium, restoring Tita's voice with the soup she brings. She informs Tita that Mama Elena has been killed by bandits, and the two decide to return to the ranch. Soon after, Pedro, Rosaura, and Esperanza, their new baby daughter, arrive as well.

In the meantime, Dr. Brown confesses to Tita that he has fallen in love with her, and before her return journey Tita agrees to marry him. Back at the ranch, however, the flames of Tita and Pedro's desire are reignited, and when Tita thinks she is pregnant with Pedro's baby, she breaks off her engagement with Dr. Brown, who insists that he will marry her regardless. Ironically, this scene is juxtaposed with a wedding sequence, but the newlyweds are revealed to be Esperanza and Alex Brown, John Brown's son, rather than Tita and the doctor. Rosaura has just died, and Tita and Pedro, now free from all constraints, dance uninhibitedly at the wedding. Later, they reaffirm their lifelong passion for each other by making love. Pedro dies in the act, and Tita swallows matches in an attempt to reignite the couple's love, recalling a pedantic lesson from Dr. Brown on the physical manifestations of passion. The room then bursts into flames when what appears to be a shower of sparks issues from Tita's body. Both lovers are cremated and the entire ranch burns down.

Tenenbaum indicates that her article will focus on how the film manages to please audiences on both sides of the border, but she writes at length explaining to the "uninitiated"—her mother and "many among the subtitle readers"—the cultural cues that she assumes they have not understood. In this role of illuminator of the "true" Mexico, Tenenbaum exposes her essentialistic approach: the film must be tested for legitimacy against what she believes to be Mexico's cultural essences. She finds a few inaccuracies but uses what she presumes to be the intentions of the filmmakers to justify them. Cultural references, for example, are drawn from central Mexico but the geographic setting for the film is the U.S. border. Tennebaum explains that this dislocation of culture and space allows the filmmakers to draw upon the more tradition-oriented culture of central Mexico to advance their argument about the power of tradition in shaping social relations.

Repeating her mother's questioning of the film, Tenenbaum asks why Tita ultimately refuses to marry Dr. Brown. Projecting her own mother's befuddlement on all citizens north of the border, Tenenbaum concludes that U.S. audiences cannot understand the passion inherent in Mexicans. "In the United States," she says, "there are many kinds of love, and a marriage based solely on passion is seen as quite a risky enterprise. In Mexico, however, love is defined by passion." She has proceeded from and arrived at what semiotics finds to be an essentialist assumption: People from the United States are intrinsically practical while people from Mexico are intrinsically passionate.[1] An essentialist disagreement with Tenenbaum might set out to prove that Mexicans are intrinsically uncalculating, not intrinsically passionate, thereby swapping one ontological essentialism for another.

We can see that Tenenbaum herself is a bit uncomfortable with this argument about intrinsic characteristics because she attempts to prove her assertion with a seemingly scientific, or at least statistical, argument. She reasserts an essentialist structure by insisting that both the cause and effect of Mexicans seeking out their identity in an indigenous past can be traced to the disproportionately lower numbers of European immigrants that Mexico received when compared with other Latin American countries like Uruguay and Argentina. Passionate love, therefore, is "truly" Mexican since every Mexican has a preponderance of indigenous, not European, heritage. Tenenbaum never defines this heritage as racial bloodlines, and she might well be thinking of it in solely cultural terms, but her failure to distinguish and clarify the issue leaves a lingering feeling of essentialism that Wade's discussion of ethnicity in Chapter 6 helps to detect.

Harmony Wu, on the other hand, is not at all concerned with judging *Como agua* by whether it represents the true Mexico. She shifts attention from testing the authenticity and verifiability of the film to testing the discourse upon which ideas of Mexicanness rest.

In "Consuming Tacos and Enchiladas" Wu attributes the success of this film to the fact that it meets the expectations of U.S. audiences regarding the otherness of Mexicans and Latin Americans. "Embedded in the melodrama," she writes, "is a representation of Mexico/Latin America that characterizes it as magic, folkloric, exotic, provincial—in short, other."[2] Wu argues that when the magical realist aesthetic is commodified for popular international consumption, it "fixes a frozen identity of Mexicanness" as well as Latinness: "In demanding and consuming endless reproductions of magic realism, the dominant U.S. culture condemns a lumpen, undifferentiated pan-Latin culture to repetition of an aesthetic that, from the point of view of the rational, industrial, and dominant cultures that consume the images, both defines it as underdeveloped and fixes its status there."[3] Wu concludes that, rather than challenge Western rationality, magical realism in commodified form reaffirms the West's position as core and Latin America's as peripheral.

The proliferation of successful Hispanic films that incorporate magical realism into their narratives might lead one to ask not whether Latin Americans are inherently mystical, but to question what it is about Mexican and U.S. national discourses that encourage the figuring of Mexican identity using magical realism as a trope. Does this not limit Mexican identity to a kind of surreal, if not irrational, sense of reality? Are movie producers and distributors, ticket buyers, and givers of film prizes simply rewarding the production of a Hispanic identity that we have already projected as primitive and exotic? Questions such as these force us to consider our own position in defining others and bring us to the crucial matter in our analysis of *Como agua para chocolate*'s role in shaping notions regarding Mexican identity. As you read Tenenbaum and Wu, consider the implicit dialogue between these two critics.

BARBARA TENENBAUM, "WHY TITA DIDN'T MARRY
THE DOCTOR, OR MEXICAN HISTORY IN *LIKE WATER
FOR CHOCOLATE*"[4]

My mother has only seen one Mexican movie—*Like Water for Chocolate*. It is understandable that she should have seen that particular picture because the film was both a commercial and a critical success. In the seven months following its February 1993 release, it had already grossed $6.1 million, the most ever by a Latin American film. Janet Maslin, film critic of the New York Times, suggests a reason for its popularity: "It relies so enchantingly upon fate, magic, and a taste for the supernatural that it suggests Gabriel García Márquez in a cookbook-writing mode." Such praise and success at the U.S. box office does not necessarily mean, however, that audiences in the United States fully understood the action presented. In fact, many among the subtitle readers proclaimed themselves perplexed. Like my mother, they asked, "Why didn't the girl marry that nice doctor?" Aside from my Jewish mother's fascination with doctors as the sine qua non of husband material, the general question underscores not only the important ways in which Mexico developed differently from many other nations in the Western Hemisphere but also how Laura Esquivel was able to adjust the screenplay of her novel of the same title to fit a crossover audience in the United States without alienating its Mexican public [. . .].

There are countless examples of spiritual restlessness throughout the movie, and, even when offered a "calm, secure, and peaceful" life through marriage to the American doctor who adores her, Tita, our heroine, eschews probable happiness or at least contentment in favor of maintaining her forbidden passion for the Pedro she fell in love with as a child. This decision generally confused viewers in the United States, yet it nevertheless embodies a traditional Mexican worldview and reflects Mexico's distinctive lack of massive European immigration.

In the period during which most of the movie takes place, 1880–1914, immigrants from Europe flooded many countries of the Western Hemisphere. Indeed, it was during that time that my mother's parents left Russia and Poland to settle in Philadelphia. While we think of the United States, Canada, Brazil, Uruguay, and Argentina as immigrant societies, we have not thought about what it meant to their counterparts—Mexico, Ecuador, Bolivia, and, to a lesser degree, Peru—not to have undergone that immigrant experience.

Of course, we well know that Mexico is not simply an indigenous society; it was conquered and colonized and mestizoized by those living in the area currently known as Spain, who came there in hopes of winning for themselves a better life. However, unlike nineteenth-century immigrants, these Spaniards came to the New World as representatives of their government and could count on its support, in most cases. They did what they did in the name of the crown or the church, which in this particular case was the same thing. They imposed, or tried to impose, their culture and way of life on the indigenous empires and tribes they found in the land that they conquered. And, over time, they blended more or less openly, and not so openly, with that population, creating something that Mexican author and statesman José Vasconcelos called "the cosmic race." [. . .]

That embrace of the indigenous past virtually closed the door to European immigration at a time when the native inhabitants of the Western Hemisphere were seen as threatening subhumans in both the United States and the Southern Cone. Mexico did attempt to attract immigrants; it offered land and other enticements but to little avail. Although European intellectuals and some members of the elite perhaps were charmed by the idea of noble savages across the sea, they were not about to leave home and settle among them. As for the real potential immigrants like my grandparents, imagine their reactions to the supposed temple of Montezuma and the full-size statue of Cuauhtémoc, the last Aztec emperor, that they would have seen at the Mexican pavilion at the 1889 Paris Exposition! How could they not have preferred the European buildings and progressive machinery found at the exhibitions from the United States or Argentina close by? Suffice it to say that Argentina did not even bother to exhibit in the 1900 Exposition; it already had more immigrants than it could ever have thought possible.

To further complicate an already complex scenario, *Like Water for Chocolate* presumably concerns itself with an area far away from the core of Mexico, where yet a very different culture evolved on what would become after 1848 the border between the Mexican world and Anglo-Saxon territory. The movie quickly introduces us to the landscape of the border state of Coahuila and the relationship between the towns of Piedras Negras and Eagle Pass in the Rio Grande Valley in 1895. In addition, it alerts us to the fact that the movie will be what used to be called a tearjerker, but a tearjerker with a twist, for tears overtly play an important part in the plot. The film begins with the contemporary narrator's putting an onion on her head to prevent tears flowing while she cuts onions. She introduces us to her tale by relating the birth of her great-aunt and our heroine, Tita, who supposedly cried so much in the womb that her dried birth water yielded a forty-pound sack of salt (only ten pounds in the book). According to Celsa, a peasant woman from whom we will hear more later, "Crying is a good way to purge your soul of evil. It's just as good a medicine as the herbal teas." Welcome to magical realism, Mexican style [. . .].

U.S. audiences watching this movie in 1993 were unable to empathize with Doña Elena, even though they could well believe that she could have demanded such daughterly devotion. What mother sitting in the audience could imagine herself uttering such a pronouncement without fear of prompting uncontrollable laughter from her offspring? Further, the beliefs in individual will and romantic love are so firmly embedded in the mythology of the United States that any cinematic parent who would try to control a child's destiny in such a way would evoke great resentment in viewers, as it is meant to do. The audience is not supposed to like Doña Elena; it is meant to side with the victimized Tita.

When we next join the family, it is 1910, the year in which the Mexican Revolution begins. We are preparing for Tita's fifteenth birthday, her *quinceañera*, when she would officially become a woman and thus marriageable. A neighbor's son, Pedro Múzquiz, sees her and, true to Nacha's prediction, falls in love with her. She returns his feelings. As Tita says, "Now I know how raw dough feels when it hits boiling oil; I expected to break out all over my body." The lovers acknowledge their passion verbally, and Pedro promises to marry Tita. But when he with his father asks for Tita's hand, Elena forbids the match and offers her eldest daughter Rosaura instead [. . .].

In a move shocking to both his father and to Tita's household at large, Pedro accepts, even though, as the servant Chencha notes, "You just can't substitute tacos for enchiladas" (that is, the plain for something fancier). At this point the audience who understands Mexican history begins to shake its collective head. As historian William French has noted for the neighboring state of Chihuahua, it was common during that period for prospective but forbidden grooms to "kidnap" their brides and marry without parental consent. Tita herself screams this to Pedro later in the movie. In this case, despite the probable approval of his father for such an action, in service to a tragic plot, Pedro agrees to marry a woman he does not love in order to be near the one he does. Yet there is precedent in central Mexico for this behavior. For example, Celsa, the protagonist of *Celsa's World: Conversations with a Mexican Peasant Woman*, suggests that Elena's laying down the law is quite reasonable if not likable.[5] According to Celsa, a peasant woman who lives in San Antonio, a village near Cuernavaca, whose comments were gathered in 1979–1980, "People have respect for you if you can manage a house or farm well and control your children. If the head of a family cannot control the children, that person loses the respect of the people. [. . .] A woman can do as good a job as a man if the children listen to her and do as she says." Elena, living alone and having three girls to raise, had to maintain the respect of her neighbors in order to survive independently. The use of this pattern of parental control common in central Mexico, rather than the bride kidnapping found on the northern border, is only one suggestion among many that Esquivel took a plot valid in the center and imposed it on the northern frontier. That explains why she did not make more of the typical aspects of the frontier, including its cuisine [. . .].

It is surprising that the revolution, the most important phenomenon in twentieth-century Mexican history, plays such a small part in the action.

If the drama had been set in central Mexico, that would have been much more understandable. It appears that residents of Mexico City, like Edith O'Shaughnessy, did not really know a revolution was taking place until 1913! Here is yet another clue that makes us realize that the book and movie only adopt the northern frontier as a backdrop, a not-so-artful disguise for the all-powerful central valley of Mexico. The food comes from there as do the customs and behavior, which seem much more Indian than is customary along *la frontera*, which even then had been strongly influenced by the United States—a typical case, then, of the center dominating the periphery as it has since 1433, when the Aztec Triple Alliance took control of the central valley [. . .].

This mixture of the spiritual, the sensual, and the emotional gives the film its poignancy and its resonance with Mexicans. It is a celebration of the female sphere—the kitchen with its smells, its wonders, its sacrifices, dangers, and pleasures, a world that for many Mexicans still exists, if in part due to the affordability of servants. For if Mexico is not an immigrant country, it is a nation that can proclaim "thirty centuries of splendor," as the 1992 exhibit at New York's Metropolitan Museum of Art called itself in hopes of winning recognition of Mexican greatness on the other side of the border. Such tradition, as Tita's plight reminds us, is not easily dismissed.

There are few nations in the world as culturally rich as Mexico, where the past so intrudes on the present that it hardly seems past. In a recent talk in Washington at the Library of Congress, Dr. María Carmen Serra Puche, director of the National Museum of Anthropology in Mexico City, spoke of her awareness of hidden spirits as she began directing the excavation of a pre-Columbian site in central Mexico in 1993, the same year that the film was released. Finally, she decided that crew members would sacrifice a turkey to the gods before they began their labors.

In that regard, Mexico is unlike any other nation in the Western Hemisphere. Although countries such as Guatemala and Bolivia have a vibrant Indian past and present, the first chooses to turn its back on its Indian heritage (as shown quite beautifully in the film *El Norte*), and the second merely tolerates it. However, Mexico has built its history as an independent nation on its Indian past. It is no accident that one of its major presidential candidates in 1988 and 1994 bore the name of the last Aztec emperor, Cuauhtémoc [. . .].

So we return to my mother's question: Why didn't Tita marry the nice Dr. Brown, who loved her? Quite apart from the fate that Tita felt bound her to Pedro, there are several other reasons in the book and film meant, at least in part, for Mexicans. The nice Dr. Brown was not brown at all; he was a *güero*—tall, blond, and Anglo even to his heavily accented fluent Spanish.

Would it not have been a repetition of the conquest for the Mexican Tita to surrender her virtue to the blond from across the border? Mexico even has a special word for women who give themselves to the enemy (and those who love foreigners too much): they are known as *malinchistas* in "honor" of Doña Marina, the hated mistress of the blond Cortés, who betrayed her people only to be cast aside herself and given to another conquistador when the mission had been completed. In one of the first silent films ever made in Mexico by a company based in the United States, an American soldier says to the Mexican girl he is embracing, "And soon you'll be Mrs. Shorty." Obviously, in a film made in Mexico, the heroine cannot become Mrs. Brown, regardless of the reason.

Of course, U.S. audiences perceive no such impediment and look at the doctor as a prize catch—he loves Tita, he is a doctor, he has a fine sense of humor, he seems to have a good character and, most important, he is an American. The book and script cheat a little; in order to make Mexican audiences more sympathetic to the gringo, the author gives him a grandmother from the Kickapoo, a tribe that voluntarily chose to abandon the United States and live in Mexico. Partly, American audiences' resonance with this character can be blamed on the appealing actor who plays the forsaken sawbones; his sweetness and gentle humor make him much more attractive than he ought to be, particularly to happily married women of a certain age. The actor who plays Pedro, by contrast, displays none of the smoldering fire that the role demands.

The book, however, leaves no doubts as to the rightness of Tita's choices. In the United States, there are many kinds of love, and a marriage based solely on passion is seen as quite a risky enterprise. In Mexico, however, love is defined by passion; whether it lasts an hour or a lifetime is of little consequence. The book revolves around the central premise that women experience love promised and not fulfilled, making them forever "like water for chocolate." Given this construct, going after the one you love, regardless of the consequences, becomes in itself a revolutionary act. All throughout the story, women think about the men whom they have loved and who loved them, and whom they have not been permitted to marry. From the servant Nacha to Mama Elena, unfulfilled passion knows no class distinctions. When the naked Gertrudis vanishes in a cloud of passion, swooped up by the Villista captain, she excites both Tita and Pedro into thinking momentarily that another course is possible for them, until Mama Elena appears to break their spell. Perhaps another meaning of the revolution is that Gertrudis, Tita, Esperanza, and Chencha will all eventually have the opportunity to be with their true loves, regardless of the cost.

296 REFRAMING LATIN AMERICA

Another thing that my mother did not understand about this movie was its ending. The book clearly informs the reader that, following Mama Elena's death, Tita and Pedro become lovers with Rosaura's knowledge. Their love continues a secret, even after Rosaura's death, until the day of the wedding of Pedro's daughter Esperanza and John Brown's son Alex, when Pedro asks Tita to marry him. The passion cooked with the *chiles en nogada* burns even more fiercely in the hidden lovers, who, at the first opportunity, go to their favorite room to indulge in the finally unguarded manifestation of their feelings. Horribly, at the triumphant moment of their union, Pedro suffers a heart attack and dies. Tita quickly decides that life without him, without someone to light the fire within her, would be torture, so she lights a fire within herself and joins Pedro as she burns to death, taking the ranch with her. Her cookbook, alone, survives.

How Mexican an ending! What other culture so teases death that it spends a whole day each year, November 2, to celebrate it? As Frances Toor, the chronicler of Mexican folkways, notes, "For days before and after, death is everywhere present. He leers invitingly from bakery windows, where there are special [. . .] breads of the dead in animal and human forms; from candy shops, in skulls with bright tinsel eyes." Families get together for a trip to the cemetery, there to clean gravestones, plant flowers, sing songs, play games, make chalk designs, and eat meals with their beloved ancestors. Whereas, across the border, the highest medical expenses are incurred in the last year of life using heroic measures to keep a person breathing, in Mexico death is not so feared. Toor notes that a typical attitude is found in "Valentina," the marching song of those who followed Carranza and Obregón in the revolution. As the soldier sings to his Valentina, "If I must be killed tomorrow/Let them kill me today." What the Mexican fears, rather, is the abandonment of the family and its inevitable alienation and loneliness. That unendurable situation is to be avoided at all costs, even to the extent of the restraint of individual desire. Tita's resolute determination to surrender to her first love, regardless of its consequences, keeps her tied to her mothers—her birth mother Elena and her kitchen mother Nacha—and to her family. After all, it is her grandniece who tells her story and cooks her recipes, a more positive equivalent to cleaning her gravestone.

And it is this feeling that ultimately has my mother and U.S. audiences stumped. What the movie evokes in them is a baffled nostalgia for a time when mothers really mattered and women's work was defined differently than it is today, when dinner all too often for all too many comes from a box and satisfies only the most elemental hunger. There is something alluring for them about a solid family tradition, according to which children live at home until marriage and do not move so far away that they cannot come back for Sunday dinner every week. Although these audiences recognize that in the real world that way of life stifled individual will and led to spiritual, if not physical, death, particularly for women, it seems sensuous and exotic while on screen. Then, as the audience emerges from the theater, it starts to tinker with the movie, trying to meld American individualism uneasily onto Mexican tradition, so that Tita too will have a happy ending. Good food and a blond doctor—what could possibly be wrong with that?

HARMONY WU, "CONSUMING TACOS AND ENCHILADAS"[6]
Revolutionary Melodrama for the 1990s?

Against this history of foundational moments and Revolutionary melodramas comes *Como agua para chocolate* (*Like Water for Chocolate*) in the early 1990s. The necessary question to ask for this film in relation to this context is, What is its agenda in appropriating the forms for reimagining nationness in 1991? *Como agua para chocolate*, directed by Alfonso Arau from the novel written by his ex-wife Laura Esquivel, who also adapted the screenplay, again returns to the Revolution with its own reimagining of the nation. *Como agua para chocolate* uses the Mexican Revolution as a backdrop, returning to this foundational moment in Mexican history, but it also returns to the foundational texts of the classic Revolutionary melodramas like *Flor silvestre* that first reimagined that moment cinematically. Almost as markers of narrative progression, Arau quotes the visual style of Fernández and Figueroa with low-angle shots and wide expanses of sky and sculptural clouds, almost requiring that *Como agua para chocolate* be read within the diverse context of its intertextuality. It is at once revising the classic Revolutionary melodramas like *Flor silvestre*, engaging in historical discourse (both in its own representations and in its references to the Revolutionary melodramas, which were themselves historically revisionist), eliciting comparisons with the novel from which the film is adapted, and activating a discourse of magic realism that necessarily invokes classics of this genre in the literary tradition. At the same time, its unique production and box office history—as a staggeringly expensive production in Mexican terms and at the time of its release the most successful foreign film ever distributed in the United States—graft additional considerations of capital (cultural and otherwise) in examinations of the film.

Given the complex intertextual matrix of *Como agua para chocolate*, it is no surprise that its ideological implications and reimagining of the modern nation are quite changed from those of *Flor silvestre*. The academic and popular discourse in the United States has articulated the ideological agenda of *Como agua para chocolate* as a liberal, feminist treatise, and the film certainly suggests these possibilities. However, I argue that the text itself doubles back against its own feminist pretensions, resulting in what is ultimately a conservative text.

Women, Nation, Revolution [. . .]

Alex Saragoza and Graciela Berkovich argue that the feminine representations in *Como agua para chocolate* constitute an ideological break with the films that portray women who are liberated but still confined within the patriarchal system. However, a close reading of *Como agua para chocolate* shows that the break is not as clean or radical as it has been figured.

Continuing in the tradition of the classic Revolutionary melodramas like *Flor silvestre,* Arau's film projects ideological issues onto the individual matters of the family. Conflict between "old" and "new" is again rendered in generational terms. The narrative of *Como agua para chocolate* concerns the subversion of the rules of Mama Elena, who has decreed that according to family tradition, her youngest daughter, Tita, may never marry and is instead condemned to care for her mother until the matriarch's death. In the repression of feminine desire and its figuration as "tradition," Mama Elena and her ideas represent outdated, patriarchal ideology. But Tita falls in love with young Pedro, and their desire to consummate and marry threaten Mama Elena's social order. As in *Flor silvestre* and the foundational fictions, it is love and the union of lovers that represent a break with the past and, in *Como agua para chocolate,* the threat of subversion to the dominant patriarchal order. But the issue here is of feminine agency and desire, not class conflict as it was in classic Revolutionary texts. *Como agua para chocolate* has appropriated the form and forum for ideological change from *Flor silvestre* and other classic Revolutionary melodramas but apparently has altered the goal of change from class to gender concerns.

Even the Revolution itself as represented in *Como agua para chocolate* is no longer associated with the agendas of class justice and land redistribution at the heart of the (historical) Revolution. Tita's magical food, into which she sublimates her own repressed desires, has an erotic effect on everyone who eats it. Tita's sister Gertrudis is so turned on by the food that she sets fire to the bathhouse with her burning desire. A Villista miles away in the midst of battle smells her passion and rides off to capture a nude and burning Gertrudis and fulfill both his and her erotic fantasies. Gertrudis joins the Revolution, not for social justice as did José Luis in *Flor silvestre* but for sexual liberation. The Revolution becomes a sexual one, reinscribed as a discourse of erotics and gender, endowing these ostensibly feminist interests with historical and national importance.

Another important marker of the text's feminine/feminist point of view is the narrative voice-over. Like *Flor silvestre, Como agua para chocolate* charts the reimagined Revolution's impact on the present through a narrative frame set in the spectator's present. The film opens with Tita's great-grandniece chopping onions, which triggers Proust-like memories and reflections on the narrative past. The great-grandniece's voice is heard throughout the master narrative, the story of Tita and Pedro, offering subjective insights and providing explanation. As narration, the voice is omniscient and powerful: this disembodied voice effectively dominates the text, suggesting that a feminine voice and a feminine perspective control the narrative.

Clearly, as demonstrated in the examples cited above, *Como agua para chocolate* figures itself as a feminine/feminist text, presenting feminine subversion of the patriarchal system in the past to realign the nation's "future ideal" (our present, figured in the frame) with feminine agency and empowerment. However, upon pressing this reading, it soon becomes clear that elements in the narrative itself frustrate this position. Sommer's paradigm of the foundational fictions is again helpful to elucidate this problem. The purpose of romances in Latin American foundational fictions, Sommer argues, is to symbolically weave together previously divided classes and races in order to produce a hybrid new generation. She writes, "Unproductive eroticism is not only immoral; it is unpatriotic." Classic Revolutionary melodrama and *Flor silvestre* follow that logic: Esperanza and José Luis's child represents the fruit of their suffering and *is* the new nation, the unity of social classes. But *Como agua para chocolate* turns problematic on this point of reproduction. Tita's only moment of maternal plentitude (which suggests alternatives to a patriarchal system) are both given to her and taken away by the patriarchal/male figures. Tita first takes on the role of productive matriarch when her virgin breast magically produces milk to feed Rosaura and Pedro's child—but this power is bestowed on her by Pedro's erotic gaze, which imparts the maternal flow. Tita's nurturing maternal agency is thus sanctioned and conferred by masculine desire. Later in the film, Tita and Pedro consummate their love for the first time, after Mama Elena has been killed by bandits. Tita thinks she is pregnant, a thought that is at first horrifying, but Tita and Pedro soon await the child with hopeful anticipation. But this promise of a new generation built on their subversive, magic love is taken away: the pregnancy was actually a hysterical one wished upon Tita by the ghost of patriarchal Mama Elena as psychological punishment for her sexual indiscretion with Pedro. Even though the text attempts to create an alternate feminine discourse through its magic realist aesthetic, one outside traditional realism aligned with patriarchy, these maternal and patriotic moments are still tightly conferred and controlled by patriarchal power—and the supposedly alternative, feminine magic is shown to be bound to patriarchy and the thrust of traditional, phallic narrative.

The power of the patriarch is shown to be still intact and potent in another significant sequence. When Tita and Mama Elena hear of the death of Rosaura's son (Elena has sent the family to live over the border so as to separate Tita and Pedro), Tita's anguish is overwhelming, but Mama Elena proclaims, "¡No quiero lágrimas!" ("I don't want any tears!") With this latest frustration by the patriarchal mother of the free flow of feminine feeling, Tita breaks down and for the first time openly accuses Mama Elena of her injustices. Elena strikes her, and Tita sequesters herself in the dovecote. Days later, when the female servant Chencha goes to her, she finds that Tita "está como loca" ("has gone crazy") and has turned mute. While on the one hand her madness and loss of voice (or agency) are consistent with other Mexican screen depictions of women going mad under patriarchal pressures, it is her "cure" from this patriarchally imposed madness that creates ideological disjunctures in this ostensibly feminist text.

Mama Elena sends Tita to an asylum across the border under the care of Dr. Brown. This young widower with a son gently cares for her, and the great-grandniece's voice-over informs us that for the first time, within the space provided her by this new, sympathetic and North American patriarch, Tita feels free. It soon becomes apparent that Dr. Brown is falling in love with Tita, as he describes pedantically how every person has a box of matches inside, which can be lit only by a true love. Tita's matches are damp, he says, and Dr. Brown implies that he would like to dry them. (Magically?) Tita recovers her voice in the very next scene. The juxtaposition of Dr. Brown's nurturing attitude and Tita's recovery suggests that the resolution of her "madness" is achieved through the protective care of this North American doctor, problematizing even further a feminist interpretation; with Tita under his wing, Dr. Brown gives her back her voice. Tita uses her reinstated but limited agency to consent to marriage with Dr. Brown, trading one patriarchy (Mama Elena's) for another. Here, the narrative recovers any residual doubt that it is the patriarch that retains the power to both take away and restore—and control—feminine agency.

Any remaining progressive message in this story about the power of Tita and Pedro's *amor loco* is effectively squelched in the final resolution of the master narrative. Free from the patriarchal impediments and the old order by the deaths of Rosaura and Mama Elena, Tita and Pedro make love for the first time without fear of patriarchal or social reprisals. This *should* be the foundational moment of the text: the final consummation of the new ideology of the nation. But Pedro's death during sex frustrates the fulfillment of both Tita's erotic desires and the foundational moment. The reimposition of patriarchy is made even more pronounced and assertive by the narrative voice-over of Dr. Brown, which reiterates the metaphor of the internal box of matches. The action on screen follows the narration on the soundtrack as if obeying orders, and the room explodes into fire. The film, which has relied on the feminine narrative throughout, in the last instance cedes control of the text to a white male North American. The ideology and the narrative are recontained within a patriarchal, conservative discourse, showing that the only thing this magical true love succeeds in ending is not a repressive patriarchy but the lives of the lovers themselves. The resolution promises that there is no danger of subversion to patriarchal order to come out of their union, making their story a cautionary tale rather than a liberating one.

The film closes with the book-ending of the frame in the present tense. Both Tita and Esperanza, Tita's surrogate daughter (Pedro and Rosaura's second child), whom she rescued from the family's repressive tradition, stand behind the narrator as spectral visions, emphasizing now visually the connections of the present with the past. But this epilogue vision of the "fruit" of the narrative suffering, however, cannot recontain the memory of the patriarchal system's nullification of the power and frustration of the desires of these fictional Revolutionary protofeminists. The would-be positive, feminist frame is "disjointed" by the discourse that unfolded in the narrative [. . .].

Eating Magical Otherness

After the film had established a word-of-mouth familiarity and had started showing its incredible box office potential, newspaper advertisements in the United States read, "Experience the Magic" and later, "Experience the Magic—Again." This zippy slogan sums up what sold American audiences on the picture: the strong element of a magical realist style. Victor Zamudio-Taylor and Inma Guiu point out the following passage in Janet Maslin's *New York Times* review:

> This film, a lively family saga that is centered on forbidden love and
> spans several generations, relies so enchantingly upon fate, magic and

a taste for the supernatural that it suggests Gabriel García Márquez in a cookbook-writing mode. (The best-selling Mexican novel by Laura Esquivel, who also wrote the screenplay, interweaves the fanciful story of "Like Water for Chocolate" with actual recipes.) Whether you approach this swift, eventful tale on the culinary or the cinematic level, prepare for a treat.[7]

Zamudio-Taylor and Guiu protest Maslin's take on the film, saying, "After all, there is more to the novel and film than magical realism and food," but their objections too easily dismiss the reality that this is the level at which a majority of U.S. filmgoers consumed the movie.[8] In fact, the distribution and promotion of the movie actually sought this kind of reception, as can be seen in the newspaper ads and other promotional materials. Whether or not this approach was anticipated or desired by the filmmaker and the author, the promotion of the film essentially plugged into an established perception of Latinness, actively courting the art house public familiar with the best-selling magical realism of Gabriel García Márquez's *Cien años de soledad* (*One Hundred Years of Solitude*) and Isabel Allende's *La casa de los espíritus* (*The House of the Spirits*). Arau and Esquivel's film even quotes the well-known literary image from *Cien años de soledad*, the magical encounter with the gypsy's block of ice, framing the erotic summer rendezvous between Pedro and Tita with fetishized closeups of a huge block of ice. Magical realism and *Como agua para chocolate* are reductively commodified as identifiable markers of Latino cultural identity, obliterating national or cultural distinctions of Mexico, Colombia, Chile. As Chencha says of the exchange of Tita for Rosaura as Pedro's bride—"You can't change tacos for enchiladas!"—but the film does just this with distinct national and cultural Latin identities [. . .].

Magical realism, author William Spindler argues, belongs to those cultures on the margins, in the "periphery," in contrast to the cultures at the center or the "core," whose Western scientific rationalism forecloses participation in this aesthetic discourse. He is very clear about where magic realism exists (Latin America, Africa, the Caribbean) and where it doesn't (Western Europe, the United States); one is periphery, the other the core. Magic realism, as exemplified by this academic typology, is a sign of primitive and preindustrial culture and its encounter with modernity, limited to and defining those nations on the margin.

While Spindler is arguing in some capacity for this marginal aesthetic's subversive potential, I suggest that when commodified for popular international consumption, magic realism fixes a frozen identity of

Mexicanness—and then by consuming popular conception, *latinidad*. In demanding and consuming endless reproductions of magic realism, the dominant U.S. culture condemns a lumpen, undifferentiated pan-Latin culture to repetition of an aesthetic that, from the point of view of the rational, industrial, and dominant cultures that consume the images, both defines it as Third World and fixes its status there. Magic realism becomes not a challenge to Western rationality and scientific discourse but rather reaffirms their hegemonic position of power. Paul Willemen calls the effect of this dynamic "cultural apartheid" and the cultural "ghetto."[9] Confining the parameters of "authentic" Mexican (and in its perceived amorphous unity, Latin American) national culture in this way denies Mexican identity in the internal sphere passage to what Homi K. Bhabha calls "the living principle of the people," whereby cultural and national identities transform and evolve in the daily performances of both culture and life.[10] *Como agua para chocolate* plugs into and perpetuates this cultural apartheid of the fossilizing magic realist aesthetic and adds fuel to the exotic fire with its fetishization and eroticization of commodified, consumable images of border life and food. And as these images are bought and eaten with U.S. dollars, they are digested and become just another ingredient in the mess of the melting pot, drained of any residual Mexican specificity. Much as the disturbing intensity of Frida Kahlo's self-portraits is transformed and resituated through the endless postcard reproductions tacked on North American walls for their chic exoticism and foreign tokenism, magic realism and Latin identity are condemned to the cultural ghetto in the name of pluralism.

Finally, we arrive at an explanation for the immense success of *Como agua para chocolate* in the usually hermetic U.S. film market. Embedded in the melodrama is a representation of Mexico/Latin America that characterizes it as magic, folkloric, exotic, provincial—in short, other. Even the film's final attempt at realigning the narrative with its glossed-over but disjointed frame elicits this subordinate national relationship: Tita's surrogate daughter, Esperanza, whose name invokes Dolores del Río's famous character in *Flor silvestre*, is explicitly figured as the "hope," the success of the new ideology. Significantly, she marries the son of North American Dr. Brown, symbolically and literally crossing the border of two national communities. If we take Doris Sommer's definition of a foundational text, it is in the marriage of Esperanza and Alex Brown that *Como agua para chocolate* becomes such a text, not in the story of Tita and Pedro. Esperanza and Alex's union is productive and marries together two classes, races, and nations, but the message is quite different from the subversive feminist one that is first promised. In the context of the early 1990s political ambitions and economic troubles, the message of the final frame set in our present evokes pre-NAFTA aspirations, laying the foundations of "natural" family bonds between Mexico and the United States in the past and justifying appeals for aid and (inter?)dependency in the present. The happy ending comes when the "hope," Esperanza, trades in Mama Elena's pre-Revolutionary patriarchy for Alex Brown's and Uncle Sam's late-capitalist patriarchy [. . .].

DISCUSSION QUESTIONS

• Wu argues that *Como agua para chocolate* doubles back against its own feminist pretensions, resulting in what is ultimately a conservative text. How does Wu "kill off" a lot of authors as she demonstrates the process whereby a discourse (patriarchy, in this case) can seep its way into an ostensibly feminist text, thwarting what seems to be the intention of the authors/directors?

• Based on Tenenbaum's article, make a list of phrases and adjectives to describe Mexico and then interpret these using a semiotic understanding of essentialism.

• Imagine that you disagree with Tenenbaum, but not from a semiotic perspective. Instead, you are an essentialist or a hermeneutician who does not concur with her depiction of Mexican identity. Construct an alternative.

• How does the fact that Tita's niece marries Alex Brown undermine the validity of Tenenbaum's insistence that Tita cannot marry Dr. Brown since this would be tantamount to the repetition of Malinche's betrayal of her people? What is Wu's argument regarding this marriage? How does this new sort of foundational fiction as defined by Wu contradict Tenenbaum's claim?

• Wu spends quite a lot of time looking at the way the film was marketed. Tenenbaum does not. Why not? Can you relate this aspect of Wu's argument back to Bary's examination of discourse and power in Chapter 10, perhaps exemplified there also in Rama's lettered city?

• Does Tenenbaum essentialize Mexican identity with regard to the issue of love and family? Does she also essentialize U.S. identity? In the examination of magical realism, how does Wu dispute Tenenbaum's notion of Mexican identity?

NOTES

1. Barbara Tenenbaum, "Why Tita Didn't Marry the Doctor, or Mexican History in *Like Water for Chocolate*," ed. Donald Stevens, *Based on a True*

Story: Latin American History at the Movies (Wilmington, DE: Scholarly Resources, 1997) 170.

2. Harmony Wu, "Consuming Tacos and Enchiladas: Gender and the Nation in *Como agua para chocolate*," ed. Chan Noriega, *Visible Nations: Latin American Cinema and Video* (Minneapolis: U of Minnesota P, 2000) 188.

3. Wu 188.

4. This excerpt is from 157–159, 161–164, 167–171.

5. Tenenbaum is referring to Thomas Tirado, *Celsa's World: Conversations with a Mexican Peasant Woman* (Tempe: Center for Latin American Studies, Arizona State University, 1991), which is excerpted and discussed in Chapter 18.

6. This excerpt is from 176–183, 185–187.

7. Janet Maslin, "Emotions So Strong You Can Taste Them," *New York Times*, 17 Feb. 1993: C13.

8. Victor Zamudio-Taylor and Inma Guiu, "Criss-Crossing Texts: Reading Images in *Like Water for Chocolate*," ed. Chon Noriega and Steven Ricci, *The Mexican Cinema Project* (Los Angeles: UCLA Film and Television Archive, 1994) 47.

9. Paul Willemen, *Looks and Frictions: Essays in Cultural Studies and Film Theory* (Bloomington: Indiana UP, 1994) 207.

10. Homi Bhabha, "DissemiNation: Time, Narrative, and the Margins of the Modern Nation," ed. Homi Bhabha, *Nation and Narration* (New York: Routledge, 1990) 29.

Film Foray: Mi familia (My Family)

Gregory Nava, a politically and socially committed Mexican-American film-maker, made a name for himself in 1985 with *El Norte*, a film about an indigenous Mayan brother and sister who fear political persecution and economic hardship in Guatemala and flee that country to seek safety and opportunity in the United States. They find neither. Nava cowrote the film with his wife, Anna Thomas, and it was nominated for an Academy Award for best original screenplay. Nava would go on to direct and write several other prominent and popular productions centered on Mexican-American themes, including *Mi familia* (1995), the focus of the analysis in this chapter. *Mi familia* is an epic drama chronicling the trials and tribulations of Mexican Americans as they are reflected in one family's struggles over three generations. As the plot unfolds, the film makes its nation-rebuilding project clear: to remind the spectator of the path that U.S. history has followed (see our discussion of Gerald Martin in Chapter 10) by reinserting U.S. Latino history and by recounting the uneasy relationship between the United States and Mexican Americans.[1] Nevertheless, by progressively narrowing the definition of Chicano identity—male, lower middle class, and unsuccessful in the eyes of Anglo-American society—the film reinscribes many discursive issues like those it challenges. At the same time, it prevents the United States from excluding Mexican Americans from its discourse of citizenship and nation and then limits who gets to be included in this definition.

Edward James Olmos, a stalwart of Latino filmmaking in the United States and well-known for his political activism, plays Paco, eldest son of José Sánchez. Paco is also the narrative voice of the film and the writer of the family history. In the opening scene, he states that "to write the story of my family, I have to begin where millions of stories have begun. In a small village in Mexico a long, long time ago." This assertion explicitly connects his family's struggle with that of all Mexican Americans, not to mention that of millions of Mexicans.

The film highlights the roles that Mexican Americans have played in various eras in U.S. history—no small feat in a two-hour film. José Sánchez crosses over into California and settles in Los Angeles with the help of a distant relative. On the job he meets María, the woman he will marry. (She is played by Jennifer López in her first significant film role.) They grow into a large family with six children, Francisco (nicknamed Paco), Irene, Jesus (nicknamed Chucho), Toni, Ernesto (nicknamed Memo), and Jimmy. Paco becomes a writer after his tour of duty with the U.S. Navy; Irene gets married, and she and her husband establish a Mexican restaurant; Chucho gets involved with a gang and is gunned down by police; Toni joins a convent and then leaves her order to marry a former priest and become a human rights activist; Memo studies constantly, becomes a lawyer, and gets engaged to an Anglo; and Jimmy ends up as a father after serving time for petty thievery.

Paco begins the story of his family by recounting how his father left his small village in Mexico and walked for months before crossing the border to enter Nuestra Señora de Los Angeles, California. "In those days, the border was just a line in the dirt," says Paco, laying bare the political discourses that create nations. From the outset, he establishes that his dad, José, is a storyteller with a vivid imagination so as to prepare the viewer for a movie filled with attempts to destabilize official versions of history in favor of multiple unsanctioned histories. Paco and the film make clear from the opening moment that one must distinguish fact from fiction. To this end the film begins with a semicomical sequence that resembles a *telenovela* or soap opera to explain the reason José left the village. Paco says that his uncle Roberto had been caught in an adulterous relationship, and Trini, Roberto's wife, took out her revenge by shooting him with her double-barrel. A shot is heard but not shown. Says Paco, "Actually nothing like that ever really happened. That's just the way my father used to tell the story."

Paco goes on to explain that his uncle Roberto died of a ruptured appendix and that economic hardship in the aftermath of the Mexican Revolution was the impetus for his father's departure. Thus, from the start, the film encourages the enjoyment of sensational stories but rejects the notion that all versions of a story are equally valid. The spectator is made aware that we must question what we only presume to have witnessed in order to investigate other possibilities, however mundane they may be.

Paco also recounts the story of his father's journey in his own words. José is shown sitting alone by a fire he has built in a serene setting, waiting for the next day to break. In voice-over, we hear Paco relate his father's stories of the perils of the passage with deliberate irony in his voice: "He was attacked by ten bandits in Sonora and had to beat them off with a cactus branch. He rode the back of a snorting mountain lion!"

These initial sequences emphasize the film's attempts to play with the conventions of narrative and its alternative account of U.S. identity. As narrator, Paco gives authorial voice to this revision of history, as he recounts forgotten details that exclude Mexican Americans in the nation's quest for singularity. His first challenge to the historical amnesia that naturalizes the myth of U.S. national origins as Anglo-Saxon and Protestant is to prove that many of the nation's original citizens actually were Mexican. To this end, Paco narrates a sequence in which his father arrives in East Los Angeles at the home of El Californio, a great uncle who soon becomes a father figure. The old man's name, Paco explains, comes from his being born in Los Angeles when it still belonged to Mexico. After the U.S.-Mexican War (1846–1848), Mexico lost nearly half its territory, and Mexicans, as casualties of hemispheric politics, were forced to change nationalities overnight. The point is that politics creates nations rather than the other way around. When El Californio dies, he specifies in his will that he wants his tombstone to be inscribed: "Don Alejandro Vazquez 'El Californio.' Died 1934. When I was born here, this was Mexico, and where I lie, this is still Mexico." In contrast to the U.S. myth of national foundation, there are no pilgrims seeking religious tolerance here and no Calvinistic work ethic; only greedy Westerners manifesting their destiny.

The film's next target is the myth of U.S. ethnic and class harmony, the proverbial melting pot supposedly well-seasoned with equal opportunity for all. Paco explains that soon after his father arrived in Los Angeles, he crossed the bridge with many other Mexican Americans from East L.A. into downtown to find a job. He ends up working as a gardener at a stately home and there meets his future wife, María, the family's maid and nanny. Paco notes that this commute reflected the hierarchical economic structure of U.S. society, since Hispanics crossed over every day to do the work of the Anglos but no Anglo ever ventured over the bridges into the barrio. Then, with two children (Paco and Irene) and another (Chucho) on the way, María is surreptitiously shipped back to Mexico by train.

It was the time of the great depression. I guess some politicians got it into their heads that the Mexicanos were responsible for the whole thing. I mean they were taking up a lot of jobs. Jobs that were needed for what they called "young Americans." So La Migra made some big sweeps through the Barrio and they rounded up everyone that they could.[2] It didn't matter if you were a citizen like my mother. If you looked Mexicano, you were picked up and shipped out. She had just been out shopping. She wasn't allowed to come home. My father was never told. She was all alone and she was pregnant. *All these things really happened.* The year was 1933. The Southern Pacific railroad made the U.S. government a deal. For $14.75 a head, they took the Mexicanos all the way back into central Mexico hoping they would never be able to get back. (italics added)

"All these things really happened" is a crucial statement here, given the first fictional scene of the film and Paco's emphasis about his father's talent for embellishment. Paco has set the stage for questioning official accounts of history, but he must also take care to distinguish fact from fiction in his promotion of alternative versions. In this case, it is clear that his father's penchant for tall tales has nothing to do with the telling of this story since José remains ignorant of María's whereabouts until she is able to complete the journey back to the family two years later with Chucho.

Another indication that these events really happened is that the film shows María's journey back to California from Mexico and without ironic commentary from Paco. She arrives at an aunt's house determined to make the trip back to Los Angeles as soon as possible. She sets off when Chucho is old enough to travel and soon arrives at a river that, because of early rains, is too dangerous to cross. María persuades the porter to take her across despite his misgivings; meanwhile, a white owl hoots portentously. Their boat capsizes after a harrowing trip down white-water rapids. María manages to save Chucho and herself but still doesn't cross the river. Back at her aunt's, two indigenous healers perform a curing rite on little Chucho to prevent the river spirit from claiming the baby's life. They tell María she must pray to the Virgin Mary. Eventually, María makes it back home, but according to her syncretic, indigenous/Catholic belief system, Chucho must ultimately be sacrificed to the river spirit. In image, word, and form—since María and Chucho's reunion with José establishes the holy family of Jesus, Mary, and Joseph—María's spiritual interpretation of events will be consistently narrated. This point of view adds complexity to the fact-versus-fiction dichotomy that Paco has established, but it also recalls the vast body of films that characterize Mexicans and Mexican Americans (particularly women) as spiritual and mystical. *Mi familia* both participates in this discourse and rejects it because, while María draws conclusions based on her indigenous/ Catholic belief system, her daughters do not. In this regard, it is worthwhile to revisit our introductions to Hall in Chapter 5 and to Martin and Bary in Chapter 10. While Martin might ultimately see these texts as a reflection of Mexicans' indigenous essence, Bary and Hall would define the genre more as a reflection of the discursive place that Mexicans temporarily inhabit.

Chucho is the character who embodies Mexican-American oppression. From the almost fatal journey he makes with his mother back to Mexico until his demise, the film makes clear that Chucho's life is compromised and his death brought on by discrimination. He turns out to be a pachuco—his baggy trousers worn tight at the ankle recall the zoot suits of the 1940s and 1950s; he uses slang typical of the pachuco subculture; and he is the leader of a gang called Los Apóstoles.[3] He and other pachuco youths are "filled with anger and hatred [against the U.S. system], and [have] nowhere to put it except into each other," according to Paco's narration. The quintessence of Mexican-American identity of this era, he is also one of the most sympathetic and romanticized characters in the film, modeling *vato* style and demeanor (*vato* is Mexican-American slang for "homeboy" or "dude") with affection for his little brother Jimmy, who idolizes him. In one memorable scene, Chucho teaches Jimmy and the other children of the barrio to dance the mambo. He openly defies the so-called U.S. work ethic that relies on his dad's backbreaking labor while ignoring Mexican-Americans' contributions to the economy. Chucho sells drugs as part of a broader counter-hegemonic impulse, entering into an alternate economy since the dominant one has shut Latinos out.

One particularly telling scene crystallizes Chucho as a symbol of Latino oppression and discrimination. This scene also affirms his doomed destiny to satisfy the river spirit, which reappears in the form of the white owl, again suggesting the multiple layers of Mexican-American identity: Mexican, American, Western, non-Western/indigenous. While the Los Angeles police hunt him down for the "cold-blooded murder" of a gang leader, cross-cuts in the film show the Sánchez family gathered around the television laughing during an episode of *I Love Lucy*, the enormously popular 1950s comedy series. The viewer knows that Chucho has actually killed the gang leader in self-defense, yet the police chief characterizes him as "a known criminal [who] is armed and extremely dangerous, [and] has killed and will kill again." He instructs his underlings "[not to] hesitate to use your weapons. . . . Your lives depend on it." They shoot Chucho through the head and back, killing him in front of little Jimmy who is playing ball in the street. Then they celebrate. The scene alludes to the notorious, decades-long

FIGURE 17.1   *The Sánchez family watches* I Love Lucy *in* Mi familia

history of police brutality against minorities in Los Angeles. Jimmy will grow up to internalize this anger against the injustices of the U.S. system that Chucho has learned to externalize through his gang.

The discursive continuity implied in this crosscutting between representations of Latinos in popular culture and their lived existence is of particular importance to the film's overall discursive position. Chucho is seen hiding out in an abandoned factory/junkyard while, back at the house, the television is turned on and a familiar jingle begins the *I Love Lucy* show. José gets up agitatedly and retreats to his bedroom as the rest of the family frowns. The dialogue between Lucille Ball and Desi Arnaz on the TV sets the scene for Chucho's death:

Ricky: "What's the matter with them?"
Lucy: "They don't want to watch, and I don't blame them!"

We then see one of the officers enter the area of Chucho's hideout as Paco joins his father in the bedroom to explain that the murder was an accident. The camera then cuts for the first time to the television screen, which displays Ricky entering into a state of rage, typical comic fodder for an episode, as Lucy tries to smooth over yet another one of her blunders. Lucy hands Ricky something to throw just after she informs him that, thanks to her, he no longer has a job at Metro, whereupon he smashes the glass table with the object. As María, her daughters, and Memo laugh at the TV screen, the latter says, "I really dig Desi." At this juncture, Chucho is being chased, and when he runs into the police chief and knocks him over, he spits in his face, further refuting his official status as armed and dangerous. Just as the episode of *I Love Lucy* is ending, the "spic son of a bitch," as the chief calls Chucho, is shot graphically in the head and chest before Jimmy's eyes, the shots ringing out over the *I Love Lucy* theme song.

The first subjective frame of the television scene invites the spectator to join the women of the family and Memo (this group will become significant later) in consuming and concretizing through humor the image of Latinos as inherently hot-tempered. However, the juxtaposition of that scene with the grave events taking place outside the home inspires the viewer to take a second critical look at this seemingly innocuous and humorous portrayal. With the deliberate crosscutting between events, the film advocates a connection between the hackneyed representations of U.S. Latinos that are sold to and bought by Anglo Americans as well as Latino Americans and the violent consequences these representations can indirectly and directly bring about once they are firmly located in the subconscious of the viewer. If U.S. television audiences believe that Ricky Ricardo can be transformed from mild-mannered musician to wild-eyed, Spanish-spewing maniac in a matter of seconds, it's only natural to also assume that a young Hispanic punk with a bad attitude can easily make the leap into violent crime. In this sense the film's project widens to include alternatives to the reified images of U.S. *Latinidad* (Latinness) as they are presented in standard cultural fare and practiced in daily life.

Clearly then, *Mi familia* is a film that seeks to establish Chicano legitimacy in the United States by presenting multiple versions of official U.S. history, consequently exposing this history as unjust.[4] Yet, while the film consciously and successfully seeks to dismantle U.S. foundational singularity, it also operates within a discursive framework of exclusion by limiting who and what define Chicano identity. To be sure, having six children who run the gamut of typical Chicano roles in the United States smacks of diversity campaigns. But like these campaigns, which attempt to increase cultural understanding but often end up further pigeonholing the individuals of any group, *Mi familia* narrows the definition of Chicano in two important ways. First, in its patriarchal structure, it masculinizes Chicano identity. The men of the family drive the plot forward. José's prominence gives way to a focus on Chucho's defiant character and then on Jimmy, the redemptive figure, all narrated by Paco's authorial and authoritative voice-over.

FIGURE 17.2   *Paco sits at a typewriter in* Mi familia

Even in the exceptions to this rule, such as the prominence given to María's harrowing journey back to Los Angeles, the focus is on women as facilitators of male agency. Women operate from within traditional spheres to maintain the unity of the patriarchal family. Since the film does not take a critical stance on this issue, as it certainly attempts to do with Latino stereotypes vis-à-vis the *I Love Lucy* show, *Mi familia* inadvertently forms part of the genre of Mexican-American films that invite its audiences to define Chicano identity as singularly masculine.[5]

The film also limits the definition of Chicano identity, while endeavoring to expand U.S. identity to include Mexican Americans, through the discourse of Chicano citizenship. *Mi familia* continually reinforces the idea that being part of the Chicano community means embracing an identity in limbo between Mexico and the United States. Consider that the one character in the film who asserts *only* his U.S. identity—Memo, the lawyer who marries an Anglo—is also the only wholly unsympathetic character in the film.

At various intervals we are invited to condemn Memo for apparently turning his back on his Mexican heritage. He lives on the wealthy West side and anglicizes his name to William Sánchez, which he proudly displays on the door to his law office. The baseball cap he wears when dressing casually, and the suit when formally, contrast with Chucho's and Jimmy's *vato* look and the guayaberas worn by Paco and José. When he takes his

FIGURE 17.3 *Memo adjusts his Anglo look in* Mi familia

Anglo fiancée, Karen Gillespie, and her parents to meet the whole family in East L.A.—their first visit to the barrio though they are native to Los Angeles—Memo ends up denying facts about the family's history. When José speaks of his great uncle El Californio being buried in the backyard, Memo vehemently contradicts his father by complaining that those are simply old family stories made up and nurtured by his father's vivid imagination, while using his tone of voice to implore his father to agree. In this way, Memo becomes aligned with amnesiac U.S. history taught in the textbooks that he furiously studied as a boy. This history dismisses any inconvenient versions to maintain one that is official and untainted. His denials prompt the spectator to condemn him not only as a traitor to his family but to all Chicanos. Paco prefaces this scene with a telling voice-over narration that undermines Memo's success. Just before the visit from the in-laws, Jimmy's reflection in his prison mirror is seen dissolving into Memo's—as if Jimmy were looking in the mirror and seeing Memo. While Memo smugly straightens his tie as he leaves his office, Paco narrates that Jimmy is the true backbone of the family. By carrying the family's burdens, Jimmy has made it possible for

Memo to be considered by José and María the "pride and joy" of the family. Thus, not only is Memo deceiving his parents at the expense of his own flesh and blood, but since the family is meant to represent all Chicanos, he and his type are traitors to Chicano identity.

If, however, we were to read against the grain of the film's overt attempt to alienate the viewer from Memo, we might agree that Memo should certainly doubt the validity of his father's stories, since José Sánchez has proven himself a talented and inventive storyteller. Born after the death of El Californio, Memo is not old enough to remember his great uncle or to verify his burial circumstances, i.e., he was not an eyewitness as we were, which allowed us to distinguish between truth and fable. In this way, *Mi familia*, like other U.S.-Latino films, narrows the definition of Latinidad to exclude anyone who attempts to mitigate his/her hyphenated status by assimilating into mainstream U.S. culture. In this genre's definition of Chicano identity, Anglo acclamation is unacceptable.

Mi familia represents an important innovation in the history of U.S. film by redressing Hollywood's endless production, and North America's eager consumption, of images of U.S. Latinos aligned with mainstream presuppositions and expectations. The film reverses Hollywood's penchant for casting Italian Americans in portrayals of Hispanics by using a cast that is all Latino, albeit not all Chicano. In both content and form, *Mi familia* consciously attempts to expand both U.S. historical dialogue and the cultural productions it engenders. Yet, as our introductory discussion regarding discourse demonstrated, each successive reading reveals another level of unconscious discursive construct, and *Mi familia* is no exception. In its deliberate attempt to promote inclusion, it unwittingly promotes exclusion.

DISCUSSION QUESTIONS

• In what ways does *Mi familia* represent and empower the nonlettered citizen?

• By portraying Mexican Americans as the new American family, how does *Mi familia* at once challenge and accept traditional notions of so-called American values?

• How does this film dialogue with the polemic ignited by Bill Cosby's criticism of the notion that African Americans equate education and studying with being white? Cosby calls on African-American parents to teach their children the value of education, but his detractors claim that African-American youth's disillusionment with education stems from the fact that the system disenfranchises them from a good education and future opportunities. How are Cosby's critics exposing his participation in the discourse of U.S. national singularity? If we define ourselves with numerous and diverse identities, how do we reconcile the oppositional requirements made by each identity group?

• The film makes it clear that seeing an event privileges the discerning of facts. What is the broader implication of this filmic assertion? Does the film encourage us to recognize that the lens we are using to view a scene might be just as discursively constituted?

• How is mainstream U.S. culture portrayed and how does it portray Latinos in the film? Explain how the film demonstrates that discourse drives perceptions rather than being derived from them.

• In writing the essay for this film, we confronted the challenge of which terms we should use to describe the people depicted in *Mi familia*—Mexicans, Mexican Americans, Chicanos, Latinos, Hispanics, etc. How does the existence of these multiple terms exemplify discourses of nationality, ethnicity, and race? In other words, how do these terms expose the semiotic nature of these identity categories?

• Thinking back to Mignolo's discussion of Chicanos in Chapter 10, how does the film *Mi familia* challenge mainstream U.S. construction of Chicanos as subalterns?

• Is it simply a coincidence that the group glued to the television enjoying the *I Love Lucy* show consists of Memo, his mother, and his sisters? How does this arrangement bolster the assertion that the film promotes a circumscribed definition of Chicano identity?

NOTES

1. In preparation for the rest of this essay, you may want to revisit our introduction in Chapter 10 to Gerald Martin's *Journeys Through the Labyrinth*. There we defined the concept of U.S. singularity and Latin American duality as master myths that attempt to naturalize the constructed notion that the United States is complete while Latin America remains incomplete. We demonstrated that master narratives articulated by dominant powers and accepted by the world form a part of hegemonic discourse that defines the very form and content of history.

2. La Migra is the colloquialism used to refer to the Immigration and Naturalization Service (INS).

3. A particular style of dress, behavior (*pachuquismo*), and language code (*pachucano*) developed among Chicano youth in the isolated barrios of the Southwest and, in particular, in Los Angeles. The dress of these young Mexican-American men imitated the zoot suit, a style made famous in Harlem among African-American youth. They were called pachucos because the style they affected was assumed to have been brought to the United

States by young male migrants from El Paso: Pasuco → pachucho. Typical *pachuquismo* behavior that develops to protect the *vato* (a homeboy or man in *pachucano*) from the harsh life of the barrio is the formation of gangs and the cultivation of reputations as being tough fighters as evidenced by their violent deeds. See Rosaura Sánchez, *Chicano Discourse: Sociohistoric Perspectives* (Houston: Arte Público, 1994) 128–129; Luis Valdez and Stan Steiner, eds., *Aztlán: An Anthology of Mexican American Literature* (New York: Random House, 1972) 174.

4. *Chicano* is a term of identity used by politically active or conscious Mexican Americans. It is a word with indigenous, not Spanish, roots, and thus is meant to reflect the pride of Mexican Americans in their indigenous heritage. One of its first and most recognized users was César Chávez, the leader of the United Farm Workers in the 1960s. The term is used to define Mexican Americans who are born in the United States, are U.S. citizens, and whose families have been in the United States for a long time. In its political context it is not used to describe recent, undocumented Mexican immigrants.

5. For further reading on Chicano identity politics reflected in film, see Rosa Lina Fregoso, "Zoot Suit: The 'Return to the Beginning,'" ed. John King, Ana Lopez, and Manuel Alvarado, *Mediating Two Worlds: Cinematic Encounters in the Americas* (London: British Film Institute, 1993) 269–278.

Are We There Yet? Testimonial Literature

The final reading in this collection is an example of testimonial literature, a genre that flourished internationally in the late twentieth century and originated largely in Latin America. Testimonials reflect the growing attempt throughout the twentieth century to seek out the voices and perspectives of people who have historically been disenfranchised. The testimonial genre emerged from the civil conflicts in Latin America in the 1970s and 1980s and represented the political act of denouncing injustices against members of marginalized groups. These personal stories are told in plain language by people who are indigenous, poor, and/or female to an ethnographer, reporter, or academic. The testimonial that gave the genre international fame is *I, Rigoberta Menchú: An Indian Woman in Guatemala*. Menchú won a Nobel Peace Prize for denouncing the human rights violations against Indians in Guatemala in the 1980s. Her story illustrates testimonial's capacity to challenge established power structures traditionally claimed by the lettered citizens who remain ironically central as well to the testimonial process. They become the transcribers, or intermediaries, who receive the testimony and then facilitate the outside world's access to it. This often involves editing, shaping, or marketing the testimonial so that the impact of the interlocutor can be quite substantial.[1]

The story of Celsa presented in this chapter is that of an indigenous poor woman who lives in rural central Mexico and speaks both Spanish and Nahuatl, her native language. The title positions Celsa as an outsider; she is, from the outset, the Other. Thomas Tirado, the author/transcriber of this excerpt, is a retired professor of history at Millersville University. He has traveled to Mexico on various occasions for research; during one of these trips he went to Celsa's village and met her. He returned to the village many times and developed a friendship with Celsa that eventually led him to accumulate her life story.

Tirado begins by introducing himself and his role in the story. He explains his methodology and describes the village and Celsa. He offers an excellent example of the claims of testimonial literature as true and unmediated narration because he portrays himself as nothing more than a conduit for Celsa's words. But unlike other testimonials in which the narrator is often invisible, Tirado admits to organizing and shaping the narrative into a form he believes his readers can grasp. For example, he provides definitions of indigenous names and food throughout the text. Like Celsa, he is pivotal in creating the published result.

An essentialist reading of *Celsa's World* would debate the extent to which Celsa's voice reflects the true Mexican nation. By the end of the twentieth century, after decades in which the literary cutting edge had been defined by the incorporation of increasingly diverse voices, most essentialists would agree that a Celsa-like testimonial dramatically advances this constant search. They might not identify her as the sole metaphor for national identity, but as a representative of the most downtrodden and most ignored, Celsa represents a sort of profundity that discussions of identity have tragically left out. This can be seen in a recent anthropological study from Mexico entitled *Mexico profundo*, which argues that the long-ignored and much-disparaged Indian heritage actually constitutes a major, or "profound" element of Mexican national culture.[2] Essentialists disagree about testimonials. Some still conceive the nation through the lens of a Sarmiento-inspired white supremacy, even if they present it in a form that appears to be more acceptable and contemporary. Others might still celebrate the mestizo as the essence of Latin America. Regardless of these disagreements, essentialists do accept the existence of a true, essential Mexico.

A semiotic reading obviously rejects the notion of a national essence, even though it celebrates the attempt to incorporate marginalized voices into the construction of the national identity. Because the subjects of testimonies have been excluded from the center for such a long time, their voices are in some ways outside discourse and have a special positioning to reveal discourse to us. This position leaps out of Celsa's testimony. She offers an interpretation of the world that is notable for its lack of reliance on the traditional essentialisms of race, class, gender, and nation. However, as a "dead" author, Celsa also advances some stereotypes and generalizations. She claims, for example, that the people of the nearby village of Santa Catarina are uncivilized, revealing that she too participates in the prevailing discourse of a struggle between civilization and barbarism. If pushed, examples such as this might expose an essentialist foundation.

A semiotic reading also focuses on Tirado's role. Tirado frames Celsa's narrative, and his target audience is lettered society, not the uneducated indigenous people that the testimonial claims to represent. Although their voices may be heard, they cannot contest their representation and, in that way, continue to be excluded. In this regard, testimonial literature is highly reminiscent of magical realism, which exhibits a similar exclusion through an apparent inclusion.

THOMAS TIRADO, *CELSA'S WORLD: CONVERSATIONS WITH A MEXICAN PEASANT WOMAN*[3]
A Preface

THE SETTING [. . .]   A personal narrative of an individual, *Celsa's World* is a firsthand account of life in an Indian-peasant community of 2500 people. The reader will see Celsa's world through her eyes, observe cultural change as it relates to her, and come to understand what change has meant for herself, her family, and her community [. . .].

As in countless other Mexican communities, the modernizing process sweeping through the country with its irreversible and irrepressible changes is forcing the peasant culture and residual Indian traditions of San Antonio to merge with the much more potent culture of modern Mexico. The mid-1970s was a time of great expectation and the beginning of rapid change, and there was the promise of a bright future due to newly discovered petroleum reserves [. . .].

Regrettably, the modernizing process has been a destructive force which threatened the very existence of the village. Though villagers had managed previously to resist those changes which would have altered drastically the peasant characteristics of life in the countryside, there is no guarantee that this will be the case now that the community has been linked to modern Mexico by a paved road. What has happened is that the rate of change has accelerated dramatically, and it is irreversible. Though most people with whom I spoke did not want to go back to the past, they did reveal ambivalence in their responses. On the one hand, they recognize the value of the improvements which have been introduced into the village, e.g., potable water, paved road, latrines, electricity, etc, but on the other hand, the villagers lament the loss of traditional institutions, the security of their families, and such intangibles as tranquility of life, isolation, and, even, innocence they believe they had before all of the recent changes [. . .].

METHODOLOGY [. . .]   Unknown to me, at the same time I was working in San Antonio, Judith Friedlander was doing a parallel investigation in a neighboring village. Though she finished her research years before I finished mine, our two studies are similar in a number of ways. The most important of these similarities is that Doña Zeferina, the main figure in Dr. Friedlander's published research on Hueyapán, is remarkably similar to Celsa. Our two studies differ, however, on the choice of storyteller. Whereas in Friedlander's book it is the author herself who narrates the story in the third person with only a few quotes from her informant, in *Celsa's World* it is Celsa who tells the story exclusively in the first person, except for this preface [. . .].

One of the valid ways of studying the past is to listen to what the actual participants have to say about it. If history is going to have any importance as a human lesson, only participants who experienced or observed an event or series of events can tell us their meaning in terms to which we can relate personally. For this reason I believe that the best way of entering Celsa's intimate world, which is alien for the most part to ours, is to let her tell the story [. . .].

THE VILLAGE   My introduction to the village of San Antonio came in 1961 when, as a member of a small anthropological field study group from the University of Illinois, I was led into the village by our professor, Dr. Oscar Lewis. In those days the community was accessible only by foot through a narrow mountain pass, along a path through cultivated fields, and over several small streams. Even though as graduate students we had studied *cultural shock* in the classroom, it remained only an academic topic until the day we arrived in the village. In no way was I prepared for the life I found in San Antonio. Its variance with the world I knew was nearly unbridgeable though the village was only 100 kilometers from downtown Mexico City. Without potable water, electricity, or road, the village seemed to belong to another time period in history. Nevertheless, one other student and I decided to live in the village for the summer; the others commuted from Tepoztlán several times a week. Needless to say, we were a novelty to the villagers and were studied as much by them as we studied the village. Living in the very heart of the community gave us a great view of everything but more importantly won the respect of the villagers who considered us as being *brave* for moving into a *poor* village.

One of the first villagers I met was Celsa. Though initially hired as a cook and laundress, Celsa soon proved to be much more valuable as an informant, and she became my primary source of information on village customs, the native language, local history, and folklore. Through my friendship with Celsa I established invaluable contacts with other villagers who, like Celsa, were active practitioners of oral tradition. Although my original assignment from Dr. Lewis had been to compile data on rural agrarian practices, which meant getting up before daybreak many mornings and spending the day learning to cultivate the fields, I spent much of my free time listening to oral remembrances of Celsa and her friends of whom many were elders and keepers of local history, in the Nahuatl language, of course [. . .].

After a month in the village, Celsa asked me to be the *padrino* (godfather) of her adopted six-month old daughter, Hilaria [. . .].

Although ignorant of my obligations at first, I soon learned that one of my duties as *padrino* was to ensure the well-being of my *ahijada* (goddaughter) [. . .].

I mention the story of my goddaughter and the institution of *compadrazgo* for several reasons: it established an important and lasting noncognate kinship relationship with my main informant; it had the effect of making me part of the community; and it increased my credibility as a recorder of life in the village. When I became Hilaria's baptismal godfather I also became a member of her family and, through her family, of the community. Acceptance of the institutional obligations of *compadrazgo* became a binding social contract by which I gained many friends, entered village life as an active participant, shared in its culture, and became a fictive kin. Furthermore, having lived in the community for three months at that time (1961) and having revisited it on six other occasions, most recently for four months, I can truly say that I feel very much *at home* with the people of San Antonio.

The reliability of Celsa's life history as an accurate description of the everyday life of a peasant woman was the primary objective of the greater part of my investigative research over the past twenty-five years. Having found a high degree of corroboration between Celsa's stories and those of other women in the village, I can safely say that *Celsa's World* is not only a representative life history of one individual but also an accurate and meaningful description of the social landscape of rural Mexico in the state of Morelos.

THIS BOOK [. . .] Although I did select material and organize her conversations into episodic accounts, which are presented as chapters in this book, as Celsa's biographer I was more a conduit for her story than a storyteller.

All names including that of the village have been changed in order to protect the identity of the principal characters.

Chapter 3. The Men in My Life

When I was thirteen the parents of several young men started asking my mother for my hand in marriage. I was supposed to marry Alfonso but that never worked out. He was a young man who came to live with his father in the village. I wasn't a woman yet but it was a custom for young girls to marry at a very young age, even before they had their first period. Most men were older when they married for the first time, but they expected their women to be younger and without any experiences. Men are strange that way. They want their wives to be pure, but then they do the same things to their young wives as they do to older women with whom they have had experiences. I really think the only reason a man wants his young wife to be a virgin, *pure*, is so that he knows that the baby is his. There is never a question in a woman's mind; she knows that the baby is hers. But a man has no way of knowing for sure. If the wife is a virgin and gets pregnant the first time, then there is no question about who the father is. Some men get impatient when it takes months and months for their wives to get pregnant. The longer it takes, some men think, the more chance there is that their women could have relations with other men. A Mexican man doesn't trust other men because he knows that they are all trying to seduce as many women as possible. And, each one of those women has to belong to someone else [. . .].

> It is very important for a mother to set a good example. It's her duty to love her children and want to keep them from harm.—Celsa

How can you be responsible if you are always drunk or if you show your children that the bottle is one of the ways to solve your problems. You can excuse drinking in men but not in women.

> Children take a much closer look at their mothers than they do their fathers.—Celsa

[. . .] In the past you heard a lot of talk about the farmer but rarely anything about the farmer's wife. When there was work to be done in the campo, however, women were always there giving their husbands the support they need to get it done. Now government agencies are actually aiming programs at the womenfolk. They want us to learn some new techniques designed to improve the quality and nutrition of the food we eat. The two projects of soybean sprouts and pedigree sows have been designed as work for the women.

Both sexes have always worked in the campo and it's not fair to overlook women. Men do not work harder than women; it's just different kind of work. The man goes out to the field and works under the hot sun. He handles the oxen and the plow, and he works the soil. Everyone recognizes that his work is very hard. But in the house the work is also hard because we get up before the men do in order to fix their breakfasts. We prepare their meals for the campo and we work all day around the house, sweeping and cleaning, washing, and especially grinding corn. There is always some grinding that has to be done. And then about 12:30 we have to go out into the field with the food for the men if they are close enough to walk to. When we return there are more chores: getting dinner ready, getting a change of clothes ready for him, and many other things. It's all work, both field and house. Yet there is more work in the house than in the field. At least one can rest out there, but here if you rest you don't get your chores done by the time the men come home. You don't want to be in the middle of washing or something like that when they get in from the field.

The work in the field is that of the oxen; it is only for brief periods of time and after that the men can go back to resting. When they do work it's intense, from sunup to sundown. For example, the soil has to be plowed while it is still moist, and that may last for only a few weeks. That means that the soil is plowed for the final time and the crops are planted all within one month. During the planting season if you never went out into the fields you would never see any men in the village; they leave before dawn and return home after nightfall. Corn doesn't take as much time as *jitomate* [tomatoes]. With jitomates there is something that has to be done to the plants, like tying them up against the poles or giving them water when they are thirsty. The yield is much greater from jitomates than corn so it is worth the extra work.

> Whereas a man's work is limited to three or four periods a year, a women's work is never done.—Celsa

We get to rest only when there is no meal to fix. And when is that? We get no vacations from work, no long breaks like the men, yet the government never mentioned us when it talked about the campo. Take Mother for example. Although she doesn't do too much any more because she is too old, in her lifetime she has never rested more than a few days when she went to visit her son Víctor in Veracruz or when she gave birth. It would be difficult to find another person in all of Mexico who has worked as hard as my mother. Her spouse, don Miguel, is also a hard worker. There are few men in the village who can work as hard as he. I have already seen the two of them fall asleep while sitting at the dinner table [. . .].

[Editor's note: Celsa has just finished telling the story of when she and her young sisters were home when their house burned down.] You know, I don't really know if what I remember is what I remember or if it is something put into my head by other people who have told me the story over and over again. I was only five years old. How could I ever remember something from when I was five were it not for people putting those ideas into my head or reinforcing my horrible memories with their own remembrances. For example, I cannot remember running around screaming and screaming. It might have happened; in fact, it sounds like what I would have done. But I think that was an idea put in my head by someone else because, truly, I don't remember running around screaming but I keep telling the story because everyone else says that's what I did. So I believe it; I believe it because I've told the story so many times that in my own mind it has become *real* even if it had never happened [. . .].

Chapter IV. When I Went to Mexico City to Work [. . .]

We were in [my friend's] village about two weeks. I nearly died. It was so remote and uncivilized. They lived like savages. There were no streets, just paths through the woods. Although my village of San Antonio is remote, it is not as sad as is hers. From what I saw the people were very timid and ignorant. And they showed no respect for you. If they got in your way you were the one who had to move, even the little ones wouldn't move and showed no respect. At least here and other places I've known when two people are on the same path each will step aside and try to accommodate the other [. . .].

I can't understand why everyone didn't leave the village and go elsewhere. It was boring. There was nothing to do except walk around. We went to the river to wash clothes twice and once we went to fish for something to eat. All there was to eat were some sick chickens. That's all [. . .].

Chapter VI. More Ignorant but More Obedient [. . .]

Nowadays, early morning is the only time there is peace in the village. Everybody has a radio or a television going all hours of the night and day. Even the motor of the neighbor's refrigerator can be heard all night long. Nature's sounds are being replaced by machine sounds. I can't help but think that Nature is not getting its proper rest and peace. The night is for making peace with the day. Can you imagine what sort of world this would be if all that we had were day and no nights? Quiet nights are for Nature to recuperate. Years ago the only man-made sound that could be heard was from the battery powered record player. There would be birthdays or special occasions when groups of people would get together for an evening. But generally even that activity would stop when it was time for the village to go to sleep. Now there are a lot of noises. Electricity has changed everything. So has the road. In the middle of the night some one will come into the pueblo in a car or a truck and wake up everyone. Can you imagine how loud those sounds are? I think they should ban motor vehicles from the streets from sundown to sunup. [. . .]

Chapter VIII. Animals [. . .]

The gifts you have given me this year have been invested in chickens, and for yours and Hilaria's birthdays we will have chicken *mole* (a sauce made with tomato, chili and other spices, peanut, chocolate, and is usually red and hot). I've managed to reinvest several times the amount you originally gave me.

The chicken coop was built from money I got from market sales of chickens. I'll never get rich raising chickens but the money I make from chicken sales combined with what I get from selling produce at Tres Marías and Tepoztlán does cover all of our basic necessities. And if I work a little extra each week I can even buy a few luxuries. For the first time in my whole life I have some savings. I don't actually have the cash in my hand but I can get it when I need it. Like don Tomás I am lending money to friends and acquaintances and charging interest. For the smallest loans over the shortest period of time—a month—I charge 10 to 15 percent interest per month. For larger amounts over longer periods, like six months, I charge 5 to 10 percent. So far I have not had enough money to go beyond family needs. You know, however, that there are hundreds of people in the village who are related to us. I never have any problem with people not paying their debts. They are so happy to be able to borrow money from someone in the village who does not ask them to fill out long forms or insist that the transaction be notarized that they gladly repay their loans or renegotiate them. It happens many times that I will renegotiate a second loan for the full amount of the first one. Some will be able to pay the interest but others will have the interest included in the new loan. I didn't invent the rules; I learned them from others in the village who lend money regularly. I have had more dealings with don Tomás than I care to remember. He used to lend us money for Margarito's education. Don Tomás always made us pay the interest each month and if we were one or two days late we had to pay interest on the interest. He is a millionaire today and we helped him get there.

Did you notice anything different about the tortillas today? Last night the corn grinder in the village broke and I had to take the *nixtamal* (Nahuatl for corn soaked in water and limestone prior to grinding) to Tepoztlán on the first bus to have it ground. They taste the same as always but their texture is different and they are sticking to the grill. Whenever our village corn grinding machine breaks down we usually buy tortillas in Tepoztlán instead of taking nixtamal there because they replace our good white corn with cheap yellow; the taste is nowhere equal. So, it's better just to buy tortillas! Enough of us went in this morning so we could watch the grinders to make sure they did not switch the corn. There was a time when all of the women of the village ground their own corn on their metates but nowadays we use the metate only in the final preparation of the corn dough into tortillas. Also, all women used to make their tortillas by hand. Few can do that today. We use these tortilla presses that take only a few seconds. The taste is the same only the noise is different. I can remember when I was a little girl I would wake up every morning to the sound of women patting corn dough into tortillas. And when there were several women in the kitchen doing it together, it sounded like soft applause.

Nowadays all you hear coming from the houses is the morning television news and weather or the sound of blenders making juice. Nature's sounds are much softer than machine noises and are usually lost. Only when there is a real bad thunderstorm does Nature win over machines. And you can't turn Nature off like you can a machine. [. . .]

Chapter IX. Mother [. . .]

The teachers and the schoolbooks create the impression that every soldier was a hero. Nobody pays any attention to the poor people who were the ones who suffered the most. Father still says that the motivation for the Revolution was the vengeance of one man upon another. The whole country was set on fire and all sorts of criminals and bandits or anyone else with a gun joined the fighting and called himself a revolutionary. One by one they eliminated each other until exhaustion set in. There were no winners in the end.

Mexico lost the Mexican Revolution.—Celsa

San Antonio has achieved a lot since the Revolution but it was more a question of doing it ourselves or doing it in spite of the Revolution. Santa

Catarina down the road has never recovered from the fighting and to this day the people are very strange and evil. They still shoot people they don't like and are very unfriendly to strangers. It's not that they would kill you if you walked down the street but they would ask you to identify yourself if they didn't know you. They don't like any outsiders in their village and they still speak *mejicano,* even the *chamaquitos* (diminutive of *chamaco* in Nahuatl for "children"). We don't have much to do with them although some of our villagers are related to them. Most of them aren't much better than animals. They are the ones who come here for water but when we go to their mountain to cut wood they charge us hundreds of pesos. That is why we don't like to give them water. They are bad people [. . .].

Chapter XI. The System [. . .]

Nowadays education is everything. You need it to get out of the village; you need it to get a good job; you need it for everything. But it costs so much to go beyond high school that few from our position can ever make it. Our ancestors used to say that it wasn't with school that one takes care of himself but with life's experiences. Well, that philosophy is fine if you never want to leave the village. For many it is a punishment to have to live their entire lives here in San Antonio. Every person I know who has been really successful in life and has made a lot of money has gotten a good education and has left the village. Few of us would stay here if it weren't for the serenity and the security that San Antonio gives us. Life is hectic outside of the valley but that is the price you must be willing to pay if you want to get ahead [. . .].

Margarito is in Tabasco working as a teacher. He is close to the Guatemalan border and works with *indígenas* (Indian, one who speaks an Indian dialect). They speak their own language and eat monkeys. I could never eat a monkey; they're too much like *seres humanos* (human beings). We speak Spanish and *mejicano.* We are not indígenas because we speak Spanish. The people he works with have a lot of strange customs which are difficult for us to understand. They think entirely different from us; they are very, very poor, sleep on boards, and eat monkeys; and they are unfriendly to outsiders. Margarito says that he has never been invited into one of their houses. They hide from him when they see him coming. All of the school teachers come from the outside. Although hard on the young teachers, spending a year there is good training. When they get back to civilization they appreciate their permanent assignments [. . .].

Nowadays you have to have more than *secundaria* [high school] to teach. You need a university degree. That has made it very difficult for the campesinos to get ahead. We will always be campesinos or day laborers unless we get help in reaching the university. Here in the village we have never had anything more than a *primaria* [grade school]. Since I can remember, and long before that, if you wanted to go to secundaria you had to travel to Tepoztlán. The majority of children go to Tepoztlán daily. It is much easier now since we have a road and the bus picks them up right here in the center of the village. Before we had to walk to *el* "15" in order to catch a bus [. . .].

The system is rotten. The rich always end up with the money in the end. Where did all of the money go we paid to the school? Hilaria was just one of several thousand students sent home when the doors opened. Tuition is only a part of the total expense. School requires a lot of extras, like for the celebrations. *Chingaderas* (slang expression meaning "to get screwed") my son calls them. And they are. The biggest expenses are not books and supplies, like paper, but those things related to activities outside the classroom. For example, I had to buy a uniform and other things for just one occasion; it was a parade [. . .].

In the farmer's market I feel very much at home and can make enough money to survive. At Tres Marías I always feel like an alien even though I have some friends there. But I earn enough money to allow me to make special purchases without feeling guilty. My boys do not know it but I am saving money for a television. I know that I should be spending it on my teeth [. . .].

DISCUSSION QUESTIONS

• Notice Celsa's careful distinction between *mejicanos* and *indigenas*, as well as between San Antonio and other towns. How does this dialogue with the discourse of nationalism and, in particular, *mestizaje*? Is she making essentialisms? Why would she feel the need to identify such groups as significantly different from each other? How does this speak to national and mestizo identity?

• What is Tirado's role in this book? Is he "more a conduit for her story than a storyteller," as he suggests?

• Even if Celsa wrote, organized, and published her own story, would she still be outside of discourse? In other words, is it ever possible for an author to escape his/her discursive "death"?

• In what ways does the genre of the testimonial at once challenge and agree with previous authors' representations of indigenous people?

• How might the text be different if its audience were the citizens of Celsa's community? Would that be a more "authentic" representation of Celsa's experience?

NOTES

1. For analyses of the dynamics of testimonial literature, see Georg Gugelberger, *The Real Thing: Testimonial Discourse and Latin America* (Durham: Duke UP, 1996) and John Beverley, *Against Literature* (Minneapolis: U of Minnesota P, 1993).

2. Guillermo Bonfil Batalla, *México profundo: una civilización negada* (México, DF: Secretaría de Educación Pública, 1987) (published in English as *Mexico Profundo: Reclaiming a Civilization* (Austin: U of Texas P, 1996).

3. Thomas Tirado, *Celsa's World: Conversations with a Mexican Peasant Woman* (Tempe: Center for Latin American Studies, Arizona State University, 1991). This excerpt is from 1, 3–4, 7–10, 12–16, 25, 45–46, 50–51, 61, 68–70, 76, 83–87, 98–99, 115–116. Professor Tirado is professor emeritus at Millersville University.

Some Closing Comments

Education is often, and paradoxically, alienating. In learning more, we often encounter ideas that challenge our assumed truths. Questioning those truths can be difficult because we are often forced to examine their sources, which might be very personal—our parents, other family members, friends, respected teachers, or religious leaders. We don't want to believe they led us astray. Even if we don't credit someone else for guiding us to a worldview, we still don't like learning that ours might be flawed. After all, nothing is more precious to our sense of self than the way we view the world. While having our view challenged is difficult, at least modernity offers us respite in knowing that we will replace it with something more accurate. Our feeling of alienation need only be temporary, therefore, for we can rest in knowing that something outdated is being replaced by something newer and better; progress is afoot.

Cultural theory and postmodernism seem to offer us no such comfort. In contending that our individuality, social norms, and moral codes are discursive constructs, cultural theory challenges our existing worldview, then seemingly fails to provide us with a solid alternative. Its offer of "constant questioning and continual revision" provides little solace to someone accustomed to believing in the existence of hard-and-fast truths, even if they remain elusive and undiscovered.[1] So, whereas the alienation accompanying modern enlightenment is fleeting, the estrangement experienced in the transition from a modernist to a postmodernist perspective seems more permanent; frankly, that can seem kind of depressing.

In the introduction we suggested that Neo's troubling discovery in *The Matrix* that his real world was not what he thought it was offers a cinematic representation of this alienation. Philosopher Martha Nussbaum offers a similar portrayal of the patriotic (i.e., nationalistic) student who is challenged to think in a broader, international cosmopolitanism:

> Becoming a citizen of the world is often lonely business. It is, in effect, as Diogenes said, a kind of exile—from the comfort of local truths, from the warm nestling feeling of patriotism, from the absorbing drama of pride in oneself and one's own. In the writings of Marcus Aurelius (as in those of his American followers Emerson and Thoreau), one sometimes feels a boundless loneliness, as if the removal of the props of habit and local boundaries had left life bereft of a certain sort of warmth and security. If one begins life as a child who loves and trusts its parents, it is tempting to want to reconstruct citizenship along the same lines, finding in an idealized image of a nation a surrogate parent who will do one's thinking for one. Cosmopolitanism offers no such refuge; it offers only reason and the love of humanity, which may seem at times less colorful than other sources of belonging.[2]

As Nussbaum says, this new perspective, whatever one wants to label it, might seem "less colorful" at first. But we would like to suggest here that, in actuality and over time, it shines much brighter than its predecessor. Perhaps the alienation that comes with moving from modernity to postmodernity is not so permanent. Perhaps it is quite temporary, and maybe even liberating and life affirming. How could this be? Simply put, cultural theory releases us from the narrow self-righteousness of modernity and reveals to us a much more open and, at the risk of sounding like a modernist, *humanitarian* place of residence.

Mark Taylor, a professor of humanities at Williams College, wrote an article in the *New York Times* in 2004 in remembrance of Jacques Derrida. Taylor wrote that Derrida's critics (who are also the critics of postmodernism, poststructuralism, cultural studies, etc.) argue that to accept Derrida's arguments is to begin sliding down a "slippery slope of skepticism and relativism that inevitably leaves us powerless to act responsibly." Taylor argued that this criticism is inaccurate. Listening to Derrida, he writes, "does not mean . . . that we must forsake the cognitive categories and moral principles without which we cannot live: equality and justice, generosity and friendship" because "there can be no ethical action without critical reflection."[3] Taylor's argument recalls Edward Said's comment we cited in the introduction. Said said he believes that any political or ethical stance must accept a position of constant criticism as its foundational position. It must be willing, even eager, to challenge its own presuppositions: "There must be critical consciousness if there are to be issues, problems, values, even lives to be fought for. . . . Criticism must think of itself as life-enhancing and constitutively opposed to every form of tyranny, domination, and abuse."[4]

Taylor and Said base their embrace of criticism and their belief in its life-affirming qualities on a fundamental aspect of cultural theory—hierarchy, power, and repression can reside in unexpected places. Derrida contended that in the process of building our social structures and moral norms something or someone is inevitably excluded. As Taylor put it, "Every structure—be it literary, psychological, social, economic, political or religious—that organizes our experience is constituted and maintained through acts of exclusion. In the process of creating something, something else inevitably gets left out."[5] If we fail to recognize this, or choose to ignore it, we are likely to suffer because acts of exclusion have the possibility, if not the likelihood, of becoming repressive; and ignored repression fights back, like a wounded animal trapped in a corner. "In a manner reminiscent of Freud," Taylor warns, "what is repressed does not disappear but always returns to unsettle every construction, no matter how secure it seems."[6] Only when we adopt a stance of constant criticism are we in a position to accept that what might seem so right, true, and moral in fact has the potential to be proven wrong, false, and immoral. Acts of liberation might, in fact, be acts of repression. Arguments about justice might, in fact, be arguments for tyranny. Actions and arguments based upon notions of unyielding and inalienable truths are likely to be incapable of realizing this paradoxical possibility.

If taken to an extreme, this position of constant questioning and continual revision could lend itself to a sort of passive nihilism. But cultural theorists reject that position. They take stands; they declare things to be right or wrong; they fight and die for causes. Said said that criticism should exist "even in the midst of a battle in which one is unmistakably on one side against another."[7] Indeed, throughout his life, Said constantly combined activism and academics. Cultural theorists do take stands from positions of temporality.

Stuart Hall argued in Chapter 5 that most cultural theorists realize that we can't enter into the free flow of discourse or adopt a position of criticism without coming from some place, without first staking out a position as a starting point, be it a cultural identity, a political stance, or a judicial verdict. This position becomes our identity at that moment, the point at which we locate our temporal selves, and the starting point for our entry into the flow of social construction and political action. This process of identification recognizes difference, both individual and collective, but it refuses to essentialize it. Once we have identified and labeled ourselves and acknowledged that our place of residence is perhaps different from that of many, if not most, other people, we are equipped to shed all or part of it when presented with information that makes it necessary to do so. At that point we will begin to reconstruct our identity anew, as we maneuver through the shifting sands and floating icebergs of discursive construction. The irony here, ultimately, is that postmodernity asks us to see security and life-affirming values in transition and temporality. The challenge is to embrace that irony and live with it, to "live with difference."[8] That should make us no less committed to fighting for what we believe to be right and against worldviews that promote themselves as all-knowing, all-seeing, and all-truthful.

In the preface to this book we said we would use a cultural theory approach to look at modern Latin American history in a different way. Sometimes, at the end of our seminar upon which this book is based, our students comment that they feel as if they learned everything and nothing about Latin America. This irony is, of course, precisely the point, and it takes us back to Daniel Mato's claim that "Latin America doesn't exist." If students enter the seminar or approach this text expecting to have Latin America defined for them, to have its identity and meaning spread out before them— to have Latin American reality constructed—it will feel as though Latin America is somehow missing from the experience. What we showed were the processes and patterns by which Latin American identities were constructed, both by Latin Americans and by foreigners. In other words, we adopted a position of constant criticism, showing that whenever someone defined the real Latin America, someone or something was being excluded. In this process of exclusion, the identities of both the included and the excluded were being created simultaneously and in mutual dependence upon one another. Furthermore, this constitutive process also carried within it the seeds of repression and hierarchy. So, throughout our term together, Latin America was at once ever-present but always being looked at from a position of what was happening behind the scenes, around the corner, and in the unconscious of those people who historically have described/defined/ pinpointed the supposedly true situation.

As we dismiss our students on the last day of the seminar, we suggest they practice the interpretive skills we have studied throughout the course. They already had been doing so, but now they would be leaving the reinforcing confines of the seminar. We tell them to go out into the world and see how identities are being made everywhere, every day, all the time; how identity is not a matter of awakening oneself to a true, ontological essence.

We tell them that our identities are being constructed in the very process of naming ourselves and being named by others. We tell them to experiment with divorcing themselves from the clues (racial, gender, national, etc.) that we have been taught to identify as real and meaningful. We encourage them to consider how we have been trained throughout our lives to see differences and to believe that these differences matter essentially rather than temporarily, and that truths are inalienable and ontological rather than temporal and socially mediated.

After all, we ask, what can it hurt? Even if following our suggestions feels uncomfortable, there is plenty of modernist reinforcement out there. There are plenty of movies, books, news programs, politicians, religious leaders, teachers, family members, advertisements, music, and friends who will gladly tell you not to worry: truth is as solid as it ever was, our selves are as secure and real as they were when Descartes revealed them to us, and you need not worry about those postmodernists who say that transitioning into postmodernity is inevitable. But try applying cultural theory to your own life. It can't hurt, and maybe you will find out that the ever-shifting space of social construction is a powerful and a life-affirming place.

NOTES

1. Mark Taylor, "What Derrida Really Meant," *New York Times*, 14 Oct. 2004: A29.

2. Martha Nussbaum, "Patriotism and Cosmopolitanism," ed. Joshua Cohen, *For Love of Country: Debating the Limits of Patriotism* (Boston: Beacon, 1996). The quote is from an online version <http://www.phil.uga.edu/faculty/wolf/nussbaum1.htm>.

3. Taylor A29.

4. Edward Said, *The World, the Text and the Critic* (Cambridge: Harvard UP, 1983) 34.

5. Taylor A29.

6. Taylor A29.

7. Said 34.

8. Glenn Ward, *Teach Yourself Postmodernism* (Lincolnwood, IL: NTC, 1997) 184.

Permissions Acknowledgments

We would like to thank the following authors and presses for granting us the copyrights to these works. We have worded the entries according to the requests of each publisher and author.

Bary, Leslie. "The Search for Cultural Identity: Concepts." *Problems in Latin American History: A Reader.* Ed. John Chasteen and Joseph Tulchin. Wilmington: Scholarly Resources, 1994. 169–197. Excerpts are from pages 169–174. Permission granted by the publisher through the Copyright Clearance Center.

Blum, Lawrence. *I'm Not a Racist But . . . The Moral Quandary of Race.* (Ithaca: Cornell University Press, 2002). Excerpts are from 127–128 and 156–160. Used by permission of the publisher, Cornell University Press.

Boland, Roy. *Culture and Customs of El Salvador.* Westport: Greenwood, 2001. Front cover photograph reproduced with permission of Greenwood Publishing Group Inc., Westport, CT.

Burton, Julianne. "Don (Juanito) Duck and the Imperial Patriarchal Unconscious: Disney Studios, the Good Neighbor Policy, and the Packaging of Latin America." *Nationalism and Sexualities.* Ed. Andrew Parker. New York: Routledge, 1992. 21–41. Excerpts are from 32–38. Permissions granted by the publisher through the Copyright Clearance Center.

Connell, R. W. *Masculinities: Knowledge, Power and Social Change.* Berkeley: University of California Press, 1995. Excerpts are from 3–7, 21–27,

67–71, and 185–194. Permission granted by the Regents of the University of California and the University of California Press to use the text and apparatus without substantive change.

Gallegos, Rómulo. *Doña Bárbara.* Gloucester: Peter Smith, 1948. Excerpts are from 23–29, 44–46, 139–140, 145, 185–186, 209–210, and 297. Used by permission of Peter Smith Publisher Inc.

Garro, Elena. "It's the Fault of the Tlaxcaltecas." *RIF/T: An Electronic Space for Poetry, Prose and Poetics.* Ed. Kenneth Sherwood and Loss Pequeño Glazier. Version 2.1, winter 1994. <http://wings.buffalo.edu/epc/rift/rift02/wahlo201.html>. Permissions granted by the Electronic Poetry Center.

Guillermoprieto, Alma. *Looking for History: Dispatches from Latin America.* New York: Pantheon, 2001. 73–86. Excerpts are from 73–83 and 85–86. Copyright © 2001 by Alma Guillermoprieto. Used by permission of Pantheon Books, a division of Random House Inc.

Hall, Stuart. "Ethnicity: Identity and Difference," *Becoming National: A Reader.* Ed. Geof Eley and R. Suny. New York: Oxford University Press, 1996. 337–349. Excerpts are from 339–341 and 344–349. Permission granted by Stuart Hall.

Martí, José. "Our America." *José Martí Reader: Writings on the Americas.* Ed. Deborah Shnookal and Mirta Muñiz. Melbourne: Ocean, 2001. 111–120.

Martin, Gerald. *Journeys Through the Labyrinth: Latin American Fiction in the Twentieth Century.* London: Verso, 1989. 8–31. Excerpts are from 8–13 and 25–29. Permission granted by Verso Press.

Mignolo, Walter. *Local Histories/Global Designs.* Copyright © 2000 by Princeton University Press. Reprinted by permission of Princeton University Press.

Parker, David. *The Idea of the Middle Class: White Collar Workers and Peruvian Society, 1900–1950.* University Park: Penn State University Press, 1998. Excerpts are from 2–3, 5–7, 9–14, 16–17, and 20–21. Permission granted by the publisher through the Copyright Clearance Center.

Pérez, Louis. *On Becoming Cuban: Identity, Nationality and Culture*. Chapel Hill: University of North Carolina Press, 1999. 5–15. Excerpts are from 5, 8, 10–11, and 12–13. Used by permission of the publisher and author.

Sarmiento, Domingo. *Life in the Argentine Republic in the Days of Tyrants or, Civilization and Barbarism*. New York: Collier, 1966. Excerpts are from 25–33, 40, 44–45, 47–52, and 58. Reprinted with the permission of The Free Press, a division of Simon & Schuster Adult Publishing Group. Copyright © 1970 by The Free Press. All rights reserved.

Sommer, Doris. *Foundational Fictions: The National Romances of Latin America*. Berkeley: University of California Press, 1991. Excerpts are from 272–279, 281, and 284–289. Permission granted by the Regents of the University of California and the University of California Press to use the text and apparatus without substantive change.

Tenenbaum, Barbara. "Why Tita Didn't Marry the Doctor, or Mexican History in *Like Water for Chocolate*." *Based on a True Story: Latin American History at the Movies*. Ed. Donald Stevens. Wilmington: Scholarly Resources, 1997. 157–171. Excerpts are from 157–159, 161–164, and 167–171. Permission granted by the publisher through the Copyright Clearance Center.

Tirado, Thomas. *Celsa's World: Conversations with a Mexican Peasant Woman*. Tempe: Center for Latin American Studies, Arizona State University, 1991. Excerpts are from 1, 3–4, 7–10, 12–16, 25, 45–46, 50–51, 61, 68–70, 76, 83–87, 98–99, and 115–116. Permission granted by the Arizona State University Center for Latin American Studies.

Wade, Peter. *Race and Ethnicity in Latin America*. London: Pluto, 1997. Excerpts are from 5 and 16–21. Permission granted by the publisher through the Copyright Clearance Center.

West, Candace, and Don Zimmerman. "Doing Gender," *The Social Construction of Gender*. Ed. Judith Lorber and Susan Farrell. Newbury Park: Sage, 1991. 13–37. Excerpts are from 14–16, 18–24, 32, and 34. Reprinted by permission of Sage Publications Inc.

Wu, Harmony. "Consuming Tacos and Enchiladas: Gender and the Nation in *Como agua para chocolate*." *Visible Nations: Latin American Cinema and Video.* Ed. Chan Noriega. (Minneapolis: University of Minnesota Press, 2000. 174–192. Excerpts are from 176–183 and 185–187. Permission granted by the publisher through the Copyright Clearance Center.

A note regarding permissions for the use of film stills in this text: We have used FRAPS 2.6.4 to capture the still images from the films we discuss and base our lawful use of the stills reproduced in this text on criteria published by the Society for Cinema and Media Studies (SCMS). According to guidelines posted in the "fair use" declaration of the SCMS website <http://www.cmstudies.org/CJdocs/Thompson2.htm>, film stills captured from VHS tapes and DVDs to be used for educational purposes fall under "fair use" for the following reasons:

a) Technically, by capturing a film still and publishing it as a frame enlargement, the legal warning against copying any part of the film is violated. However, the intention of this warning was to prevent the pirating of the films in their entirety to be sold and/or projected. The publishing of film stills does not in any way violate the intention of this legal prohibition.

b) Journals and books published by not-for-profit university presses use frame enlargements to enhance the educational/analytical/critical purposes of the text. These still images are in no way a duplication or replication of the film since they are devoid of movement and comprise less than one one-hundredth of one percent of a single film. It thus follows that use of the images does "not harm the potential market for or value of the copyrighted work," one of the fundamental criteria determining unlawful use of copyrighted material. On the contrary, the publishing of film stills arguably acts as a form of publicity, not piracy, often promoting the viewing of the film in its entirety by the journal and book readers.

For more information, please consult the SCMS "fair use" guidelines <http://www.cmstudies.org/CJdocs/Thompson2.htm>.

Index

Page numbers in italics refer to photographs or figures.